Selected Writings of
Albert Gallatin

THE AMERICAN HERITAGE SERIES

THE

American Heritage

Series

UNDER THE GENERAL EDITORSHIP OF
LEONARD W. LEVY AND ALFRED YOUNG

Selected Writings of
Albert Gallatin

EDITED BY

E. JAMES FERGUSON
Queens College

THE BOBBS-MERRILL COMPANY, INC.

INDIANAPOLIS AND NEW YORK

Foreword

Surely Albert Gallatin deserves better of posterity! As Secretary of the Treasury, Gallatin served as brilliantly under President Thomas Jefferson as Alexander Hamilton served under President George Washington. From 1801 to 1813, Gallatin was not only the most influential Secretary after Hamilton, but a major shaper of public policy as a whole under Presidents Jefferson and Madison. As a diplomat of the first order, his talents in negotiating the Treaty of Ghent that ended the War of 1812 were recognized by no less a statesman than John Quincy Adams. His career, moreover, spanned two political generations. In the Jacksonian era he emerged from private life as a banker to voice the views of important segments of northern opinion on the central economic questions of the day: "the bank war," currency, and the tariff. At 85, he ended his public career writing lucid political tracts denouncing President James Polk's belligerent diplomacy on the Oregon question and the wanton expansionism of the War with Mexico.

His brilliant intellectual endowments allowed Gallatin to express himself in clearly reasoned prose whether it was his speeches to Congress during the 1790's, public papers written as Secretary, private letters, or political pamphlets. He therefore left a body of writing that enables students to examine the thought of a relatively unappreciated thinker and mover of the young republic. Through Gallatin's writing we are permitted to study a kind of Jeffersonianism that is too often ignored by those who would take John Taylor of Caroline as typical. Gallatin was never a pure agrarian, a states rightist, or an advocate of laissez-faire; he combined a true devotion to

v

democratic institutions with a highly enlightened commitment to government encouragement of economic growth.

His later career almost defies categorizing. At first a partisan of the second Bank of the United States, he later became disillusioned with it. He warmed to free trade, becoming an ardent foe of the protective tariff. In opposing the idea circulating in the 1840's that it was the "manifest destiny" of the United States to expand, he rejected aggressive imperialism in favor of the older Jeffersonian idea that the United States by the attraction of its just institutions would become the rallying point for the peoples of the western hemisphere newly freed from the yoke of European empires.

In making Albert Gallatin's opinions and thoughts more available for study this volume helps to break Henry Adams' "monopoly" on Gallatin. That famous historian wrote what long served as the standard biography of Gallatin until Raymond Walters' volume appeared in 1954. Adams also edited the only edition of Gallatin's writings, a three-volume collection available only in libraries. In selecting Gallatin's most important and representative writings, Professor Ferguson brings to this collection the knowledge of an outstanding student of American public finance and of early American history.

This book is one of a series whose aim is to provide the essential primary sources of the American experience, especially of American thought. The series, when completed, will constitute a documentary library of American history, filling a need long felt among scholars, students, libraries, and general readers for authoritative collections of original materials. Some volumes will illuminate the thought of significant individuals, such as James Madison or Louis Brandeis; some will deal with movements, such as the Antifederalists or the Populists; others will be organized around special themes, such as Puritan political thought, or American Catholic thought on social questions. Many volumes will take up the large number of subjects traditionally studied in American history for which surprisingly there are no documentary anthologies; others will pioneer in introducing new subjects of increasing importance to scholars and to the contemporary world. The series aspires to maintain the high standards demanded of contemporary editing, providing authentic texts, intelligently and unobtrusively edited. It will also have the distinction of presenting pieces of substantial length which give the full character and flavor of the original. The series will be the most comprehensive and authoritative of its kind.

Leonard W. Levy
Alfred Young

Contents

THE PUBLIC LANDS

INTERNAL IMPROVEMENTS

MANUFACTURES

THE BANK OF THE UNITED STATES

Part Five: Secretary of the Treasury, 1801–1813 (II)

AMERICAN RIGHTS: THE LEOPARD-CHESAPEAKE AFFAIR, 1807

THE TARIFF OF 1816

Introduction

The Rousseauian idealism that impelled Gallatin as a young man to leave his native Switzerland in 1780 and cast his lot on the American frontier had a decisive influence in shaping his career. Like Lafayette he fled from the protection of an aristocratic family, lured by the Arcadian image that America presented to European liberals of his generation. Although his antecedents were commercial, his Genevan family having been engaged in trade and in the watch-making industry, Gallatin passed up the kind of career open to a youth of his education and ability in the coastal cities and elected to try his fortune as a land speculator and farmer. In 1786 he settled in Fayette County, Pennsylvania, a frontier area. When drawn into politics, as was nearly inevitable in view of his superiority in accomplishments over his fellow frontiersmen, he represented the agrarian West.

Ideological sympathy as well as political affiliation threw him into the company of the great Virginians who molded the rising opposition to the Federalist regime. He shared their antistatism and their responsiveness to the democratic ideas of the time. Yet there was always an incongruity in this association, for Gallatin's mind lacked the stamp of native agrarian prejudice. His aptitudes might easily have gained him a high place among the elite of the commercial cities. Particularly in his youth he was inclined like Jefferson to romanticize agriculture, yet he had no aversion to commerce or manufactures. He regarded unsound paper money as destructive of common morality, but he seldom ranted over the evils of stock speculation,

nor did he share Jefferson's dislike of banks and finance capitalism. He had no difficulty becoming a close friend of the great
financier John Jacob Astor, and he spent ten years of his later
life as a bank president without ever finding it necessary to
justify his profession. Even during the 1790's his politics lacked
the extremism generated by the party struggle. With other
Republicans he opposed the "monarchists," but he was seldom
guilty of the vindictive and irresponsible statements, or the
attribution of base motives to political foes that characterize
the writings of the period. Conversely, although he responded
in full measure to the democratic ideas of the French Revolution, he was not so ingenuous or so long an admirer of revolutionary France as many Republicans. It is noteworthy that
although his culture and native language were French, he did
not care to participate, as many Republicans did, in the Gallic
enthusiasm rampant in Philadelphia nor cultivate the society
of French émigrés and diplomats resident in the United States.

Gallatin's personality was distinguished by a refinement and
a sense of decorum rare among American politicians. Apparently almost devoid of personal vanity, he was temperate in
debate, never confused his ambition with the success of the
cause, entered into no feuds, and carefully avoided exaggerated statements. Although a brilliant conversationalist, he was
reserved in his associations with other people. One of the outstanding features of his early career was his indifference to the
conventional opportunities for advancement for which his
background and education fitted him. He made no effort to
take advantage of the usual letters of introduction to prominent men or the solicitation of patronage to which his family
rank entitled him. He chose the West rather than the commercial East as the locus of his career, and his first marriage was
to a Richmond girl of French descent but no fortune whose
mother kept a boarding house. In his correspondence he sometimes referred to his natural indolence, but since he had a
capacity for sustained work resembling that of Alexander

Hamilton, he was indulging a fancy or it may be that he was expressing his distaste for the drudgery of calculated self-advancement in business or in politics.

The same qualities of even-tempered rationality and lack of driving ambition characterize his political career. He was an excellent member of a team. During the 1790's he accepted Republican party discipline and after 1800 played the good servant to Jefferson and Madison. Although in disagreement with some of their measures, he always gave his best. As Secretary of the Treasury he eschewed any attempt to establish a reputation independent of the administration. Except in the case of the recharter of the Bank of the United States, on which he took an unequivocal stand, his advice to the President and his reports to Congress were an exploration of alternatives, leaving the decision to their judgment rather than a summons to a particular course of action. His thick French accent, a constant reminder of his foreign origin, was an obstacle to his becoming a national leader of first rank. But in any case, he was not very adept at the political game. He held no elective office after 1800, and to please his second wife[1] cut himself off from his political base in western Pennsylvania, moving first to Baltimore then to New York City. As Secretary of the Treasury, he apparently took no great pains to keep his fences mended and was victimized by intrigues within the Republican Party. After he left the Cabinet in 1813 his only public service was in diplomacy, which was congenial to his taste and sufficient for his ambition. Gallatin's temperament was not really well suited to democratic politics. It may be that he would have risen to greater heights as the minister of a European prince.

In intellectual capacity Gallatin was surely the equal of

---

[1] Gallatin's first wife died in 1789, five months after their marriage. His second wife, Hannah Nicholson, whom he married in 1793, linked him with a prominent New York Republican family.

any American leader of the period. It is enough that John Quincy Adams admitted that he gained a dominant influence over the American peace commission at Ghent, of which Adams was a member; an Adams seldom recognized a peer, let alone a superior. But Gallatin's pamphlets and speeches display the brilliance of his rational faculties. His writings are like lawyers' briefs, devoted to the question at hand, well reasoned, addressed persuasively to the intellect, exhaustively researched, and full of information. Except for a few things he wrote late in life they seldom rise to eloquence or contain any revelation of personality. Apparently the obligation he felt to truth compelled him to embrace reason alone. He once said, "I have always felt conscientious with respect to facts." His propensities led him to become the Republican expert on public finance during the 1790's, later he became an authority on such matters as the northeast boundary question, the tariff, and money and banking. He wrote treatises on American Indian tribes which place him among the founders of American ethnology. Yet there was a miniscule quality to his prose, a passion for detail, that made him a powerful advocate of a cause but deprived his works of literary appeal.

A GLANCE AT
GALLATIN'S POLITICAL CAREER

Gallatin entered politics in 1788 as a radical Antifederalist, a position out of harmony with the general cast of his mind and the course of his later development. His Antifederalist views probably owed less to youthful romanticism than to the influence of his western constituents—a political career in his district would have been difficult on any other basis. Pennsylvania was one of the few states in which something like organized political parties existed, founded on hostility between East and West going back to the colonial era. The western part of the state was Antifederalist and after the formation of the national government it gravitated toward the Republican Party.

Fayette County elected Gallatin to the Antifederalist Harrisburg Convention in 1788, to the state constitutional convention in 1790, and in the same year to the state assembly. As a legislator Gallatin was the spokesman of his western constituents, but his capacity for work and the essential balance of his mind won the confidence of all parties. In his first session he was appointed to forty committees. His greatest accomplishment was in sponsoring the reorganization of state finances. Gallatin's program included final retirement of the state paper money, placing fiscal operations on a specie basis financed by bank loans rather than by paper anticipations, rapid extinction of the state debt, payment of compensation to state creditors who had subscribed their securities to the federal loan of 1790 (even though most of the creditors were easterners and speculators) and, finally, the incorporation of a state bank on terms that made it a fiscal partner of the government. With state finances in a sound and prosperous condition, all direct taxes were discontinued. This program accommodated a variety of economic and sectional interests, but it transcended them in its commitment to general principles of financial solvency and responsibility. It was a departure from agrarian modes of finance of which any Federalist might have approved. Ironically, it was made possible largely by the income the state derived from Hamilton's funding program.

As Gallatin pushed the state into new paths of financial orthodoxy, he allowed his western affiliation to draw him into what he afterward said was his "only political sin," failing to add that it was the price he paid for pursuing his political career. Opposition to the federal excise tax of 1791 on whiskey was so widespread in western Pennsylvania that no local politician could directly challenge it, and in 1792 Gallatin had some share in inciting resistance to the law. When resistance flared into insurrection, however, he worked frantically, at the risk of personal injury and even death, to induce the people to submit. Never afterward, even amidst the highly charged atmosphere created by the Sedition Act and the election crisis of 1800, did Gallatin ever contemplate a resort to extra-legal tactics or physical force.

In 1793 the Pennsylvania legislature elected Gallatin to the national Senate, but he was expelled after a few months. Although he had resided continuously in the United States since 1780 he had neglected to apply for citizenship until 1785, and in the application he then made in the state of Virginia there were technical irregularities. Gallatin contended that he was a citizen as defined by provisions of the Articles of Confederation, but the Federalist-controlled Senate ejected him on the grounds that he had not fulfilled the Constitutional requirement of nine years' citizenship. His expulsion interrupted his political career only temporarily. In 1795 his western constituents sent him to the House of Representatives in which he served until his appointment as Secretary of the Treasury in 1801.

GALLATIN IN POLITICS, FINANCE, AND ECONOMICS

Before foreign affairs became the chief issue in national politics, the rising party opposition to the administration centered on Hamilton's financial policies: the funding of the depreciated Revolutionary debt without revaluation or a discrimination in favor of original creditors, the assumption of state debts, and the establishment of a national bank. A closely related issue was the inordinate influence of the Treasury department upon the national legislature. This influence was in part the consequence of the act establishing the Treasury department which gave its secretary a unique position among cabinet officers. The duty of submitting financial reports and recommendations allowed him to share with the House of

Representatives the power of initiating tax legislation and appropriating money. In its first session the House had appointed a committee to handle such matters, but at Hamilton's request it was disbanded. Congress fell under Hamilton's sway, referring financial matters directly to him and accepting his proposals as the basis for deliberation. Some Federalists argued that a numerous body like the House was by its nature incompetent to deal with matters of finance, which required expert knowledge, and that in any case the legislature was obliged to provide funds to carry out policies to which the executive was committed, provided that these policies met the approval of the country. Otherwise, the Federalists said, the executive branch would be crippled and the balance of government destroyed. Republicans, on the other hand, perceived in Treasury initiation of financial policy a destruction of balanced government from the opposite—executive usurpation of the powers of the legislative branch. Declaring that the Secretary should be the servant not the master of Congress, they demanded that the House initiate its own money bills.

Another source of contention was the Treasury's loose accounting of the expenditure of money. Until 1797 Congress appropriated a maximum for various purposes, leaving the Secretary considerable latitude in determining for what purposes to spend it. Republicans wanted detailed and specific appropriations limiting the Secretary's discretion. They also criticized Hamilton's neglect while in office to submit reports clearly setting forth the government's over-all financial condition, its income and expenditure, loans contracted at home and abroad, and the progress made in discharging the national debt.

Upon entering the House of Representatives in December 1795, Gallatin became the leading Republican expert on government finance, a role for which he was fitted by talent and by his experience in the Pennsylvania legislature. By this time Hamilton had retired from office so the Republicans, with a majority in the House, had to contend only with the lesser figure of Oliver Wolcott.[2] In December 1796, upon Gallatin's motion, the House appointed a Committee on Ways and Means. It became a permanent fixture of legislative machinery. In 1796 Gallatin managed for the first time to write specific appropriations into the revenue measures of that year.

In November 1796, not in time for the national elections, but early enough to influence the choice of President, Gallatin published A *Sketch of the Finances of the United States.* The pamphlet documented several Republican charges against the Federalist administration, but it represented Gallatin's independent thought and was far more than a party tract. Gallatin's avoidance of the usual shibboleths and his studied effort to state and meet the issues fairly were calculated to persuade all but extreme Federalists.

Gallatin's critique of Federalist finance was built around two allegations. The first was that a premature assumption of state debts in 1790, in advance of the final settlement of Revolutionary accounts between the states (completed in 1793) had needlessly increased the federal debt by $11,000,000. Conceding for the sake of the argument that assumption was in itself a justifiable measure, Gallatin argued that its essential purposes could have been realized without this additional debt. Secondly, Gallatin demonstrated that from 1790 the national debt had increased by another $6,000,000, despite the application of a sinking fund. He attributed the increase to military and naval expenditures and to the disproportionate military force used to crush the Whiskey Rebellion, both of which he believed excessive. His main criticism, however, was that the government met increased expenses by anticipations and loans rather than by taxation,

[2] Oliver Wolcott succeeded Hamilton as Secretary of the Treasury in January 1795, serving under Washington and John Adams until the Republicans took over the administration in 1801. Wolcott was a competent administrator, but lacked Hamilton's political influence.

and that by questionable accounting methods it concealed the growth of the debt from the American people. As a solution he proposed a reform in accounting methods and the levying of taxes in advance of anticipated expenditures. Since in his opinion import duties were about as high as they could be raised without injury to commerce and indirect taxes were relatively unproductive, the government should resort to direct taxes on real estate.

Direct taxes were a thorny issue on which there was no agreement in either party, but Gallatin's criticisms of Federalist finance were unanswerable on their own ground. They furnished valuable ammunition for the Republican leadership. From the standpoint of his later career, however, and for the light thrown on incipient divergences within the Republican Party, the pamphlet is more illuminating in its departures from the party line than in its support of it. Republican propagandists in their general indictment of Hamilton's funding program, usually made much of Madison's effort in 1790 to discriminate between original and secondary holders of federal securities. In his *Sketch of the Finances* Gallatin left the point undiscussed except to say that Hamilton's provisions for funding the public debt "were adopted by a very large majority, and seem, so far as can be judged from the rapid appreciation even prior to its being funded, to have been supported in great degree by public opinion." (See Document 7.) Justifying Hamilton's measures because they raised security values was a kind of reasoning foreign to the mental processes of the Virginia ideologues and indeed most members of the Republican Party. A further indication of Gallatin's particular attitude was his failure to declaim against speculators, or raise suspicion as to the rectitude of the Treasury department, or indict Hamilton's use of the sinking fund. On the last issue, in fact, he expressed agreement with Hamilton's policy of employing the fund to appreciate the value of federal securities.

Similarly, he had nothing but praise for Jefferson's *bête*

noire, the Bank of the United States. Far from condemning it
or raising the cry of special privilege, he complained that the
government was victimizing the Bank by excessive borrowing. His only reference to that corrupt union of government
and business—for which the Bank was a symbol in Republican minds—was to acknowledge briefly that fear of the government's using the Bank as a political weapon, in some instances justified, and doubts as to its constitutionality had
raised many enemies against it. But Gallatin was not one
of them. In his opinion the Bank had proved beneficial to the
country. "The accommodations which the government receives from that institution in almost all its financial operations
are not only useful when resorted to with moderation, but
under our present system and in our situation may be deemed
necessary." Nor could anyone doubt, he continued, that "like
all other banks, this is of great commercial utility by bringing into circulation moneys which otherwise would remain
inactive, and especially by increasing the rapidity of circulation. Banks, indeed, are perhaps still more useful for this
purpose in America than in Europe." (See Document 7.)

Gallatin's commercial orientation, while not incompatible
with Pennsylvania's varieties of Republicanism, was distinct
from the narrow tradition that Jefferson's ascendancy first
imposed upon the party. The later evolution of the party is
largely told in the amplification and nationalization of its
program.[3]

With Madison's departure from Congress in 1796, Gallatin
became the main leader of the Republican forces in the House
of Representatives. He operated in the milieu of organized
party divisions precipitated by the debate over the Jay Treaty
and the continuing crises of the French Revolution. Gallatin

---

[3] In *Views of the Public Debt, Receipts & Expenditures of the United
States* published in 1800 Gallatin repeated and brought up to date his
charges that assumption had needlessly increased the debt and that the
debt had continued to grow under Federalist auspices.

was a disciple of the rights of man. He had thrilled to the arrival of Citizen Genêt in 1793, first envoy of the French Republic. But he had endorsed Washington's Proclamation of Neutrality, and although foreign-born he was more discriminating than many Republicans, including Jefferson and certainly James Monroe, in his attachment to France. After 1795, however, he was scarcely a free agent, and it is questionable whether he would have taken the stand he did on some issues except for his party affiliation. Thus he backed every Republican maneuver against the Jay Treaty, holding out against it until the last minute, notwithstanding the views of many of his western constituents. He took high constitutional ground in opposing a relatively innocuous proposal to increase the rank and pay of the foreign diplomatic corps. He changed position on direct taxes, advocating them in 1796 when the Republicans were strong in Congress and the potential enemy was Great Britain, opposing them in 1798 when the Federalists were in control and the enemy was France. He manned the barricades against executive encroachment on the legislature. He failed to react to the XYZ affair with the same indignation he was to display a decade later on the occasion of the *Leopard-Chesapeake* incident, which occurred when he was in the Cabinet. Although the international situation was critical, he tried with every argument in his power to minimize Federalist increases in the army and navy. In 1798 he stoutly resisted the Federalist program of domestic repression initiated by the Alien and Sedition Acts.

Gallatin, Jefferson, and other Republicans subscribed to principles that set them apart from their Federalist adversaries. If they embraced French equalitarianism as a political gambit, they honestly opposed the elitism that was the underlying code of the Federalist leadership. If they were guilty of adjusting their beliefs to party purposes, they were more sensitive than the Federalists to the implications of increasing debt, the dangers inherent in military force and in the sup-

pression of political dissent. The means they employed sometimes exposed them to the Federalist jibe that their principles
masked a simple hunger for power and public office. Certainly their attacks upon individuals were frequently unjust,
not to say outrageous, and in a world at war they played a
dangerous game in exploiting popular sympathy for France.
Although in opposing the Jay Treaty few Republicans wanted
war, and they took the position that rejection of the treaty
would not mean war, they were willing to risk it with the only
foreign power capable of inflicting serious injury upon the
United States. Yet they were on firm ground in resisting the
organization of a provisional army in 1798, an army not very
relevant to the existing conflict with France and which in the
minds of some Federalists (but not President Adams) had a
sinister purpose. They were on the best ground of all in opposing the Alien and Sedition Acts. The logic of their position
forced Gallatin and a few other Republicans into definitions
of the right of free speech and free press more advanced than
the general thought of the time.

Gallatin's career entered upon a new phase with the Republican triumph in 1800. He was appointed Secretary of the
Treasury, in which position he served until 1813. Since their
parties represented antagonistic systems of government from
which the people had made their choice, Gallatin's administration of the Treasury invites comparison with that of Alexander Hamilton. In many of their views the two men were
not far apart. They were both alert to the welfare of commercial capitalism, its need for capital and credit. Gallatin no
less than Hamilton was concerned with promoting the growth
of manufactures. And there is little to be distinguished in
their willingness to employ government to sponsor economic
development. They were also alike in placing a high value on
the economic functions of banks, and Gallatin was if anything
more devoted than Hamilton to maintaining public credit,
financial solvency, and a stable currency. In their administra-

tion of the Treasury, both were superb executives with an infinite capacity for detail. Where they differed most was in their attitude toward the exercise of power and the value they placed upon democratic institutions. Hamilton was a statist, unwilling to submit to legislative direction and the uncontrolled will of the people. Gallatin was more scrupulous. During his term as Secretary of the Treasury, he adopted a liberal construction of the Constitution when it suited his purposes, and he went along with the arbitrary assumption of power involved in the enforcement of the Embargo. Yet he was a dedicated Republican and counted it his duty to accept the decision of the majority. And unlike Hamilton he had a sincere aversion toward the European state systems. He was therefore more truly committed to economy, the avoidance of large bureaucratic and military establishments, and to the reduction of the national debt.

Hamilton took office as the executor of a program endorsed by the great majority of the Federalist Party. The funding of the federal debt at face value, and by that means the establishment of a national system of currency and credit, was a formula already imbedded in the movement for the Constitution. The assumption of state debts had been anticipated during the Confederation and was a logical corollary of the Federalist economic program, as was the establishment of a national bank. But Hamilton's recommendations to Congress were operative, not only because they conformed to the views of his party, but also because he made himself the party's leader and saw to it that his program was enacted. He retired early in 1795 with nothing more to add.

Gallatin also came in with a mandate from his party. It was to practice economy, dismantle the military establishment, get rid of internal taxes, and reduce the debt. These reforms were accomplished or set in motion during the first years of his administration. The program was ameliorative, however, rather than creative; and not content with this, Gallatin addressed himself to far-reaching positive goals: the promotion of manufactures by continuing federal subsidies, construction at federal expense of a nationwide system of roads and canals, and a reorganization of the national bank along lines that might have enabled it to withstand the sectional animosities and private jealousies that led to its extinction in 1811 and again in 1836. The program failed—victim of the disunity of the Republican Party and the divergence of interest within it.

Gallatin lacked the will and the opportunity to become leader of the party. In pushing his measures he tried to exert influence directly on members of Congress, but by circumstances and one suspects by choice he remained subordinate to Jefferson in both the party and in the administration. With Madison's accession to the Presidency the party lacked strong leadership and Gallatin's effectiveness declined. Except in the case of the Bank of the United States, Gallatin was in general agreement with most policies of both administrations. He disliked the Embargo, but thought it was the alternative to war and hence did all he could to enforce it. He was helpless to arrest the drift toward war in 1811 and 1812, although he apparently thought it could be averted. Confining himself to his Treasury duties, he merely reminded Congress of the necessity of financing a war once begun and the advisability of levying taxes in advance. His admonitions were of no avail, and from the beginning of the war the Treasury was in hard straits. No doubt it was because his principles of finance were violated and his position was undermined by political intrigue that he requested a diplomatic assignment in 1813.

GALLATIN AS A DIPLOMAT

After a brief mission to Russia Gallatin was appointed to the commission charged with making peace. Besides himself, it included John Quincy Adams, Henry Clay, James A. Bayard, and Jonathan Russell. The negotiation was in some ways the most difficult that American envoys have ever faced, for the United States was losing the war. Superficially, at least, all the advantages lay with the British, who were determined to accept nothing less than a victor's peace. As events proved, the main task of the American commissioners was to keep their nerve, maintain agreement among themselves, and withstand British pressure while still holding the negotiation open. Gallatin was no novice in diplomacy, having immersed himself in various aspects of foreign affairs during his twelve years in the Cabinet. His perspicuity and even temper were invaluable in this delicate business, and he became the leading influence among the American delegates. The equal treaty they finally achieved owed rather less to their efforts than to a conjunction of events that persuaded the British government to call off the war. Under the circumstances, however, the treaty was a diplomatic triumph for the United States.

For most of the next fourteen years Gallatin remained in diplomacy, pretty well removing himself as a major figure on the domestic political scene. Monroe offered him the Treasury in 1816, but he had no taste for it. Approached again in 1825 he declined, feeling that the changes which had taken place in American politics had made his views obsolete or at least inapplicable. In the political caucuses preceding the election of 1824 he was named as a candidate for Vice-President on a ticket to be headed by William H. Crawford. Out of friendship for Crawford and opposition to Andrew Jackson he reluctantly consented, but he was relieved when his supporters changed their minds and sought a more popular candidate.

From 1815 to 1823 Gallatin served as minister to France. His greatest accomplishments, however, were in diplomatic relations with Britain. In 1815 he negotiated a convention with Britain restoring commercial relations as they had existed before the War of 1812. Sent to London in 1818, he joined Richard Rush in the role of senior diplomat in the conversations that led to the confirmation of American fishing rights in Canadian waters, the location of the northern boundary at the 49th parallel west of the Lake of the Woods, and to the joint occupation of Oregon. He was less successful in his French mission. His efforts to get indemnities for the spoliation of American vessels led to nothing but procrastination by the French government. He struggled to no avail to secure reciprocal tariff reductions, and in 1821 a treaty was finally signed in Washington without his participation. In 1826 he was back in England assisting the regular minister, Rufus King. They managed to obtain renewal of the joint occupation of Oregon and made some progress in settling the northeast boundary dispute. Gallatin's long service in diplomacy did not bring any great issues to a successful conclusion, but his part in establishing the northern boundary of the Louisiana Purchase and in providing for the joint occupation of Oregon contributed notably to American expansion to the Pacific coast.

Gallatin retired permanently from public service in 1831. It was at this time that he seriously embarked upon the studies that rank him among the founders of American ethnology. Over the years an early romantic interest in the American Indians had matured into scientific curiosity as a result, most particularly, of his long friendship with the great naturalist, Alexander von Humboldt, who first revealed to him the possibility of employing scientific methods in ethnology. Encouraged by scholarly recognition of an essay he wrote in Paris in 1823, Gallatin began research for a major work which was published in 1836. It was a description of Indian history and culture accompanied by a detailed analysis of tribal languages. Gallatin continued with his Indian studies for the remainder of his life, publishing two more pioneer works that contributed importantly to American ethnology, especially in its philological aspects. In 1842 he helped to found and was first president of the American Ethnological Society.

GALLATIN AND THE
JACKSONIAN BANKING CONTROVERSIES

At the invitation of his old friend, John Jacob Astor, Gallatin in 1831 became president of the National Bank of New York, a position which he retained until 1839 when he stepped down in favor of his son James. Although he was in his seventies and head of only a minor institution among the city's nineteen banks, his energy, reputation, and intelligence made him a spokesman of the New York financial community.

Gallatin had already gotten involved in the banking and currency controversies of the Jacksonian era. In 1831 he published *Considerations on the Currency and Banking System of the United States,* a treatise on the second Bank of the United States, supporting renewal of its charter. In this work Gallatin said that in principle he was an "ultra bullionist." Apart from checks drawn upon bank credits or deposits, he held that the currency should consist only of gold and silver. This position was singularly at odds with the fact that for over a century the country had relied on some kind of paper currency for a circulating medium, that gold and silver coins were not in general use, and that for thirty years the currency had consisted largely of bank notes of large and small denominations. Gallatin also opposed the usual procedure of incorporating banks by special legislative acts. Banking he thought should be "free," that is, open to individuals like any other business without special charter and thus divorced from government as well as the currency.

These views had a Jeffersonian savor. Gallatin, however, had not always held them, as they are not present in his previous writings. During his years in the Pennsylvania legislature, he had registered disapproval of state paper money by his eagerness to secure its withdrawal, but in his 1796 pamphlet on finance he took for granted that the country would rely on bank paper. In fact he expressed satisfaction in having helped to secure a charter for the Bank of Pennsylvania, and he had nothing but praise for the first Bank of the United States. Later, during his twelve years as Secretary of the Treasury, although state banks multiplied, he uttered no warnings about excessive issues of bank notes. Indeed, in his efforts to finance the War of 1812 he inaugurated the practice of emitting Treasury notes, perilously like federal paper money and so, in the end, subject to depreciation.

The suspension of specie payments in 1814 was obviously a great shock to him. Afterward Gallatin urged immediate resumption of specie payments without consideration of possible adverse effects upon the economy. His bullionist views probably date from this era.

In 1831 Gallatin understood that a hard money system of currency could be no more than an ideal. He acknowledged that whatever banks did in Europe, American banks had always issued circulating notes, and although he believed Congress had the constitutional authority to suppress bank notes, he felt that the right would not be exercised. Hence, he addressed himself to the problem of ensuring a sound currency by maintaining the convertibility of bank paper into specie on demand. The best means to this end, he thought, was a powerful central bank, in this case the second Bank of the United States, an institution powerful enough on the one hand to discipline state banks and on the other to support them with its resources in time of fiscal crisis. Gallatin thus became a partisan of Nicholas Biddle in his dispute with President Jackson.

He soon parted company with Biddle, as he strongly disapproved of the speculative enterprises in which Biddle engaged after the Bank of the United States lost its charter in 1836. What really outraged him, however, was Biddle's refusal to join with New York banks in bringing about an early resumption of specie payments after their suspension in 1837. Gallatin was a leader in the movement to restore specie payments, which Biddle and the Bank of the United States opposed. In May 1838 the New York banks proceeded independently, forcing specie resumption in Boston and Philadelphia. In October 1839, however, the Bank of the United States discontinued specie payments and was followed by other banks in Pennsylvania as well as banks in the South and West. In 1841 Gallatin published an indictment of Biddle and the Bank of the United States, a pamphlet entitled *Suggestions on the Banks and Currency of the Several United States, in Reference Principally to the Suspension of Specie Payments.* By this time Gallatin had lost confidence in the regulative capacity of a central bank and was inclined to put his faith in strict regulation by state governments.

The determination of Gallatin and the conservative eastern bankers associated with him to force resumption of specie payments at the earliest possible moment very likely prolonged the Panic of 1837. It is certainly true that Gallatin's zeal for curbing state banks was at odds with the intense speculative spirit of an age when American economic enterprise was bursting with energy and the foundations were being laid for the phenomenal industrial advance that followed the Civil War. Gallatin's writings show he was aware that his position was not consistent with the realization of maximum economic potential. Yet almost in the spirit of the Federalists of 1787, he felt that an unsound currency violated the moral order upon which society was based, that wild speculation brought its own retribution, and that whatever economic gains were achieved, they were not commensurate with the damage inflicted upon the community. He wrote in his pamphlet on banks and currency: "Independent of every temporary party consideration, there are questions of right and wrong, of what is just or unjust, which must be settled on that principle alone. . . . With a debased coinage or a fluctuating depreciated paper you subvert every private and public engagement, impair the performance of every contract, make invariably the ignorant and the weak dupes of the shrewd and wary, and demoralize the whole community."

TARIFF AND FREE TRADE

His views on banking had hardened through the years as had his stand on the tariff question. As Secretary of the Treasury he had indicated mild disapproval of protective tariffs by failing to endorse them. On the other hand, he had proposed federal subsidies to manufactures and in 1816 he did not speak up against the first protective tariff laid in the United States. But his ideological commitment to free trade deepened as he grew older, possibly as he read more widely in economic theory. In 1830 he served as a New York delegate to a free trade convention at Philadelphia and wrote the convention's memorial to Congress, which was published in pamphlet form. The memorial was in fact a treatise on political economy, a masterful statement of the free trade argument in terms of the history and development of the United States. But it was characteristic of Gallatin, more so in these later years, that he would not accommodate his views to a factional position. The southern-dominated convention had held protective tariffs unconstitutional. Although Gallatin agreed that they discriminated against the south, he would not go along on the constitutional point. Writing in the context of the developing Nullification Controversy, he took pains to affirm the constitutional right of Congress to levy protective tariffs.

OREGON AND THE WAR WITH MEXICO

Gallatin was quite an old man when, in 1846, he published *The Oregon Question* and *War Expenses*, which announced his final entry into public controversy. These were first issued as newspaper articles, then published as a pamphlet. They condemned President Polk's announced policy of terminating the joint occupation of Oregon with Britain and taking possession of the territory by force. The next year, in the closing months of the Mexican War, Gallatin published *Peace with Mexico,* an appeal for peace without territorial annexations. These productions fed Whig criticism of the expansionist and alleged southern orientation of the Polk administration.

It would be erroneous, however, to regard these writings as mere party tracts. The pamphlet on Oregon was antiwar, not antiexpansionist. Gallatin believed that unilateral action by the United States was certain to bring on a conflict with Britain which he regarded as unnecessary. His point was that Oregon would soon be inhabited by emigrants from the United States. He wanted nothing to interrupt the process; moreover, he did not want the territory divided. Inevitably, he thought, it would become an American or Anglo-American state on the Pacific coast, either independent and friendly to or annexed by the United States. A war over it could only have destructive results. Significantly, he excluded California from the scope of American expansion, regarding it as given over to an alien and inferior people.

Peace with Mexico was written amidst growing public sentiment for annexing the whole of Mexico, a sentiment propagated by westerners and also by many northerners who had come to the conclusion that slavery could not exist south of the Rio Grande. Gallatin's pamphlet, however, was concerned neither with the slavery issue, the Wilmot Proviso, nor any of the sectional issues generated by the Mexican War. It was an indictment of what Gallatin considered wanton military aggression, the first stain upon the record of the American republic. He urged that the wrong be mitigated as far as possible by keeping annexations to a minimum, confining them at most to the nearly uninhabited provinces of what was then northern Mexico.

As Gallatin hated slavery, he could hardly have been absolutely neutral in the sectional controversy. Yet, if one can judge from his writings, his major reaction to the events of the 1840's was not to the sectional implications of territorial expansion but to what he regarded as a new imperialism. Like many, and perhaps most, Americans of his time he believed that it was America's destiny to spread through the wilderness and create a great nation or nations in the vast space of the continent. Coupled with this belief, however, was the old ideal of the virtuous republic. What he saw in the 1840's he interpreted as a corruption of the original mission, a reversion to the age-old pattern of conquest and rule over subject peoples with its concomitants of militarism and war. When he died in 1849 Gallatin felt that he had outlived his time.

E. James Ferguson

Great Neck, New York
December 1965

Chronology

1761   January 29, born, Geneva, Switzerland.

1770   Orphaned, educated by a distant relative.

1779   Graduates from the Academy at Geneva.

1780   Leaves Geneva, arrives in Massachusetts.

1781   Gives an "extension course" in French for Harvard College students. Serves as interpreter and companion for agent of Lyons firm. Acquires part interest in land purchase in western Pennsylvania.

1784   Migrates to Fayette County, Pennsylvania; establishes a general store.

1785   Establishes farm and home, "Friendship Hill" on the Monongahela River.

1788   Member of the Antifederalist Harrisburg conference to consider ways of revising the Constitution of the United States.

1789   Marries Sophia Allegre, of Richmond, his landlady's daughter; she dies several months after migrating to "Friendship Hill."

1789 TO 1790   Delegate to the convention to revise the Pennsylvania State Constitution.

1790   Elected to the state legislature as a representative from Fayette County, reelected in 1791, 1792.

1792 Clerk of meeting of "Whiskey rebels" at Pittsburgh, "my only political sin."

1793 February 28, elected by legislature to the United States Senate. November 1, marries Hannah Nicholson, daughter of James Nicholson, well-to-do New York City merchant and naval hero. December—Federalists challenge his eligibility to the Senate.

1794 February 28, Senate votes 14 to 12 which deprives him of seat. April—sells his western Pennsylvania lands to Robert Morris, returns to Fayette County with his wife. Active as a moderating influence in the "Whiskey Rebellion" of western Pennsylvania. Elected to House of Representatives, reelected twice, serves three terms, 1795–1801.

1796 Publishes *A Sketch of the Finances of the United States.*

1797 Recognized as a leading Republican in the House, especially in field of finance.

1798 Leader of the Republican resistance to the Federalist
TO   "quasi-war" with France and the Alien and Sedition
1800 Laws.

1800 Publishes *A View of the Public Debt, Receipts & Expenditures of the United States.* Active in the House for Jefferson in the deadlock between Jefferson and Burr for the presidency.

1801 Appointed Secretary of the Treasury by Jefferson. Launches policy featuring reduction of the public debt. Leader in Cabinet.

1804 Advocates liberalization of the public land laws.

1807 Endorses Embargo; reluctantly enforces it.

1808 Issues Report advocating federal aid to internal improvements.

1809 Issues Report favoring a second charter for the Bank of the United States on altered terms.

1810 Issues Report on Manufactures, urging government support.

1811 Renews appeal for Bank of the United States which fails of rechartering.

1812 Opposes "war hawks" but supports the War of 1812. Faces bitter factional opposition in Congress over his plans for financing the war.

1813 At his request is appointed by President Madison to diplomatic mission to Russia who had offered to mediate the war; takes temporary leave of absence from the Treasury. Six months in St. Petersburg; mission unsuccessful.

1814 February—resigns as Secretary of the Treasury after twelve-year tenure. Serves on five-member commission to negotiate peace treaty with Britain. December 24, signs Treaty of Ghent, "the special and peculiar triumph of Mr. Gallatin" (Henry Adams).

1815 Visits Geneva and Paris. With John Quincy Adams negotiates favorable commercial treaty with Great Britain. September—returns to United States.

1816 Accepts appointment as minister to France. James Madison asks him to return as Secretary of the Treasury following resignation of Alexander Dallas; Gallatin refuses. Serves as minister to France until 1823; in diplomatic deadlock, unsuccessful in securing compensation for American commercial losses in Napoleonic Wars.

1818   Assists Richard Rush, the American minister in successful negotiations with Great Britain over fishing rights, northern boundary and joint occupation of Oregon.

1823   Returns to United States.

1824   Unwilling Vice-Presidential candidate on "regular Republican" ticket headed by William H. Crawford, accedes to withdrawal of his name.

1826   Drafted by President John Quincy Adams as minister to England; successful in several projects.

1827   Returns to United States; settles in New York City.

1831   Chosen president of National Bank of New York City (later named Gallatin Bank) at request of John Jacob Astor; serves to 1839. First president of the council of the University of the City of New York.

1832   Publishes *Considerations on the Currency and Banking System of the United States,* a defense of the Bank of the United States. Attends national Free-Trade Convention in Philadelphia as New York delegate to protest high tariff; writes its memorial to Congress.

1836   Publishes "A Synopsis of the Indian Tribes," an important pioneer work in American anthropology.

1840   Publishes *The Right of the United States of America to the North-Eastern Boundary Claimed by Them,* as the leading American authority on the question.

1841   Publishes *Suggestions on the Banks and Currency of the Several United States,* a critique of Nicholas Biddle and the Bank of the United States.

1842   Founder and first president of the American Ethnological Society.

1843 President of the New York Historical Society. Publishes "Memoir on the North-Eastern Boundary."

1844 Presides over and addresses New York City meeting held to protest territorial annexations.

1845 Publishes "Notes on the Semi-Civilized Nations of Mexico, Yucatan, and Central America."

1846 Publishes *The Oregon Question* against unilateral occupation of Oregon.

1847 Publishes *Peace with Mexico* and *War Expenses,* opposing war and territorial annexations.

1848 Publishes 166-page introduction to "Hale's Indians of North-West America."

1849 August 12, dies at Astoria, Long Island, aged 88 years.

Selected Bibliography

Extended studies of Gallatin are not numerous. An admirable bibliography of manuscript and published sources relative to his career is in Raymond Walters, Jr., *Albert Gallatin* (New York: The Macmillan Co., 1957), upon which I relied heavily. It supersedes the classic Henry Adams, *Life of Albert Gallatin* (Philadelphia and London: J. B. Lippincott Co., 1879). Special studies are Frederick Merk, *Albert Gallatin and the Oregon Problem* (Cambridge: Harvard University Press, 1950) and Alexander Balinsky, *Albert Gallatin: Fiscal Theories and Policies* (New Brunswick, N. J.: Rutgers University Press, 1958). Leonard D. White, *The Jeffersonians* (New York: The Macmillan Co., 1951) treats Gallatin's career in the Treasury. Russell J. Ferguson, *Early Western Pennsylvania Politics, 1773–1823* (Pittsburgh: University of Pittsburgh Press, 1938) contains a good deal on his early political career.

Numerous letters and pamphlets written by Gallatin are published in Henry Adams, *The Writings of Albert Gallatin*, 3 vols. (Philadelphia: J. B. Lippincott Co., 1879), from which many of the selections in this work are drawn. Adams has a list of Gallatin's published works at the end of the third volume. A supplementary list is in Walters, *Albert Gallatin*, page 438. The New York Historical Society has the central collection of his unpublished correspondence, as well as published works not always available elsewhere. Most of his speeches in the House of Representatives can be read, however, only in the *Annals of Congress: The Debates and Proceedings in the Congress of the United States* . . . 42 vols. (Washington: Gales and Seaton, 1833–1861). His reports as Secretary of the Treasury are in the several publications of the *American State Papers: Documents, Legislative and Executive of the Congress of the United States,* 38 vols. (Washington: Gales and Seaton, 1833–1861). Beyond the material published in Adams, *Writings of Albert Gallatin,* the source material bearing on his diplomatic career may be found in *American State Papers: Foreign Relations,* 6 vols. (Washington: Gales and Seaton, 1832–1859) and in the State Department's records at the National Archives.

Editor's Note

Gallatin used modern spelling, correct punctuation, and good grammar, so it has seldom been necessary to alter his text. The material taken from Henry Adams' three-volume work, the only previous edition of Gallatin's writings in print, has been reproduced without substantial changes. The present edition, although limited in many cases to extracts, is in some ways more comprehensive than Adams and affords a broader delineation of Gallatin's career. It contains certain manuscript pieces, speeches Gallatin made in Congress, reports as Secretary of the Treasury, and Gallatin's important pamphlet on free trade, all of which Adams omits. On the other hand, certain aspects of Gallatin's career are not represented. His diplomatic reports from France and England after 1814, his essays on the northeastern boundary question, and his ethnological studies were considered too narrowly detailed to interest any but a specialist.

I would like to thank the people at the New York Historical Society and the federal documents division of the Library of Congress for their courteous assistance.

Selected Writings of
Albert Gallatin

PART ONE

A Career in Retrospect

1. GALLATIN'S GENEVA ORIGINS.

LETTER TO EBEN DODGE

January 21, 1847

Late in life Gallatin wrote a few notes on his early career. With some nostalgia and a tendency to idealize the past, he paid tribute to the "self-created aristocracy" of wealth, talents, and public office from which he sprang. In his native city of Geneva this eighteenth-century elite existed in its most virtuous form.

There was in Geneva neither nobility nor any hereditary privilege but that of citizenship, and the body of citizens assembled in council general had preserved the power of laying

Henry Adams, ed., *The Writings of Albert Gallatin*, 3 vols, II (New York: J. B. Lippincott Co., 1879), 647–650, hereafter referred to as *Writings*.

taxes, enacting laws, and ratifying treaties. But they could originate nothing, and a species of artificial aristocracy, composed of the old families which happened to be at the head of affairs when independence was declared, and skilfully strengthened by the successive adoption of the most distinguished citizens and emigrants, had succeeded in engrossing the public employments and concentrating the real power in two self-elected councils of 25 and 200 members respectively. But that power rested on a most frail foundation, since, in a state which consists of a single city, the majority of the inhabitants may in twenty-four hours overset the government. In order to preserve it, a moral, intellectual superiority was absolutely necessary. This could not be otherwise attained than by superior knowledge and education; and the consequence was that it became disgraceful for any young man of decent parentage to be an idler. All were bound to exercise their faculties to the utmost; and although there are always some incapable, yet the number is small of those who, if they persevere, may not by labor become, in some one branch, well-informed men. Nor was that love and habit of learning long confined to that self-created aristocracy. A salutary competition in that respect took place between the two political parties, which had a most happy effect on the general diffusion of knowledge.

During the sixteenth and the greater part of the seventeenth century the Genevese were the counterpart of the Puritans of Old and of the Pilgrims of New England—the same doctrines, the same simplicity in the external forms of worship, the same austerity of morals and severity of manners, the same attention to schools and seminaries of learning, the same virtues, and the same defects, exclusiveness and intolerance, equally banishing all those who differed on any point from the established creed, putting witches to death, &c., &c. And, with the progress of knowledge, both about at the same time became tolerant and liberal. But here the similitude ends. To the Pilgrims of New England, in common with the other English colonists, the most vast field of enterprise was opened which ever offered itself to civilized man. Their mission was to conquer the wilderness, to multiply indefinitely, to settle and inhabit a whole continent, and to carry their institutions and civilization from the Atlantic to the Pacific Ocean. With what energy and perseverance this has been performed we all know. But to those pursuits all the national energies were directed. Learning was not neglected, but its higher branches were a secondary object; and science was cultivated almost exclusively for practical purposes, and only as far as was requisite for supplying the community with the necessary number of clergymen and members of the other liberal professions. The situation of Geneva was precisely the reverse of this. Confined to a single city and without territory, its inhabitants did all that their position rendered practicable. They created the manufacture of watches, which gave employment to near a fourth part of the population, and carried on commerce to the fullest extent of which their geographical situation was susceptible. But the field of active enterprise was still the narrowest possible. To all those who were ambitious of reknown, fame, consideration, scientific pursuits were the only road that could lead to distinction, and to these, or other literary branches, all those who had talent and energy devoted themselves.

All could not be equally successful; few only could attain a distinguished eminence; but, as I have already observed, a far greater number of well educated and informed men were found in that small spot than in almost every other town of Europe which was not the metropolis of an extensive country. This had a most favorable influence on the tone of society, which was not light, frivolous, or insipid but generally serious and instructive. I was surrounded by that influence from my earliest days, and, as far as I am concerned, derived more benefit from that source than from my attendance on academical lectures. A more general fact deserves notice. At all times, and within my knowledge in the years 1770–1780, a great many distinguished foreigners came to Geneva to finish their education, among whom were nobles and princes from Germany and other northern countries; there were also not a few lords and gentlemen from England (even the Duke of Cambridge, after he had completed his studies at Göttingen); besides these there were some from America, amongst whom I may count before the American Revolution those South Carolinians, Mr. Kinloch, Wm. Smith—afterwards a distinguished member of Congress, and minister to Portugal— and Colonel Laurens, one of the last who fell in the war of independence. And when I departed from Geneva I left there, besides the two young Penns, proprietors of Pennsylvania, Franklin Bache, grandson of Dr. Franklin—Johannot, grandson of Dr. Cooper, of Boston, who died young. Now, amongst all those foreigners I never knew or heard of a single one who attended academical lectures. It was the Genevese society which they cultivated, aided by private teachers in every branch, with whom Geneva was abundantly supplied.

2. THE MAKING OF A FINANCIAL

EXPERT. AUTOBIOGRAPHICAL SKETCH

1849

In these fragments, written the year of his death, Gallatin traced his career as a freshman legislator, describing how he became a specialist in public finance.

Gallatin Papers, New York Historical Society. Reprinted with the permission of the New York Historical Society.

I feel the necessity of leaving behind me some account of my public life. The part I took in the political affairs of the United States during a period of fifty years was such, that I cannot escape notoriety; and for the sake of my children, I undertake a task long delayed, because none can be more irksome to me than to speak of myself. Yet I have nothing to reproach myself with, in that respect, but errors of judgement, nothing to regret but that my life should not have been more useful.

I was born in Geneva on the 29th of January 1761. My family came originally from Bresse, a province on the right bank of the Rhone, now Department of Ain in France, but then part of the dominions of the House of Savoy. My ancestor John Gallatin, formerly Secretary of the Duke of Savoy, settled in Geneva of which he became a citizen in 1510, and, having embraced the reformation, was one of the magistrates of the City in 1535, when, by the expulsion of its Prince Bishop, Geneva became an independent Republic. The numerous descendents of John Gallatin subdivided into four branches had ever since maintained a respectable standing in Geneva as faithful citizens and of great integrity.

My grand father, Abraham Gallatin, was a merchant and had for partner his only son, John, who married Sophia Albertina Rolaz of Pays, now Canton of Vaud. They had two children, a daughter five years older than me and myself. My father died in the summer of 1765, and my mother who had talent and great energy undertook to carry on his share of the business in her own separate name. She died in March 1770: my sister who was afflicted with a nervous disease had been sent to Montpellier under the care of a celebrated physician; but she never recovered and died a few years after. Since my father's death, I never saw her but once, and have but a faint recollection either of him or of her. Left an orphan, when nine years old, I would naturally have fallen under the care of my paternal grand parents who were both alive and died at an advanced age in 1791: but I was already otherwise provided for.

My mother had a most intimate friend, a distant relation of my father, and who, when he died, seeing her overwhelmed with the cares which my sister required and those of the business she had undertaken to manage, insisted on taking me under her charge. When five years old, I came to live with her; and from that time, she was my mother. . . .

Public Functions

In April 1784, I crossed for the first time the Allegheny mountains, and became permanently established, in Feby. 1786, on a farm which I had purchased in Fayette County Pennsylvania.

Octr. 1789. I was elected member of the Convention which formed the Constitution of Pennsylvania. This was my apprenticeship. I took some share in the debates, but did not act a leading part.

1790, 1791, 1792. Three successive years, elected a Member of the House of Representatives of the State Legislature of Pennsylvania, the first year by a majority of two thirds, afterwards without any opposition.

I acquired an extraordinary influence in that body, the more remarkable, as I was always in a *party* minority. I was indebted for it to my great industry, and to the facility with which I could understand & carry on the current business. The labouring oar was left almost exclusively to me. In the session of 1791–1792, I was put on 35 Committees, prepared all the reports and drew all their bills. Absorbed by those details, my attention was turned exclusively to administrative laws and not to legislation properly so called. The great reforms of the penal code, which to the lasting honour of Pennsylvania originated in that State, had already been carried into effect, principally under the auspices of William Bradford. Not being a professional lawyer, I was conscious of my incapacity for digesting any practicable and useful improvement in our civil jurisprudence. I proposed that the subject should be referred to a Commission, and Judge Wilson was accordingly appointed for that purpose. He did nothing and the plan died away. It would have been better to appoint the Chief Justice & the Attorney General of the State (M'Kean & Bradford) and, in the first instance at least, to have confined them to a revision of the Statute law, whether Colonial, State or British still in force.

I failed, though the Bill I had introduced passed the House, in my efforts to lay the foundation for a better system of education. Primary education was almost universal in Pennsylvania, but very bad; and the bulk of school masters incompetent, miserably paid & held in no consideration. It appeared to me that, in order to create a sufficient number of competent teachers and to raise the standard of general education, intermediate academical education was an indispensable preliminary step: and the object of the bill was to establish in each County an Academy, allowing to each out of the Treasury a sum equal to that raised by taxation in the County for its support. But there was at that time in Pennsylvania, a Quaker and a German opposition to every plan of general education.

The spirit of internal improvements had not yet been awakened. Still the first turnpike road in the U. States was that from Phila. to Lancaster, which met with considerable opposition. This, as well as every temporary improvement in our communications roads & rivers and preliminary surveys, met of course with my warm support. But it was in the fiscal department that I was more particularly employed; and the circumstances of the times favoured the restoration of the finances of the State.

The report of the Comee. of Ways & Means of the Session 1790–1791, (presented by Gurkey Chrisman) was entirely prepared by me, known to be so, and laid the foundation of my reputation. I was quite astonished at the general encomiums bestowed upon it and was not at all aware that I had done so well. It was perspicuous and comprehensive: but I am confident that its true merit and that which gained me the general confidence was in its being founded in strict justice, without the slightest regard to party feelings or popular prejudices. The principles assumed, and which were carried into effect, were, the immediate reimbursement and extinction of the State Paper money, the immediate payment in specie of all the current expenses or Warrants on the Treasury (the postponement and uncertainty of which had given rise to shameful and corrupt speculations), and provision for discharging without defalcation every debt and engagement previously recognized by the State. In conformity with this, the State paid to its creditors the difference between the nominal amount of the State debts assumed by the United States and the rate at which it was funded by the Act of Congress.

The proceeds of the public lands, together with the arrears, were the fund which not only discharged all the public debts but left a large surplus. The apprehension that this would be squandered by the Legislature was the principal inducement for chartering the Bank of Pennsylva., with a capital of two millions of dollars of which the State subscribed one half. This and similar subsequent investments enabled Pennsylva. to defray out of the dividends all the expenses of Govt. without any direct tax, during the forty ensuing years and till the adoption of the system of internal improvement which required new resources.

It was my constant assiduity to business and the assistance derived from it by many members, which enabled the republican party in the Legislature, then a minority on a joint ballot, to elect me and no other but me of that party, Senator of the United States. This choice made in February 1793 was

contrary to my wishes and opinion. For the subsequent opposition to it and its being set aside were altogether due to
objections raised by myself and publickly expressed prior to
the election, which in Feby. 1794 was declared null and void
by the U. S. Senate.

Octr. 1794. I was reelected Member of the State Legislature in Fayette County for the ensuing session: and, on the
same day I was, without my knowledge, elected Member of
Congress for 1795–1797, by the western district of Pennsylvania, (Washington, Allegheny & from Lake Erie to Virg.
Line) in which I did not reside; the only instance of the kind
I believe that has ever occurred.

Decr. 1794. The House of Repr. & the Senate of Pennsylvania, in clear violation of the Constitution, (but a most
fortunate circumstance for me), set aside all the western
elections under pretence of the late insurrection. The same
members were immediately reelected, and the election for
Congress was not questioned.

Decr. 1795. I took my seat in Congress, to which I was reelected 3 times Octr. 1796, 1798, 1800, by the same district:
but I resigned, before taking it, my seat for 1801–1803, on
account of my accepting the office of Secy. of the Treasury:
so that I was only six years a Member of Congress.

The ground which I occupied in that body is well known;
and I need not dwell on the share I took in all the important
debates, & on the great questions which during that period
agitated the public mind, in 1796 the British treaty, in 1798–
1800 the hostilities with France and the various unnecessary
& obnoxious measures by which the Federal party destroyed
itself. It is certainly a subject of self-gratification that I should
have been allowed to take the lead with such coadjutors as
Madison, Giles, Livingston & Nicholas, and that when deprived of the powerful assistance of the two first who had
both withdrawn in 1798, I was able to contend on equal terms
with the host of talents collected in the Federal party, Gris-

wold, Bayard, Harper, Goodrich, Otis, Smith, Sitgreaves, Dana and even J. Marshall. Yet I was destitute of eloquence and had to surmount the great obstacle of speaking in a foreign language with a very bad pronunciation. My advantages consisted in laborious investigation, habits of analysis, thorough knowledge of the subjects under discussion, & more extensive general information due to an excellent early education; to which I think I may add quickness of apprehension and a sound judgment.

A member of the opposition, during the whole period, it could not be expected that many important measures should have been successfully introduced by me. Yet an impulse was given in some respects which had a powerful influence on the spirit & leading principles of subsequent administrations. The principal questions in which I was engaged related to constitutional construction or to the finances. Though not quite so orthodox in the first subject as my Virginia friends, (witness the U. States Bank & internal improvements) I was opposed to any usurpation of powers by the General Government. But I was specially jealous of executive encroachments; and to keep that branch within the strict limits of constitution and of laws, allowing no mere discretion than what appeared strictly necessary, was my constant effort.

The financial depart. in the House was quite vacant, so far at least as the Opposition was concerned: and, having made myself complete master of the subject, and occupied that field almost exclusively, it is not astonishing that my views should have been adopted by the Repn. Party, and acted upon when they came into power. My first step was to have a Standing Comee of Ways & Means appointed. That this should not have been sooner done proves the existing bias in favour of increasing as far as possible the power of the Executive Branch. The next thing was to demonstrate that the expenditure had till then exceeded the income: the remedy proposed was economy. Economy means order & skill; and after having determined the proper & necessary objects of expense, the legislature cannot enforce true economy, otherwise than by making *specific* appropriations. Even these must be made with due knowledge of the subject, since, if carried too far by too many subdivisions, they become injurious if not impracticable. This subject has ever been a bone of contention between the legislative & the executive branches in every representative Govt.; and it is in reality the only proper & efficient legislative check on executive prodigality.

Respecting the objects of expenditure, there was not (apart from that connected with the French hostilities) any other subject of division but that of the Navy. And the true question was whether the creation of an efficient navy should be postponed to the payment of the public debt. To do both with a surplus, not yet existing, & which after the year 1801. . . .

PART TWO

Back Country Delegate, 1788–1794

ANTIFEDERALIST

3. DRAFT OF A REPORT OF

THE HARRISBURG CONFERENCE

September 3, 1788

Gallatin was elected by Fayette County as delegate to the Antifederalist convention held at Harrisburg, Pennsylvania in September 1788. The meeting assembled too late to forestall the adoption of the Constitution. Gallatin presented resolutions which envisaged nationwide action by Antifederalists to call a second constitutional convention. Possibly the resolutions were drafted before the meeting and at the behest of his western constituents. The procedure he recommended by-passed state legislatures, calling for direct popular initiative, and hence was radical in its implications. It amounted in fact to an invitation to quasi-revolutionary action. In his

Writings, I, 1–2.

*speech to the assembly Gallatin backed down from his reso-
lutions. Voicing criticism of the Constitution, he suggested
only that the Pennsylvania legislature be requested to with-
hold its ultimate consent to the Constitution until an amend-
ing convention could be held. The resolutions finally adopted
at Harrisburg did not go even this far. The convention proposed a number of amendments and adopted a request, never
acted upon, that the Pennsylvania legislature issue a call for
a second convention. At its first session the new federal Congress considered the amendments proposed at Harrisburg as
well as those attached to ratification by several of the states.
Those affecting the structure or functions of the new government were discarded. Ten amendments, of which all but the
tenth related to individual civil and judicial rights, were eventually incorporated into the Constitution as the "Bill of
Rights."*

. . . WE, &c., . . . are united in opinion that a federal government is the only one that can preserve the liberties and secure
the happiness of the inhabitants of such an extensive empire
as the United States, and experience having taught us that the
ties of our Union, under the Articles of Confederation, were
so weak as to deprive us of some of the greatest advantages we
had a right to expect from such a government, therefore are
fully convinced that a more efficient one is absolutely necessary. But at the same time we must declare that although the
constitution proposed for the United States is likely to obviate
most of the inconveniences we labored under, yet several
parts of it appear so exceptionable to us that nothing but the
fullest confidence of obtaining a revision of them by a general
convention and our reluctance to enter into any dangerous measures could prevail on us to acquiesce in its organization in this
State. We are sensible that a large number of the citizens,

both in this and other States, who gave their assent to its being carried in execution previous to any amendments, were actuated more by the fear of the dangers that might arise from any delays than by a conviction of its being perfect. We therefore are convinced that they now will concur with us in pursuing every peaceable method of obtaining a speedy revision of the Constitution in the mode pointed out by the same, and when we reflect on the present situation of the Union we can entertain no doubt that motives of conciliation and the dictates of policy and prudence will conspire to induce every man of true federal principles to give his support to a measure not only calculated to recommend the new constitution to the approbation and support of a numerous class of American citizens, but even necessary to prevent the total defection of some members of the Union. Strongly impressed with those sentiments, we have resolved as follows:

1. *Resolved,* That in order to prevent a dissolution of the Union and to secure our liberties and those of our posterity, it is necessary that a revision of the Federal Constitution be obtained in the most speedy manner.

2. That the safest manner to obtain such a revision will be in conformity to the request of the State of New York, to use our endeavors to have a federal convention called as soon as possible.

3. That in order that the friends to amendments of the Federal Constitution who are inhabitants of this State may act in concert, it is necessary, and it is hereby recommended to the several counties in the State, to appoint committees who may correspond, one with the other, and with such similar committees as may be formed in other States.

4. That the friends to amendments of the Federal Constitution in the several States be invited to meet in a general conference to be held at   , on   , and that   members be elected by this conference, who or any   of them shall meet at said place and time, in order to devise, in concert with

such other delegates from the several States as may come
under similar appointments, on such amendments to the Federal Constitution as to them may seem most necessary, and
on the most likely way to carry them into effect.

THE WHISKEY REBELLION

4. PETITION AGAINST EXCISE

1792

*In 1790 Gallatin was elected to the first of three successive
terms as delegate to the Pennsylvania House of Representatives. The issue that most agitated his western constituents at
this time was the federal excise tax on whiskey enacted in
1791 to support the assumption of state debts. In August 1792
Gallatin attended a meeting of western politicians at Pittsburgh and drafted an able petition to Congress. It was considerably more judicious than the actual resolutions passed
which called for popular resistance to the excise law.*

To the Honorable, the Speaker and House of Representatives
of the Congress of the United States.

The Petition of the subscribers, inhabitants of the western
counties of Pennsylvania, most respectfully showeth:

That your Petitioners have been greatly alarmed by a law of
Congress which imposes a duty on spirituous liquors distilled
from produce of the United States. To us that act appears
unequal in its operation and immoral in its effects. Unequal
in its operation, as a duty laid on the common drink of a nation,

---

Writings, I, 2–4.

instead of taxing the citizens in proportion to their property, falls as heavy on the poorest class as on the rich; immoral in its effect, because the amount of the duty chiefly resting on the oath of the payer, offers, at the expense of the honest part of the community, a premium to perjury and fraud.

Your Petitioners also consider this law as dangerous to liberty; because the powers necessarily vested in the officers for the collection of so odious a revenue are not only unusual, but incompatible with the free enjoyment of domestic peace and private property; because these powers, to prevent evasions of the duty, must pursue the endless subtleties of the human mind, and be almost infinitely increased; and because we are apprehensive that this excise will by degrees be extended to other articles of consumption, until everything we eat, drink, or wear be, as in England and other European countries, subjected to heavy duties and the obnoxious inspection of an host of officers.

Destitute of information of the real deficiencies of the revenues of the United States, of the proportion which the probable proceeds of the excise bear to them, and doubtful whether those deficiencies could not have been supplied by other resources sufficiently productive and less obnoxious and oppressive, we want those motives which alone can reconcile us to the collection of a duty so odious in its nature and dangerous in its tendency.

Our peculiar situation renders this duty still more unequal and oppressive to us. Distant from a permanent market, and separate from the eastern coast by mountains which render the communication difficult and almost impracticable, we have no means of bringing the produce of our lands to sale either in grain or in meal. We are therefore distillers through necessity, not choice, that we may comprehend the greatest value in the smallest size and weight.

The inhabitants of the eastern side of the mountains can dispose of their grain without the additional labor of distillation at a higher price than we can, after we have bestowed that labor upon it. Yet with this additional labor we must also pay a high duty from which they are exempted, because we have no means of selling our surplus produce but in a distilled state.

Another circumstance which renders this duty ruinous to us is our scarcity of cash. Our commerce is not, as on the eastern coast, carried on so much by absolute sale as by barter, and we believe it to be a fact that there is not among us a quantity of circulating cash sufficient for the payment of this duty alone.

We are not accustomed to complain without reason; we have punctually and cheerfully paid former taxes on our estates and possessions, because they were proportioned to our real wealth. We believe this to be founded on no such equitable principles, and are persuaded that your Honorable House will find on investigation that its amount, if duly collected, will be four times as large as any taxes which we have hitherto paid on the whole of our lands and other property.

Submitting these considerations to your honorable body, we respectfully apply for a total repeal of the law, or for such modifications thereof as would render its principles more congenial to the nature of a free government, and its operation upon us less unequal and oppressive. And as in duty bound shall forever pray, &c.

5. DECLARATION OF THE
COMMITTEES OF FAYETTE COUNTY

September 1794

President Washington issued a proclamation on September 25, 1792 denouncing the Pittsburgh resolutions and warn-

ing against combinations to obstruct enforcement of the law. Attributing the disorder to the influence of pro-French "Jacobin Clubs" and believing that its aim was to bring down the government, Washington prepared to crush the resistance by force. But first he sent commissioners into the disaffected counties in August 1794 to determine whether troops would be necessary. The commissioners were authorized to extend pardon for past offences if the inhabitants would sign a declaration that they would not oppose the execution of the excise law. The response to this offer was minimal, and in September 1794 Washington despatched troops.

As the issue became one of civil obedience or defiance of federal authority, Gallatin urged compliance with the law and tried to check the extremists. That an open clash was prevented was in no small degree the result of his efforts, along with those of William Findley and Hugh Henry Brackenridge. In September Gallatin drafted the following statement, which advised the people to sign the declaration. Not many signed, but when federal troops came in, Fayette and other counties quietly submitted.

At a meeting of committees from the several townships of the county of Fayette, held at Uniontown the 10th day of September, 1794, twenty-one members present;

The following declaration was taken into consideration and unanimously adopted by the meeting:

We trust that the citizens of Fayette County will feel no more reluctance in declaring their intention to submit to the laws of the United States than we do in making the declarations required by the Commissioners. It is doing no more than expressing by a vote what the great body of them have heretofore proved by their conduct. We think it, however, our duty to state to them some of the reflections which must suggest themselves to every thinking mind upon the present occasion. That if the western counties will resist the execution of the laws, a civil war must be the consequence, no person, who will reflect, can doubt; for if any one part of the Union are suffered to oppose by force the determination of the whole, there is an end to government itself, and of course to the Union. The excise law is obnoxious to us, another law may equally be so in another part, a third one in a different quarter, and if every corner of the United States claim a right to oppose what they dislike, no one law will be obeyed. The existence of government, therefore, depends upon the execution of the laws, and they are in duty bound to enforce it. The President has, in consequence, sent Commissioners, in the first place to try by conciliatory means to obtain a submission; but if it is not so obtained, he will proceed by coercion. We could have wished, indeed, that more time had been given to the people to reflect, and we think that in this country it would have had a happy effect; for we are sure that arguments and the good sense of the people themselves, provided they had time to cool, would have a greater influence in convincing their minds than the fear of bayonets will. But the President was better acquainted with the general situation of the United States (though perhaps less with that of this country) than we can pretend to be. He has thought it his duty, and he has declared it to be his intention, to attempt a military coercion, if an explicit answer is not now given. He cannot at present recede without exposing government, and it remains with us only to consider what the consequences will be if resistance is attempted by the people.

We might expatiate on the improbability that such a small number as the inhabitants of the Western country, unprepared as they are for such an event, having but a scanty supply of arms and ammunition, and with the Indians on their back, could succeed against the whole force of the Union. We might represent how ruinous, at all events, to this country a contest would be. But your judgment and your patriotism we mean to address, and not your fears. Resistance by force against oppression is lawful only when no legal and constitutional remedy is within the reach of the people, and when the evils arising from the oppression are excessive, when they far surpass those that must ensue from the resistance. Such was the case of America at the beginning of the Revolution, when they took up arms against Great Britain. Such was the case of France when they overset their despotic government. Can the situation of the people of America or of France on those two occasions be compared to our own at present? You had your full share of representation in the Legislature which enacted the law we complain of. You are not deprived of the right of electing in future for that body the proportion of members your population entitles you to. Every mode of redress which can exist under a republican form of government is still open to you. Violence and resistance on your part would be the attempt of a minority to overrule, and, in fact, to oppress the majority of the people of the United States; an attempt to destroy every principle of that constitutional and rational liberty which we now enjoy. But, supposing there were some cases in which intolerable oppression on the part of the majority would justify resistance or secession in the minority, is the present one of them? The question which every man before he decides must answer is this,—Is the oppression arising from the excise law sufficient to justify me, before my own conscience and my God, in taking up arms against my fellow-citizens? Are the evils that will arise from the payment of that tax equal to those which a war must bring upon myself and upon my country? What is then the just value of the oppression and evils arising from the excise law? Nothing more nor less, at present, than paying seven cents for every gallon of whiskey we consume. We feel the probable consequences of that kind of taxation, once introduced, as warmly as you do yourselves. We think it a part of a more extensive system, and we look upon it only as the forerunner of a premeditated extension to numerous other articles. But those consequences, however probable, have not yet taken place; and although, from a fear of their ensuing, we have a right to be suspicious and to use our best endeavors to have the root of the fatal tree eradicated, yet we cannot count suspicions and fears amongst our present grievances and oppressions, and it is only in case they shall be realized that it may become justifiable to resent and perhaps to resist. Till then we must take things just as they are, and the actual evil, as already stated, will be the mere payment of the duty; for as to that oppression more dangerous to your liberties than the excise law itself, the power of dragging you at a distance from your own neighborhoods in order to be tried for real or supposed offences, the President has declared that he will relinquish its exercise as long as our own courts shall do justice,—that is to say, as long as yourselves shall please,—for upon you, who compose those courts and juries, must depend whether justice shall be done or not. That great and important point is, therefore, fully obtained, that grievance is now redressed, and the payment of the duty alone must be put in the scale against all the evils arising from resistance and a civil war. Those evils, in our opinion, are nothing less than anarchy and ruin to ourselves, be the event what it will, and a probable annihilation of the Union; for, in order to conciliate so many and various interests as those of the several parts of the Union, mutual forbearance, manifestations of good will one to another, and reciprocal acts of friendship are as essentially necessary as a strict adherence to that Constitution which binds us together; and if ever the fatal lesson is taught the inhabitants of this extensive republic to shed one another's blood, we may forever bid farewell to harmony, to mutual confidence, and to peace. The seeds of dissension, a spirit of hatred and revenge, will be implanted in every man's heart, and whatever might be the future duration of a nominal Union, its reality would no longer exist. If, therefore, you wish to preserve to yourselves and to your fellow-citizens the inestimable benefits that arise from our being united; if you wish, through the Union, to obtain, by a restoration of the Western posts and a free navigation of the Mississippi, the full enjoyment of those advantages to which nature has entitled you; if you wish not to destroy, along with the federal republic of North America, the finest monument which men have yet erected to liberty; if you wish not to become a prey to your natural enemies, the British, ready to take every advantage of our internal dissensions and to hunt down liberty in every corner of the globe, we entreat you to accede to the honorable terms proposed by the Commissioners, and not to hesitate in giving that testimony of your attachment to your country which is at present required of you.

By such an explicit declaration you will adopt the best possible means to obtain a repeal of the law, for previous submission is essentially necessary, that our friends and the friends of our principles throughout the Union may act in concert with us. We cannot expect either that they will join any but constitutional measures, or that Congress should yield anything to threats and violence, or even hear our complaints, until they are satisfied of our disposition to obey the laws. The privilege of petitioning and of adopting any other constitutional measure is expressly reserved to you in case of submission, but cannot be exercised except in that case. Time does not permit us to detail the many other reflections and arguments which crowd on our minds upon this subject, your own good sense will doubtless suggest them to you; suffice it to say, that when we earnestly recommend to you the adoption of pacific measures, we feel ourselves forcibly urged to it by a serious consideration of the private interest of every individual amongst you, of the interest of the Western country, of the interest of the United States, and of that solemn duty which you, as well as ourselves, owe to the government under which we live, to our fellow-citizens here and throughout the Union, and to that Being who has poured His choicest blessings upon us, by permitting us to live in this land of happiness and liberty.

Having thus concluded what we had to say to our immediate constituents, shall we be permitted to add a few words to those amongst our brethren of the neighboring counties who, under the present impulse of their passions and resentment, may perhaps blame us for that moderation which we trust their cool judgment will hereafter approve? The only reflection we mean to suggest to them is the disinterestedness of our conduct upon this occasion. The indictable offences, to be buried in oblivion, were committed amongst them, and almost every civil suit that had been instituted, under the revenue law, in the federal court was commenced against citizens of this county. By the terms proposed, the criminal prosecutions are to be dropt, but no condition could be obtained for the civil suits. We have been instrumental in obtaining an amnesty, from which those alone who had a share in the riots derive a benefit, and the other inhabitants of the Western country have gained nothing for themselves. Have those who were immediately concerned a right to require anything more from us? Let themselves give the answer. This address, we know, cannot reach them till after the time when they shall have given their vote; but if, contrary to our expectations, there shall be any townships that shall have expressed sentiments different from our own, we entreat them by every tie of common interest and fraternal union that connects us to reconsider their proceedings, to recede before it is too late, to avert from themselves and their country the horrors of a civil war, to relinquish every idea of violence and of resistance, and to join us in those legal and constitutional measures which alone can procure us redress, and which alone are justifiable in our present circumstances.

Signed by order of the committee,

JOHN McGAURRAUH, *Chairman.*

Attest: ALBERT GALLATIN, *Secretary.*

6. LETTER TO

GOVERNOR THOMAS MIFFLIN

September 17, 1794

Gallatin explained to the governor why the citizens had re-fused the oath, and pleaded unsuccessfully against the use of federal troops.

I am directed by the committee of townships for this county to transmit to you a copy of the declarations agreed upon by them on the 10th instant, which were read on the fol-lowing day to the people convened in their respective elec-tion districts, and the return of the sense of the people of this county on the question of submission, so far as we have yet been able to ascertain it. We have, through every step during the course of the late disturbances, taken those measures which, from our knowledge of the sentiments of the people and of the heat which prevailed among them, appeared to us best calculated to allay by degrees the flame, to promote peace and submission to the laws, and to preserve this country and Pennsylvania from the disgraceful necessity of a recourse to military coercion; and we are happy to be able to inform you that the present appearances are as favorable as we had any right to expect. It was an effort too great, perhaps, to be expected from human nature that people should at once pass from an avowed intention of resisting to the signing a test of

Writings, I, 9–12.

absolute submission, and to a promise of giving active support to the laws. The change could be operated only by degrees; and after having convinced the understanding of the most enlightened, it was a more difficult task to persuade those whose prejudices were more deeply rooted and means of information less extensive. The great body of the people, which consist of moderate men, were also for some time afraid to discover their sentiments, from a want of knowledge of their own strength, and were in fact kept in awe by the few violent men. This was one of the principal reasons which prevented so many from attending the general meetings on the day on which the sense of the people was taken; to which may be added, in this county, the unconcern of a great number of moderate men, who, having followed peaceably their occupations during the whole time of the disturbances, did not think themselves interested in the event, and were not sufficiently aware of the importance of the question to the whole country. Although, however, all the warmest persons attended, we had a very large and decided majority amongst the actual voters, and great many of those who had come with an intention of testifying their intention to resist were convinced by the arguments made use of, though their pride would not suffer them to make a public retraction on the moment, and they went off without giving any vote. A very favorable and decisive change has taken place since, and has indeed been the result of the event of that day. The general disposition seems to be to submit, and great many are now signing the proposals of the Commissioners, not only in the neighboring counties, but even in this, where we had not thought it necessary. We have, therefore, thought the moment was come for the people to act with more vigor, and to show something more than mere passive obedience to the laws, and we have recommended associations for the purpose of preserving order and of supporting the civil authority by the resolutions herein enclosed, and which we hope will be attended with salutary effects. As whatever heat existed in this county was chiefly owing to what had passed in the neighboring counties, we have no doubt of peace being fully reestablished and a perfect submission taking place here, provided it is not interrupted by some new acts of violence elsewhere. It is well known that from sundry local causes, which we have not now time to detail, the heat was much greater there than amongst us; but there, also, it was confined to a certain number, and we have the best information of its daily subsiding. Still, however, a certain degree does exist both here and in the other western counties, and some time will be necessary to operate a complete restoration of order and a perfect submission to the laws. The great question now is, whether there are sufficient assurances of that submission and of its sincerity to justify government in not making use of military coercion. Mr. James Lang, one of our number, and whose efforts for the restoration of peace have been unremitted during the whole course of the late disturbances, has undertaken to deliver this letter and the enclosed papers, and we must beg leave to refer you to him for a full communication of our sentiments on that head. We will only observe that punishment of past offences cannot be now the design of government, since all those who might have been proper objects of resentment have taken advantage of the proposals of the Commissioners by signing the declaration required; and that if the submission is not sincere now, military coercion, although it may, by operating on the fears of the people, cause a more general and temporary acquiescence, will, so far from rendering it more sincere, increase the discontents, embitter the minds, and disgust many good citizens, so that if there is any danger of new outrages being again committed, that danger will be the greatest the moment the military force is withdrawn. When to that observation we add the consideration of the possibility of tumults and riots breaking out on the approach of an army, even if its march did not again promote actual resistance; of the danger to which those citizens who have taken an active part in restoring peace will be thus exposed; of the difficulty the officers will find in restraining a militia, but newly organized, and inflamed by exaggerated representations, from committing outrages against the innocent citizens; when we reflect on the necessity of cultivating harmony between the different States and between the different parts of the same State, and on the local reasons which enjoin that duty still more forcibly in regard to the Western country; when, finally, we recollect the peculiar situation of this country, once claimed by Virginia, and the danger of old broils and intestine dissensions being again renewed, we cannot too explicitly express our opinion that nothing less than a conviction that submission cannot be obtained through any other means, and that every conciliatory measure would prove abortive, can justify government in adopting that last and desperate resource.

Under the impression of those sentiments we have, we trust, discharged our duty as citizens by taking the most active part in trying to compose the disturbances, and we mean to persevere to the last in our endeavors, be the event what it will. We are also fully sensible of the propriety of the measures heretofore adopted, and of the paternal indulgence shown by the President and by yourself in everything relative to this unfortunate business, and the confidence we have in both the State and General Government convinces us that nothing but dire necessity will induce them to embrace a measure which must unavoidably be attended with great mischiefs; and that if they think themselves bound in duty to do it, they will use every method to lessen the evil, by not sending troops from another State unless those of this State are found insufficient; by subjecting them to the strictest discipline; by rendering them altogether subservient to the civil authority alone, and by putting them under the command of an officer who, as a man, as a citizen, and as a friend to order and discipline, may, as far as it is possible with such a commission, attract the confidence of the people amongst whom he shall be obliged to act.

PART THREE

Republican Stalwart in Congress
1795–1801

FEDERALIST FISCAL POLICY

7. A SKETCH OF THE FINANCES
OF THE UNITED STATES

1796

*This pamphlet established Gallatin as the chief Republican
expert on government finance. The first two sections, not included here, present an intricately reasoned analysis of Federalist finance from 1789 on, listing receipts and expenditures
and discussing returns from various taxes. Reviewing the
origins and history of the national debt, Gallatin asserted on
the basis of elaborate and imposing calculations that the debt
had been gratuitously enlarged by the assumption of state*

A Sketch of the Finances of the United States (New York: William A.
Davis, 1796) as reprinted in Writings, III, 143–168.

debts prior to the final settlement of Revolutionary accounts between the states. All the legitimate purposes claimed for assumption could have been accomplished at a saving of more than $11,000,000. Moreover, the nominal debt of the United States had increased by 1790 by more than $6,000,000.

In the following extract Gallatin explored the consequences of increasing indebtedness. He denied several major premises of the Federalists, including the idea that funding the debt created new capital. The appreciation in value of federal securities represented merely a redistribution of capital, and the taxation necessary to support the debt was a drain on the productive part of the community. He conceded that foreign investment in the domestic debt may have gained the use of new capital, but felt that it came at high rates of interest and that most of it was not applied to American production but to extravagant consumption. Gallatin argued strongly for a rapid extinction of the debt. To this end he proposed a radical and somewhat Antifederal crash program, by which part of the debt, the 3% stock, would be received at artificially high values in the sale of western lands and ten years' credit given the purchaser.

Effects of the Public Debt, and Resources applicable to its Extinguishment.

Almost all the expenses of government, but especially that species which most usually engenders a public debt, viz., the expenses of war, are a destruction of the capital employed to defray them. The labor of the men employed in the public service, had it been applied in the pursuits of private industry, would not only have supported them, but probably afforded them some reward beyond mere sustenance, and therefore would have produced an excess beyond their consumption, an addition to the national wealth, an increase of the capital of the community. The whole of their labor, however useful and necessary it may be, being totally unproductive, not only the community is deprived of that increase of capital which otherwise would have taken place, but their consumption, together with all that waste which necessarily attends the most economically managed war, must be supplied out of the resources of the community at large, out of some capital which is annihilated by being applied to that purpose. This evil, an evil of the first magnitude, is the consequence of the expenditure itself, and not of the means by which that expenditure is discharged. The capital, whether it has been raised by taxes or by loans, is destroyed on account of its being applied to an unproductive purpose; and that destruction of capital is to be charged to the object of expense, to the war, and not to the public debt which is commonly contracted for supplying the expense, for procuring the capital thus devoted to destruction. In that point of view, the only evil which arises from a habit of recurring to loans is that, by facilitating the means of raising capital, it tends to enlarge the scale of expenses, it encourages unnecessary ones; it thus indirectly promotes a greater destruction of capital than would otherwise have taken place.

If it was possible, however, to defray the expenses of a war by applying thereto a capital which would at all events have been consumed, it is evident that such a mode would in a great degree repair the evils occasioned by the war. This effect is produced to a certain extent by taxes, which always fall in part upon such parts of the revenue of the nation as would have been consumed in as unproductive a way as the expenses of the war itself. But loans uniformly are supplied not by a revenue which would have been expended, but by a capital which was before that time employed to some useful and productive purposes. To support a war, to defray any kind of public expense by taxes, is to do it by the resources of economy, by retrenching the consumption of individuals, the consumption of the nation. To defray it by loans is the mode of the spendthrift; it is irretrievably to destroy the principal rather than to diminish our immediate consumption and enjoyments. But this evil is the consequence of contracting and not of funding a debt.

When the first measures of the present government in relation to the public debt were adopted, seven years had elapsed since the conclusion of the war. It was that war which had consumed the capital of the nation; it was during, or at least in consequence of, that war that the debt had been contracted. The most sensible evils which usually accompany a public debt had preceded by many years the provisions made for the American debt; they were already in a great measure cured by the exertions of private industry. The funding of the debt was therefore attended with no immediate evil, except that arising from the taxes necessary to pay the interest. But was that measure productive of any positive good?

It has been said that it had created a large productive capital which did not exist before. How this could have been effected does not appear. The owners of the debt have in their possession certificates, bonds given by the community, but if they are richer than they were before they had obtained that security for a regular payment of interest, the community who gave the bonds are certainly the poorer. If those certificates of debt are a capital more to the holders, they are a capital less to the debtors; and the nation is exactly, in that point of view, in the same situation in which they were before; with this difference, however, that the taxes necessary to pay the interest tend in part to prevent an accumulation of capital, fall perhaps in some degree upon the necessaries of the industrious part of the community, to a certain extent oppress and impoverish the nation, are paid but in part out of a revenue which would at all events have been consumed, whilst their whole amount is consumed by the holders of the debt. There is no more capital created by those certificates, by those bonds, than would be created if a number of individuals were, in consequence of any contract, to be indebted to other members of the community and to give them their bonds to an amount equal to that of the public debt. If a holder of the public debt sells his certificates to another member of the community, he acquires indeed a capital, but he does not create it. The purchaser must pay it with a capital previously existing in the country. A public debt does not increase the existing amount of cultivated lands, of houses, of consumable commodities; it makes not the smallest addition either to the wealth or to the annual labor of a nation. It does not appear that it can in any way be an additional national capital, unless it be supposed to operate, like money, as the means of facilitating exchanges; unless it be supposed to supply the place of a circulating medium.

Supposing that to be the case, it would not be to a larger amount than the demand of the country for that medium; and as the amount of the debt is much greater than the quantity of circulating specie required, it follows that only a part of it could be employed to that purpose, and that whenever a greater part was put in circulation than was required by the actual demand, its price would sink, and it could no longer answer the very purpose to which it was designed. In fact, the paper money of the banks and the increase of circulation they produce are in general fully sufficient for the demands of the country. Whenever, from some sudden drains of specie, or from that most common evil in America, "over-trading," a greater demand for specie takes place, one of the first effects is to sink the price of the public debt. So far from adding to the capital of a nation, it would seem that a nation must have a large capital in order to support the price of a public debt, in order to give to that price that *fixture* which is an essential requisite to render it a proper substitute for a circulating medium. It is well known that that part of the capital of the

Bank of the United States which consists of public stock does not answer to that institution the purpose of a capital in specie, of a circulating medium; that it does not enable them to increase their discounts. Although the evidences of the debt may occasionally and when at a fixed price answer the purposes of money, yet generally, and whenever variations take place in that price, it becomes an article of barter, an object of speculation, calls for, instead of giving, additional supplies of money, and is well known upon many occasions to have caused some of the greatest distresses which the mercantile world has experienced.

But although the funding of the American debt neither could nor did create any additional capital, yet it became the means of drawing to America a foreign capital to a large amount. It may be seen by the statement (B) that the foreign debt properly so called, that is to say, the debt immediately consisting of moneys borrowed abroad, and upon which the interest must be paid in Europe, amounts at this time to about the same sum which it did when the present government was established. But very large sums in the present domestic debt of the United States are owned by foreigners residing in Europe. The two millions of dollars, five and half and four and half per cent. stocks, created in order to extinguish the debt due to France, are principally held by foreigners. A large amount of the original domestic debt was purchased by citizens of Holland before it had raised to its nominal value; and from that time it has been usual for merchants to make remittances to Europe in public stock. The government of the United States alone have remitted during the year 1795 near one million and a half of dollars in six per cent stock. Thus America has received from foreigners a capital of several millions of dollars, which has appeared in the light of a great acquisition of wealth, which has had some dazzling temporary effect, but which has been an acquisition of wealth to the speculators in stock alone, and not to the nation. For the nation owes to foreigners those millions; the nation must yearly pay to Europe the interest of those millions, and it cannot get rid of the payment of that interest and of the taxes necessary to pay it until it shall have returned to Europe not only the capital received by America, but a capital equal to the nominal amount of the public stock purchased by Europe.

If it be insisted that the sales of stock to Europeans, being nothing more than a certain mode of borrowing money in Europe, are advantageous to America, since we have so much demand for capital and can employ it in so profitable a way, still two circumstances must concur in rendering borrowing useful,—a low rate of interest and a proper application of the capital borrowed. The rate of interest, as it depends upon the price obtained for the stock, is uncertain. Yet it must be recollected that the purchases by foreigners began at a very early period, and that during the six years that have elapsed since the funding system was proposed, the six per cent. stock has not been at par or above par more than eighteen months, viz., from the latter end of July, 1791, to the beginning of January, 1793. The probability is that we pay from 7 to 8 per cent. on the capital which we have thus borrowed. Had, however, the whole of that capital been applied to productive purposes, it would have enabled the nation to pay the interest, high as it was, and perhaps to make some profit. But it cannot be denied that a small proportion, indeed, has been so applied as to increase the cultivation and improvement of lands, the erection of manufactures, the annual income of the nation. Acquired suddenly by individuals, that capital has been applied in the same manner as every other sudden acquisition of wealth; it has enabled those individuals to consume, to spend more, and they have consumed and spent extravagantly. Taking in the great number of elegant houses which have been built within a few years in all the large cities, and which, however convenient to the inhabitants, afford no additional revenue to the nation, it may be asserted that the greater part of the capital thus drawn from Europe for purchases of stock has been actually consumed, without leaving in its stead any other productive capital, and that as the nation still owes the whole, it has been impoverished even by the only consequence of the funding system that has made any temporary addition to the apparent wealth of the country. That wealth is, in a great degree, consumed and destroyed, and the whole debt remains to be paid. Still it is not astonishing that those who have been thus enabled to consume that capital should not have attended much to the manner in which it was to be replaced and repaid by the nation, and should have finally persuaded themselves and many others that the funding of the debt was a real and permanent increase of the national capital, a national acquisition of wealth.

Let it not be supposed that any of those reflections are intended to convey a censure on that part of the funding system which provided for the payment of the interest of the proper debt of the United States. They are designed merely to show that the propriety of that measure must have depended solely on its justice. Whether the debt had been funded on the plan of discrimination in favor of the original holders of those who had performed the services, or, as has been the case, in favor of the purchasers of certificates, the general effects would have been nearly the same; and unless the American government had chosen to forfeit every claim to common honesty, it must necessarily provide for discharging the principal or paying the interest to one or the other of two descriptions of persons.

Whatever difference of opinion may heretofore have existed on that subject, on the propriety of paying those who had purchased the debt so much under its value, it now exists no more, it has ceased with the cause; for all the present owners have, or may be supposed to have, purchased the debt at the market price, which, since it has been funded, has been obtained for it. The solemn obligations, superadded by the present government to those contracted before, never can be set aside without the most flagrant and pernicious breach of public faith and of national morality.

If the public debt is not an additional national capital, no other disadvantage can result from its extinction except the increase of taxes necessary for that purpose, and the annual loss which will be suffered by replacing to Europe the capital borrowed there, either under the denomination of foregn debt or by the sales of domestic debt. So far as the taxes necessary for that purpose will check consumption, the capital to be thus repaid abroad will be supplied by economy, and its payment will in no shape whatever impoverish the country. So far as those taxes will fall, not on that portion of the annual revenue which would have been consumed, but on that part which would have been saved and have become an addition to the permanent wealth of the nation, so far the progress of the country will, in a certain degree, be checked by the withdrawing and paying the capital due to Europe. To do this too suddenly would certainly be injurious to the community. But any evil that may arise from a gradual extinction of the debt, from a gradual repayment of the capital borrowed in Europe, will be more than counterbalanced by the natural progress of America, will free us from the payment of interest upon that capital, and will, at the same time, strengthen the bonds of our Union and give additional vigor and respectability to the nation.

It may have been supposed by some that the debt, by rendering the creditors dependent on government, gave it an additional stability. But it should be recollected that although an artificial interest is thereby created, which may at times give an useful support, it may at some future period lend its assistance to bad measures and to a bad administration. So far as that interest is artificial, so far as it is distinct from the general interest, it may perhaps act against that general interest and become as pernicious as it is supposed to have been useful. At all events, who can doubt that the jealousies, the apprehensions, the discontents excited by the public debt have been more injurious to our domestic peace, have gone farther to weaken our real union, than any other internal cause? It is a lamentable truth that the Americans, although bound together by a stronger government, are less united in sentiment than they were eight years ago. Every source of discontent, every permanent cause of taxation which can be removed, adds to the strength of the Union and to the stability of its government.

But, in regard to our strength and consequent respectability and independence in relation to other nations, as speedy an extinction of the debt as circumstances will admit becomes indispensable. As there is not the smallest probability that we ever shall be involved in any war except in self-defence, and as the exhausted situation of all the European nations seems to warrant, at the conclusion of the present war, a continuance of peace for at least ten or twelve years, we should by all means improve that period to discharge the heaviest part of our debt. It requires no argument to prove, it is a self-evident truth, that, in a political point of view at least, every nation is enfeebled by a public debt. Spain, once the first power of Europe,—Spain, with her extensive and rich possessions, Holland, notwithstanding her immense commerce, still feel the effects of the debts they began to contract two centuries ago, and their present political weakness stands as a monument of the unavoidable consequences of that fatal system. Yet what are those instances when compared with that of France, where the public debt, although once discharged by the assistance of a national bankruptcy, has at last overwhelmed government itself! The debt of Great Britain, which began at a later period than that of any of those three nations, has not yet produced such visible effects. The unexampled prosperity of that country has heretofore been sufficient to support its strength and to increase its wealth, notwithstanding the weight of that burden. Yet the revenue now necessary to discharge the interest annually payable on that debt and to support the peace establishment of that nation, that is to say, the annual revenue now raised by taxes in Great Britain, would, if unencumbered, discharge the yearly expenses even of the war in which she is now engaged.

The sum necessary to pay the annuity and interest on the debt of the United States constitutes more than two-thirds of their yearly expenditure; and it is presumable that we would not be much exposed to the wanton attacks, depredations, or insults of any nation was it not known that our revenue and resources are palsied by an annual defalcation of five millions of dollars. It does not seem that any possible object of expense, without even excepting the creation of a navy, can be so eminently useful in adding to our external security and respectability as that which, by paying the principal of our debt, will give us the command of an unimpaired revenue, and enable us to dispose, if necessary, of all our resources.

A circumstance which seems to render this still more requisite in America, is the difficulty for the United States of raising moneys by loans, except in time of profound peace. It is well known that the great demand for capital in America, the usual high market rate for interest, the peculiar circumstances of the country, render it nearly impossible to borrow any large sums at home; and experience has lately proved that the circumstance of an European war, even though we ourselves were not engaged, was sufficient to prevent us from any farther loan in Europe. Hence it results that as we cannot in case of any emergency put much reliance on that resource, we should during our state of peace and prosperity hasten to disencumber our domestic resources. We have, indeed, severely felt the obligation of repaying during the present European war the anticipation at home and the instalments of the foreign debt abroad. We have thereby been compelled to borrow on the most disadvantageous terms, to contract the obligation of paying an interest of at least six per cent. for 24 years, and to remit to Europe stock purchased at par, and which will probably sell there under its nominal value. These considerations, supported, it is believed, by the general opinion of the people of America, forcibly point out the necessity of an immediate recourse to our domestic resources, of an immediate increase of revenue.

It has already been shown that our present receipts are hardly adequate to our present expenditure; in fact, that we have heretofore made only a nominal provision far paying the principal of any part of our debt. For although (supposing the present receipts to be equal to the present rate of expenditure) it may be said that we have provided for the yearly payment of 2 per cent. on the principal of our six per cent. debt bearing a present interest, yet we have not made any provision whatever for the payment of the annuity payable after the year 1800 on the deferred stock. Indeed, the interest (exclusively of the additional 2 per cent.) payable on this stock exceeds the yearly payments of 2 per cent. upon the six per cent. stock; and the fact is that our present revenue is not even sufficient to pay after the year 1800 the interest on our debt. Our faith is now pledged to pay from after that year an annuity of 8 per cent. upon both stocks; and whatever difference of opinion may exist upon the extinguishment of other parts of the debt, it is necessary to increase our revenue from after that year by a sum sufficient to discharge that annuity, which has already been stated at about 1,100,000 dollars.

This increase will enable the United States to extinguish the whole of the six per cent. stock by the year 1818, and the whole of the deferred stock by the year 1824. No farther provision seems necessary on that part of the debt, which amounts to about forty-two millions of dollars, except the very important one to find the additional revenue of 1,100,000 dollars.

The parts of the debt which will remain unprovided for are:

1st. The foreign debt, which on the 1st of January, 1796, consisted of about twelve millions of dollars, but which, by the payment of the instalment that falls due during the year 1796, and has been provided for by the five million loan, will be reduced to about 11,600,000 dollars.

2dly. The five and a half per cent. and four and a half per cent. stocks, amounting to about 2,000,000 dollars.

3dly. The instalments due after the year 1796 to the bank, and not provided for by the five million loan, amounting to 1,600,000 dollars.

4thly. The anticipations necessary during the years 1796 and 1797 (exclusively of the loans that may be requisite to pay any part of the principal of the debt), estimated at 800,000 dollars.

5thly. The new five million loan, which, being irredeemable for twenty-three years, cannot be extinguished except by purchases.

6thly. The three per cent. stock, amounting to about 19,300,000 dollars, which, on account of its low rate of interest, is not susceptible of any extinguishment, except by purchases or by a new modification of the debt.

Those different sums somewhat exceed forty millions of dollars; but the four first items, which seem alone to be the object of redemption by an application of revenue, amount altogether to sixteen millions of dollars. They are all, the five and half per cent. and four and half per cent. stocks excepted, payable by instalments due before the year 1810; and although the amount of the yearly payable instalments is not equal every year, yet as some of the Dutch loans may, according to the terms of the contract, be discharged by government as much earlier as they please, the total sum to be paid each year may be so equalized and modified as to render the discharge of the whole practicable before the year 1810, with an uniform revenue. It is proposed to make provision for that payment during that period by an additional revenue, and as it is not possible that any new revenue, even if raised by Congress at their next session, can be productive before the year 1798, the term proposed for the redemption of those sixteen millions will be twelve years from the first of January, 1798, to the first of January, 1810.

The interest payable on those sixteen millions may, when calculating the revenue necessary to discharge the principal, be estimated at an average of about five per cent. A debt of sixteen millions, bearing an interest of five per cent., will be discharged in twelve years by a revenue somewhat exceeding one million of dollars. But as the eleven hundred thousand dollars necessary to pay the annuity on the deferred stock will not be wanted till the year 1801 for that purpose, and, if raised from the year 1798, may in the mean while be applied to discharge three millions and a half of the debt of sixteen millions; this, being thus reduced to twelve millions and a half, will be discharged in twelve years by a revenue of about 800,000 dollars. This sum added to the 1,100,000 dollars, which are at all events necessary to pay the annuity on the deferred stock, form an aggregate of 1,900,000 dollars, the revenue necessary to be raised for twelve years.

Through the means of that revenue not only sixteen millions of the debt shall have been redeemed, but an annuity equal to about 780,000 dollars, the interest payable thereon, will be liberated and form an actual addition to our present revenue. If during the same period the resources to be derived from the lands of the United States, which will next be taken under consideration, are applied to the three per cent. stock so as to liberate an annuity of 320,000 dollars, these two sums will be sufficient to pay the annuity on the deferred stock, and the whole of the additional revenue of 1,900,000 dollars may cease after the year 1809. On the other hand, if only the 1,100,000 dollars are raised from the year 1801, that additional revenue must continue till the year 1824. The difference between raising what must at all events be raised, to wit, 1,100,000 dollars, only from after the year 1800, putting off the increase of taxes and revenue to the last moment, and raising

1,900,000 dollars from the year 1798, consists in the difference between taxes of 1,100,000 dollars for twenty-four years and taxes of 1,900,000 dollars for twelve years; or (as 1,100,000 dollars must by both plans be raised for twelve years) it consists in the difference between immediate taxes of 800,000 dollars for twelve years and taxes of 1,100,000 dollars also for twelve years, but beginning twelve years hence. Supposing the country to be so fast progressing in prosperity that 1,100,000 dollars of taxes will not be more heavy twelve years hence than 800,000 dollars now are, still the sole advantage which arises from a postponement is present enjoyment, and putting off a burden which must necessarily come at that time. The loss is manifest; for although the same burden must then be borne, the debt remains unpaid. Should we not raise that revenue at present, to a momentary relief we shall have sacrificed sixteen millions of dollars, we shall have lost the present time, we shall have lost an almost certain period of peace and prosperity; and although we cannot command future events, we shall have to encounter them at that time as unprovided and as enfeebled as we now are.

Independent of any additional revenue to be raised by taxes, the lands of the United States will afford another resource. Those now at the disposal of Congress do not amount to ten millions of acres; but the quantity might be enlarged without any difficulty was there any real demand for more. Lands are so much more valuable to us than to the Indians, that whenever they are actually wanted we may afford to pay for them a much higher price than they ever do ask. The actual demand, which must regulate the price that may be obtained by Congress for the lands belonging to the public, is determined itself by the increase of population and by the direction of emigrations. Lands of good quality and in actual demand for settlers will fetch about four dollars per acre, payable in about five years by instalments. If sold upon shorter terms of credit, or in large tracts, the persons who settle the lands and can afford to give the highest price are generally excluded from the competition, and the lands will only bring such a price as will leave to the purchaser (who is to sell again to settlers) the usual profit upon capital employed in similar speculations. Should the lands be sold before there is an actual demand by settlers, they will bring a price proportionably less as the prospect of settlement may be farther distant. Congress have directed their lands to be sold partly in small and partly in large tracts; one half of the purchase-money to be paid at the time of sale, and the other half within one year after; no lands to be sold under two dollars per acre. The credit is so short that the class of people who usually begin settlements will be nearly altogether excluded. The provision which fixes the price at two dollars at least will exclude, to a certain degree, the speculators. And the sales will probably fall short of the actual yearly demand for settlers and be confined to the very best tracts.

About ten thousand families migrate every year to the westward of the Alleghany Mountains. Although all of them cannot purchase lands, all of them increase the demand for land, as they enable those who can purchase to cultivate more and therefore to purchase more. Of those ten thousand families, three-fourths at least will be fixed in the States of Tennessee, Kentucky, Virginia, and Pennsylvania, and in those parts of the North-West Territory already ceded by the United States and by Virginia. The yearly migration to the lands of the United States will be probably about 2600 families; the yearly actual demand for lands may vary from 500,000 to one million of acres. Although various circumstances render it impossible to form any tolerably correct conjecture on the amount of sales, it is not probable that, on the plan which has been adopted, they will upon an average exceed 250,000 acres, yielding a revenue of 500,000 dollars. The first year, on account of the great demand for the valuable low lands on the Ohio and other rivers, will perhaps be more productive than the succeeding ones.

The lands may be applied in two ways to the payment of the debt, either indirectly or immediately: indirectly, by selling the lands for the best price that can be obtained, and applying the moneys to the redemption of the debt; immediately, by inducing the holders of some species of debt to exchange it for lands, by making the price of lands payable in certificates of debt of that species. By the first mode it is probable that a higher price will be obtained for the lands, as they will only be sold from time to time as they rise in value, and as some advantages must be given to the holders of the debt to induce them to make the exchange. But, on the other hand, the second mode will secure a proper application of the proceeds of the land; the land itself will pay the debt without coming into the Treasury in the shape of money, which, upon the first emergency, might be applied to some other purposes. Another peculiar advantage would arise if the land was immediately applied to the extinguishment of the debt bearing an interest of three per cent. Was a redemption of this debt to be attempted by purchases, it would necessarily raise its price beyond its usual market price and beyond what it is supposed to be really worth. It would, therefore, require so much larger a sum for its redemption. Supposing that stock to be worth sixty per cent. upon its nominal value when six per cent. stock is at par, the 19,300,000 dollars now existing are worth only something more than eleven millions and a half of dollars. But although the lands should bring that money, it would undoubtedly require a greater sum to purchase the whole of the stock. A variety of plans might be formed for a commutation of that stock into lands. The following sketch is offered merely to show in what manner the operation might be effected.

Let the lands, after they shall have been surveyed, be divided into ten large lots of 960,000 acres each, as equal in quality and value as the nature of the case will admit; and each of the said large lots be subdivided into townships, and these into tracts of 640 acres. Let then a subscription be opened for the sale of the large lots successively, beginning with the most valuable; each purchaser to subscribe for at least a tract of 640 acres; the price of the subscription to be two dollars per acre, with interest at the rate of three per cent. a year from the time of the sale, payable in any species of stock of the United States at its nominal value; with liberty to the purchaser to discharge the debt in specie at the rate of one dollar and a half per acre; one-tenth part of the purchase-money to be paid at the time of the subscription, and the remainder part in nine yearly instalments, or sooner, at the option of the purchaser: possession of the land to be given immediately, but the land to remain mortgaged in security for the purchase-money. As soon as the subscription to one of the large lots is filled, let the subscribers draw lot for their respective shares, under such modifications as will secure to subscribers for one township, or quarter of a township, the whole in one tract.

The most weighty objection against this plan is, perhaps, the lottery and speculation to which it will give rise; yet it will be found difficult to devise any plan for the sale of lands and for the redemption of the public debt which will not, in some degree, be liable to the same objection. The number of acres, price, interest, time of payment, &c., in the above have been inserted merely for the sake of conveying clearer ideas; but they should be considered as blanks that can be filled only upon an investigation of all the details of the subject.

The advantages for the public, supposing the whole of the subscription to be filled, would be the certainty of the redemption of the whole debt bearing an interest of three per cent. and an immediate liberation of the annuity of 580,000 dollars necessary to pay the interest thereon, since the interest payable for the land would always be equal to the interest payable on the three per cent. stock in circulation.[1] This sum might, there-

---

[1] Ten lots of 960,000 acres each are 9,600,000 acres; which, if all sold at two dollars per acre, would bring dollars 19,200,000. The amount of three per cent stock is about 19,800,000.

fore, be applied in part of the additional revenue of 800,000 dollars wanted to extinguish the debt of sixteen millions; I say of the 800,000 dollars, for it could not be applied in part of the 1,100,000 dollars necessary to pay the annuity on the deferred stock, the faith of the Union being pledged to discharge that annuity out of the revenues of the Union, and to apply, *in addition to it,* the proceeds of the public lands towards the extinguishment of the public debt. Thus, if that subscription was to be filled, the lands would in twelve years extinguish both the debt bearing three per cent. interest and a great part of the above-mentioned sixteen millions of dollars; it being necessary to add (for that purpose and exclusively of the 1,100,000 dollars requisite to pay the annuity on the deferred stock) only a yearly revenue of 220,000 dollars for those twelve years. Those advantages would more than counterbalance to the public the advantages offered to the subscribers by the low rate of the lands.

The advantages to subscribers would be obvious. The average price of lands equal in situation and quality, but either settled or capable of being immediately settled, is now four dollars per acre. In all probability ten years, and at farthest fifteen, will settle the whole of the ten millions of acres offered for sale, or at least will raise the whole of it to what may be called the settlement price, an average of four dollars per acre. A part might now be sold above that price; a great proportion of the lands will attain it within a shorter period than ten years; the most remote situation will be worth it at the expiration of that time. And this must take place, according to the natural course of events, by the natural increase of population, without giving any farther trouble of management to the purchasers than that of selling the lands again to actual settlers. Those amongst the purchasers who will become settlers will affix that price to the land as soon as they improve it; and at the price they give will be enabled to pay three-fourths of the purchase-money out of the proceeds of the land itself. The land may therefore be considered as being, upon an average, worth four dollars per acre within eight years after the time of purchase; which, discounted at the rate of six per cent. compound interest, is equal to about two dollars and a half at the time of purchase. For this the subscribers will give, at most, one dollar and a half, bearing, in fact, only four per cent. interest, payable in nine years, and not worth much more than one dollar and a quarter at the time of purchase.

Although the success of a plan something similar to this may not be complete, yet so far as it will succeed, so far the extinguishment of the debt bearing an interest of three per cent. will be promoted, and so far the amount of the additional revenue necessary for the payment of the annuity on the deferred stock, and for the extinguishment of the above-mentioned debt of sixteen millions of dollars, may be diminished. The sources from which that additional revenue, whatever its amount may be, can be derived remain to be examined; still recollecting that at least 1,100,000 dollars must necessarily be raised, and that the ability of the United States to raise the highest required sum, viz., 1,900,000 dollars, cannot be denied.

This revenue may be raised either by indirect or direct taxes. A difficulty, inherent in the Constitution, will always render a recurrence to direct taxation the last resort of the general government. For, it being provided that such taxes shall be apportioned among the several States according to their respective population, those States who have a less extent of territory in proportion to their numbers will think themselves aggrieved by a species of tax which must reach their lands, not in the ratio of their value, but in that of the whole number of inhabitants.

Labor being the only source of wealth, the annual quantity and produce of labor was the best general rule which could be established for fixing the respective ability of paying taxes in the several States. Nor does it appear that any better criterion

could have been adopted, in order to ascertain that annual produce of labor, than the number of inhabitants, making the
same allowance with the Constitution by estimating the net
produce of the labor of five slaves (after deducting that part
necessary for their sustenance) equal to the net produce of
the labor of three freemen. Yet that general rule, like all others,
is liable to some exceptions. The labor of the same number of
men may, according to the differences in the nature of their
employment, in their skill and industry, in the government
under which they live, in the quantity of active capital existing
in the country, and in several other circumstances, vary in
different countries. The labor of the inhabitants of Great
Britain is certainly far more productive than the labor of the
inhabitants of Poland, who are at least equal in number. It
does not, however, appear that the differences existing in the
respective circumstances of the several States are so great as
to render the operation of the rule more unequal than the
operation of most indirect taxes. Their government is similar,
and the most sensible difference is, that the Southern States
have a larger capital in land, and the Northern States have
both more industry and a larger circulating capital. Hence it
results that a tax merely on lands might perhaps bear more
heavily on the landholders of the North than on those of the
South; not but that a tract of land, without reference to its
size, is usually equally productive in both places when cultivated by an equal number of persons; but because there is a
less proportion of the inhabitants employed in the cultivation
of land to the North than to the South. The operation of a tax
merely on land might therefore be unequal on that description
of persons in the several States, but not on the States themselves. A direct tax upon the whole property, although perhaps liable to still greater objections, would not, in that point
of view, be unequal either on the States or on any particular
description of people. And it is worthy of remark that, whatever inequality may result from the operation of direct taxes

proceeding from the difference in the nature of the capital and in the application of the labor in the different States, as great a one, but operating in the very reverse, must result from indirect taxes on consumable commodities imported into the Union. For, if taxes on land, laid according to the rule prescribed by the Constitution, bear more heavily in some one quarter because the proportion of persons employed in the cultivation of lands is less there than in other parts of the Union, on the other hand the proportion of persons employed in manufactures in the same place must be greater.

The consumption, therefore, of imported manufactures, and the amount of duties paid on that consumption, will be proportionably less. If a land tax presses harder upon the landholders of the North, it is because the proportion of cultivators is less and that of manufacturers is greater than to the South. If the proportion of manufacturers is less to the South, the people there must consume a greater quantity of foreign goods and pay a larger proportion of the impost. By combining the two modes of taxation, a more equal effect will probably be produced than can be by either singly. This opinion is confirmed by the experience of all other nations; it is not believed that any instance can be adduced of a nation raising any considerable revenue without having resorted to direct taxation, to land taxes. Nor have these, when laid judiciously and with moderation, ever been complained of as unequal or oppressive. It is, however, proper to examine what additional resources can be derived from indirect taxes.

The duties upon importations are, of all others, those which seem best adapted to our situation. As we import more and manufacture less, in proportion to our consumption, than almost any other country, the impost must necessarily be far more productive than any internal duties on our own manufactures. The collection of the impost, being confined to a few seaports, requires but few officers and a small expense. The merchant is liable to no vexation from the officers except at the time of landing the goods and on board of his vessel; and he is always a man of sufficient information to understand thoroughly the duties required of him by the law, and to repel any attempt by the officer to oppress. In those particulars the manufacturers who pay internal duties are generally placed in a worse situation, for the act of manufacturing not being, like that of landing goods, the work of a day, but that of the whole year, it is necessary, in order to know the quantity manufactured, that the workshop of the manufacturer should be perpetually opened to the inquisitorial inspection of the collector. Nor must it be forgotten that, in America, the few extensive manufactures are carried on by a great number of persons, many of whom,[1] from their situation in life, may often involuntarily omit some of the numerous duties prescribed by the most complex of all revenue laws, and are also more exposed to the oppressions of subaltern officers. Although few manufactures are yet carried on upon a large scale in the United States, yet a great proportion of the most essentially necessary articles are made at home, and the greater part of the importations may justly be termed luxuries, and are amongst the most proper objects of taxation. Thus the impost, at the same time that it possesses the same general advantages with other taxes upon consumption, is free of the most weighty inconveniences which may be objected to the other species; it is, in our present situation, of all others the most productive, the cheapest to collect, the least vexatious, and in general the least oppressive.

This resource has, therefore, been resorted to and carried already pretty generally as far as its own limits will permit. For there is a certain rate of duty beyond which the high temptation offered to smuggling or a diminution of consumption must necessarily decrease the revenue. It cannot be said

---

[1] Distillation of spirits and tanning leather, chiefly south of the Delaware.

that the present duties have, upon all those articles which are fit objects of taxation, been carried to the utmost extent of which they are susceptible. Perhaps a judicious selection may be made amongst the most bulky of those articles which now pay ten per cent. *ad valorem,* and the duty increased to the same rate paid upon printed cotton goods, viz., twelve and a half percent perhaps sugar, which is now thought to pay the lowest duty amongst those articles charged with specific duties, might, without oppression, as it can without danger, be taxed half a cent. higher; perhaps some of the articles which now pay duties *ad valorem* might be classed amongst those paying specific duties, so as to be made to contribute something more to the revenue; perhaps the system is susceptible of some farther improvements. But it will be generally allowed that there would be a great risk of diminishing, instead of increasing, the revenue was any considerable extension of the impost to be attempted, and that it would be a large computation to suppose that 300,000 additional dollars could be raised in that manner. Yet it may be safely predicted that, unless recourse be had to direct taxes, the unavoidable consequence will be an undue and dangerous augmentation of the present duties on importation, amongst which the most oppressive, viz., an increase of that upon salt, is already contemplated.

The next class of indirect taxes are the internal duties on the use or consumption of consumable articles. The only tax which has been suggested, in addition to that on carriages, upon the use of anything is one upon horses; but it must be remembered that, in order to be an indirect tax, it should be confined to saddle-horses.[1] For the horses employed in agriculture or in the transportation of merchandise are not an object of expense, but a productive capital, an object of revenue, an object of direct taxation only. It is presumable that a

---

[1] The use of coach-horses is already taxed by the duty on pleasurable carriages.

tax confined to saddle-horses would be difficult in its execution, liable to be evaded, and very unproductive.

The little success which taxes upon consumption, laid on the manufactures, have heretofore met with does not seem to afford much encouragement for similar attempts in future. Men who are earnestly wishing to derive new revenues from internal sources and by indirect taxes have not been able to suggest, in addition to those already liable to the excise, more than two American manufactures productive enough to be proper objects of taxation, that of leather and that of hats.

The manufacture of leather is, without doubt, one of the most extensive in the United States. It is presumed that a duty of ten per cent. on that article might, if duly collected, yield about 500,000 dollars. It is liable to two weighty objections: it is a tax which would, at least in the first instance, fall with nearly equal weight on every individual; it is properly a tax upon labor, always oppressive in its first operation, and the final effect of which cannot be calculated. In the next place, it does not seem practicable to raise the duty in any other mode than upon the tanner himself; and the manufacture in many parts of the Middle and almost universally in the Southern States is a family one, carried on by every planter and farmer. Its collection would therefore be expensive, and a great proportion of the duty evaded.

A tax upon hats would be less unequal and more easily collected; but, on the other hand, far less productive. It is believed that a duty of ten per cent. on this article would not in practice yield more than 100,000 dollars.

The last tax of indirect taxes includes all the duties laid upon a variety of transactions in life, which are commonly taxed by the operation of licenses or of stamps.[1] Amongst these, law proceedings, transfers of property, and contracts or obligations for money are the most usual objects of taxation.

---

[1] Duties upon sales at auction, and licenses to retailers when no consideration is paid to the quantity retailed, cannot be said to be duties upon consumption, and must be ranked in this class.

Taxes upon law proceedings may deservedly be ranked amongst the most unequal, unjust, and oppressive. Those upon contracts in general, although always to a certain degree unequal, are, perhaps, liable to less objections than most other indirect taxes. Yet in America they could not, without injustice, be extended to all species of contracts. Transfers of all real property especially are so much more frequent in those parts of the Union which are newly settled, that a stamp duty upon them would be in proportion not to the wealth, but to the poverty, of the contributors. A necessity of limiting the number of species of contracts to be taxed would diminish the productiveness and increase the expense of collection; and as in mere contracts for money the only penalty attached to the omission of taking out a stamp depends on the subject-matter of the contract becoming a subject of discussion in a court of justice, the confidence of the parties in one another will sometimes, and their negligence often, tend to diminish the revenue. From those causes this class of duties has not been supposed to be likely to produce more than 150,000 dollars at most, and would not probably yield above 100,000.

It therefore appears that the only new indirect taxes that can be resorted to are an addition to the impost, an excise on leather and hats, and a stamp duty; all of which would not yield above one million of dollars, and would therefore fall short of the revenue wanted.[1] Yet could a sufficient sum be

---

[1] No notice is taken here of a duty of two per cent. proposed during the last session of Congress upon testamentary dispositions, descents, and successions. As it is not intended to extend to those to parents, husbands and wives, and children, it is evident that in the present state of society in the United States it would be quite unproductive. But a tax of this kind is to all intents and purposes a direct tax. It falls upon capital, upon revenue, and not upon expense. Should the definition of direct taxes, given in the first section, be thought incorrect, yet it is believed that, upon whatever principle a classificaion is attempted, this must necessarily be arranged under the head of direct taxation. Thus it falls finally and solely upon the person who pays it.

raised by those means, the people of the United States may decide which would be most oppressive, these including an additional duty on salt, or a direct tax. The objection arising from a supposed inequality has already been noticed, and it must be farther observed that if some States have stronger objections against that species of taxation than others, they are generally those which have been mostly relieved, by the assumption of the State debts, from the heaviest individual burden. Had not that assumption taken place, the Union, indeed, might have proceeded to the extinguishment of their proper debt without wanting additional revenues and without resorting to direct taxation. But those States who were oppressed under the weight of their own debts must, in that case, have raised a larger revenue than will now be their proportion of a general tax. After having urged, as the most powerful argument in favor of the assumption, that it would liberate the resources of each State from local demands and enable the Union to use them all, it would seem unfair, at present, to refuse to the general government the command of the most productive internal branch of revenue. In fact, the very objections against that assumption which have been so much insisted upon must lose a great part of their strength if an adequate revenue is raised. They are mostly grounded upon the increase of the general debt and the greater difficulty for the Union effectually to command all the resources of the country. Give the Union that command, prove that its ability of paying the principal of the debt is not impaired by having assumed the State debts, and the measure will stand almost justified.

How far the lands belonging to the United States, the additional resources to be derived from indirect taxes, and the savings which may be effected in our present rate of expenditure, may reduce the amount of revenue to be raised by a direct tax, cannot be ascertained. But it cannot be supposed that even a tax of 1,600,000 dollars could be oppressive in the smallest degree. From the year 1785 to the year 1790, at a time when the situation of the United States was less prosperous than now, when their population, the quantity of cultivated land and of circulating capital, the annual income of the people, and their consequent ability to pay, may fairly be stated as inferior to what they now are, a tax was raised in Pennsylvania without oppression and paid with punctuality, the amount of which was nearly equal to the present proportion of that State of a Federal tax of 1,600,000 dollars.[1] Perhaps it would not be amiss, in order to insure the greatest possible economy, to make all the payments of the interest and principal of the public debts out of the duties on imports, appropriating the surplus of those duties, the internal existing duties, and the new taxes, to the discharge of all the current expenditures, and especially of the military and naval establishments.

A direct tax imposed by the Union may be laid either uniformly on the same species of property in all the States, or upon that species in each State which has usually been directly taxed there. In favor of the last mode it may be said that it will altogether remove the inequality apprehended from a land tax, and, above all, that it will better accommodate to the habits and prejudices of each State. This last argument carries so much weight with it that the House of Representatives have directed the Secretary of the Treasury to prepare a plan upon that principle, to be laid before them at the ensuing session. The materials which will then be collected may enable Congress to form a final determination on the subject; and it is not the intention of this sketch to anticipate, by any remarks on details, the deliberations which must then take place.

---

[1] During the war Pennsylvania raised some enormous taxes, far beyond her abilities, the arrearages of which are not yet finally paid. These, which were certainly highly oppressive, were often collected at the same time with the tax here mentioned, but should by no means be confounded with it.

Yet, opinions having been expressed here upon most species of taxation, a general remark will also be added on the comparative merits of the two modes of laying direct taxes, without any reference to the local causes which may influence a final decision.

A direct tax is laid upon property in proportion either to its capital value or to the revenue it affords. It is, therefore, necessary not only to collect the tax, but previously to assess it; in other words, to estimate the value of the property or of the income derived from it. The collection of the tax itself is everywhere cheaper than that of any other tax, because the officers employed may always be temporary ones, there being no necessity, as in the case of indirect taxes, to keep a watch over the contributors. It costs less to collect in England and in France than any other species of tax. Even in Pennsylvania, where the system was complained of on account of its being expensive, the charges of collection were but five per cent. But the assessment must necessarily increase to a certain degree the expense, and this will vary according to the species of property taxed. Real property, being of a permanent nature, may be valued once in five or ten years without any great inequality resulting therefrom. The assessment of England, which, it is true, is now very unequal, has stood for near a century without variation. Personal property, perpetually shifting, requires a yearly valuation. But it is not only in the article of expenses in collecting that direct taxes upon real property possess a great comparative advantage. In order to assess, to estimate the capital or the income of an individual, that capital, that income, must be known. His real property is visible and can always be estimated with certainty. But the greatest part of his personal property may with propriety be denominated invisible. His capital employed in commerce, the debts which are due to him (from which must be deducted those he owes), his money, and even his stock in goods, must either be assessed according to his own declaration, or be estimated in an arbitrary manner. And when the tax is laid upon the revenue and not upon the capital of persons, when the profits of their industry are also to be calculated, it may truly be asserted that, was it not for the permanence of the vexations of excises, the most odious of these would be less oppressive, unequal, and unjust than a direct tax levied in that manner. Experience justifies those assertions. In England, where direct taxes fall almost exclusively upon lands and houses, they never have given cause to any just reason of complaint. In France, the taxes called *personal, taille* and *capitation,* which were laid with a regard to the conditions of persons, and assessed according to a conjectural proportion of fortunes, industry, and professions, were equally oppressive to the contributors and injurious to the nation. Although there are some species of personal property which may be estimated and taxed in a more certain and less arbitrary manner than others, yet it may be laid down as a general rule, liable only to local exceptions, that lands and houses are the proper objects of direct taxation, that almost every other species of property must be reached indirectly by taxes on consumption.

To conclude: the resources to which it appears that the Union should resort are those of the most general nature, leaving all the lesser, all the local subjects of taxation, to the individual States. There are at present but two species of wealth of a general nature in the United States, viz., lands and capital employed in commerce. It has already been stated that in proportion to our population we were one of the first commercial nations. It cannot be denied that we are by far the first agricultural nation. It must be acknowledged that we are not yet a manufacturing nation. Our capital in commerce is great; our capital in lands is immense; it can hardly be said that we yet have any capital in manufactures. Taxes must be raised from that fund which can afford to pay; taxes must be laid, even in the first instance, where capital does exist. The impost is productive, because our commerce is extensive; every effort, in our present situation, to raise a considerable revenue from our manufactures will prove abortive, because there is no capital there to pay it; because the income drawn from those manufactures which are proper objects of taxation is yet inconsiderable. The same taxes upon consumption, which in manufacturing countries are raised by excises, are in America very properly raised by impost.[1] When the impost is carried as far as prudence will dictate, the great source of taxes upon consumption may, in this country, be considered as nearly exhausted, and the other general species of American capital, the other great branch of national revenue, lands, must be resorted to; must be made to contribute by direct taxation.

THE FRENCH REVOLUTION

Republicans made little headway against the Federalist regime until they were able to capitalize on the vast sympathy of the American people for the French Revolution. This sympathy was not an active force until 1793, after the French beheaded King Louis XVI, declared a republic, and went to war against a European coalition which was soon joined by Great Britain. Despite the shocking atrocities of the revolution, Americans were emotionally drawn to France in her defense of the republic against Old World kings. Her struggle against the ancien régime *corresponded to American ideals. Most*

---

[1] If soap, leather, and beer pay a duty in England which is not paid in the United States, on the other hand, a great proportion of our clothing of every description pays a duty to which the inhabitant of Great Britain is not subject.

Americans felt a sense of gratitude for French aid during the American Revolution, and on the other hand they had a residual hatred of Britain. But France proved more than a match for her adversaries, and as the years passed the dynamism of the revolution was subtly converted from the realization of social reform to the achievement of French hegemony over Europe. Even before this transformation occurred, Americans were divided over France.

Federalists were more attached than Republicans to elite rule and social gradation, principles that were ultimately threatened by the spread of French equalitarianism. The party was commerce oriented, and thus more alert to America's dependence upon amicable relations with Britain for economic prosperity. Unblinded by visionary enthusiasm, Federalists were able very early to take a rational attitude toward the French Revolution, to recognize its corruption, and to expose the danger that French aggrandizement posed for the United States. Republicans, on the other hand, were not so easily disillusioned. To them the epochal struggle for the rights of man was more important than its lapses from rectitude. Their genuine enthusiasm for France was prolonged beyond its natural term, however, by political considerations. Like the patriots of 1776 they could only unseat an established government by cultivating the support of the people, hence they played upon sympathy for France and invoked the slogans of liberty and equality on their side of the political battle.

Although some allowance must be made for political motive, Gallatin was unquestionably a devotee of the rights of man. As the following letters show, he was disposed like most Republicans to extenuate the atrocities of the revolution and defend the conduct of the French government. It is interesting that he approved of the democratic upheaval accom-

panying French "liberation" of his native Geneva, which brought down the aristocratic class into which he had been born. The slave uprising in Haiti, which drove thousands of white refugees to America in 1793, he attributed, not as most Federalists did to French doctrines of equality, but to the intrinsic evil of slavery itself, thus throwing the onus on the ancien régime. *In time, like all but the extremists in the Republic camp, he distinguished between the rights of man and French imperialism.*

8. LETTER TO JEAN BADOLLET

March 9, 1793

Hardly had the Swiss troops left Geneva in conformity with the agreement made with France, when the looks, the discourse, & the rising commotions of the mass of the people began to foretell a storm. The magistrates, for once, were wise enough to avert it by yielding before it was too late. An almost unanimous vote of the three Councils has extended the right of citizenship to every native & has given a representation to the people who are now acting under the name of Genevan Assembly. I believe, the fear of the people joining France has been the real motive which has induced their proud Aristocracy at last to bend their necks.

Gallatin Papers, New York Historical Society. Reprinted with the permission of the New York Historical Society.

9. LETTER TO THOMAS CLARE

May 3, 1793

You must have seen that France is now at war with Prussia, Austria, Germany, Sardinia, Great Britain & Holland, to which host of enemies must now be added Spain & Russia. The French Nation seem to be still in high spirits, but they must bear with many defeats & much distress before they can establish their freedom. It is the most infamous combination of Kings and Despots against People, and if those Tyrants happen to be so successful as to re-establish the old Government in France, I am much afraid that our turn will come next. French armies have been defeated in the . . . [torn] Netherlands, which they conquered last fall, and I believe they will be obliged to retreat to their own territories. The Irish nation, a while ago, seemed disposed to make an effort in order to recover and establish upon a solid foundation their Liberties. But the war has given additional strength to the Government and the volunteers are every where delivering up their arms to the regular troops sent for that purpose.

10. LETTER TO JEAN BADOLLET

February 1, 1793

Who has been right or in the wrong in the lamentable scene of Hispaniola no body can tell; but to view the subject inde-

---

Documents 9 and 10 from *Gallatin Papers,* New York Historical Society. Reprinted with the permission of the New York Historical Society.

pendent of the motives & conduct of the Agents who may
have brought on the present crisis, I see nothing but the natural consequences of slavery. For the whites to expect mercy
either from mulattoes or negroes is absurd and whilst we may
pity the misfortunes of the present generation of the whites
of that island, in which, undoubtedly, many innocent victims
have been involved, can we help acknowledging that calamity
to be the just punishment of the crimes of so many generations
of slave traders and slave holders. . . .

If there be another campaign [in Europe], as there is little
doubt of at present, our situation next summer will be truly
critical. France, at present, offers a spectacle unheard of at
any other period. Enthusiasm there produce an energy equally
terrible & sublime. All those virtues which depend upon social or family affections, all those amiable weaknesses which
our natural feelings teach us to love or respect, have disap-
peared before the stronger, the only, at present, powerful
passion the *Amor Patrie*. I must confess my soul is not enough
steeled, not sometimes to shrink at the dreadful executions
which have restored at least apparent internal tranquillity to
that Republic. Yet, upon the whole, as long as the combined
despots press upon every frontier & employ every engine to
destroy and distress the interior parts, I think they & they
alone are answerable for every act of severity or injustice,
for every excess, nay for every crime which either of the contending parties in France may have committed.

11. DEBATE ON PEACE OR WAR

WITH FRANCE, SPEECH IN

HOUSE OF REPRESENTATIVES

March 27, 1798

The House was deliberating over President Adams' message of March 19, 1797. The question was whether to adopt a resolution disavowing intent to go to war with France or to declare war.

Mr. G. concluded, by observing, that the conduct of France must tend to destroy that influence which gentlemen had so often complained of as existing in this country. Indeed, he was convinced that at the commencement of her revolution there was a great enthusiasm amongst our citizens in favor of her cause, which naturally arose from their having been engaged in a similar contest; but he believed these feelings had been greatly diminished by her late conduct towards this country. He thought, therefore, that whether we engaged in war, or remained in a state of peace, much need not be appre-

---

The Debates and Proceedings in the Congress of the United States, 1789–1824. Joseph Gales and W. W. Seaton, eds., 42 vols. Washington, 1834–1856. (5 Cong., 2 Sess., 1798), pp. 1329–1330. Hereafter cited as *Annals of Congress.*

hended from the influence of France in our councils. The
business had come to a mere matter of calculation, as to what
course will be best to be taken for the interest and happiness
of the country. If he could separate defensive from offensive
war at sea, he should be in favor of it; but he could not make
the distinction, and therefore he should be in favor of pursuing measures of peace.

THE JAY TREATY

*The events leading to the negotiation of the Jay Treaty consti-
tuted a major crisis in foreign relations. After the outbreak of
war between Britain and France in 1793, the British government issued orders in council which completely violated American conceptions of neutral rights. Without warning 250
American vessels trading with the French West Indies were
seized. About the time the seizures were reported in the
United States news arrived that the Governor-General of Canada, Lord Dorchester, was preparing the Indian tribes for
war on the northwest frontier. In a last effort to avoid an encounter that was certain to ruin American commerce and
bring down the funding system, President Washington sent
John Jay to England as a special minister. When the terms of
the treaty he signed on November 19, 1794 became known,
however, a wave of indignation swept the country at what was
generally considered an abject surrender of American interests. Convinced that war was the alternative, Washington
signed the treaty, and his influence secured ratification by the
Senate June 24, 1795, with certain reservations, by a bare
two-thirds majority. Because a money appropriation was required to execute it, the treaty was still subject to an adverse
vote by the House, in which the Republicans had a majority.
With national elections coming up, they were eager to exploit
popular hostility toward the treaty.*

12. HOUSE DEBATE ON RESOLUTION

TO EXAMINE JAY PAPERS

March 9, 1796

The House debate began March 2 with Edward Livingston's motion requesting the President to lay before the House Jay's instructions and the papers relative to the negotiation. This motion raised constitutional questions of considerable magnitude. Could the House by requiring the President to reveal diplomatic papers supervise his execution of the treaty-making function? When called upon to appropriate money to carry out a treaty, did the House have a discretionary right to decide on the treaty and annul it by refusing an appropriation? Federalists were indignant at what they considered an attempt to invalidate the constitutional separation of powers and claim unbounded authority for the "popular branch." The House, they contended, had no business investigating treaties. The only subject within its purview to which the Jay papers were relevant was impeachment of the President, and if this were the object let the Republicans declare it. Federalists argued that as long as the President and Senate acted constitutionally in making treaties, their acts could not be reviewed by the House. Once signed and ratified, treaties were the supreme law, obligatory upon the United States. The House had no

---

Annals of Congress (4 Cong., 1st Sess., 1796), pp. 464–469.

He wished gentlemen had defined what they understood by a Constitutional Treaty; for, if the scope of their arguments was referred to, it would not be found possible to make an unconstitutional Treaty. He would say what he conceived constituted the unconstitutionality of a Treaty. A Treaty is unconstitutional if it provides for doing such things, the doing of which is forbidden by the Constitution; but if a Treaty embraces objects within the sphere of the general powers delegated to the Federal Government, but which have been exclusively and specially granted to a particular branch of Government, say to the Legislative department, such a Treaty, though not unconstitutional, does not become the law of the land until it has obtained the sanction of that branch. In this case, and to this end, the Legislature have a right to demand the documents relative to the negotiation of the Treaty, because that Treaty operates on objects specially delegated to the Legislature. He turned to the Constitution. It says, that the President shall have the power to make Treaties, by and with the advice and consent of two-thirds of the Senate. It does not say what Treaties. If the clause be taken by itself, then it grants an authority altogether undefined. But the gentlemen quote another clause of the Constitution, where it is said that the Constitution, and the laws made in pursuance thereof, and all Treaties, are the supreme law of the land; and thence, they insist that Treaties made by the President and Senate are the supreme law of the land, and that the power of making Treaties is undefined and unlimited. He proceeded to controvert this opinion, and contended that it was limited by other parts of the Constitution.

That general power of making Treaties, *undefined* as it is by the clause which grants it, may either be expressly *limited* by some other positive clauses of the Constitution, or it may be *checked* by some powers vested in other branches of the Government, which, although not diminishing, may control the Treaty-making power. Mr. G. was of opinion that both positions would be supported by the Constitution; that the specific Legislative powers delegated to Congress were limitations of the undefined power of making Treaties vested in the PRESIDENT and Senate, and that the general power of granting money, also vested in Congress, would at all events be used, if necessary, as a check upon, and as controling the exercise of the powers claimed by the PRESIDENT and Senate.

The Treaty-making power is limited by the Constitution, when in the first section it is said that all Legislative power is granted to Congress. To construe the Constitution consistently, we must attend to all the sections of it. If it is attempted to be construed by referring to particular portions, and not attending to the whole, absurdities must arise. So in the present case, by the mode of construction advanced by the gentlemen opposed to the motion. By one section it is declared that a Treaty is the supreme law of the land, that it operates as a law; yet it is to be made by the PRESIDENT and Senate only. Here will be an apparent contradiction; for the Constitution declares that the Legislative power shall be vested in the three branches. By this construction there would appear to be two distinct Legislatures. How shall this apparent contradiction be reconciled? Some gentlemen, to solve the difficulty, had declared the Treaty-making power to be an Executive power; but a power of making laws cannot be termed Executive without involving an absurdity; the power of making Treaties, although called an Executive power, is transformed into a Legislative one by those gentlemen.

The power of making Treaties is contended to be undefined, then it might extend to all subjects which may properly become the subjects of national compacts. But, he contended, if any other specific powers were given to a different branch of the Government, they must limit the general powers; and, to make the compact valid, it was necessary that, as far as those powers clashed with the general, that the branch holding

the specific should concur and give its sanction. If still it is insisted that Treaties are the supreme law of the land, the Constitution and laws are also; and, it may be asked, which shall
have the preference? Shall a Treaty repeal a law or a law a
Treaty? Neither can a law repeal a Treaty, because a Treaty is
made with the concurrence of another party—a foreign nation—that has no participation in framing the law; nor can a
Treaty made by the PRESIDENT and Senate repeal a law, for
the same reason, because the House of Representatives have a
participation in making the law. It is a sound maxim in Government, that it requires the same power to repeal a law that
enacted it. If so, then it follows that laws and Treaties are not
of the same nature; that both operate as the law of the land,
but under certain limitations; both are subject to the control
of the Constitution; they are made not only by different powers, but those powers are distributed, under different modifications, among the several branches of the Government. Thus
no law could be made by the Legislature giving themselves
power to execute it; and no Treaty by the Executive, embracing objects specifically assigned to the Legislature without
their assent.

To what, he asked, would a contrary doctrine lead? If the
power of making Treaties is to reside in the PRESIDENT and
Senate unlimitedly: in other words, if, in the exercise of this
power, the PRESIDENT and Senate are to be restrained by no
other branch of the Government, the PRESIDENT and Senate
may absorb all Legislative power—the Executive has, then,
nothing to do but to substitute a foreign nation for the House
of Representatives, and they may legislate to any extent. If
the Treaty-making power is unlimited and undefined, it may
extend to every object of legislation. Under it money may be
borrowed, as well as commerce regulated; and why not money
appropriated? For, arguing as the gentlemen do, they might
say the Constitution says that no money shall be drawn from

the Treasury but in consequence of appropriations made by law. But Treaties, whatever provision they may contain, are law, appropriations, therefore, may be made by Treaties. Then it would have been the shortest way to have carried the late Treaty into effect by the instrument itself, by adding to it another article, appropriating the necessary sums. By what provision of the Constitution is the Treaty-making power, agreeably to the construction of the gentlemen, limited? Is it limited by the provisions with respect to appropriations? Not more so than by the other specific powers granted to the Legislature. Is it limited by any law past? If not, it must embrace every thing, and all the objects of legislation. If not limited by existing laws, or if it repeals the laws that clash with it, or if the Legislature is obliged to repeal the laws so clashing, then the Legislative power in fact resides in the PRESIDENT and Senate, and they can, by employing an Indian tribe, pass any law under the color of Treaty. Unless it is allowed that either the power of the House over the purse-strings is a check, or the existing laws cannot be repealed by a Treaty, or that the special powers granted to Congress limit the general power of Treaty-making, there are no bounds to it, it must absorb all others, repeal all laws in contravention to it, and act without control.

To the construction he had given to this part of the Constitution, no such formidable objections could be raised. He did not claim for the House a power of making Treaties, but a check upon the Treaty-making power—a mere negative power; whilst those who are in favor of a different construction advocate a positive and unlimited power.

Since this is the striking difference between the doctrine held by the friends and by the opposers of the present motion, why, added Mr. G., with some warmth, are the first endeavored to be stigmatized as rebellious, disorganizers, as traitors against the Constitution? Do they claim a dangerous active power? No, they only claim the right of checking the exercise of a general power when clashing with the special powers expressly vested in Congress by the Constitution.

He should not say that the Treaty is unconstitutional, but he would say that it was not the supreme law of the land until it received the sanction of the Legislature. He turned to the Constitution. That instrument declares, that the Constitu-ion, and laws made in pursuance thereof, and Treaties made under the authority of the United States, shall be the supreme law of the land. The words are, "under the authority of the United States," not signed and ratified by the PRESIDENT: so that a Treaty, clashing in any of its provisions with the express powers of Congress, until it has so far obtained the sanction of Congress, is not a Treaty made under the authority of the United States.

Gentlemen had dwelt much on that part of the Constitution which had declared the Constitution, Laws, and Treaties, laws of the land; but they had avoided reading the whole of the clause, and had not given to it its obvious meaning. Why should the Constitution barely declare the Constitution the law of the land, the laws the law of the land, or Treaties the law of the land? All know that they are so. In all countries they are so, because made by the supreme authority: but, by adverting to the latter part of the clause, the meaning of the former must immediately become obvious. It runs as fol-lows: "And the Judges in every State shall be bound thereby; any thing in the Constitution or laws of the individual States to the contrary notwithstanding." It would have been childish if the Constitution had confined itself to expressing the first part of the clause; because no doubt could arise whether the Constitution, laws, and Treaties, were the supreme law of the land. But, as the General Government sprung out of a confed-eration of States, it was necessary to give that Government sufficient authority to provide for the general welfare, that the laws of the Union should supersede those of the particu-lar States. There was thus a valuable purpose to be obtained by the latter part of the clause, viz: a positive provision declaring which authority should be supreme in case of clashing powers.

But the clause does not compare a Treaty with the law of the United States, or either of them with the Constitution: it only compares all the acts of the Federal Government with the acts of the individual States, and declares that either of the first, whether under the name of Constitution, law, or Treaty, shall be paramount to and supersede the Constitution and laws of the individual States. In that point of view are Treaties said to be the supreme law, to wit: when standing in competition against acts of the several States; but the clause by no means expresses that Treaties are equal or superior to the laws of the Union, or that they shall be supreme law when clashing with any of them.

To illustrate: He supposed that the Pennsylvania Legislature were to pass an act incorporating the city of Philadelphia, granting to certain bodies the power to make regulations which should be the supreme law of the land: this would mean only that they were so within their proper sphere, and not that they were paramount to the laws of the State or of the Union. The same of Treaties: they are declared to be the supreme law of the land, within the provisions of the Constitution, and agreeably to the modifications therein provided; but they are not declared to be supreme when compared, or paramount to the laws of the United States. The Constitution is paramount to both laws and Treaties; and, when gentlemen ground their arguments on the position that Treaties are superior or equal to the laws of the Union, they take for granted the very thing which is to be proved. The natural construction of the Treaty-making power was this, he contended, that, as far as a Treaty negotiated by the Executive embraced Legislative objects, so far it required the sanction of the Legislature. . . .

13. HOUSE DEBATE ON

THE JAY TREATY

April 26, 1796

The House passed Livingston's motion March 24, 1796 by a vote of 62 to 37. Washington promptly sent in his refusal to submit the Jay papers, concluding with the observation: "It is essential to the due administration of the Government, that the boundaries fixed by the Constitution between different departments should be preserved." (See Document 13.) Delivering one of the few rebuffs Washington ever received at the hands of the legislature, the House resolved 57 to 35 that it had a right to pass on treaties requiring a money appropriation.

On April 13 debate began on the Jay Treaty itself. Federalists who had once expected that the House would approve the treaty as a matter of course were infuriated and seriously alarmed by the succession of votes indicating a hostile majority. Despite able speeches by Gallatin and others, however, the Republicans weakened. The majority of the American people still followed where Washington led and believed him when he said that the alternative to the treaty was war. Westerners had also come to realize that if the treaty failed Britain would continue to occupy the Northwest posts. They were

---

Annals of Congress (4 Cong., 1st Sess., 1796), pp. 1183–1202.

*afraid that its defeat would impair the Pinckney Treaty, cur-
rently under consideration by the House, and thus forfeit the
cherished right to navigate the Mississippi. Petitions in support of the Jay Treaty poured in from every quarter, and the
Republicans were intimidated. Finally, on April 29 the House
resolved to carry the Jay Treaty into effect. The vote was 49
to 49. The tie was broken by the affirmative ballot of Chairman Frederick Muhlenberg, a Pennsylvania Republican. The
Republicans had the strength to defeat the treaty but not the
courage.*

*In the following speech Gallatin delivered a long indict-
ment of the treaty. Significantly, however, he declared that
"acquiescence" in the treaty, no matter how bad it was, might
be better than outright rejection. He argued for a postponement until Britain ceased her depredations on American commerce and until certain clauses were renegotiated.*

MR. GALLATIN said he would not follow some of the gentlemen who had preceded him, by dwelling upon the discretion
of the Legislature—a question which had already been the
subject of their deliberation, and been decided by a solemn
vote. Gentlemen who had been in the minority on that question might give any construction they pleased to the declaratory resolution of the House; they might again repeat that, to
refuse to carry the Treaty into effect, was a breach of the
public faith, which they conceived as being pledged by the
PRESIDENT and Senate. This had been the ground on which a
difference of opinion had existed since the beginning of the
discussion. It was because the House thought the faith of the
nation could not, on those subjects submitted to the power of
Congress, be pledged by any constituted authority other than
the Legislature, that they had resolved that, in all such cases,
it was their right and duty to consider the expediency of car-

rying a Treaty into effect. If the House thought the faith of the nation already pledged, they could not claim any discretion; there would be no room left to deliberate upon the expediency of the thing. The resolution now under consideration was merely "that it was expedient to carry the British Treaty into effect," and not whether they were bound by national faith to do it. He would, therefore, consider the question of expediency alone; and, thinking as he did, that the House had full discretion on the subject, he conceived that there was as much responsibility in deciding in the affirmative as in rejecting the resolution; that they would be equally answerable for the consequences that might follow from either.

It was, however, true that there was a great difference between the situation of this country in the year 1794, when a negotiator was appointed, and that in which we were at present; and that consequences would follow the refusal to carry into effect the Treaty in its present stage, which would not have attended a refusal to negotiate, and to enter into such a Treaty. The question of expediency, therefore, assumed before them a different and more complex shape than when before the negotiator, the Senate, or the PRESIDENT. The Treaty, in itself, and abstractedly considered, might be injurious; it might be such an instrument as, in the opinion of the House, ought not to have been adopted by the Executive; and yet, such as it was, they might think it expedient, under the present circumstances, to carry it into effect. He would, therefore, first take a view of the provisions of the Treaty itself, and in the next place, supposing it injurious, consider, in case it was not carried into effect, what would be the natural consequences of such refusal.

The provisions of the Treaty relate either to the adjustment of past differences or to the future intercourse of the two nations. The differences now existing between Great Britain and this country arose either from the non-execution of some articles of the Treaty of Peace, or from the effects of the

present European war. The complaints of Britain in relation
to the Treaty of 1783 were confined to the legal impediments
thrown by the several States in the way of the recovery of
British debts. The late Treaty had provided adequate remedy
on that subject; the United States were bound to make full
and complete compensation for any losses arising from that
source, and every ground of complaint on the part of Great
Britain was removed.

Having thus done full justice to the other nation, America
had a right to expect that equal attention should be paid to
her claims arising from infractions of the Treaty of Peace,
viz: compensation for the negroes carried away by the British;
restoration of the Western posts, and indemnification for their
detention.

On the subject of the first claim, which had been objected
to as groundless, he would observe, that he was not satisfied
that the construction given by the British Government to that
article of the Treaty was justified even by the letter of the
article. That construction rested on the supposition that slaves
came under the general denomination of booty, and were
alienated the moment they fell in the possession of an enemy,
so that all those who were in the hands of the British when
the Treaty of Peace was signed, must be considered as British,
and not American property, and were not included in the
article. It would however appear, by recurring to *Vattel,* when
speaking of the right of *postliminium,* that slaves were not
considered as part of the booty which was alienated by the act
of capture, and that they were ranked rather with real property, to the profits of which only the captors were entitled.
Be that as it may, there was no doubt that the construction
given by America was that which had been understood by the
parties at the time of making the Treaty. The journals of Mr.
Adams, quoted by a gentleman from Connecticut, [Mr. Corr,]
proved this fully; for when he says that the insertion of this
article was alone worth the journey of Mr. Laurens from Lon-

don, can it be supposed that he would have laid so much stress on a clause which, according to the new construction now attempted to be given, meant only that the British would commit no new act of hostility? would not carry away slaves at that time in possession of Americans? Congress had recognised that construction by adopting the resolution which had been already quoted, and which was introduced upon the motion of Mr. Alexander Hamilton; and it had not been denied that the British Ministry, during Mr. Adams's embassy, had also agreed to it.

But when our negotiator had, for the sake of peace, waived that claim; when he had also abandoned the right which America had to demand an indemnification for the detention of the posts, although he had conceded the right of a similar nature, which Great Britain had for the detention of debt; when he had thus given up every thing which might be supposed to be of a doubtful nature, it might have been hoped that our last claim—a claim on which there was not and there never had been any dispute—the Western posts should have been restored according to the terms of the Treaty of Peace. Upon what ground the British had insisted, and our negotiator conceded, that this late restitution should be saddled with new conditions, which made no part of the original contract, Mr. G. was at a loss to know. British traders were all allowed, by the new Treaty, to remain within the posts without becoming citizens of the United States, and to carry on trade and commerce with the Indians living within our boundaries, without being subject to any control from our Government. In vain was it said, that if that clause had not been inserted we would have found it our interest to effect it by our own laws. Of this we were alone competent judges; if that condition was harmless at present, it was not possible to foresee whether, under future circumstances, it would not prove highly injurious; and, whether harmless or not, it was not less a permanent and new condition imposed upon us. But the fact was, that by the introduction of that clause, by obliging us to keep within our jurisdiction, as British subjects, the very men who had been the instruments used by Great Britain to promote Indian wars on our frontiers, by obliging us to suffer those men to continue their commerce with Indians living in our territory, uncontrolled by those regulations, which we had thought necessary, in order to restrain our own citizens in their intercourse with these tribes, Great Britain had preserved her full influence with the Indian nations; by a restoration of the posts under that condition, we had lost the greatest advantage that was expected from their possession, viz: future security against the Indians. In the same manner had the British preserved the commercial advantages which resulted from the occupancy of these posts, by stipulating as a permanent condition a free passage for their goods across our portages, without paying any duty.

Another article of the new Treaty, which was connected with the provisions of the Treaty of 1783, deserved consideration—he meant what related to the Mississippi. At the time when the navigation of that river to its mouth was, by the Treaty of Peace, declared to be common to both nations, Great Britain had communicated to America a right, which she held by virtue of the Treaty of 1763, and as owner of the Floridas; but since that cession to the United States, England had ceded to Spain her claim on the Floridas, and did not own at the present time an inch of ground, either on the mouth or any part of that river. Spain now stood in the place of Great Britain, and by virtue of the Treaty of 1783, it was to Spain and America, and not to England and America, that the navigation of the Mississippi was at present to be common. Yet, notwithstanding that change of circumstances, we had repeated that article of the former Treaty in the late one, and had granted to Great Britain the additional privilege of using our ports on the eastern side of the river, without which, as they owned no land thereon, they could not have navigated it. Nor was this all. Upon a supposition that the Mississippi did not extend so far northward as to be intersected by a line drawn due west from the Lake of the Woods, or, in other words, upon a supposition that Great Britain had not a claim even to touch the Mississippi, we had agreed, not upon what would be the boundary line, but that we would hereafter negotiate to settle that line.

Thus leaving to future negotiation what should have been finally settled by the Treaty itself, in the same manner as all other differences were, was calculated for the sole purpose either of laying the foundation for future disputes, or of recognising a claim in Great Britain on the waters of the Mississippi, even if their boundary line left to the southward the sources of that river. Had not that been the intention of Great Britain, the line would have been settled at once by the Treaty, according to either of the two only rational ways of doing it in conformity to the Treaty of 1783, that is to say, by agreeing that the line would run from the northernmost source of the Mississippi either directly to the western extremity of the Lake of the Woods, or northwardly till it intersected the line to be drawn due west from that lake. But by repeating the article of the Treaty of 1783; by conceding the free use of our ports on the river, and by the insertion of the 4th article, we had admitted that Great Britain, in all possible events, had still a right to navigate that river from its source to its mouth. What might be the future effects of those provisions, especially as they regarded our intercourse with Spain, it was at present impossible to say; but, although they could bring us no advantage, they might embroil us with that nation, and we had already felt the effect of it in our late Treaty with Spain, since we were obliged, on account of that clause of the British Treaty, to accept as a gift and favor the navigation of that river, which we had till then claimed as a right.

The seventh article of the Treaty was intended to adjust those differences which arose from the effects of the present

European war. On that article, it might also be observed, that whilst it provided a full compensation for the claims of the British, it was worded in such a manner, when speaking of the indemnification for spoliations committed on the American commerce, as would render it liable to a construction very unfavorable to our just claims on that ground. The Commissioners to be appointed by virtue of that article, were to take cognizance, and to grant redress only in those cases where, by reason of irregular or illegal captures or condemnations made under color of authority or commissions from the King of Great Britain, losses had been incurred, and where adequate compensation could not now be actually obtained by the ordinary course of judicial proceedings. If Great Britain should insist that, since the signing of the Treaty, they had, by admitting appeals to their Superior Courts, afforded a redress by the ordinary course of judicial proceedings; if those Courts were to declare, that the captures complained of, were neither illegal nor made under color, but by virtue of authority or commissions from the King; and if that construction should prevail with the Commissioners, the indemnification which our plundered merchants would actually receive, in consequence of the provisions of this article, would fall very far short of their expectations and of their just claims. Yet that article, considering the relative situation of the two countries, at the time when the negotiation took place, was as much as could reasonably have been expected by America. When a weak nation had to contend with a powerful one, it was gaining a great deal if the national honor was saved even by the shadow of an indemnification, and by an apparent concession on the part of the aggressor; and however objectionable that article might appear at first view, he was on the whole satisfied with it.

The remaining provisions of the Treaty had no connexion with past differences; they made no part of the Convention which had been the avowed object of Mr. Jay's mission; they applied solely to the future intercourse of the two nations as relating to commerce and navigation; and had they been entirely omitted, our differences would have been nevertheless adjusted. It was agreed on all hands, that so far as related to our commerce with Great Britain, we wanted no Treaty. The intercourse, although useful perhaps to both parties, was more immediately necessary to England, and her own interest was a sufficient pledge of her granting us at all times a perfect liberty of commerce to her European ports. If we want to treat with her, it must be in order to obtain some intercourse with her colonies, and some general security in our navigation.

The twelfth and thirteenth articles had been obtained by our negotiator with a view to the first object. The twelfth article, however, which related to our intercourse with the West Indies, was found, upon examination, to be accompanied by a restriction of such a nature, that what had been granted by Great Britain as a favor, was rejected by the Senate as highly injurious. The thirteenth article, which related to the East Indies, and remained part of the Treaty, was, like the twelfth, conferring a favor limited by restrictions, and so far as he could depend upon the opinion of the best-informed judges on that subject, those restrictions put the trade in a more disadvantageous situation than it was before the Treaty. As the West India article had declared that we should not re-export any produce of those islands to Europe, so the East India article, at the same time it granted us the privilege, which we enjoyed before, and which we enjoyed because it was the interest of the East India Company to grant it to us, that of being admitted in the British seaports there, had forbidden our carrying any articles from thence to any place except to America; which regulation amounted to a total prohibition to export East India articles to China, or to obtain freights back to Europe; and, upon the whole, he could not help thinking, from what had fallen on that floor, and what he had heard elsewhere from gentlemen of great commercial knowledge, that if the East India Commerce had been as generally understood in America as the West India trade, that so much boasted-of article would have met the same fate in the Senate with the twelfth article.

But if, leaving commercial regulations, we were to seek in the Treaty for some provision securing to us the free navigation of the ocean against any future aggressions on our trade, where were they to be found? He could add nothing to what had been said on the subject of contraband articles: it was, indeed, self-evident, that connecting our Treaty with England on that subject with those we had made with other nations, it amounted to a positive compact to supply that nation exclusively with naval stores whenever they were at war. Had the list of contraband articles been reduced, had naval stores and provisions—our two great staple commodities—been declared not to be contraband, security would have been given to the free exportation of our produce; but instead of any provision having been made on that head, an article of a most doubtful nature, and on which he would remark afterwards, had been introduced. But he meant, for the present, to confine his observations to the important question of free bottoms making free goods. It was with the utmost astonishment he had heard the doctrine advanced on this floor, that such a provision, if admitted, would prove injurious to America, inasmuch as, in case of war between this country and any other nation, the goods of that nation might be protected by the English flag. It was not to a state of war that the benefits of that provision would extend; but it was the only security which neutral nations could have against the legal plundering on the high seas, so often committed by belligerent Powers. It was not for the sake of protecting an enemy's property; it was not for the sake of securing an advantageous carrying trade; but it was in order effectually to secure ourselves against sea aggressions that that provision was necessary. Spoliations might arise from unjust orders given by the Government of a belligerent nation to their officers and cruisers, and these might be redressed by application to and negotiation with that Power. But no complaints, no negotiations, no orders of Government itself, could give redress, when those spoliations were grounded on a supposition that the vessels of a neutral nation had an enemy's property on board; as long as such property was not protected by the flag of the neutral nation, as long as it was liable to be captured, it was not sufficient, in order to avoid detention and capture, to have no such property on board. Every privateer, under pretence that he suspected an enemy's goods were part of a cargo, might search, vex, and capture a vessel; and if in any corner of the dominions of the belligerent Power, a single Judge could be found inclined if not determined to condemn, at all events, before his tribunal, all vessels so captured would be brought, and the same pretence which had caused the capture would justify a condemnation. The only nation who persisted in the support of that doctrine, as making part of the Law of Nations, was the first maritime Power in Europe, whom their interest, as they were the strongest, and as there was hardly a maritime war in which they were not involved, led to wish for a continuation of a custom, which gave additional strength to their overbearing dominion over the seas. All the other nations had different sentiments and a different interest.

During the American war, in the year 1780, so fully convinced were the neutral nations of the necessity of introducing that doctrine of free bottoms making free goods, that all of them, excepting Portugal, who was in a state of vassalage to, and a mere appendage of Great Britain, had united in order to establish the principle, and had formed for that purpose the alliance known by the name of the Armed Neutrality. All the belligerent Powers, except England, had recognised and agreed to the doctrine. England itself had been obliged, in some measure, to give for a while a tacit acquiescence. America had completely, at the time, admitted the principle, although they were then at war [Mr. G. quoted on this subject the Journals of Congress of the year 1780, page 210, and of the year 1781, page 80] and it had been introduced in every other Treaty we had concluded since our existence as a nation. Since the year 1780, every nation, so far as his knowledge went, had refused to enter into a Treaty of Commerce with England, unless that provision was inserted. Russia, for that reason, would not renew their Treaty, which had expired in 1786, although he believed that, during the present war, and in order to answer the ends of the war, they had formed a temporary Convention, which he had not seen but which, perhaps, did not include that provision. England had consented to it in their Treaty with France in 1788, and we were the first neutral nation who abandoned the common cause, gave up the claim, and, by a positive declaration inserted in our Treaty, had recognised the contrary doctrine. It had been said, that under the present circumstances, it could not be expected that Great Britain would give up the point; perhaps so; but the objection was not, that our negotiator had not been able to obtain that doctrine, but that he had consented to enter into a Treaty of Commerce (which we did not want, and which had no connexion with an adjustment of our differences with Great Britain) without the principle contended for making part of that Treaty. Unless we could obtain security for our navigation, we wanted no Treaty; and the only provision which could give us that security, should have been the *sine qua non* of a Treaty. On the contrary, we had disgusted all the other neutral nations of Europe, without whose concert and assistance there was but little hope that we should ever obtain that point, and we had taught Great Britain that we were disposed to form the most intimate connexions with her, even at the expense of recognising the principle the most fatal to the liberty of commerce, and to the security of our navigation.

But, if we would not obtain anything which might secure

us against future aggressions, should we have parted, without receiving any equivalent, with those weapons of self-defence, which although they could not repel, might, in some degree, prevent any gross attacks upon our trade, any gross violation of our rights as a neutral nation? We had no fleet to oppose or to punish the insults of Great Britain; but, from our commercial relative situation, we had it in our power to restrain her aggressions by restrictions on. her trade, by a total prohibition of her manufactures, or by a sequestration of the debts due to her. By the Treaty—not satisfied with receiving nothing; not satisfied with obtaining no security for the future—we had, of our own accord, surrendered those defensive arms for fear they might be abused by ourselves. We had given up the two first for the whole time during which we might want them most—the period of the present war—and the last, the power of sequestration, we had abandoned forever: every other article of the Treaty of Commerce was temporary, this perpetual.

Mr. G. was not going to enter into a discussion of the immorality of sequestering private property. What could be more immoral than war? or the plundering of the high seas legalized under the name of privateering? Yet self-defence justified the first, and the necessity of the case might, at least in some instances, and where it was the only practicable mode of warfare left to a nation, apologize even for the last. In the same manner the power of sequestration might be resorted to, as the last weapon of self-defence, rather than to seek redress by an appeal to arms. It was the last peace-measure that could be taken by a nation; but the Treaty, by declaring that in case of national differences it should not be resorted to, had deprived us of the power of judging of its propriety, had rendered it an act of hostility, and had effectually taken off that restraint which a fear of its exercise laid upon Great Britain.

Thus it appeared that, by the Treaty, we had promised full

compensation to England for every possible claim they might have against us, that we had abandoned every claim of a doubtful nature, and that we had consented to receive the posts, our claim to which was not disputed, under new conditions and restrictions never before contemplated. That, after having obtained, by those concessions, an adjustment of past differences, we had entered into a new agreement, unconnected with those objects, which had heretofore been subjects of discussion between the two nations; and that, by that Treaty of Commerce and Navigation, we had obtained no commercial advantage which did not enjoy before; we had obtained no security against future aggressions, no security in favor of the freedom of our navigation, and we had parted with every pledge we had in our hands, with every power of restriction, with every weapon of self-defence, which was calculated to give us any security.

There was yet another article which stood by itself, unconnected either with adjustment of past disputes, or with commercial regulations; he meant the ninth article, which provides that British subjects now holding lands in the United States should continue to hold them, and might sell or devise the same, and that neither they, nor their heirs or assigns should, so far as might respect the said lands, and the legal remedies incident thereto, be regarded as aliens. Mr. G. said he was not a lawyer, and, in expressing an opinion, he meant nothing more than to communicate his doubts, and ask for an explanation. There would be no difficulty in finding the meaning of the article, did it apply only to those British subjects, who had acquired lands under the laws of the States; but the former connexion of this country with England rendered the subject difficult to be explained, even by men of legal abilities; for its explanation must depend on the consequences of a principle unknown to the laws of England.

The principle of the English law was, that no subject could shake off his allegiance; that is to say, that no man, who was once a citizen, could become an alien. Yet, by the effect of the Revolution, British subjects, who before 1776, had a right to hold lands in America as part of the British Empire, had become aliens in the United States, and the effect of that alienage upon their titles to such lands and how far that effect was changed by the operation of the Treaty, seemed to him to be questions of a very nice nature. He would, however, beg leave to suggest, what to him appeared to be the effect of the Treaty. So far as lands had been confiscated by the laws of any State, and those laws carried into effect, and so far as, such lands having been considered as escheated, an office had been found and the escheat been completed, he conceived the Treaty would create no alteration; but where the lands had not been confiscated, either because no laws had been passed for that purpose, or because they had not been carried into effect before the Treaty of 1783, and where the legal formalities of finding an office, &c., necessary to complete an escheat had been neglected, it seemed to him the Treaty might operate in three ways. Firstly, it would prevent any State from completing an escheat by finding an office, &c., when they had neglected doing it. Secondly, it would enable the British subjects to sell or devise, and therefore to convert their life estate into a fee-simple forever. And thirdly, it would enable those subjects to institute suits in Courts for the recovery of those lands, providing them with a legal remedy they had not before, since their alienage would have been a sufficient bar against bringing real actions. If the Treaty might be supposed to have that effect, its tendency, so far as related, not to private estates, but to the former proprietary estates, might prove vexatious and injurious to several of the States. It would strengthen the proprietary claims of the Penn family, not in Pennsylvania, but in the State of Delaware. It might have some effect on the decision of the Fairfax claim in Virginia, and even on such parts of the lands of Maryland which had been sold, although formerly the property of the

Baltimore family, as vacant lands, and not as confiscated lands.

In North Carolina the proprietary claim of the Grenville family, which included the best half of that State, and of the Southwestern Territory, might be revived by the Treaty; for although a law had passed in that State to confiscate the lands of all the British subjects who would be absent on a certain day; yet the proprietary lands were not meant to be comprehended within that provision; the Commissioners, who were to sell the confiscated property, never disposed of a sin- gle acre of the lands which were granted by another law of the State as vacant, and not as confiscated lands, without hav- ing been actually escheated to the State by an office being found, or any other formality whatever; and they were even expressly distinguished from land to be confiscated by the very act passed for the purpose of confiscating. [Mr. G. here read the clause of the act he alluded to.] Supposing, however, every thing he had said on that subject as very doubtful, it was not less true that this article, which under an appearance of reciprocity, granted a positive advantage to Great Britain, without any equivalent being given, was, if not an infraction, at least a restriction over the Legislative powers; and an ex- ception to the laws of the different States on a subject of a delicate nature, might involve not only some of our citizens, but even several of the States, in complex law suits and serious embarrassment, and, although it might thus create much mis- chief, would give us no possible benefit.

From the review he had taken of the Treaty, and the opin- ions he had expressed, Mr. G. said, it was hardly necessary for him to add that he looked upon the instrument as highly injurious to the interests of the United States, and that he earnestly wished it never had been made; but whether, in its present stage, the House ought to refuse to carry it into effect, and what would be the probable consequences of a refusal, was a question which required the most serious at- tention, and which he would now attempt to investigate.

Should the Treaty be finally defeated, either new negotiations would be more successful, or Great Britain would refuse to make a new arrangement, and leave things in the situation in which they were, or war would be the consequence. Mr. G. said that he would, in the course of his observations, make some remarks on the last supposition; he did not think that the first would be very probable at present, and he was of opinion that, under the present circumstances, and until some change took place in our own or in the relative political situation of the European nations, it was to be apprehended that, in such a case, new negotiations would either be rejected or prove unsuccessful. Such an event would have perhaps followed a rejection of the Treaty even by the Senate or by the PRESIDENT. After the negotiator employed by the United States had once affixed his signature, it must have become very problematical, unless he had exceeded his powers, whether a refusal to sanction the contract he had made would not eventually defeat, at least for a time, the prospect of a new Treaty. He conceived that the hopes of obtaining better conditions, by a new negotiation, were much less in the present stage of the business than they had been when the Treaty was in its inchoate form before the Executive; and in order to have a just idea of the consequences of a rejection at present, he would contemplate them upon that supposition which appeared to him most probable, viz: that no new Treaty would take place for a certain period of time.

In mentioning his objections to the Treaty itself, he had already stated the advantages which, in his opinion, would result to the United States from the non-existence of that instrument; he would not repeat but proceed at once to examine what losses might accrue that could be set off against those advantages.

As he was not sensible that a single commercial advantage had been obtained by the Treaty, he could not mention the loss of any, as a mischief that would attend its rejection. If, however, the East India article was supposed to be beneficial, it must, on the other hand, be conceded that we had enjoyed every benefit arising from it for a number of years, without Treaty, and consequently, because it was in the interest of the East India Company that we should enjoy them; and that it was not probable that circumstances would so far change there, during the short period to which that article was limited, as to induce that Company to adopt a different policy towards us.

The indemnification to be obtained from Great Britain for spoliations on our trade, if considered as a national reparation for a national aggression, was, certainly, as he had already stated it, an important object gained by the Treaty. But if it was to be viewed as a money transaction, and its loss as a national loss of money, it would be well to examine, whether in that point of view, that of money, we would not be the gainers, on the whole, by not carrying the Treaty into effect? Mr. G. said that he had made no objection to that article of the Treaty which relates to British debts. Whatever the amount might be, if it was just that we should pay them, it was just to pay that amount; but when we were examining the situation in which we should be, if we had no Treaty, when we were calculating the losses we were to experience by obtaining no compensation for our claims, it was right to consider the amount of those claims, and to compare it with the probable amount of the claims of the other party, and of the sums of money which a non-execution of the Treaty, and a refusal on the part of Great Britain to do us justice, to indemnify us for our own losses, and to enter into new negotiations, would justify us in withholding. That subject had already undergone a full discussion, and he would recall the attention of the Committee only to the demand of Great Britain for interest on the British debts. It was well known that our Courts had uniformly refused to allow the British creditors the interest which had accrued on their demands during the late war, that is to say, during eight years. Although we had contended that those decisions could not be considered as legal impediments, yet it had been insisted by Great Britain that they were. The two Governments had come to issue on that point, as might be seen, by recurring to the printed correspondence of Mr. JEFFERSON. It was one of the points to which the jurisdiction of the Commissioners must extend, since, on account of decisions of our Courts, it was one of the cases where compensation could not be obtained, and had been refused by the ordinary course of judicial proceedings; and for greater security the Commissioners were, by the Treaty, empowered to take into their consideration all claims, whether of principal or interest, or balances of principal or interest. Those Commissioners must be considered less as/judges than as political agents, who would come with a determination to support the claims contended for by their respective nations. They would, therefore, disagree on the subject of war-interest, and it would be left solely to the fifth Commissioner— that is to say, to lot—to decide whether that interest should be paid by the United States or not. Eight years' interest amounted to one half of the whole amount of debts due by America to Great Britain at the beginning of the war; for it must be remarked that that claim extended to all debts, whether good or bad, because it had been refused on all, and could be recovered by the ordinary course of judicial proceedings on none. What those debts amounted to was very uncertain, and he had seen a variety of calculations on that subject. If they were estimated, as they had been by some, at five millions sterling, one half of them would amount to more than twelve millions of dollars; and when we took into consideration the amount of principal we should have to pay, on the principles stated by a gentleman from Virginia, [Mr. NICHOLAS,] his calculation of near fifteen millions of dollars in the whole would not be exaggerated. But even taking the amount of those debts at the lowest estimate, the amount of

war-interest, and of the principal we would have to pay, far
exceeded the amount which the most sanguine amongst us
expected to recover from the Government of Great Britain,
by virtue of the Treaty, on account of the spoliations committed on our trade.

The only positive loss, therefore, which in his opinion would
arise from our having no Treaty, was that of the Western
posts. He had already stated that, surrendered in the manner
settled by the Treaty, he conceived them to be of very insignificant value in a commercial point of view, and of little
use, if any, as a security against the Indians; for it must be remembered that our own laws, for the purpose of preserving
peace with those tribes, had enacted, under severe penalties,
that our own citizens should, on no account whatever, cross
over the boundary line between them and ourselves, (although
within the territory ceded to us by Great Britain,) unless they
had special licenses from our Government. It was, therefore,
our own opinion that peace could not be preserved with the
Indians, if ever our own citizens had a free and uncontrolled
intercourse with them. And yet it was a positive condition of
the Treaty, that the British traders settled at Detroit and the
other posts—men, who from habit, were attached to Great
Britain and inimical to the United States, who had given repeated proofs of that enmity, who possessed an unbounded
influence amongst the Indians, and had been the chief pro-
moters of the Indian war—that those men should remain there
as British subjects; and that they and all other British subjects should have the privilege forever to pass over that line,
which we had forbidden our citizens to cross, and should
continue to carry on with the Indians living within our territory a free trade and commerce, uncontrolled by our laws and
by those regulations which we had imposed or might impose
on our citizens. In other words, we had agreed that these men
should preserve their baneful influence over the Indians, and
their allegiance to Great Britain; and we might, therefore, ex-

pect that influence to be exerted as would suit the interest, and in conformity to the directions of their Sovereign.

He must therefore repeat that, as he had thought that at any time since 1789, we might have had the posts without those conditions, provided we had then agreed, as we had by the late Treaty, to make a compensation for the British debts, he had much rather that we could again be placed in the situation in which we were two years ago. And he would not hesitate to declare that, in his opinion, our claim to the posts and the chance we had to claim them, by negotiation, in the year 1793, was better than their possession upon the terms of the Treaty. But as the question now was not what would be best to be done if no Treaty had been made—as the negotiator had put us in a worse situation than we were in before that Treaty; as the subject of the present examination shows the consequences that would follow, if no Treaty at all was made; and as one of those consequences would undoubtedly be a further detention of the posts, and less hope to obtain them in future—he would certainly agree that it was better to have them, even encumbered with these conditions, than not to have them at all. For although they might not be of any immediate advantage, either as a commercial object or as giving security against the Indians, their possession would enable us to prevent a further extension of the British settlements within our territory, and, by forming settlements of our own, to acquire, by degrees, sufficient strength in that quarter to have nothing to fear either from the British or from the Indians.

The further detention of the posts, the national stain that would result from receiving no reparation for the spoliations on our trade, and the uncertainty of a final adjustment of our differences with Great Britain, were the three evils which struck him as resulting from a rejection of the Treaty; and when to these considerations he added that of the present situation of the country, of the agitation of the public mind,

and of the advantages that would arise from union of sentiments, however injurious and unequal he conceived the Treaty
to be, however repugnant it might be to his feelings and perhaps to his prejudices, he felt induced to vote for it, and would
not give his assent to any proposition which would imply its
rejection. But the conduct of Great Britain since the Treaty
was signed, the impressment of our seamen, and their uninterrupted spoliations on our trade, especially by seizing our
vessels laden with provisions—a proceeding which they might,
perhaps, justify by one of the articles of the Treaty—were
such circumstances as might induce them to pause awhile, in
order to determine whether it was proper, immediately, and
without having obtained any explanation thereon, to adopt
the resolution on the table, and to pass at present all the laws
necessary to carry the Treaty into effect.

The 18th article of the Treaty, the provision article, as it
was called, had already been fully investigated by a gentleman from Virginia, [Mr. NICHOLAS,] and he had been astonished that those gentlemen who had spoken in favor of the
Treaty, had given no direct answer to his remarks on that
point.

Mr. G. proceeded then to state the second clause of that
article, which declares, that "whenever provisions becoming
contraband according to the existing Laws of Nations, should
for that reason be seized, the same should not be confiscated,
but the owners indemnified;" and said that this clause of the
article did not contemplate provisions, or other articles not
generally contraband, when attempted to be carried to a besieged place; for the third clause of the same article provides
for the last mentioned case, and declares "that a vessel thus
laden, and sailing for a beseiged place, shall not be detained,
nor her cargo, if not contraband, confiscated, unless, after
notice, she shall again attempt to enter:" which implies that,
in case of notice thus given, provisions may be confiscated,
whilst the provisions contemplated in the second clause are

not to be confiscated. It is therefore admitted by that article, that there are cases, other than that of provisions and other articles not generally contraband, carried to a besieged place, in which those provisions and articles may be regarded as contraband. It was admitting a principle unknown to the Laws of Nations, infringing our neutrality, destructive of our trade, and liable to every misconstruction. The British had shown what they meant by provisions becoming contraband according to the existing Laws of Nations, when they had taken our vessels laden with provisions, and given us an indemnification of ten per cent. So immediately connected was that proceeding of the British and that article, that even the gentleman from Connecticut [Mr. HILLHOUSE] could not separate them in his own mind; and when speaking of the indemnification we were to obtain in such cases as were contemplated by the article, he had repeatedly called it "ten per cent.," thinking only of the compensation given by the British in the case before mentioned, as one contemplated in the article, since the words ten per cent. were not to be found in the clause itself. It was not, however, material at present to decide whether a fair construction of the article justified the conduct of the British or not. The fact was uncontroverted; they still continued to impress our seamen and to capture our vessels. If they pretended to justify that conduct by the Treaty, it became necessary to obtain an explanation of the doubtful articles; if there was nothing in the Treaty to justify it, their acts were acts of hostility—were an infraction of that Treaty. And, even according to the doctrine of those gentlemen who thought that, in common cases, the House had no discretion, the Treaty once broken by one party was no longer binding on the other; and it was the right as well as the duty of this House not to proceed to pass the laws necessary to carry it into effect, until satisfactory assurances were obtained that these acts should cease, and until Great Britain had evinced a friendly disposition towards us.

Whatever evils might follow a rejection of the Treaty, they would not attend a postponement. To suspend our proceedings would not throw us in a situation which would require new negotiations, new arrangements on the points already settled, and well understood by both parties. It was merely a delay until an explanation of the late conduct of the British towards us was obtained, or until that conduct was altered. If, on the contrary, we consented to carry the Treaty into effect, under the present circumstances, what would be our situation in future? It was, by committing the most wanton and the most unprovoked aggressions on our trade; it was, by seizing a large amount of our property as a pledge for our good behaviour, that Great Britain had forced the nation into the present Treaty. If, by threatening new hostilities, or rather by continuing her aggressions, even after the Treaty was made, she could force us also to carry it into effect, our acquiescence would be tantamount to a declaration that we meant to submit in proportion to the insults that were offered to us; and this disposition being once known, what security had we against new insults, new aggressions, new spoliations, which, probably, would lay the foundation of some additional demands on the part of the aggressor, and of some additional sacrifices on ours? It had been said, and said with truth, that, to put up with the indignities we had received, without obtaining any reparation, which would probably be the effect of defeating the Treaty, was highly dishonorable to the nation. In his opinion, it still was more so, not only tamely to submit to a continuation of those national insults, but whilst they thus continued uninterrupted, to carry into effect the instrument we had consented to accept as a reparation for former ones. When the general conduct of Great Britain towards us, from the beginning of the present war, was considered; when the means by which she had produced the Treaty were reflected on; a final compliance, on our part, while she still persisted in that conduct, whilst the chastening rod of that nation was still held over us, was, in his opinion, a dereliction of national interest, of national honor, of national independence.

But it was said that war must be the consequence of our delaying to carry the Treaty into effect. Did the gentlemen mean that, if we rejected the Treaty, if we did accept the reparation there given to us, in order to obtain redress, we had no alternative left but war? If we must go to war in order to obtain reparation for insults and spoliations on our trade, we must do it, even if we carry the present Treaty into effect; for the Treaty gives us no reparation for the aggressions committed since it was ratified, has not produced a discontinuance of those acts of hostility, and gives us no security that they shall be discontinued. But the argument of those gentlemen, who supposed that America must go to war, applied to a final rejection of the Treaty, and not to a delay. He did not propose to refuse the reparation offered by the Treaty, and to put up with the aggressions committed; he had agreed that that reparation, such as it was, was a valuable article of the Treaty; he had agreed that, under the present circumstances, a greater evil would follow a total rejection, than an acquiescence to the Treaty. The only measure which had been mentioned in preference to the one now under discussion, was a suspension, a postponement whilst the present spoliations continued, in hopes to obtain for them a similar reparation, and assurances that they would cease.

But, was it meant to insinuate that it was the final intention of those who pretended to wish only for a postponement, to involve this country in a war? There was no period of the present European war at which it would not have been weak and wicked to adopt such measures as must involve America in the contest, unless forced into it for the sake of self-defence; but, at this time, to think of it, would fall but little short of madness. The whole American nation would rise in opposition to the idea; and it might, at least, have been recollected that war could not be declared except by Congress, and that two of the branches of Government were sufficient to check the other in any supposed attempt of that kind.

If there was no necessity imposed upon America to go to war; if there was no apprehension she should, by her own conduct, involve herself in one, the danger must arise from Great Britain; and the threat is, that she shall make war against us, if we do not comply. Gentlemen first tell us that we have made the best possible bargain with that nation; that she has conceded everything, without receiving a single *iota* in return; and yet they would persuade us that she will make war against us, in order to force us to accept that contract, so advantageous to us, and so injurious to herself. It would not be contended that a delay, until an amicable explanation was obtained, could afford even a pretence to Great Britain for going to war; and we all knew that her own interest would prevent her. If another campaign took place, it was acknowledged that all her efforts were to be exerted against the West Indies.

She had proclaimed her own scarcity of provisions at home, and she must depend on our supplies to support her armament. It depended upon us to defeat her whole scheme, and this was a sufficient pledge against open hostility if the European war continued. If peace took place, there would not be even the appearance of danger; the moment when a nation was happy enough to emerge from one of the most expensive, bloody, and dangerous wars in which she ever had been involved, would be the last she would choose to plunge afresh in a similar calamity.

But to the cry of war, the alarmists did not fail to add that of confusion; and they had declared, even on this floor, that, if the resolution was not adopted, Government would be dissolved. Government dissolved in case a postponement took place! This idea was too absurd to deserve a direct answer. But he would ask those gentlemen, by whom the Government was to be dissolved? Certainly, not by those who would vote against the resolution; for, although they were not, perhaps, fortunate enough to have obtained the confidence of the gentleman who voted against them, still, it must be agreed, that those who succeeded in their wishes, who defeated a measure they disliked, would not wish to destroy that Government, which they held, so far, in their hands, as to be able to carry their own measures. For them to dissolve the Government would be to dissolve their own power. By whom, then, he would ask again, was the Government to be dissolved? The gentlemen must answer, by themselves, or they must declare that they meant nothing but to alarm. Was it really the language of those men, who professed to be, who distinguished themselves by the self-assumed appellation of friends to order, that if they did not succeed in all their measures, they would overset the Government? And had all their professions been only a veil to hide their love of power? a pretence to cover their ambition? Did they mean, that the first event which would put an end to their own authority, should be the last act of Government? As to himself, he did not believe that they had such an intention; he had too good an opinion of their patriotism to permit himself to admit such an idea for a single moment; but he thought himself justifiable in entertaining a belief, that some amongst them, in order to carry a favorite, and what they thought to be an advantageous measure, meant to spread an alarm, which they did not feel; and he had no doubt that many had contracted such a habit of carrying every measure of Government as they pleased, that they really thought that everything must be thrown into confusion the moment they were thwarted in a matter of importance. He hoped that experience would, in future, cure their fears. But, at all events, be the wishes and intentions of the members of this House what they may, it was not in their power to dissolve the Government. The people of the United States, from one end of the Continent to the other, were strongly attached to their Constitution; they would restrain and punish the excesses of any party, of any set of men in the Government, who would be guilty of the attempt; and on them he would rest as a full security against every endeavor to destroy our Union, our Constitution, or our Government.

But, although he was not afraid of a dissolution, he felt how highly desirable a more general union of sentiment would be; he felt the importance of an agreement of opinion between the different branches of Government, and even between the members of the same branch. He would sacrifice much to obtain that object; it had been one of the most urging motives with him to be in favor, not of a rejection, but only of a suspension, of a delay. But even as a matter of opinion, it was difficult to say which mode of proceeding, in this House, would best accord with the general sentiments of the people. So far as related to the petitions before them, the number of signatures against the Treaty exceeded, at the moment he was speaking, the number of those in favor of the Treaty. Amongst the last, some had come from one part of the Union, where it would seem, both from the expressions in the petition itself, and from the proceedings there, that a great inducement in the petitioners to sign, was a wish to carry the Treaty with Spain into effect, as they appear to have supposed that its fate depended upon that of the British Treaty. How they would have acted upon the British Treaty alone, and unconnected with the other, he did not know, nor had he any evidence which could enable him to form an opinion thereon. All he knew was, that, until the Spanish Treaty was made, they had been perfectly silent on the subject of the other Treaty, and had never expressed an opinion upon it alone.

True it was, that an alarm which had produced a combination, had lately taken place amongst the merchants of this and some other seaports. What effect it would have, and how successful they would eventually be, in spreading this alarm amongst the people at large, he could not tell; but there were circumstances accompanying their petition, which, in his opinion, much diminished the weight they otherwise might have had. They had, undoubtedly, a right to petition upon every public measure, where they thought themselves interested, and their petitions would deserve equal regard, with those of their fellow-citizens throughout the United States. But, on this occasion, in order to create an alarm, in order to induce the people to join them, in order to force the House to pass the laws relative to the Treaty, they had formed a dangerous combination, and affected to cease insuring vessels, purchasing produce, and transacting any business. A gentleman from New York [Mr. WILLIAMS] had been so much alarmed himself, that he had predicted a fall in the price of every kind of produce, and seems, indeed, to have supposed, that the clamors of a few individuals here, would either put an end to, or satisfy the wants of those nations which depended on us for supplies of provisions. Yet, it had so happened, and it was a complete proof that the whole was only an alarm, that, whilst they were debating, the price of flour, which was of very dull sale two weeks ago, had risen in equal proportion with the supposed fears of the purchasers.

He could not help considering the cry of war, the threats of a dissolution of Government, and the present alarm, as designed for the same purpose, that of making an impression on the fears of this House. It was through the fear of being involved in a war, that the negotiation with Great Britain had originated; under the impression of fear, the Treaty had been negotiated and signed; a fear of the same danger, that of war, had promoted its ratification; and now, every imaginary mischief which could alarm our fears, was conjured up, in order to deprive us of that discretion, which this House thought they had a right to exercise, and in order to force us to carry the Treaty into effect.

If the people of the United States wished this House to

carry the Treaty into effect immediately, and notwithstanding the continued aggressions of the British; if their will was fairly and fully expressed, he would immediately acquiesce; but since an appeal was made to them, it was reasonable to suspend a decision until their sentiments were known. Till then, he must follow his own judgment; and, as he could not see that any possible evils would follow a delay, he would vote against the resolution before the Committee, in order to make room, either for that proposed by his colleague, [Mr. MAC-LAY,] or for any other, expressed in any manner whatever, provided it embraced the object he had in view, to wit: the suspension of the final vote, a postponement of the laws necessary to carry the Treaty into effect, until satisfactory assurances were obtained, that Great Britain meant, in future, to show us that friendly disposition, which it was his earnest wish might, at all times, be cultivated by America towards all other nations.

THE FRENCH WAR AND
DOMESTIC REPRESSION

The Jay Treaty caused a rupture in Franco-American relations that widened in 1798 to the point of undeclared war. John Adams spent nearly his entire term as President coping with the crisis. Before Adams took over his post, Washington had recalled James Monroe as minister to France on the charge that he had made an improper display of his French sympathies and had subverted the Administration's diplomacy. His replacement was Charles Coatesworth Pinckney, a solid Federalist and no enthusiast for France. The French Directory considered the appointment an affront, and it deemed the completion of the Jay Treaty a virtual treaty of Anglo-Ameri-

can alliance. Therefore the French Directory broke off diplomatic relations and ordered Pinckney out of France. A new decree authorized the seizure of all American vessels bound to or from a British port or carrying British goods.

Upon assuming the Presidency, Adams called a special session of Congress and delivered a bellicose message which convinced the Republicans that he intended to take the country into war. However, as a final effort to negotiate, he sent a commission to France consisting of Pinckney, John Marshall, and Elbridge Gerry.

During 1797 Gallatin and his fellow Republicans fought against warlike measures. Because negotiations were still in progress and because French military victories in Europe gave reason for hesitation, they were for a time successful. As the year closed, however, the Federalists prepared to introduce bills to arm American merchantmen, to increase the army and navy, and to levy direct taxes and contract loans to support military operations. Republicans assumed that the administration did not really want peace, that its efforts to negotiate were insincere. Therefore, when Adams did not communicate despatches belatedly received from the commissioners in France, Republicans sponsored a resolution in April 1798 requesting him to lay all the documents pertaining to the negotiation before the House. Unlike Washington in a similar situation, Adams was glad to comply. The famous XYZ despatches disclosed a shocking tale of French arrogance and American humiliation. The commissioners had been refused official recognition. Agents of the French foreign minister Talleyrand had demanded, as the price of any negotiation, a bribe of $250,000 for the Directory, the promise of a loan of several million dollars (which would have violated American *neutrality and linked the United States with France), and a public disavowal by Adams of derogatory remarks he had made about the French government.*

Capitalizing on the indignation that swept the United States, the Federalists abrogated the French alliance of 1778 and pushed a military program through Congress. The Alien and Sedition Acts were passed to stamp out opposition at home. American naval vessels and privateers soon engaged French ships at sea. However, there was no declaration of war. A few Federalist leaders actively desired to broaden the conflict. Most were content with the results already achieved. The people had become gratifyingly loyal to the government, the military and naval establishments had been strengthened, Federalists were sustained in power, the Republicans discredited, and the noxious principles of French equalitarianism stigmatized as enemy doctrine.

While keenly appreciative of these facts, President Adams did not see eye to eye with the extremists in his party. In his view, defense preparations and a show of determination had been necessary to convince France that Americans were united behind their government and would not be intimidated. With the British navy on the seas, he never believed seriously in the threat of French invasion. When toward the close of 1798 Adams received unequivocal information that France wanted to negotiate, he considered the game won. His bluff had worked. He was not willing to perpetuate the conflict for purely domestic purposes; hence, breaking with the extreme Federalists, he proposed in February 1799 a renewal of negotiations. The resulting agreement with France dispelled the crisis and gave the Republicans their opportunity to win the election of 1800.

14. HOUSE DEBATE ON THE

FOREIGN INTERCOURSE BILL

March 1, 1798

Although not of first importance, the Foreign Intercourse Bill raised a number of constitutional questions and gave Republicans another opportunity to resist what they deemed executive usurpation. On January 15, 1798 the bill was introduced to provide for the salaries of foreign ministers. It left the President free to appoint as many ministers as he chose and at any rank, but, the suggested appropriation ($40,000 plus an additional $28,000 for the year 1798) was calculated only to sustain the existing corps and raise the rank of American representatives at Lisbon and Madrid from Ministers Resident to Ministers Plenipotentiary, with an increase in pay from $4,500 to $9,000. Until 1796 only ministers at Paris and London held the higher rank; in that year a Minister Plenipotentiary had been appointed to Berlin.

John Nicholas, a Republican, moved to amend the Foreign Intercourse Bill in such a way as to reduce the establishment to what it had been before 1796. He perceived in the bill an extension of executive patronage that would increase Presidential influence over the legislature and undermine the sep-

---

Annals of Congress (5 Cong., 2 Sess., 1798), pp. 1118–1139.

*aration of powers, particularly since, as he said, it was clear
that only persons willing to become the "creatures" of the
Executive (i.e., staunch Federalists) would be appointed. In
any case, he thought a staff of foreign ministers largely unnecessary and that the country would do better not to keep
too many agents abroad. Federalists replied that the House's
meddling with the diplomatic establishment invaded the
President's constitutional authority to conduct foreign relations. Since the President regarded the existing foreign appointments and the level of rank proposed for them as auxiliary to his task, his judgment must be accepted. In effect, they
said, the House was obliged to vote the necessary funds and
could not refuse without undermining the Constitution.*

*In his long summation for the Republicans, Gallatin opened
with a lengthy discourse on the constitutional aspects of the
question, followed this with a commentary on Adams' foreign
policy and the principles laid down by George Washington in
his Farewell Address, ending with a warning on the dangers
of executive corruption in a Republic.*

Mr. GALLATIN rose, and addressed the Chair as follows:

Mr. Chairman: The amendment proposed to this bill fixes
the salary of Ministers employed at foreign Courts, not according to the grade of those Ministers as has heretofore been
the case, but according to the Courts to which they may be
sent. Its object is to reduce the diplomatic establishment
nearly to what it was before May, 1796, by confining the salary of $9,000 a year to the Ministers at London, Paris, and
Madrid, and allowing only $4,500 to all others. The shape of
the bill precludes an amendment more simple in its nature,
and by which the same object would have been attained. The
present permanent establishment, which the framers of the

bill mean to support, requires an annual appropriation of $64,000; and yet $24,000 of that sum are thrown into a separate section, as a temporary grant for the present year, thereby preventing us from proposing a reduction in the sum which is openly asked for the support of the permanent establishment.

Before we are permitted to enter into the merits of the question, we are arrested in the threshold of discussion by Constitutional objections. It is not, indeed, insisted that the amendment itself is unconstitutional; it is not denied that the Legislature has a right to fix the salaries of public Ministers; but the reduction of the establishment is supposed, in its operation and tendency, to affect the legitimate authority of the President. We are charged with a design of subverting by our doctrine the principles of the Constitution, and we are thus drawn, in an incidental manner, into a previous discussion of a Constitutional question.

The 2d section of the 2d article of the Constitution, among other things, provides, that "the President shall nominate, and by and with the advice and consent of the Senate, shall appoint Ambassadors, other public Ministers and Consuls, Judges of the Supreme Court, and all other officers of the United States, whose appointments are not herein otherwise provided for, and which shall be established by law." The first inference attempted to be drawn from the clause is, not only that the appointment of Ministers is exclusively vested in the Executive, which position is self-evident, but that an unlimited number of officers, of Ambassadors, and other diplomatic agents, is created by the Constitution itself, and that the President, in appointing, only fills those preexisting offices. It appears to me that it would be more correct to say, that the possible existence of those officers is recognised by that section, but that the office of Minister to any foreign Court, where we have not had any before, is created by the President making the appointment. And it may even be thought doubtful whether a law may not be necessary to create the office before an appointment takes place. This clause recognises the existence of Judges of the Supreme Court, as well as that of foreign Ministers, and gives the same unlimited power of appointment in both cases to the Executive. Nay, the case of Judges is stronger than that of Ministers; for upon these the Constitution is silent in every other part, whilst not only it is here declared that Judges of the Supreme Court, as well as public Ministers, may exist, but the 3d article of the Constitution positively enacts that there shall be a Supreme Court, and fixes its jurisdiction. Yet it has not been contended that the office of Judges of the Supreme Court was created by the Constitution, or could be created by the mere appointment of the President, without the previous authorization of a law. It has not been contended that the President had, by the Constitution, the power of appointing any unlimited number of those Judges, to be fixed by his own discretion. On the contrary, a law had passed defining their number, before any appointment took place; and it is not insisted that the Executive can appoint more than six, as fixed by that law. Had that power, contended for in relation to public Ministers, existed in the case of Judges, that part of the law which declares that there shall be six Judges, and no more, must be unconstitutional, as we have no right by law, and even with the consent of the President, to divest him of any of his Constitutional authorities. Still, it is not my intention to lay any stress upon this argument; some nice discrimination may perhaps be drawn between the two offices; a different construction has heretofore prevailed in the case of Ministers; and it is not necessary, in order to prove the constitutionality of our doctrine, to contend for the construction of this section. I would not, therefore, have made these preliminary observations had it not been to show that the power of the Executive to appoint Ministers without the previous sanction of a law, from which it is attempted to derive by implication the right of controlling the Legislature in the exercise of its own Constitutional powers, is itself of a doubtful nature, and can only be admitted by a very liberal construction of that clause of the Constitution.

On the other hand, the Constitution has expressly and exclusively vested in Congress the power of raising, granting, and directing the application of money. The 8th section of the 1st article declares, that "Congress shall have power to lay and collect taxes, duties, imposts, and excises, and to borrow money on the credit of the United States." The 1st section, emphatically states, that "All legislative powers herein granted shall be vested in a Congress;" and the 9th section provides, that "no money shall be drawn from the Treasury, but in consequence of appropriations made by law."

We say that Congress, having the sole power of granting money, are judges of the propriety or impropriety of making a grant, and that they have a right to exercise their discretion therein; whilst those who oppose the amendment upon Constitutional grounds, contend that the power of creating the office of public Ministers, vested in the President, imposes an obligation upon Congress to provide an adequate compensation for as many as he shall think fit to appoint. We say that the power of granting money for any purposes whatever belongs solely to the Legislature, in which it is literally vested by the Constitution. They insist that that power in this instance attaches, by implication, to the President, and that Congress are bound to make provision, without having a right to exercise their own discretion.

In order to establish this doctrine, it is asserted that, by our Constitution, each department may have checks within itself, but has none upon the others; that each department is self-independent, has its own share of powers, and moves uncontrolled within its sphere; that, therefore, whenever a certain authority is, by the Constitution, vested in any one department, it must possess the means to carry that authority into effect, and that the other departments are bound to lend their assistance for that purpose.

Those positions will not stand the test of investigation. Whenever the powers vested in any one department are sufficient to complete a certain act, that department is independent of all the others, and it would be an unconstitutional attempt in any of the others to try to control it. But whenever the powers have been so distributed between two departments, in relation to another certain act, that neither of the two can complete the act by virtue of its own powers, then each department is controlled by the other, not in relation to the operation of its appropriate powers, but in relation to the act itself. Each department, in that case, may go as far as its own authority will permit, but no further. The refusal of the other department to exercise its powers in relation to that act, in the same direction, and in concurrence with the first department, is no abridgement of the legitimate powers of the first. It is the Constitution which, in that case, abridges the powers of both, and which has rendered the concurrence of both necessary for the completion of the act. If either of the departments, in that case, after having exercised its own authority towards the completion of the act, shall pretend to have a right to force the powers of the other in the same direction, so as to have the act completed against, or without its voluntary consent, it is that department which abridges the legitimate exercise of the powers of the other. Thus, in the instance before us, the President may appoint as many public Ministers as he thinks fit, and if he can send them to their intended mission without the assistance of any act of the Legislature; if he can, as in the case of Consuls, find men who will serve without a salary, he has a right to do it, and thus to act uncontrolled by the Legislature; because, in this supposed instance, his own authority is sufficient to carry into effect his intentions. But further than that he cannot go; for the Constitution, in no part, gives him any power to force the Legislature to grant the money which may be necessary to pay the Ministers. In the same manner the Legislature have a right to appropriate a sum of money for the purpose of paying twenty public Ministers, if they shall, in their judgment, think so many necessary. But further than that they cannot go; they cannot force the President to appoint twenty Ministers, if he does not think them necessary. In this instance the act is placed partly under the jurisdiction of the Executive, and partly under that of the Legislature—under the jurisdiction of the Executive so far as relates to the creation of the office and to the appointment—under the jurisdiction of the Legislature so far as relates to granting the money—and the concurrence of both departments is necessary to complete the act.

The contrary doctrine leads to a palpable absurdity, for if it be true that any department, having expressed its will in relation to an act upon which it can operate but partially, binds the other departments to lend their assistance, in order that its will may be completely carried into effect; it follows that whenever two departments shall differ in opinion as to a certain act, we shall have two different wills acting in contrary directions, and each, however, binding the other respectively; that is to say, that there is a necessity that the act should, at the same time, be done in two different ways, or in some instances, that it should, at the same time, be done and not be done. But the fact is, that the true doctrine of those gentlemen, though not openly avowed on the present occasion, is not, that each department may act uncontrolled in the exercise of its own appropriate powers; but that they have two standards, one of which they apply to the Executive, and another by which they measure the powers of the Legislature; and that, in their opinion, the powers of the Executive are paramount, and must limit and control those of the Legislature, whenever they happen to move in the same sphere, whenever the execution of an act depends upon the concurrence of both.

This doctrine is as novel as it is absurd. We have always been taught to believe, that, in all mixed Governments, and especially in our own, the different departments mutually operated as checks one upon the other. It is a principle incident to the very nature of those Governments; it is a principle which flows from the distribution and separation of Legislative and Executive powers, by which the same act, in many instances, instead of belonging exclusively to either, falls under the discretionary and partial authority of both; it is a principle of all our State constitutions; it is a principle of the Constitution under which we now act; it is a principle recognised by every author who wrote on the subject; it is a principle fully established by the theory and practice of the Government of that country from which we derive our political institutions. In Great Britain the power of declaring war is vested in the King; but the power of granting supplies, in order to support the war, is vested in Parliament. It has never been contended there that Parliament were bound by the act of the King in granting money for that purpose; it is, on the contrary, fully understood that a concurrence of opinion is necessary before a war can be carried into effect; that the two departments, in that respect, control and check each other, and that war is never declared by the King, unless he can depend on the support of Parliament.

When it is found that the Constitution has distributed the powers in a manner different from that contended for, although there is no clause which directs that Congress shall be bound to appropriate money in order to carry into effect any of the Executive powers, some gentlemen, recurring to metaphysical subtleties, and abandoning the literal and plain sense of the Constitution, say that, although we have a Constitutional power, we have not a moral right to act according to our own discretion, but are under a moral obligation in this instance to grant the money. It is evident that where the Constitution has lodged the power, there exists the right of acting, and the right of discretion. Congress is, upon all occasions, under a moral obligation to act according to justice and propriety. We do not claim the absurd privilege of acting without sufficient motives, but we wish every proper motive to have its due weight. The opinion of the Executive, and, where he has a partial power, the application of that power to a certain object, will ever operate as powerful motives upon our deliberations. I wish it to have its full weight; but I feel averse to a doctrine which would place us under the sole control of a single force impelling us in a certain direction, to the exclusion of all the other motives of action which should also influence us.

The last clause of the 8th section of the 1st article of the Constitution, which declares that "Congress *shall have power* to make all laws which shall be necessary and proper for carrying into execution the foregoing powers, and all other powers vested by this Constitution in the Government of the United States, or in any department or officer thereof," was introduced yesterday in order to prove that Congress were bound to pass the laws necessary to carry into execution any of the powers vested by the Constitution in the President. But it is evident that this clause gives a power and does not impose a duty; it does not say that Congress *shall make laws,* but *shall have power to make laws*—that is to say, shall exercise their own discretion. This clause, contrasted with the language of the Constitution in another part, affords an additional proof in support of our arguments.

It cannot have escaped observation that the doctrine of some gentlemen on this floor would, by transferring to the Executive the power of determining the amount of an appropriation, give him a Legislative power, the power of doing what is within the province of a law, the power of fixing the rule by which a certain act is to be executed; whilst the Legislature, being bound to carry into effect the intention of the President, would, in that instance, be transformed into an Executive power. That such was not the intent of the Constitution appears from its not using, in the last mentioned clause, the same mode of expression which is applied to mere Executive duties. The 3d section of the 2d article directs that "the President shall take care that the laws be faithfully executed." Here no discretion is left. The Constitution does not here say that the President shall have power to execute the laws; but, by the phraseology, he is bound to have them executed. When, therefore, the Constitution means to impose a duty, it is sufficiently explicit, and positively directs the act to be done; and we may safely conclude, that where it gives no such discretion, where it empowers instead of commanding, the reason is that it meant to leave a discretion.

It is also objected that Congress cannot, in every case, exercise that discretion we contend for, as those clauses of the Constitution which provide "that the President and Judges shall receive, for their services, a compensation, which shall not be diminished, &c.," would be defeated, by the refusal of the Legislature to appropriate for that purpose.

The Constitution recognises the existence of public Ministers as well as that of the President and Judges. It goes no farther on the subject of Ministers; but declares that the President and Judges shall have salaries, &c. Had the framers of the Constitution also intended that Congress should be bound to make provision for Ministers, they would have introduced a similar clause in respect to them. The Constitution is explicit in one case, and declares that salaries shall be given; it is silent in the other, and does not declare that salaries shall be given. The objection, therefore, cannot reach farther than the specific case upon which it is grounded. Permit me to add, that, in respect to the President and Judges, the discretionary power of the Legislature to grant money is limited only by the Constitution, and is not transferred to any other department. For the number of those officers being determined, in respect to the President by the Constitution, and in respect to the Judges by *law,* the amount of money necessary for their support, which must be in proportion to their number, is fixed in the first instance by the Legislature, and not by the Executive. The limitation of the Legislative power does not go farther there, than to bind subsequent Legislatures for a certain time by the acts of former ones. But, in respect to public Ministers, should the doctrine, against which we contend, prevail—as their number would be fixed, not by the Legislature, but by the President—the amount of money necessary for their support would also depend upon him; and the power of granting money, in that instance, would be transferred from the Legislature to the Executive.

Some gentlemen, embarrassed by the clause respecting appropriations, have attempted to diminish its force by correcting it with the following one, which directs the publication of the accounts of receipts and expenditures of the public money, and by representing it as a mere matter of form. It is strange, indeed, that an attempt should be made to represent appropriation clauses in the Constitution as mere matters of form, as nominal provisions, whilst the only security against standing armies, contained in the Constitution, consists in the clause which provides that "no appropriation of money to raise and support armies shall be longer than two years." But the ingenuity of those gentlemen cannot erase the obnoxious clause; and so long as it shall remain a part of the Constitution, so long shall it be necessary that a law be passed before any money can be drawn from the Treasury, to be applied only in such manner, to such extent, and for such purposes, as shall have been ascertained previously by law. It is this clause which completes the power vested in Congress over money. And it should be well understood that the doctrine for which we contend is that Constitutional principle which gives to the Legislature an exclusive authority of raising and granting money—an authority which our opponents wish to place, in several instances, (the present one, and that of treaties,) in the hands of the Executive, allowing him thereby to raise and to expend money without the control of Congress. I say to raise money—for it is immaterial to me whether he does it directly, or whether the Legislature are bound to do it according to his discretion.

In this investigation, I have confined myself strictly to the Constitutional question, wishing to ascertain what the Constitution was, and not what it should be. Before I make any observations on the tendency and consequences of the two opposite constructions, I wish to make some on the merits of the amendment itself.

We conceive that the effect of the amendment will be to prevent an extension of our political connexions with foreign nations, at the same time that it will reduce an expenditure of money, which, if unnecessary, may be applied to give an undue influence to the Executive, through the means of patronage, even over the Legislature. But we do not believe that this amendment will injure our commercial intercourse with those nations, or cause any prejudice to our commercial interests.

The commercial intercourse between nations is regulated by the law of nations, by the municipal laws of the respective countries, and by treaties of commerce. The application of those different laws to individual cases, the protection of individuals against acts of oppression not consonant with those laws, the protection of our seamen and of our citizens trading to foreign countries, fall within the province of those agents known by the name of Consuls. Consuls are appointed for that specific purpose; we have them in all countries with which we trade, whether we have there public Ministers or not; they protect our commerce as effectually at Hamburg, in Denmark, or Sweden, where we have no diplomatic characters, as it is protected in Spain, or Holland, where we have Ministers. It is only when we wish to obtain a change in the regulations provided by the acknowledged law of nations, or by the municipal laws of the country, that public Ministers are necessary, as they alone can negotiate with a foreign Government, as they alone can form treaties of commerce. But it is only the application of laws and treaties to individual cases which requires a continual attention and a permanent residence. The extraordinary occasions on which it may be necessary to negotiate treaties may be provided for by special missions, by extraordinary Envoys; and it is worthy of remark that the two only treaties which have yet been made, under the present Constitution, with foreign nations, those with Great Britain and Spain, have both been formed by extraordinary Envoys, (Mr. Jay and Mr. Pinckney,) although we had at that time public Ministers at those two Courts. The proposed amendment affects only the permanent diplomatic establishment; it applies neither to Consuls, nor to such extraordinary missions as circumstances may render necessary.

It must be acknowledged, however, that it is not improbable that the extension of our diplomatic establishment may tend to increase the number of our commercial treaties beyond those which might result from extraordinary missions. But is this a desirable object? It would, indeed, be extremely advantageous to obtain from all nations such general alterations in the law of nations as would secure the freedom of the seas, and effectually protect the flag of neutral Powers against the danger of capture of detention, in all possible cases. But have we ever yet formed a commercial treaty, in which those provisions were not connected with some commercial restrictions of a different nature, and which did not even contain some causes of a political nature? I will go farther, and I will ask whether we have derived any commercial advantage from the commercial treaties we have heretofore made? Let me remind gentlemen on this floor with the situation of our commerce before the organization of this Government. The treaties of commerce we had at that time with France, Holland, Sweden, and Prussia, had not prevented its depression. And to what cause must we ascribe the vigor it had acquired before the present European war? Not to commercial treaties; for we had formed no new ones. To the want of a General

Government, having a power of making general commercial regulations, was due the languid situation of our trade; and its revival was owing to the adoption of that Government, to our own regulations, to ourselves, and not to the compact made with foreign nations.

The restrictions which we had laid upon ourselves, by our commercial treaties, have been attended with political consequences fatal to our tranquillity. We had made two treaties with France—one of alliance, avowedly of a political nature, another of commerce unconnected with the first. I need not remind the House of the difficulties in which we have been involved by several clauses of the Commercial Treaty. The articles relative to the admission of prizes of one nation into our ports, and of the exclusion of those of another, were the cause of long and critical diplomatic discussions. We have now extended to the other belligerent Power the same clauses with a reservation of our prior engagements, but to the exclusion of nations with whom we had no treaties, and have not thereby lessened our difficulties.

But, I will again ask, what commercial advantage have we derived from our commercial treaty with France, which we would not have enjoyed without that treaty? Have we derived any from the commercial part of our treaty with Great Britain? Is our commerce with that nation on a better footing than it was without the treaty? I do not mean to allude to the conventional part of that treaty, by which our differences were arranged. I do not mean to allude to the political consequences of that treaty: they are foreign to the present discussion. I speak only of commercial advantages. All we know on that subject is contained in the two acts of Parliament communicated to us by the President. It results from them that England has opened the East India trade to us under the restrictions provided by the treaty, and to all neutral nations without those restrictions. Whether she means to include us in the general provision, which relates to all neutral nations, or to keep us under the treaty restrictions, I will not pretend to say, and is not material to the present question. But it is evident that we are placed, by the treaty, in a worse commercial situation, in respect to the East Indies, than we were in fact before the treaty, or than we might be by the sole effect of the municipal laws of Great Britain. It also appears, by that act of Parliament, that England has laid a countervailing duty on our imports there in American vessels. This they had a right to do without the treaty; but they had not attempted to do it until the treaty took place, because we had till then the natural right of defeating that measure, by our own regulations here. We have abandoned that right by the treaty: we have, in order to obtain some supposed commercial advantages, laid a restriction upon our natural power of making our own general commercial regulations. This act of Parliament, however, is the only effect, in relation to commerce, which has yet resulted from the treaty. What its consequences upon our trade may be, I cannot judge; but it places us precisely in the situation in which we were before the year 1789, when we had no efficient General Government, when we could not make commercial regulations of a general nature. If the commercial part of our former treaties had not been attended with any beneficial consequences; if, on the contrary, it has involved us in a critical situation, we may be permitted to doubt whether commercial treaties are not as likely to check as to protect our commerce.

It is not denied that an extension of our political connexions with Europe would be injurious to us; but it is said that our having no Ministers in foreign countries will not prevent foreign nations sending their Ministers here, and that our Ministers abroad will not increase our political foreign connexions. I do not mean to make any personal allusions to the conduct of our Ministers in Europe; but we may judge from past events, we may judge from the conduct of foreign Ministers here, that diplomatic characters are not likely to be inactive.

From the nature of their appointment, from the nature of man, we know that they will try to acquire importance with their own Government and credit to themselves; they are placed in a dangerous vortex, and they will all, more or less, according to circumstances and to their personal character, take a part in the political intrigues or quarrels of Europe. They will attempt to do something; they will attempt to involve us in the political vortex of Europe; they will try to make for us new connexions, or to break ancient connexions.

Whether foreign nations, with whom we have no public Ministers, will send Ministers here, cannot be absolutely foretold; but we know that it is not usual. At all events it cannot be wise to invite a greater number of foreign Ministers here, by extending our diplomatic establishment to countries where we have not heretofore sent Ministers. The amendment under consideration has no tendency to annihilate that establishment, but it will effectually check its extension. If our Ministers abroad are necessary for the protection of our commerce, or on account of our political situation in respect to the belligerent Powers, this amendment will not withdraw their compensation. Its avowed object, its only possible effect, is to reduce the establishment to what it was in 1796, when we had no Minister at Berlin, and when our Minister at Lisbon, with a salary of $4,500, rendered us the same services as if he had had $9,000.

But we are told that this is not the time to make a reduction; that our situation in respect to Europe forbids it; and that our differing in opinion with the President on this subject, will prove us to be a divided people. I am much afraid, that if now is not the time, it will be with this reform, as with all others, it will never be time. To evince to European nations that we wish not to mix in their political sphere of action; that we are not desirous of forming political connexions; that we will not interfere, especially at this time, with their political interests, is, in my opinion, the best mode in our power to prevent their interfering with us, and the most likely to produce a termination of our present dispute. Nor can I conceive how our expressing, on this ground, a difference of opinion with the Executive, will tend to prove that we are not united on the subject of self-defence. But I believe that now is the time to express our opinion, because the object of the extension of our diplomatic establishment having been explained to us by the President, it is our duty, if we think the object contemplated to be dangerous, not to be silent upon this occasion. Our information is derived from the following paragraph of the President's Speech at the opening of the last extraordinary session of Congress:

"Although it is very true that we ought not to involve ourselves in the political system of Europe, but to keep ourselves always distinct and separate from it, if we can; yet, to effect this separation, early, punctual, and continual information of the current chain of events, and of the political projects in contemplation, is no less necessary than if we were directly concerned in them. It is necessary, in order to the discovery of the efforts made to draw us into the vortex, in season to make preparations against them. However we may consider ourselves, the maritime and commercial Powers of the world will consider the United States of America as forming a weight in that balance of power in Europe which never can be forgotten or neglected. It would not only be against our interest, but it would be doing wrong to one half of Europe at least, if we should voluntarily throw ourselves into either scale. It is a natural policy for a nation that studies to be neutral, to consult with our nations engaged in the same studies and pursuits. At the same time that measures ought to be pursued with this view, our Treaties with Prussia and Sweden, one of which is expired, and the other near expiring, might be renewed."

Permit me, before I proceed to make any remarks upon that part of the President's Speech, to contrast the sentiments contained in the late President's Address to the People, on his retiring from office:

"The great rule of conduct for us, in regard to foreign nations, is, in extending our commercial relations, to have with them as little political connexion as possible. So far as we have already formed engagements, let them be fulfilled with perfect good faith. Here let us stop."

"Europe has a set of primary interests, which to us have none, or a very remote relation. Hence she must be engaged in frequent controversies, the causes of which are essentially foreign to our concerns. Hence, therefore, it must be unwise in us to implicate ourselves by artificial ties, in the ordinary vicissitudes of her politics, or the ordinary combinations and collisions of her friendships or enmities."

"Our detached and distant situation invites and enables us to pursue a different course. If we remain one people, under an efficient Government, the period is not far off when we may defy material injury from external annoyance. Why forego the advantages of so peculiar a situation? Why quit our own to stand upon foreign ground? Why, by interweaving our destiny with that of any part of Europe, entangle our peace and prosperity in the toils of European ambition, rivalship, interest, humor, or caprice? It is our true policy to steer clear of permanent alliances with any portion of the foreign world, so far, I mean, as we are now at liberty to do it. Let those engagements be observed in their genuine sense. But, in my opinion, it is unnecessary, and would be unwise to extend them."

Supported by this authority, may I hope to escape the censure of arrogance, if, on this occasion, I dare express an opinion in some degree opposed to the very respectable authority of the President of the United States.

The object of both the late and the present President is perfectly the same; it is that we may not be involved in the political system of Europe, that we may not be drawn into the vortex. But they do not seem altogether to agree on the means by which to obtain that object.

The President of the United States conceives that it is a

natural policy for us to consult with other nations engaged in the same studies and pursuits, and that measures ought to be pursued with this view. The late President thinks it unwise, by interweaving our destiny with Europe, to entangle our peace—unwise to implicate ourselves by artificial ties—unwise and unnecessary to extend our engagements. His opinion is emphatically expressed by these words: "Here let us stop."

As to that balance of power in Europe, which never can be forgotten or neglected, it is a system which, so far as it relates to Europe itself, it is not necessary for us to discuss. And yet, without examining all the useless wars to which it has served as a cause or a pretence, we must recollect, at what late period the British Ministry wanted to involve the British nation in a war with Russia for the purpose of preserving that balance, which might, in their opinion, be affected by the transfer of Oczackow, situated as it is in a remote corner of the Black Sea, from the hordes of Tartars which rule Turkey, to the Tartar hordes which inhabit Russia. But, however interesting that balance may be to Europe, how does it concern us? We may lament the fate of Poland and Venice, and I never can myself see, without regret, independent nations blotted from the map of the world. But their destiny does not affect us in the least. We have no interest whatever in that balance, and by us it should be altogether forgotten and neglected. If we ever think that we have an interest in it, shall we not be induced to throw our weight in the scale; shall we not involve ourselves in the destinies and the wars of Europe? If we act on our own ground, is it likely that other nations will ever consider us as forming a weight in their balance?

But, if we adopt the policy to consult with other nations—if measures are to be pursued with that view—if we are to form a new foreign political connexions, how can we hope to escape being unavoidably drawn into the vortex? It was, after having thus communicated his intention, it was in pursuance of that plan, that the President thought fit to send a

Minister to Berlin. With Prussia we have no commerce. Had commerce been the object of that embassy, Sweden, Denmark, the Hanse towns, or Italy, would have been preferred. The mission is avowedly and evidently of a political nature; and if we are to consult and to form connexions with nations who may, in our opinion, be engaged in similar pursuits with ourselves; if Prussia is considered as such, with what nation in Europe may we not, and shall we not, according to circumstances consult, concert measures, and form political arrangements? It is from this view of the subject that I have been induced, however reluctantly, fully to state all the reasons which impress upon my mind conviction of the importance of the present amendment, of the importance of checking at this time, and in its birth, a system which tends to increase our political connexions with Europe.

So much has already been said on the subject of patronage, or the danger which might hereafter result from an influence obtained through those means over the Legislature, and on the system said to be adopted by the Administration, to exclude from every description of office men who do not subscribe to a certain political creed, that I think it useless to add any observations on that subject. As, however, the patronage now vested by law in the Executive has been stated as very insignificant, I will merely state its real extent.

It consists in appointment to offices and in the disposal of public moneys by contracts. The annual pay of the officers in the different departments—of the Treasury, of State and of War—and all the subordinate offices, of Loans, Mint, &c., of the officers in the Northwest Territory, of the Attorney General, Surveyor General, Indian agents, diplomatic characters, agents for the protection of seamen, agents and commissioners appointed by virtue of certain treaties; in fine, the pay of all civil officers, whose appointment depends upon the Executive or some branch of the Administration, including therein all the clerks, but excluding the Judiciary department, added to the pay and emoluments of the commissioned officers of the Army and Navy, forms an aggregate of about $420,000. The salary and other emoluments of the officers employed in the collection of the impost and of the internal revenues, including therein postmasters, amount to about $430,000. These two sums amount together to $850,000 yearly, received by officers who derive their appointment from the Executive.

The amount of moneys disposed of by contracts, and it is well known that lucrative contracts may be made a powerful engine of influence; that amount, calculated on some objects upon an average of three years, and including those relative to the Mint, to the printing of the several offices, to the printing of the laws, for the transportation of the mail, for supplying the provisions, clothing, horses, medicines, cannons, arms of the Army, for Indian goods, and all the immense details of the Quartermaster's department; for building and furnishing all the supplies of the Navy; for building light-houses, and for several other contingent expenses exceeds $1,200,000 a year.

The aggregate of the two sums exceeds two millions of dollars, a sum by no means despicable, when compared with our population and wealth, when compared with a revenue which, till this year, never exceeded seven million of dollars. After having stated these considerations, which appear to me immediately applicable to the present discussion, I would not encroach any longer on the patience of the committee, had not some gentlemen brought into view a number of topics of a more general nature, in which it may not be altogether useless to follow them.

The first position they assume is, that there is a natural tendency in the Legislative department to encroach upon the Executive, and they attempt to prove by historical facts, that, in all countries, where a Republican form of Government ever existed, the Executive has in fact been swallowed up by the Legislature. The instance of the Greek Republic and their subversion by Philip of Macedon, and that of Rome, have been chiefly insisted upon. Both are altogether inapplicable to the American Constitution. The question is not, whether Governments, constructed on different principles from ours, have been destroyed by the effect of those principles, but whether the history of those similar to our own will support the assertion.

The small Greek Republics, Athens especially, were governed directly and immediately by the people themselves. In Rome, where the Constitution, though imperfectly, was better balanced, the popular branch of Government was also an assembly of the whole people of the city; and when their virtues and their manners, which could alone support such a system, had been corrupted by the spoils of a conquered world; when the dregs of every other town of Italy, admitted to the rights of citizenship, had resorted to a corrupt metropolis; when a few citizens, enriched by the treasures of Asia, had it in their power to bribe that mixed mass, which alone, and without being controlled by the other parts of an extensive empire, disposed of every office of honor or power; when these offices thus obtained placed ambitious leaders at the head of the standing armies, which constituted at that time, the sole military force of the nation; we cannot be at a loss to discover the causes of the civil wars and contests for power which terminated in the establishment of despotism.

These instances are inapplicable to our own situation, because those Governments essentially differed from that of America in this, that the Legislative power was there lodged in the people residing in a single city, and that it is here vested in the Representatives of the whole people. *There* not only was there no proper or precise distribution of powers, but *there* also the people themselves had the authority of deliberating and of enacting laws, and *here* they have only that of electing the persons who are to make laws for them. All that can be proved by this is, that power ought to be vested in the body of the people. But because the heterogeneous

mass which constituted the body of citizens in Rome, abused
the power they had, ought we to conclude that the people of
America will abuse the power they have not? Or that, because
a Government, where the principle of representation was unknown, was destroyed by the corruption of the people, and
the ambition of their demagogues, the representative Government of the United States will be destroyed by the Representatives themselves? The history of those ancient republics may
indeed teach us to cherish that principle of representation,
which is the leading feature of our Constitution, and the safeguard of our liberties. It may teach us another lesson, applicable to all times and to all men—that money accumulated
in the hands of a single man, or of a few, may be applied with
success to the destruction of any Government. The foreign
gold of Philip gave the last blow to the expiring liberty of
Athens. And the same engine in the hands of the citizens of
Rome was not attended with less fatal effects.

But if we turn our attention from a view of obscure antiquity
to modern Europe, how shall the assertion be supported, that,
in representative Governments, the Legislature usually swal-
lows up the Executive? History tells us that, three centuries
ago, representative forms of government existed throughout
Europe, in which the representatives of the people, or a part
of the people, had more or less power and influence, according
to the various circumstances under which they respectively
arose. But if we look at the present situation of that country,
such at least as it was before the French Revolution, where
can we discover traces of those institutions? What has become of the Cortes of Spain? Of the States General of France?
Of the Diets of Denmark? Everywhere we find the Executive
in possession of Legislative, of absolute powers. The glim-
merings of liberty, which for a moment shone in Europe, were
owing to the decay of the feudal system. When the princes
were deprived of the personal services of their vassals, and
of the revenues derived from their ancient domains; when

industry and commerce rendered money the principal engine of power, those popular assemblies which had the till then unimportant right of raising taxes and granting supplies, arose at once into consequence. And as the Executive, either by force, or by fraud, or by the folly of the people themselves, succeeded in wresting that power from them, they fell again into misuse or insignificance.

The fate of the European Republics would lead us to similar conclusions. Venice, the greater part of Switzerland and Holland, would show us the Legislative powers equally merging into the Executive, and a self-created council or hereditary Stadtholder, usurping by artifice the legitimate authority of representative bodies. Almost every vestige of liberty was erased from the continent of Europe; and it is to England that we are indebted for the preservation of those principles which form the basis of our Constitution.

It is from England that we have borrowed our political institutions. Taught by her example, we have improved them and adapted them to our own situation; but her history is still that which is most applicable to ourselves; for, notwithstanding the happy modifications which we have introduced, the great outlines of representation and distribution of powers are the same, and notwithstanding the strong distinguishing features, there has never existed a Government more similar upon the whole to our own than that of that country.

Some gentlemen, leaving out of view that period in the British history which should naturally attract our attention, have attempted to draw from the events of the reign of Charles the First, a proof of their favorite doctrine, the danger to be apprehended from the encroachment of the Legislature. They have forgotten that those events were not the effect of the slow progress of an established Government, but the result of an unsettled Constitution. The precise boundaries of power were not ascertained; Parliament contended for the acquirement of rights which had been usurped or enjoyed by the

Kings. In its beginning, the contest was between the King in his own right, and Parliament in the right of the people. Convulsions, a civil war, a revolution ensued. But the position, which we controvert, is not that the people or a popular assembly may, by a convulsion, wrest from the Executive powers originally obtained by fraud or violence. It is that, when a representative Government, with properly distributed powers, is once established, the Legislature will finally encroach upon the Executive. This position cannot be illustrated by the events of Charles's reign; but that period, which extends from the revolution of 1688 to the present reign, after the Constitution had been ascertained and settled, is that to which we must recur as immediately applicable to our own situation.

It is during that period that a progressive patronage, and a systematic, corrupting influence have sunk Parliament to a nominal representation, a mere machine, the convenience used by Government for the purpose of raising up supplies; the medium through which the Executive reaches with ease the purse of the people. And now, when the farce of obtaining even the nominal consent of Parliament is sufficiently understood, the Ministry dispense with the ceremony, and have carried so far their contempt for that body, that the sum spent during the last year, without the consent, exceeds the amount spent with the consent of Parliament. The Executive there have acquired the unlimited and uncontrolled power of raising and expending money, and the House of Commons is under a moral obligation of making the necessary appropriations.

But, is it to be apprehended, from the structure of our own Constitution, that the Executive will be destroyed by the Legislature? The Legislative powers, vested in Congress, seem to have been given under such efficient checks, as should remove any fears of that nature. They are not given to a single popular branch, but to two distinct bodies. The consent of both is necessary to do any act, and one of them, elected not immediately by the people, but through the medium of State Legislatures, is, at the same time, united with the Executive in the exercise of its most important powers, that of appointing to offices, and that of making treaties. Thus no encroachment can be made upon the Executive powers, without the consent of the Senate; and this body never will give their assent to any act, which, by weakening the Executive, would necessarily diminish their own authority. But should ever such an act pass both Houses of Congress, it must not be forgotten that the Constitution has vested the President with a modified negative. That negative, already twice exercised, was, on both occasions, effectual; and it is an absurd supposition that, at any time, the President should not be supported by at least one-third of the two branches of the Legislature, against any unconstitutional attempt to deprive him of his legitimate authority.

To these Constitutional barriers, may be adduced, in respect to any supposed encroachments of this House, the greater degree of permanency in the Senate and President, and the systematic line of conduct which a single magistrate, whose powers are always in action, and a permanent body, who, like the Senate, are only renewed by thirds, are enabled to pursue; contrasted with the insulated efforts of this House, liable to a total renovation every two years, and composed of members occasionally in session, but dispersed through this extensive country the greater part of the year. Nor should the gentlemen who attach so great a degree of influence to the supposed popularity of this House, forget, that to us belongs the most obnoxious share of Government, that of laying taxes, whilst the Executive enjoys the more grateful employment of the individual application of the public money.

The object of our Constitution has been to divide and distribute the powers between the several branches of Government. With that distribution, and with the share allotted to us, we are fully satisfied. We only wish to preserve the equilibrium intended by the Constitution. The Constitutional right which is the subject of this discussion is of a negative kind. By its exercise we may prevent, but we cannot act; nor is there any power claimed by us which does not equally attach to the Senate, and lay us under their control. In this instance we ask only that the powers which the Constitution has separated, may not be blended; that the power of raising and granting money may remain inviolate in the Legislature, and that of appointing to offices, or even in the case of public Ministers, of creating offices, in the Executive. But the doctrine introduced by some gentlemen tends, in its immediate effects, to blend those powers, and, by vesting that Legislative authority which they represent as so formidable, in the same hands where the Executive power is lodged, to overset every barrier and to destroy the most fundamental principles of our Constitution.

In the same manner, as in this instance, they insist that we are bound to appropriate, they, in the case of treaties, also claim for the Executive a power of abridging the Constitutional authority of Congress of raising and granting money, and vest in that department what they take from this. Nor do they stop there. The most important powers entrusted to Congress, exclusively of that over money, consist in regulating commerce, raising armies, providing a navy, and declaring war. And all these are swept away, and transferred to the Executive, by the construction put upon the treaty-making power, which rests on the same foundation with that which is now claimed. The Executive has the power of appointing public Ministers, of making commercial treaties, of making subsidiary treaties, and of making treaties of alliance, offensive and defensive. The same principle which should bind us in one case, binds us in every other. If we are under a moral obligation to lend our assistance, in order to carry into effect the Constitutional powers of the Executive; if we have no discretion left in the exercise of our own; if it be not true, that when an act, in order to be completed, requires the concurrence of two departments, each department has an equal right to give or to refuse its assent; if in the instance of public Ministers, we are bound to appropriate; if in the instance of commercial treaties, we are bound to repeal or to make commercial regulations, in conformity with the provisions of the treaties, the inference is unavoidable, that where the Executive has formed a subsidiary treaty, we are also bound, without any discretion being left to us, to appropriate the sums of money necessary to pay the subsidy, to raise the required number of auxiliary troops, and to provide the stipulated number of ships of war; that where a treaty of alliance offensive has been made, we are under a moral obligation to make war. Thus would the important powers entrusted to Congress by the Constitution be reduced to those of coining money, passing penal laws, granting patents, and establishing post-roads. The rule of construction which, in one instance, vests in the Executive the power of granting money, or any other Legislative authority, makes the transfer in all the cases I have enumerated. Any construction which shall except a single case, shall restore our discretion in all.

Can any fatal consequences attend the full exercise of the Constitutional discretion of Congress, in granting money? Its general effect must be to diminish the expenditure of public money. By restraining it, you take away the most efficient check, provided by the Constitution, to control and to keep within proper bounds that expenditure. Thus, applied to the present amendment, the exercise of that discretion may prevent too large a sum of money being applied to the support of foreign Ministers. It never can be used to increase that sum. Thus it may prevent an appropriation for the payment of a subsidy to a foreign nation; it may prevent an extension of our political foreign connexions; it may prevent the raising of troops, or the equipping of a fleet; it may prevent a war. But it never can create an expenditure of money, an army, a navy, a war, which, upon the ground of the doctrine supported by our opponents, would not equally take place. The checks intended to prevent those evils, and their inseparable attendants, taxation and public debts, cannot be too strong. For it is the natural tendency of Governments, and, I will add, it is the natural tendency of every Administration, and of every Executive, to increase the rate of expenditure beyond the necessary demands, and the real abilities of the nation. It is here, indeed, that we may appeal to the history of other countries: it is here that it will afford us instructive lessons, applicable to all times, and to every form of Government.

Wherever the Executive have acquired an uncontrolled command over the purse of the people, prodigality, wars, excessive taxes, and ever progressing debts, have unavoidably ensued. Not to speak of Spain and Holland, weakened by those causes; not to speak of France, whose example is still more awful, the fate of England is sufficient to warn us against the dangers of that system. In vain did the insular situation of that nation preserve it from foreign invasions; in vain did she alone, among the great Powers of Europe, enjoy the advantages of laws which protected property and encouraged industry; in vain did her agriculture arrive to a superior degree of perfection; in vain did she obtain the commerce of the world; in vain were the treasures of India poured in her bosom; in vain did the industry of her inhabitants, and the incalculable effects of machinery, raise her manufactures to their unrivalled present state; in vain did she enjoy a century of uninterrupted and unparalleled prosperity. The folly and extravagance of Government have kept pace with all the efforts of industry, with every improvement of the individuals. The whole surplus of the labor of the industrious part of the community has been destroyed by expensive wars; or, if any part escaped annihilation, it was what was plundered by the direct or indirect agents of Government, and was applied to the accumulation of wealth in the few unproductive consumers. And now she stands on the brink of ruin, overburthened by a debt of four hundred and fifty millions sterling, and by taxes amounting to twenty-five millions sterling a year, and yet insufficient to support her peace establishment.

Can we hope for a greater prosperity—for a more fortunate concurrence of circumstances? Have we any security that we shall be preserved from those evils? And yet, this is the system which flows from the doctrine which would wrest from the Legislature their exclusive control over the expenditure of money; that would vest in the Executive, in certain specific but widely extended cases, the power of raising and applying money. It is the system which seeks for support in the influence of patronage, by increasing the number of offices, and avowing a determination to distribute them exclusively as rewards, amongst men of a certain description. It is the system which entangles us in new political connexions, raises standing armies, builds navies, squanders the public money, swells the public debt, and multiplies the burdens of the people.

Shall we be told that the frequent elections of the Executive are a sufficient safeguard against every danger? Doubtless they are, provided we are not altogether lost to ourselves. They afford us that remedy to which hereditary Governments cannot resort. But should we, on that account, suppose that we are not open to danger? No one can set a higher value on the benefits resulting from an elective Government than myself. But let us never forget that the forms of a Constitution afford us security, only as they preserve us from abuses, and that they will become useless, whenever they shall be applied to cover, protect, and defend abuses.

May we not be alarmed, when we hear the gentleman from Delaware, (Mr. BAYARD) in accents of regret, telling us that our Executive is the most weak, the infirm branch of Government, and that danger is to be apprehended from its weakness; contrasting the scanty provision and insignificant patronage of our Executive, with the immense army, the incalculable navy, the church patronage, the nobility-creating power and the civil list of the monarch of Great Britain? And concluding, by delivering an opinion that, notwithstanding all those sources of corrupting influence, the House of Commons, were the venal boroughs abolished, would lop off every prerogative of the Crown, till, though the features of monarchy might remain, the substance would be gone.

A Government, which loses the substance, however it may retain the features of monarchy, is in substance a Republic; and the least idea of that gentleman is only, that a pure representation and monarchy are incompatible. But in his opinion, provided an equal representation is established, monarchy is destroyed, and a substantial Republic may exist, notwithstanding an accumulation of power and influence equal to those possessed at present by the King of England. And, when this follows his declaration of the dangers to be feared from the weakness and infirmity of our Executive, are we not irresistibly forced to infer, that he thinks that the introduction of armies, navies, patronage and civil list, are necessary to strengthen our Executive, and would not injure the principle of our Constitution?

To such doctrines avowed on this floor, to such systems as the plan of Government which the late Secretary of the Treasury (Mr. Hamilton,) had proposed in the Convention, may perhaps be ascribed that belief in a part of the community, the belief, which was yesterday represented as highly criminal, that there exists in America a Monarchico, Aristocratic Faction, who would wish to impose upon us the substance of the British Government.

I have allowed myself to make this last observation, only in reply to the gentleman who read the paper I alluded to. It is painful to recriminate, I wish denunciations to be avoided, and I am not in the habit of ascribing improper motives to gentlemen on the other side of the question. Never shall I erect myself into a High Priest of the Constitution, assuming the keys of political salvation and damning without mercy whomsoever differs with me in opinion. But what tone is assumed, in respect to us, by some gentlemen on this floor?

If we complain of the prodigality of a branch of the Administration, or wish to control it by refusing to appropriate all the money which is asked, we are stigmatized as disorganizers; if we oppose the growth of systems of taxation, we are charged with a design of subverting the Constitution and of making a revolution; if we attempt to check the extension of our political connexions with European nations, we are branded with the epithet of Jacobins. Revolutions and Jacobinism do not flow from that line of policy we wish to see adopted. They belong, they exclusively belong, to the system we resist; they are its last stage, the last page in the book of the history of Governments under its influence. It is after centuries of extravagance, vice, and oppression, that the people make revolutions, and it is then, it is during the general convulsion that ensues, that the dregs of the nation rise to the surface, and overwhelm in a common ruin both the oppressors and the deliverers of the people.

Are gentlemen serious in their fears? Do they, from us, apprehend revolutions, plunder, and massacre? Have we not an equal stake with themselves? I speak not of myself; but I will ask, what benefit could those men, who are commonly called Jacobins, derive from a convulsion? Have they less property? Have they less to lose or more to hope from a change? If you think us deprived of common integrity, you might at least allow us some share of common sense. But if no confidence is to be placed in ourselves, some might be put in the people of America and in their situation. In a country, where a scattered population covers an extensive territory; where the means of subsistence are easy; where the dangerous class which constitutes an European mob does not exist; where actual oppression is yet unknown, the people who enjoy those advantages, who enjoy a better Government and more happiness than any other nation of the globe, are not the people ready for a revolution. Nor should it be forgotten that those parts of the Union that are commonly charged with a design of oversetting the Constitution are those which, on account of their peculiar situation, on account of the unhappy race of men they contain, would be exposed to the most dangerous convulsion by an internal revolution. . . .

15. HOUSE DEBATE ON THE

PROVISIONAL ARMY

May 8, 10, 16, 1798

The House of Representatives, May 8, 1798

On April 24, 1798 the House took up a bill introduced from the Senate to raise a provisional army. It authorized the President to call 20,000 men into service "whenever he shall judge the public safety to require the measure." It also authorized him to accept within the next three years the enlistment of an undetermined number of volunteers to be officered but held in inactive status until called into service by the President. Republicans would have liked to defeat the bill for raising a provisional army, but with the country in a frenzy over the XYZ disclosures they had to be content with modifying certain features. They attacked the discretionary power

---

Annals of Congress (5 Cong., 2 Sess., 1798), pp. 1631–1634.

given to the President, holding that the surrender of Congress's authority to raise an army was unconstitutional. They declared that the vague wording of the bill left the President free to summon the army not merely to repel invasion, which to them seemed remote, but to suppress political opposition at home. Federalists in reply harped on the imminence of invasion and danger of subversion by a pro-French faction in the United States. They accused the Republicans of intent to block necessary preparation for national defense—a hint that Republicans were the very sort of people whose activities might oblige the President to invoke the public safety clause. As to the discretionary authority conferred upon the President, the Federalist argument was that if Congress could give the President power to raise an army immediately, it could within the Constitution give him a contingent power to do so.

A select committee reported the bill on May 8. An amendment proposed to limit the President's authority to summon the army to specific contingencies: a declaration of war against the United States, actual invasion, or "imminent danger of such invasion, discovered, in his opinion, to exist."

Mr. GALLATIN said, if this amendment was adopted, it would prevent a motion being made to strike out the first section of the bill. This amendment would certainly make the bill better than it is at present, as it goes to define, in some measure, the cases in which the provisional army may be raised; yet, as he conceived the amendment did not go far enough, and that, under our present circumstances, it is not necessary or proper to pass this bill, he would move to strike out the first section of the bill, which would supersede the motion under consideration. He would briefly state his reasons for the motion.

He had said that the amendment removed, in some degree,

the objections against the bill; but it was far from removing them altogether. He allowed the two first contingencies, viz: a declaration of war or actual invasion were definite, and therefore the Constitutional objection which lay against the bill, as to its transferring a power to the Executive which is vested by the Constitution in Congress, viz: to judge of the propriety of raising an army, does not lie against them; but the third, viz: when imminent danger of such invasion, discovered, in his opinion, to exist, is liable to the same Constitutional objection to which the original bill was liable, as it left it to the opinion of the President to decide the proper time of raising an army.

Undoubtedly, the Constitution has foreseen, that in cases of imminent danger, the United States would need a standing army, but it makes Congress the judge of this necessity; but this bill went to make the President the judge; yet he knew, if there were no other objection to this bill, the most usual course would have been to have moved to strike out the latter part of the amendment.

But he conceived it was not proper, at present, to pass this bill; he believed it would be time enough to do it when we were convinced of the existence of danger. And he did not think there were any serious apprehensions to be entertained of an invasion during the present session. The danger to be apprehended was upon our trade; but he expected no attack upon our territory beyond predatory excursions, the landing of a dangerous class of persons from the West India islands, or an attack on the coast by some detached frigates. But, in every case, short of an actual invasion by an army, he conceived the militia would not only be competent to repel the attack, but more so than a regular army. If an invasion or insurrection took place in the Southern States, where the danger seems most to be apprehended, the militia in the neighborhood would be ready, immediately, to repel or suppress it. If these could not do so, neither could a regular army. The danger to be apprehended, in case of an insurrection, or an attack of that kind, is what would take place immediately, and this could only be prevented by the militia who are on the spot; for, an army could not be supposed to be always at hand to meet any sudden emergency. He had no doubt, therefore, the militia of the country would be fully equal to its defence. But if they were not, the volunteer corps of cavalry, accoutrements for which were proposed to be provided by this bill, might be called in, and would be more effectual than any other force. He thought, therefore, it would be better to negative this bill, and to adopt the regulations recommended by the select committee, in a separate bill.

If the militia was equal to the repelling of any attack, except from a regular army, it could not be apprehended that an invasion of that kind could take place during the present session. The attention of France is at present engaged on very different objects; and, if it was in their power, which he did not think it was, yet as the whole of their marine strength is engaged in a different object of much greater importance to them than the invasion of this country could be, they would not attempt it at present. This must be evident when it is recollected what a small force they have employed against the West India islands, which they wish to conquer. We do not know that the French mean to invade this country; everything on this subject arose from apprehension, but we do know they wish to take their possessions in the West Indies, since they have made their restoration a *sine qua non* condition of peace; and we all know the force they have been able to send against them. And what does it amount to? In the course of a year two or three frigates and a few hundred men with arms. This is all the force they are able or willing to send from home. In the East Indies, where they have colonies to conquer for themselves or the Dutch, the same want of force is to be seen. It is certain that while the European war lasts, they are either unable or unwilling to make any great exertions at a distance from Europe. Indeed, if all the force they have employed out of Europe were to come against this country, it would be repulsed by the militia in any part of the country where it might make its attack. If, then, any invasion of this country is to be expected, it must take place at the conclusion of the European war; and, if it was then made, he had no doubt of our being able to repel it. But, in such case, the contingency on which the raising of this army by this bill rests, would not take place till the next session of Congress. He was not, however, under any apprehension of its taking place even at this time; and, when he said this, it was not because he differed in opinion with gentlemen as to the ambition of France, but because he thought it was neither their interest nor in their power to effect an invasion of this country. He believed the French nation to be as ambitious as the gentleman from South Carolina represented it to be, and he believed every nation intoxicated with victory as she is, and possessing power equal to her, would also be as ambitious as she is. If, said he, this country was situated as near to France as Italy and Switzerland are, and our resources were no greater than theirs, he would agree that we should be in some danger; but, situated as we are, he believed it would neither be in the power of France, nor would it be her interest if it was, to invade this country in any formidable manner.

It is not the interest of France to make an attempt to invade this country, because we have no business in the political scale or vortex of Europe. It was to increase their power in Europe that the French have taken those steps which were so often reprobated in that House; but they could have no such views in sending a force against us. And though they may not always be guided in their conduct by the principle of interest, their ambition must be limited by the extent of their power. And if, twenty years ago, when our population, and consequently our strength, was not half what it is at present, the attack of a nation whose force, as applicable to any maritime exertion and to an invasion, was greater than that of France and all her allies, and whose money resources were far superior to theirs, was not able to make an impression upon this country, it held out no flattering encouragement to France to make the attempt. He must confess he looked upon all that was said of an invasion by France as a mere *bugbear.* He did not believe any attempt would ever be made, and if it was made that the militia alone would be sufficient to repel it. Yet were there anything like certainty of such an event, he would not trust wholly in the militia, but would call the whole of our resources into motion—he would have a standing army as well as the militia.

Under these impressions, it was clear he could not vote for this bill, because it goes upon the idea of an army being necessary to meet an invasion, of which he thought there was no danger; but if there are gentlemen who are of a different opinion, who think that an invasion will take place, and, if so, that we must have an army, he would ask if it could take place without being known some time before hand? It certainly could not, as such an undertaking would not be entered upon without immense previous preparation.

What is the intention of this bill? It is, that if the President shall think danger exists, he shall begin to raise an army. When will he do this? He supposed when he first heard of preparations making for an invasion. But, in that case, Mr. G. wished to know whether the first step of the President would not be to call Congress together? Congress were called together last Spring, upon an occasion far less important, and when no imminent danger existed. When it was known that the President could convene Congress within six weeks after he was convinced the danger of an invasion existed, he submitted to the committee, whether it was proper to place the power in the hands of the President which the Constitution has placed alone in Congress, of judging when it is proper to raise an army?

Mr. G. said, the question was, whether an army of 10,000 men should be raised for six years, according to the discretion of the President, or whether Congress would reserve to itself the discretion of raising an army or not, as it shall think proper. He said six years, because, though the enlistments are only to be for three years, yet the power of enlisting was vested in the President for three years. Ten thousand men, according to the gentleman from Maryland, (Mr. SMITH,) would cost four millions dollars a year. If gentlemen really believed there was at present danger of an invasion, they would immediately order an army to be raised; but if they do not, and choose to say the President shall decide on the danger, as he conceived this to be a dereliction of duty, he could not agree to it, and therefore he wished to destroy the bill.

The House of Representatives, May 10, 1798

Debate continued over the constitutionality of giving the President power to call forth the army. Supporters of the bill argued that the contingent power was necessary in order to prepare the country in advance of hostilities and that knowledge of the measures taken would be a deterrent to France. A previously organized and trained force was essential for, as the American Revolution had proved, the militia was not adequate. Republicans countered with allegations that the Federalists intended to have a standing army, that the invasion threat was fictitious, and that, as the American Revolution had demonstrated, the militia was thoroughly competent for local defense.

Mr. GALLATIN said, he would not take much of the time of the committee in relation to what might be called the Consti-

---

Annals of Congress (5 Cong., 2 Sess., 1798), pp. 1655–1660.

tutional question under consideration; yet he found, from the manner in which his arguments had been noticed, it would be necessary to make a few additional observations on this subject.

He understood that the object of a constitution was to secure a proper distribution of power among the different branches of a government. It was a security never possessed by any country before the constitutions of the United States were formed. In Great Britain, whatever distribution of powers may exist, an act of Parliament may transfer any power from one department to another. The only check, then, upon the use of that power is public opinion. But, in this country, the principle of the Constitution is, that no department of Government can exercise that power which has been given to another department. Gentlemen, however, seem to suppose the Constitution may remain inviolate so long as there is no forcible assumption of power by any branch of Government from the other, and that a transfer or free gift of such power would not be a violation of the Constitution. He considered the effect to be precisely the same whichever way it was done. The object of the Constitution was to assign forever certain specific Legislative powers to Congress, and certain other powers to the Executive, and whenever one department shall exercise the powers of the other, in whatever way it shall be done, the Constitution will be broken, and the security intended by it will no longer exist.

If these remarks are applied to the case under consideration, it would be found that one of the most important powers that could be vested in Congress, viz: the power of raising an army, is, by this bill, proposed to be transferred from Congress to the President. This he considered as a dangerous principle, and if once admitted, it would be in the power of Congress to destroy the Constitution. Yet the committee are told that there are precedents to authorize this procedure. He knew the line which separates Executive from Legislative duty is sometimes very indistinct; and in some cases of not very great importance, where the distinction might not be very striking, or had not perhaps been attended to, powers which, strictly speaking, were Legislative, may have been improperly given to the Executive; but is an instance of this kind to be brought as a precedent for passing a bill of so important a nature as is the present. Because power has been given to the President to build ten galleys, if he shall think them necessary, and to spend $80,000, should it now be inferred that there would be no impropriety in giving him the power to judge of the necessity of raising an army of 10,000 men, which are to cost the United States at least four millions of dollars a year? If that conclusion was drawn, he would ask whether Congress might not also transfer any of the other important powers vested in them, such as the power of laying and collecting taxes, and that of declaring war? And if so, it was admitted that Congress have the power of destroying the Constitution; for limitation clauses to laws were frequently opposed as improper, and if a single Congress passed without any limitation clause an act similar to this, or giving forever to the Executive the power of judging of the necessity of raising an army, or of laying a tax, or of declaring war, or of enacting laws, he asked whether the Legislative power of Congress would not be annihilated? And yet this is the objection which some gentlemen call it ridiculous to entertain, while others charge the supporters of it with a want of candor and sincerity.

After stating this, Mr. G. said, he believed he need not answer the objections of the gentleman from Connecticut, (Mr. Dana,) who seemed to think that he (Mr. G.) had relied upon a mere verbal difference in the wording of some of the clauses in the Constitution. He would now see that he did not raise his objections on so slight a ground, but that they arose from the general principles and spirit of the Constitution itself. Mr. G. said, he might be told that no danger would arise from this transfer of power, as it was not to be supposed the President would abuse it, and that he ought not to suppose the case of future Legislatures passing such improper acts as he had mentioned, or at any rate transferring other powers to the Executive, because this Congress was going to transfer the specific discretionary power contemplated in the section under consideration. But ought they to put more trust in future Legislatures than in themselves? And if the galleys were brought as a precedent to induce Congress to pass this bill, would not it be brought as a precedent to induce future Legislatures to make still further and more dangerous transfers of power? Were not evident symptoms of that disposition discernable in this very discussion? A gentleman from Massachusetts (Mr. OTIS) had positively asserted, that if the President was to give information to Congress, that, in his opinion, there was imminent danger of an invasion, Congress, without examining the grounds of that opinion, must necessarily act in conformity to it. The same gentleman had said, that if the validity of the objections urged against this bill were admitted, it would declare all former laws enacted upon the same principle null, and of course the whole of our present army would be dissolved. This could not be the case; for if there was anything unconstitutional in the law fixing the Military Establishment, it was the power which was given to the President to forbear raising, or to discharge the men when he should think them unnecessary, which power had never been executed, and therefore could in nowise affect the Military Establishment now existing.

But the committee are told that the present dangerous situation of our country renders it necessary to pass a law of this kind. It appeared to him that when gentlemen were called upon to show where this danger exists, they were at a loss how to answer. They had not shown where it is; almost all concurred in an opinion that there would be no invasion by an army this season. After a peace was concluded in Europe,

some gentlemen were of opinion there might be danger, but
not at present. The gentleman from South Carolina had indeed pointed out a part of the country where he supposes
there is at present some danger, and it was the only quarter in
which he himself expected any annoyance at present, and
upon which he had already made some observations. That gentleman had, however, gone on to detail the manner in which
the French may land, and the points most likely to be attacked.
If that gentleman be sincere in his fears, and really thinks
that imminent danger exists, he ought to vote for the raising
of the army immediately, otherwise the force which he wished
to raise would be too late for the quarter in which this danger
is said to be so imminent. But the gentleman in the whole
course of his observations, has spoken of this section as giving
to the President a power, whenever danger shall appear, of
calling these men out, or embodying them, as if the proper
power of raising an army was suddenly to embody men together in an emergency; whereas it must be clear to him that
these men must first be enlisted and collected; while, on the
contrary, the militia alone could be called out or embodied
immediately. Indeed, a militia force might be called out, and
might repel a predatory attack, before five hundred of this
provisional army could be raised. He conceived only two things
were wanting to make militia more effective than at present,
which were provided by the additional sections reported to
this bill by the select committee, which were to furnish them
with arms, and also the equipments for cavalry, in the Southern States. He hoped those sections would be agreed to, and
then he thought the gentleman from South Carolina (Mr.
HARPER) might be perfectly easy on account of the safety of
the Southern States. If we were to be engaged in war, not
only by sea but by land, and an invading army was to land
under an idea of subjugating the country, or of bringing us
to a dishonorable peace, he would then agree that a standing
army would be necessary to aid the militia; but at present he

did not think there would be any reasonable expectation of such an event.

Mr. G. said he had been told that he might consider himself safe on his farm on the Monongahela, and that the people of the South would not be very thankful for the opposition he made to this force for their defence. But was it proper to introduce circumstances of this kind into debate? He did not believe, that, by any vote which he had ever given on that floor, he had shown any unjustifiable attachment to his constituents to the injury of other parts of the Union. He should undoubtedly, on all occasions, support their interests, so far as he understood them, whenever it could be done consistently with the good of the whole, but never in opposition to that good.

Mr. G. supposed, that if the danger were very great on the Southern coast, more would have been heard of it than by the private letter of the gentleman from South Carolina (Mr. HARPER.) He himself did not believe there was any great danger to be apprehended at present from invasion. But the arguments of gentlemen went to show that the danger is now imminent, and consequently that the army ought now to be raised; and yet, instead of acting consistently with their own arguments, they support a bill by which an army is to be raised only in case of a change of circumstances. When gentlemen wish to establish the belief of a probability of an immediate invasion, they refer to the conversations which passed in Paris between our Ministers and X, Y, and Z. If they believe that they see, and the President believes that he sees in that conversation, a threatened invasion, he supposed the army would be immediately raised. Indeed, from what he daily heard and saw, he was of opinion that the President believed imminent danger now to exist. But the section under consideration went, taking the arguments of the gentleman to be well grounded, to throw the responsibility of a measure,

which, in their opinion, was now necessary, from themselves
on the President.

But the committee had been told by the gentleman from
New York (Mr. BROOKS) that the militia are more expensive
than regular troops. Mr. G. believed, that while they were in
service, they were more expensive, on account of their marching to and from home; but the great difference between the
two forces was, the militia were only called into actual service
and paid when actual danger exists, but an army receives pay
all the time it is in being. Of course an army, if considered a
cheaper weapon of defence, ought only to be raised in time
of actual danger, and discharged when it ceases to exist.

Shall I, said Mr. G., be told it is improper to speak of expense in a business of this kind? He said he knew well enough,
that in case of actual war, or invasion, it would be ridiculous
to talk of the expense of defence. And if the committee now
believe that we are in imminent danger, they ought immediately to raise an army; but as they suppose the danger does
not at present exist, the expense was a proper subject of discussion. He would not, however, on the subject of this bill,
have said anything about it, had it not been asserted that no
expense could be incurred on account of this law. He wished
to know why gentlemen had so earnestly insisted upon a permanent land-tax, in order to insure a permanent loan? That
loan and that tax were wanted for the sole purpose of supporting this army, as all the expenses at present incurred are
provided for by the present revenue and one year's land-tax.
Without this army there would be no necessity for a permanent land-tax. Let not gentlemen amuse themselves with the
idea that at the time they are giving the President a power to
raise an army of 10,000 men, it will be attended with no expense. If they give the authority, they must reckon upon paying the men, and this can only be done by a permanent land-
tax. He had therefore voted against making the land-tax

permanent, because he was against raising this army, and he could not conceive how gentlemen who had agreed with him on that question could consistently be in favor of this. If they were in favor of the army, they ought, in order to provide the means, to have voted for the permanent land-tax. As to the distinction made by the gentleman from South Carolina between the troops proposed to be raised by this bill, and a standing army, he looked upon it as frivolous; the words *standing army* meant a regular force as distinguished from the militia; you may call it by that name, or simply an army, which are the words used by the Constitution, it will not change its substance—and in Great Britain, where its existence, on account of the annual supply bill, was always limited to one year, it was always called a standing army.

He would add one remark with respect to standing armies. Military men on this floor, in favor of an establishment of this kind, judge of a regular army from what they saw of the Revolutionary army—but such an army, he apprehended, would not again be seen in this country, except in case of invasion, when the same spirit would animate our citizens which inspired them heretofore; but a standing army, in time of peace, would always be found very different from the patriotic army with which those gentlemen were acquainted. With respect to militia, he believed most of those gentlemen were better acquainted with their merits than he could pretend to be, yet they have not only denied that the militia of the United States are capable of serving against a regular army, for any length of time, but also of repelling an invasion. He believed, with his friend from Tennessee, that very many instances in our Revolutionary war spoke a contrary language. If he recollected right, the enemy was kept in Boston for more than a year, and at last driven from thence by the militia; and he believed the State of New Jersey was recovered in 1777 by the militia, when hardly the appearance of a regular army existed. Advancing to another period of the war, which perhaps decided it, he asked whether the standing army would have been able to stop the course of General Burgoyne, had it not been for the militia, which poured from all quarters, checked his progress, and so eminently contributed to his capture. He knew great services were performed by regular troops, and that in case of actual war they were necessary; but he believed the militia were equal to the repelling of any invasion which could, under present circumstances, be contemplated.

The House of Representatives, May 16, 1798

The Republicans lost 48 to 41 on a motion to eliminate Presidential discretionary power. The wording as reported by the select committee was allowed to stand. Motions were then entertained to reduce the number of troops. Gallatin spoke in favor of 5,000 alleging no danger of invasion. Robert G. Harper replied with the warning that 150,000 to 200,000 French troops were mobilized on the channel coast to invade England and might be turned against the United States.

The House decided on a provisional army of 10,000 men. A resolution authorizing the President to call forth and train in rotation, not exceeding 20,000 men at any one time, the militia authorized by the act of June 24, 1797 was negatived by a large majority. Discussion then ranged over the volunteer corps to be officered and held in readiness.

Harper taunted Gallatin for having alluded to the violent suppression of political dissenters in England as an example of what would result from the organization of a volunteer corps in the United States. Gallatin, said Harper, was really concerned because such a corps would put an end to sedition

---

and French intrigue. For his part, Harper said he would like to see such a suppression in this country.

Gallatin's rebuttal did not prevent the provision for a volunteer corps from being enacted by a vote of 56 to 37.

Mr. GALLATIN said, he should disappoint the member from New York, in some degree, as he expressed an expectation that he (Mr. G.) should answer what might fall from him; but when a member so far abandoned every rule of common decency, so far forgot the respect due to this House, and so far insulted the understanding of members, as to pay no attention to the question under discussion, but, laying argument aside, goes merely into a wide field of abusive declamation, he conceived him entitled only to silent contempt, and that, and that alone the member from New York would receive from him.

The gentleman from South Carolina, Mr. G. said, had not made any reply to the leading arguments urged against the section under consideration.

He would once more ask whence arose the particular partiality which is shown to the proposed organization of these corps? Are gentlemen afraid that the present militia officers will not be so good as those appointed by the President of the United States? Or are they afraid that if these corps are organized agreeably to the existing laws of the United States, that they will not be so good a defence as if organized according to the present bill?

When gentlemen speak of the Western insurrection, and of volunteer corps, why do they not say there was only one volunteer corps not attached to the militia out of 12,000 men, and he adduced this as a proof to show that, whatever disorders might take place in the country, the militia would be sufficient to quell them. They seemed to think differently, and that they are not to be trusted.

Gentlemen opposed to this motion charge the supporters of it with being afraid to put arms into the hands of the citizens. The charge was unfounded. They are not afraid of putting arms into the hands of our citizens, but they do not wish to put them into the hands of a few chosen persons, to the exclusion of others. The reliance of the supporters of this motion is in the people at large; that of the opposers of it in these few. Mr. G. wished gentlemen to show the difference between these corps and militia, and what are the great advantages in favor of these, and then the committee may judge between the merits of each. He could see no advantage from the present plan; all that he could conceive from it was, that its supporters believe there is more safety in arming a select few, than in depending upon the whole people.

But the committee are told that, these volunteers, thus organized, are the best calculated for suppressing perturbators and disorganizers. But this was a mere assertion, and no argument had been adduced to prove that they would be better calculated for that purpose than the people at large, or more likely to exert themselves in support of the Constitution and liberties of the country. The gentleman from South Carolina had said, there were disorganizers and seditious persons in the country, and that he was determined to support the present system of alarm; and yet he has not shown where these disorganizers and perturbators exist. Is there anything known, Mr. G. asked, to induce a belief that there are persons of this description in any part of the United States? And when gentlemen, without any proof, insist that if those volunteers shall consist of men of greater property, they will, on that account, be the most proper to suppress sedition, he would not hesitate to say that the assertion implied an illiberal and unfounded insinuation against all the other classes of the community, and was a calumny on the great mass of the people of the United States.

But the gentleman from South Carolina went on to support

the justice and policy of a similar plan adopted in England, the effect of which, he supposes, has been to suppress insurrection, and to save that country from that general system of devastation which has taken place throughout Europe. But what, Mr. G. asked, are the effects which we see arising from this system? From that system of alarm and from that combination against France, which went hand in hand, at the commencement of the European war? The consequence has been that France has not rested satisfied with making regulations in her own Government, but has subjugated some of the finest countries in Europe, and subverted their Governments, and she now threatens Great Britain herself with a similar fate. This, Mr. G. said, we know has been the effect of those measures; but the gentleman from South Carolina, in order to reconcile us to a similar plan, sets up his supposition against fact, and tells us what might have happened, in his opinion, had not this system of alarm been adopted in England. He knew what had happened in consequence of those fatal steps; what might have happened had they not been adopted, was a matter of conjecture. It was but a poor consolation to that nation to be told by its Minister, "matters would have been worse, had I not taken such and such measures." And if a similar conduct was now pursued by this country, and should be attended with similar calamities, it would afford but a miserable comfort to America to hear, two years hence, the gentleman from South Carolina assert that a contrary course would have produced, in his opinion, still greater evils. It could not be denied that that system of alarm which the gentleman from South Carolina commended, had, in England, increased that disaffection which it was its object to suppress, and the same effect would be produced here by similar measures. How was the alarm in England supported? By means similar to those adopted in this House this day. A gentleman rises from his seat, and tells the committee he saw five or six men in the streets of this city with French cockades in their hats. He says that some one had reported, that it was said that somebody had heard that one of them had said, he would join the French if they landed here; the gentleman immediately concluded that there is a deep conspiracy in the country, and thousands ready to do the same. The same things were done in England at the beginning of the war; the Tower was fortified on account of an insurrection which no one had ever heard of. Every member on this floor might remember the numerous artifices used there at that time; and it was in order to avoid the evils which had been produced in England by that system that he wished it to cease here; that he wished, instead of placing these young men in corps separate from the militia, to have them joined to it, so as to make one undivided general defence for the country, instead of separating them in the way proposed, which could only produce divisions and uneasiness among the people.

Mr. G. said he would make no remark upon what fell from the gentleman from South Carolina, as to the unfairness of this motion to strike out the section, instead of endeavoring to amend it. He thought it was not less unfair for gentlemen to wish a contrary course to be taken, while they declare themselves unwilling to agree to any amendments which would make it more agreeable to those who oppose it. Nor should he make any remarks on what had fallen from that gentleman on the subject of Ireland, in respect to the Executive Directory sitting there, or of the day appointed for a general massacre. He had seen such things in the papers. How true or false they were, he could not say. But he did know that there had been for a long time in existence there a system of military coercion, which had doubtless increased the disaffection which before existed, and which will in the end prove fatal to the Government of Ireland. Yet the gentleman from South Carolina says there may be a time when it will be proper that the same military coercion should exist here. He trusted that gentleman was the only one who anticipated such an event, and he did not think it necessary to refute or comment on that observation.

For a number of years, Mr. G. said, attempts had been made, in different shapes, to give to the President of the United States a standing army, or select corps of militia. Ever since the organization of the present Constitution these attempts had been on every occasion repeated and defeated. This kind of half-way army and militia would effect the purpose, and might become the most dangerous of all others; and whatever might be the fate of this motion, he never would repent to have exerted himself as far as he was able in order to prevent its introduction.

Mr. G. concluded with saying that he was sorry he had taken up so much of the time of the committee on this question. He had spoken three times, which he would not have done had any other gentleman answered the observations which had been made in opposition to this motion by the gentleman from South Carolina. But however disagreeable it was to him to be obliged to rise so often, not only to meet the arguments of some gentlemen, but the abuse and impertinent allusions of others, nothing should prevent him from doing it, while he had hopes that the fatal measure now proposed might be defeated.

THE ALIEN AND SEDITION ACTS

Federalists took advantage of the war with France to try to crush their domestic political foes. In May and June 1798 antisubversive bills were introduced into both houses of Congress. From Washington's first term the Federalists had regarded opposition to the administration as essentially treasonous, imputing to it the ultimate aim of destroying the government established by the Constitution. When Republicans embraced the cause of France, which soon became the world's foremost military power, Federalists saw a definite pattern of subversion and conquest emerging, a pattern clearly articulated in Europe where pro-French sympathizers undermined resistance to French invasion. The repressive legislation adopted by the Federalists in 1798 rested on the widely-held conviction, partly genuine, partly inspired, that a conspiracy existed to overturn the government with the aid of French arms.

16. HOUSE DEBATE ON

THE ALIEN FRIENDS ACT

June 19, 1798

As it was presumed that Frenchmen and Irish political refugees were active in the conspiracy, a number of laws were passed with respect to aliens. A new naturalization law raised the residence requirement for citizenship from five to fourteen years, the purpose being to deprive newcomers of political rights. An Alien Enemies Act authorized the President in event of war to confine and deport enemy aliens whose presence he considered inimical to national security. A second Alien Act applied to all aliens, including nationals of countries friendly to the United States. It gave the President authority to banish any alien he thought dangerous to the safety of the United States or whom he suspected of being engaged in "treasonable or secret machinations against the government."

Annals of Congress (5 Cong., 2 Sess., 1798), pp. 1973–1983.

Gallatin spoke powerfully against this last bill. His main argument was that Congress lacked constitutional authority to remove aliens of friendly countries; it was a matter reserved to the states. Also, he warned that the violation of the civil rights of aliens might set a precedent for invalidating rights of native Americans.

Mr. GALLATIN rose, and repeated the remarks he was making yesterday, when twice interrupted. He said he could not discover the reason why the bill which was under discussion on Saturday, was postponed for the purpose of taking up this. Both contained the same principle. They differed only as to the mode of carrying it into effect. The first and third sections of the other bill were the same in substance as the first section of this. The discussion on this first section, therefore, must be the same as before; and the question is not whether the measure is expedient, but whether this Government has any power, under the Constitution, to remove alien friends out of the United States, or whether the power over aliens does not belong exclusively to the individual States. He was himself clearly and decidedly of opinion that no such authority was vested in the General Government, and that this bill, if passed, will be a gross violation of the Constitution. Mr. G. referred to arguments which he had used on the former bill. All the powers vested in the General Government are either positively specified by the Constitution, or they are such as are necessary and proper for carrying into effect some of those specific powers. For the Constitution provides that the powers not delegated by it to the United States are reserved to the States. It is not contended, in this instance, that a power over aliens is specifically and positively given to the Union; but an attempt is made, to show that it is given by implication. In order to establish this position, let gentlemen remember that it is necessary not only to assert in a vague manner that the authority contended for may be derived from some specific power, but to prove that, in the words of the Constitution, the present law is necessary and proper for carrying into effect some one specific power expressly given by the Constitution. Let the arguments of the supporters of this bill be examined by that test.

It has been declared by the gentleman from Massachusetts (Mr. SEWALL) that this power over aliens is included in the power given to Congress to regulate commerce; the gentleman from Delaware believes it to be contained in that clause of the Constitution which gives to Congress the power to lay and collect taxes, by which he argues power is also given to provide for the common defence and general welfare; but another gentleman from Massachusetts (Mr. OTIS) and a gentleman from Connecticut (Mr. DANA) drew this power from that which they say every Government must have to preserve itself.

Mr. G. said, he would offer a few remarks upon each of these reasons. In the first place, the power was said to be included in the power to regulate commerce. But this bill is not intended for any commercial purpose; it is wholly of a political nature, intended to effect political ends, and does not relate to aliens as merchants. It is a power to be given to the President to remove all aliens dangerous to the peace of the United States, and cannot by any one be considered as a commercial regulation. If Congress has any power which they can exercise on the persons of alien merchants it must relate to them as merchants—to their professions, not to their existence as men; if the power was derived from this source, it must be confined in its operation to alien merchants, and could not be applied to aliens of other descriptions. But this general authority over aliens, not only is not now intended, but it is not necessary for carrying into effect the power given to regulate commerce. Will the regulations of this bill in any way determine how commerce shall be carried on with foreign countries, or from one State to another?

With respect to the clause of the eighth section, contended for by the gentleman from Delaware, it was in the following words: "Congress shall have power to lay and collect taxes, duties, imposts, and excises, to pay the debts, and provide for the common defence and general welfare of the United States; but all duties, imposts, and excises, shall be uniform throughout the United States," and that no gentleman contended that its meaning was to give power to Congress, in the first place to lay taxes, and in the next place to provide for the common defence and general welfare of the United States. But the obvious and universally received meaning of the last words was not to give a general power altogether unconnected with the remaining part of the sentence, but to define the purpose for which taxes should be laid. Had the construction of the gentleman from Delaware been intended, the power would have been given in a distinct paragraph, in the same manner as all the other powers are given, instead of placing the words in this way in the middle of a paragraph relating to a quite different subject. If this new construction was adopted, there would have been no need to have enumerated the powers given to Congress in this and other sections, because such a broad power as that contended for, would have embraced every other.

Nor is this all. The twelfth amendment of the Constitution seems to have apprehended some improper use being made of the sweeping clause, by taking it as a ground for power never intended to be given, and, therefore, it declares that "the powers not delegated to the United States by the Constitution, nor prohibited by it to the States, are reserved to the States respectively, or to the people; but if the construction now spoken of were to prevail, this amendment could have no application; for if all the powers are delegated to Congress by that clause, how could it be said that the powers not delegated were reserved to the States?

To show that at the time the Constitution was adopted, no such opinion as this prevailed, Mr. G. referred to the debates had upon it in the Pennsylvania Convention. He particularly quoted the sentiments of Mr. Wilson, who spoke of this provision for raising taxes as being necessary for the common defence and general welfare. Mr. Wilson expressed himself as follows: "Certainly Congress should possess the power of raising revenue from their constituents for the purpose mentioned in the eighth section of the first article, that is, to pay the debts and provide for the common defence and general welfare of the United States;" and again, "I think it would be very unwise in this Convention to refuse to adopt this Constitution, because it grants Congress power to lay and collect taxes for the purpose of providing for the common defence and general welfare of the United States." Mr. G. also made the following quotation from the essay signed Publius, and called the Federalist, written by the members of the Federal Convention, in defence of the Constitution before its adoption:

"Some, who have not denied the necessity of the power of taxation, have grounded a very fierce attack against the Constitution on the language in which it is defined. It has been urged and echoed that the power to lay and collect taxes, duties, imposts, and excises, to pay the debts, and provide for the common defence and general welfare of the United States, amounts to an unlimited commission to exercise every power which may be alleged to be necessary for the common defence or general welfare. No stronger proof could be given of the distress under which these writers labor for objections, than their stooping to such a misconstruction. Had no other enumeration or definition of the powers of Congress been found in the Constitution, than the general expressions just cited, the authors of the objection might have some color for it; though it would have been difficult to find a reason for so awkward a form of describing an authority to legislate in all possible cases. A power to destroy the freedom of the press, the trial by jury, or even to regulate the course of descents, or the forms of conveyance, must be very singularly expressed by the terms 'to raise money for the general welfare.' But what color can the objection have, when a specification of the objects alluded to by these general terms immediately follows, and is not even separated by a longer pause than a semicolon? If the different parts of the same instrument ought to be so expounded as to give meaning to every part which will bear it, shall one part of the same sentence be excluded altogether from a share in the meaning, and shall the more doubtful and indefinite terms be retained in their full extent, and the clear and precise expressions be denied any signification whatsoever? For what purpose could the enumeration of particular powers be inserted, if these and all others were meant to be included in the preceding general power? Nothing is more natural or common than first to use a general phrase, and then to explain and qualify it by a recital of particulars. But the idea of an enumeration of particulars, which neither explain nor qualify the general meaning, and can have no other effect than to confound and mislead, is an absurdity which, as we are reduced to the dilemma of charging either on the authors of the objection, or on the authors of the Constitution, we must take the liberty of supposing had not its origin with the latter."

Mr. G. said he was well informed that those words had originally been inserted in the Constitution as a limitation to the power of laying taxes. After the limitation had been agreed to, and the Constitution was completed, a member of the Convention, (he was one of the members who represented the State of Pennsylvania,) being one of a committee of revisal and arrangement, attempted to throw these words into a distinct paragraph, so as to create not a limitation, but a distinct power. The trick, however, was discovered by a member from Connecticut, now deceased, and the words restored as they now stand. So that, Mr. G. said, whether he referred to the Constitution itself, to the most able defenders of it, or to the State Conventions, the only rational construction which could be given to that clause was, that it was a limitation, and not an extension of powers.

Another gentleman from Massachusetts (Mr. Oтis) has taken a kind of general ground, supposing that there must exist certain general powers in Congress which are equal to meet any possible case. He could not say that he rightly understood the meaning of that gentleman. If he meant that all power should be vested in Government, because it is possible that occurrences may arise which will call for the exercise of them, he would not hesitate to say that doctrine is contrary to the Constitution, for that has put limits to the powers of the Government, and has said certain things shall not be done by it. For instance, it might be thought necessary, though neither an invasion nor a rebellion had taken place, to suspend the Habeas Corpus Act, as had been the case in Great Britain some time ago. It was there represented that a dangerous conspiracy existed against the Government, and that, in order to meet it with effect, it was necessary to suspend the Habeas Corpus Act. Reasoning on the same ground, the gentleman from Massachusetts might say that a dangerous conspiracy now exists here, that he has got hold of the threads of that plot which the gentleman from South Carolina has pledged himself to this House a few days ago to pursue through all its ramifications, and move for a suspension of the Habeas Corpus Act. But the Constitution would be directly against such a motion, as it is there said "it shall not be suspended, but in cases of actual rebellion or invasion." So that this Government cannot do everything which the gentleman may suppose necessary to be done. Or did the gentleman mean that Congress ought to exercise all the powers that may be vested in Government in this country? Such a sentiment is also flatly contradicted by the Constitution, as it recognises a division of powers between the General and State Governments. Thus, in the instance before the committee, Congress has the power to declare war, and to punish any persons guilty of treasonable practices, but what relates to aliens as suspicious characters, the Government of the United States has no cognizance of. It is a matter which remains with the State Governments; and if there was any necessity for passing a law on the subject, there could be no doubt it would be done by the proper Constitutional authority—the State Governments. Or did gentlemen mean that the power for providing for the common defence should absorb all other powers, and that if this power was limited, the Constitution is not worth a farthing, or not worth having, as the gentleman has said. Did he wish, except the Constitution would authorize an act of this sort, it should be overset? Did he like the Constitution only for the powers it gave, and not for the restraints it put on power? Did he intend to declare himself an enemy to every part of the Constitution which restrains the power of the General Government? He could not suppose that this was his opinion; and if it was not, he did not understand what he meant.

As to the general declaration contained in the preamble of the Constitution, he would remark that the articles of Confederation under the old Congress, had several expressions of the same nature. The power was there said to be given for the general defence, showing that to have been the object of the Union. The same articles gave power to Congress to declare war, and several other powers of a general nature, in which such a power might equally be supposed to be included; and it was on this account that he stated that the old Congress never acted on this subject, merely because the general powers of both Governments being nearly similar, the opinion of the old Congress, in relation to their own authority, was applicable to the present instance.

In opposing this bill, it might not be supposed to be necessary to go further than to show that the power of passing a law like the present, had not been given to this Government. But it so happened that, supposing he was mistaken in that position, another clause expressly prohibited the exercise of that power for the present, even if it did exist at all. He would, therefore, proceed to notice some of the objections which had been urged against his observations on the 9th section of the 1st article of the Constitution, which says that Congress shall not prohibit the migration of such persons as the States choose to admit. It was insisted, by a new construction of the word *admit*, that it required a positive law of a State to show that a State exercised this power, and that so long as a State had not passed a law upon the subject, declaring that they do admit persons of the description mentioned in this bill, Congress have a right to pass a law upon it. By this doctrine a new kind of construction of the Constitution will result; for there must not only be a concurrent authority between the States and the United States, but also contradictory powers. So that, if Congress were to pass a law on the subject before the committee, the States might each of them pass a law to repeal it.

But Mr. G. took it for granted that, whatever is not prohibited is permitted; and, so long as no law of any State prohibits the admission of aliens, he supposed all are admitted. Indeed, the admission is recognised by laws in every State. Of that description were the laws in which some States allow aliens to possess lands; in other States declare that the estate of an alien dying in this country, and leaving no heirs here, will go to his nearest of kin in a foreign country, &c.

Again, it was said, that this clause relates solely to slaves, as an exception granted to the power of regulating commerce. He allowed this provision was chiefly intended to secure the importation of slaves. He believed the regulation of the migration of persons to the United States was not included in the power regulating commerce, because the voluntary migration of free persons was not, like the importation of slaves, an object of trade, and, therefore, that it was unnecessary to have introduced this clause, in relation to the migration of free persons, as an exception to a power which did not exist. In-

deed, the gentleman from Massachusetts mentioned this as
an argument to show that the general power of regulating
migration existed in the General Government. If not, why,
he asked, was this article introduced? In answer to this argument, which supposes that this clause relates to free people,
he would only refer the gentleman to the Constitution, which
had expressly guarded against the danger of a similar construction, by declaring, in the eleventh amendment, that "the
enumeration in the Constitution of certain rights, shall not
be construed to deny or disparage others retained by the
people."

But the only use he meant to make of this clause, in support of his opinion, was this: Whether it was necessary, in relation to free persons, or not; and, whatever might have been
the intention of the framers of the Constitution, it must be
taken as it now stands. The word *migration,* as contradistin-
guished from the word *importation,* could only apply to a
free act of the will, and to the voluntary arrival of free persons coming to this country, in the same manner as the word
importation could only apply to slaves brought into the United
States without their consent; and the word *persons* was of
the most general acceptation, and could by no means exclude
free emigrants. That this even was well understood, at the
time of the adoption of the Constitution, he would prove by
the following quotation from Mr. Wilson's speech, in the debates of the Pennsylvania Convention: "The gentleman (Mr.
Findley) says, that it is unfortunate in another point of view;
it means to prohibit the introduction of white people from
Europe, as this tax may deter them from coming amongst us;
a little impartiality and attention will discover the care that
the Convention took in selecting their language. The words
are the *migration* or *importation* of such persons shall not be
prohibited by Congress prior to the year 1808, but a tax or
duty may be imposed on such *importation;* it is observable
here, that the term *migration* is dropped, when a tax or duty

is mentioned; so that Congress have power to impose the tax only on those imported."

The argument, therefore, stood thus: Either the general power of preventing the migration of aliens is included in the powers given by the Constitution to Congress, or it is not. If it is not included, and that was his decided opinion, the present bill is unconstitutional. But if, by implication, it may be derived from any of the specific powers given to Congress, whether that of regulating commerce, of declaring war, or of any other, or if it be included in a supposed general power of providing for the common defence and general welfare, even, in that case, its exercise is prohibited to Congress, by this clause, till the year 1808, and, on this ground, the present bill is also unconstitutional.

Mr. G. thought, when a constructive power of this kind was claimed, it was time that a stand should be made against it. He looked upon the provision not only as unconstitutional, but as of a most arbitrary nature, grounded upon a supposition which has not been proved, and upon another which does not exist. The supposition is not proved that the measure is necessary on account of danger to be apprehended, from there being aliens resident in the country dangerous to its peace. The persons from whom this danger is apprehended, are either alien friends or alien enemies. So far as relates to the latter, they are provided for in another bill. The whole of the arguments on this bill, therefore, are applicable only to alien friends. And here he must take notice that, although Congress has not the power to remove alien friends, it cannot be inferred, as had been objected, that it had not the power to remove alien enemies; this last authority resulted from the power to make all laws necessary to carry into effect one of the specific powers given by the Constitution. Among these powers is that of declaring war, which includes that of making prisoners of war, and of making regulations with respect to alien enemies, who are liable to be treated as prisoners of war.

By virtue of that power, and in order to carry it into effect, Congress could dispose of the persons and property of alien enemies as it thinks fit, provided it be according to the laws of nations and to treaties.

No facts had appeared, with respect to alien friends, which require these arbitrary means to be employed against them. If there are gentlemen possessed of facts of this kind, it is their duty to lay them before the House. But whilst these proofs are held back, gentlemen have a right to say no necessity exists for such a measure. He supposed gentlemen who spoke with so much confidence on this subject, must be possessed of facts unknown to him, otherwise they would be unjustifiable in creating a groundless alarm; but the House had a right to inquire what the facts are, if they did exist, and whether they relate to alien friends or alien enemies.

He would not only say that this bill was founded on a supposition which was not proved, but, also, that it took for granted another position which did not exist. If there be any danger, it is certainly such as may be punished by the laws of our country, without adopting a measure of this kind. The laws of the United States will reach alien friends if guilty of seditious or treasonable practices, as well as citizens. And if the law is not at present sufficient to reach every case, it might be amended. He wished all crimes and punishments to be accurately defined; and he hoped gentlemen who profess to be warm supporters of this Government and Constitution, will not say that it is not in our power to reach the object. And if it be necessary to send certain persons out of the country, on account of their mal-practices, he trusted laws would be framed for the purpose of punishing them, and that they would not be left without trial, subject to the arbitrary control of one man only.

This bill not only was grounded upon a supposed necessity which did not exist, but it appeared to him that if it was passed, a bill of a similar nature may be brought in, in rela-

tion to citizens of the United States. This bill is called a bill
concerning aliens; but in its consequences it affects citizens as
much as aliens; for he called upon the supporters of this bill
to show him a single clause in the Constitution which has been
referred to in support of this bill, which would not equally
justify a similar measure against citizens of the United States.
And, so far as relates to the necessity of the bill, the plea may
be equally made against citizens as against aliens; for what is
the ground upon which this power is claimed? It is by virtue
of the power vested in Congress to regulate commerce. And
what is this power? It is "to regulate commerce with foreign
nations, and among the several States, and with the Indian
tribes." Therefore, if by virtue of the power of Congress to
regulate commerce with foreign nations, they can remove foreigners from the country by the same reasoning, (bad reasoning he knew it was,) they had a similar power of removing
citizens of the several States. And when another gentleman
tells us that the power is claimed under certain powers given
to Congress to provide for the common defence and general
welfare, will it not apply to citizens as well as aliens? It certainly would, since they might argue that seditious and turbu-
lent citizens might be as dangerous to the peace of the country,
as aliens of a similar description; and when gentlemen are disposed to treat the Constitution in this way to come at aliens,
he had no doubt they would be equally ready to do it against
citizens whenever they shall wish to do so.

Or will gentlemen say that the Constitution affords a security to citizens which it does not extend to aliens? He knew
the rights of aliens are limited; but if we can dispense with
the law towards them, we may also do it with respect to citizens. The trial by jury does not speak of citizens, but of
persons. What security, said Mr. G., can citizens have, when
they see a bill like the present pass into a law? What, said he,
have we heard on this floor? The member from Connecticut
(Mr. ALLEN) objected to the bill for preventing and restrain-

ing seditious persons. What were his objections? That the Constitution of the United States had, in all criminal cases, said the trial by jury should remain sacred. By that bill power was given to the Judges to determine certain facts; and, in order to remedy that objection, and to provide a better security for the persons amenable to that law, what did he propose? To take the power from the Judges, and give it entirely to the President of the United States.

Again, with respect to the writ of habeas corpus, what do gentlemen say? They say it is only to prevent any man from being imprisoned in an arbitrary manner; and that, as the present bill describes the cases in which a man is liable to arrestation and imprisonment, it cannot be a suspension of that law; that is to say, the writ of habeas corpus is designed to prevent arbitrary illegal imprisonment, or what the gentleman calls illegal imprisonment; but, according to this doctrine, if you give, by law, the power to the President of arbitrary imprisonment, that power being thus given by law, is on that account no longer illegal nor arbitrary. That was the kind of security which citizens might expect to derive from the clause of the Constitution which related to the writ of habeas corpus. That privilege was to be done away by a legal distinction.

By the seventh amendment to our Constitution, it is provided that "no person shall be deprived of life, liberty, or property, without due process of law." According to the doctrine of the gentleman, Congress may give, by law, the power to the President, or any one else, to deprive a citizen of his liberty or property, and the act of giving that power by law, will be called the due process of law contemplated by the Constitution.

The gentleman from Massachusetts allowed that there exists in the State Governments a power to regulate the migration of aliens, and to admit the arrival of such as are described in this bill; but he said that, as they had forborne to exercise the power, the United States might, with propriety, pass a law on the subject; but that any one of the States might prevent its execution. He therefore allowed a power in the States to prevent the execution of the law, and the only reason why, in his opinion, if this bill passed, it would not be at once a dead letter, was grounded on the construction he put on the word "admit."

But Mr. G. would go further, and say that the States and the State Judiciary would, indeed they must, consider the law as a mere nullity, they must declare it to be unconstitutional; for no one, except the gentleman from Massachusetts, ever would suppose that aliens were not now admitted by the States, and, on his own ground, whenever they were thus admitted, the law was at an end.

A gentleman had said that States must claim only local powers, general ones being placed in the General Government. But the present bill was more of a local than of a general nature. Those States whose population is full, and to which few migrations take place, are little concerned in this question, unless, indeed, to check the population of other States, and to keep a preponderance in their hands, be an object with them. It was of consequence only to those States whose population is thin, and whose policy it has always been to encourage emigration. Amongst these, he placed the State of Pennsylvania. Indeed, he had always thought it was the general policy of this country; he believed it had only been the violence of party which had created any difference of opinion on the subject. It had been an established principle in Pennsylvania, from its first establishment to the present time, and every encouragement had been held out to emigrants of all nations. On this account, if this bill passes, there will be ten times the number of people under its operation, and the arbitrary power of the President in this State, than there will be in all the New England States put together. Emigration, he said, had been very useful to Pennsylvania. It is owing to it that its population had, within a little more than a century, reached its present extent. Nor had the mixture of emigration from Great Britain and Germany produced any bad effect upon the policy of the State. He believed it could boast of civil establishments as wise and as good as any of her sister States.

A temporary sacrifice has already been made by that State, by the new naturalization law, which makes it necessary for a foreigner to reside fourteen years in the country before he can become a citizen. When that bill was under consideration, the friends of it said, they wished to give security to the persons and property of aliens, but they did not wish them to have any political influence in the country. That point was yielded without a struggle, although, from the establishment of the Province of Pennsylvania to this day, no more than two years' residence had ever been required by the Provincial or State laws, to naturalize a foreigner; and let it be remembered that the Declaration of Independence, in the enumeration of the complaints of America against the King of Great Britain, states that "he has endeavored to prevent the population of these States, for that purpose obstructing the laws for the naturalization of foreigners, refusing to pass others to encourage their migration hither," &c. The present bill related not to any political rights; it affected the civil rights, the personal liberty, the property of aliens. It subjects them to a removal, upon suspicion, and that at the will of one man. It was not only a refusal to encourage migrations, it was a bill to prevent migrations. And in such a bill, assuming a power belonging to herself and not to the United States, and affecting her population and prosperity to such an extent, Pennsylvania was immediately and deeply concerned.

Mr. G. admitted, there might be cases in which it might be proper to transport persons for crimes, but the punishment should in that case be inflicted upon conviction of crimes, and not as a measure of caution, to be effected on mere suspicion, by the arbitrary power of one individual.

Mr. G. concluded by saying, that he was at a loss for the

cause of the introduction of this bill. No ground had been shown for it; if any reason could be adduced, he supposed the States, whose duty it is, would be as ready to guard against the dreaded evils, as the General Government, whose duty it is not; and he thought any evils which may exist would be better provided for in the usual way, than by placing so extraordinary a power in the hands of the President of the United States.

17. HOUSE DEBATE ON

THE SEDITION ACT

July 5, 10, 1798

The House of Representatives, July 5, 1798

Gallatin's best efforts were reserved for the debate on the Sedition Bill which came down from the Senate on July 5. The bill made it a crime punishable by $5,000 fine and six months to five years imprisonment to oppose the measures of the government or obstruct the execution of its laws. Persons who should "write; print, utter, or publish . . . any false, scandalous, and malicious writing . . . against the government of the United States" were liable to a $2,000 fine and two years imprisonment. This feature of the bill was intended to silence the Republican press.

Annals of Congress (5 Cong., 2 Sess., 1798), pp. 2107–2111, 2156–2164.

The Sedition Bill was vehemently supported by John Allen of Connecticut, who in a highly emotional speech disgorged the rage that had for years festered in Federalist hearts. Reading passages from Republican newspapers, notably the Aurora *and the New York* Time Piece, *he invited the House to decide whether the lies and abuse inflicted upon the government and its faithful officers could be interpreted as anything but a deliberate attempt at subversion. Gallatin delivered a rebuttal.*

Mr. GALLATIN wished that the bill had been committed before any debate had taken place, as, in its present stage, any observations on details susceptible of amendment would be out of order; and he must now confine himself to the general question Does the situation of the country, at this time, require that any law of this kind should pass? Do there exist such new and alarming symptoms of sedition, as render it necessary to adopt, in addition to the existing laws, any extraordinary measure for the purpose of suppressing unlawful combinations, and of restricting the freedom of speech and of the press? For such were the objects of the bill, whatever modifications it might hereafter receive.

The manner in which the principle of the bill had been supported, was perhaps more extraordinary still than the bill itself. The gentleman from Connecticut, (Mr. ALLEN,) in order to prove the existence of a combination against the Constitution and Government, had communicated to the House—what? a number of newspaper paragraphs; and even most of those were such as would not be punishable by the bill as it now stands. The object of that gentleman in wishing a bill of this nature to pass, extended far beyond the intention of the Senate who had sent down this bill; far beyond, he would venture to say, the idea of any other member upon this floor, besides himself. His idea was to punish men for stating facts which he happened to disbelieve, or for enacting and avowing opinions, not criminal, but perhaps erroneous. Thus one of the paragraphs most obnoxious to the gentleman from Connecticut, was that in which the writer expresses his belief that Mr. Gerry may yet make a treaty with the French Government, his powers being sufficient for that purpose. [Mr. ALLEN said, his charge was against persons making this assertion, when they knew it to be unfounded.] Mr. G. said, he did not understand the gentleman's explanation. He now says that the act he condemns is the assertion of a fact, which may be true, but which the writer himself disbelieves: and thus he wished to punish such men as, according to his caprice, he may suppose guilty of expressing opinions not consonant with their own sentiments. For by what rule of evidence could he discover and know what was really the writer's belief. But, to return, was there any thing criminal in that paragraph: It asserted that Mr. Gerry had powers sufficient to treat. The gentleman from Connecticut denies this to be true. Mr. G. would aver that it was an undeniable fact, as appears evidently from the documents now on the table. They showed that the powers given to the Envoys were joint and several. And, if Mr. Gerry had powers to treat, how could it be criminal to say that he might treat? Or supposing the writer of the paragraph to have said, that he believed Mr. Gerry would treat, could the opinion be charged with anything but being erroneous? When a paragraph of this nature was held out as criminal, what writings, what opinions, could escape the severity of the intended law, which did not coincide with the opinions, and which might counteract the secret views of a prevailing party?

The gentleman from Connecticut had also quoted an extract of a letter said to be written by a member of Congress from Virginia, and published in last Saturday's Aurora. The style and composition of that letter did the highest honor to its writer. It contained more information and more sense, and gave more proofs of a sound understanding and strong mind, than ever the gentleman from Connecticut had displayed, or could display on this floor. So far he would venture to say, although he had given but a cursory reading to the letter, and he was altogether at a loss to know what was criminal in it, though he might easily see why it was obnoxious. Was it erroneous or criminal to say that debts and taxes were the ruinous consequences of war? Or that some members in both Houses of Congress uniformly voted in favor of an extension of the powers of the Executive, and of every proposed expenditure of money? Was it not true? Gentlemen of that description avow that, in their opinion, the Executive is the weakest branch of Government; and they act upon the ostensible principle that, on that account, its influence and powers must be increased. Look at the laws passed during this session. Look at the alien bill, at the provisional army bill, look at the prodigious influence acquired by so many new offices, and then deny that the powers of the Executive have not been greatly increased. As to the increased rate of expenditure, and the propensity of these gentlemen to vote money, they would not themselves deny it. Was it criminal to say that the Executive is supported by a party? when gentlemen declared that it must be supported by a party. When the doctrine had been avowed on this floor that men of a certain political opinion, alone ought to be appointed to offices; and when the Executive had now adopted and carried into practice that doctrine in its fullest extent?

Mr. G. acknowledged that some of the newspaper paragraphs quoted by Mr. ALLEN were of a very different nature from that letter. One of them, taken from the *Timepiece*, was extremely exceptionable; most of them contained sentiments different from his own, and expressed in a style he never would adopt. Yet in almost every one of them there was a mixture of truth and error; and what was the remedy proposed by the gentleman from Connecticut, in order to rectify and correct error? Coercion: a law inflicting fine and imprisonment for the publication of erroneous opinions.

Was the gentleman afraid, or rather was Administration afraid, that in this instance error could not be successfully opposed by truth? The American Government had heretofore subsisted, it had acquired strength, it had grown on the affection of the people, it had been fully supported without the assistance of laws similar to the bill now on the table. It had been able to repel opposition by the single weapon of argument. And at present, when out of ten presses in the country nine were employed on the side of Administration, such is their want of confidence in the purity of their own views and motives, that they even fear the unequal contest, and require the help of force in order to suppress the limited circulation of the opinions of those who did not approve all their measures. One of the paragraphs says, that it will soon become a question whether there will be more liberty at Philadelphia or Constantinople. The gentleman from Connecticut bitterly complains of this, as insinuating that some persons in Government intend to establish a despotic power; and in order to convince the writer of his error, that gentleman not only supports the bill, but avows principles perfectly calculated to justify the assertions contained in the paragraph. [Mr. ALLEN said, he stated all these things to show the temper of certain seditious persons in the United States.] Mr. G. remarked that if the gentleman from Connecticut, by that explanation, meant to say that the paragraphs he had quoted were not criminal, but only evidences of a general seditious temper, it was extraordinary that in order to prove the existence of certain criminal combinations, which, in his opinion, it was necessary to punish, he had brought in evidence only writings which he now acknowledged ought not to be punished. But, at all events, that gentleman supposed the existence of a certain seditious spirit, which in his opinion ought to be crushed.

And how has that seditious spirit been exhibited? The only evidences brought by the supporters of this bill consist of writings expressing an opinion that certain measures of Government have been dictated by an unwise policy, or by improper motives, and that some of them were unconstitutional. This bill and its supporters suppose, in fact, that whoever dislikes the measures of Administration and of a temporary majority in Congress, and shall, either by speaking or writing, express his disapprobation and his want of confidence in the men now in power, is seditious, is an enemy, not of Administration, but of the Constitution, and is liable to punishment. That principle, Mr. G. said, was subversive of the principles of the Constitution itself. If you put the press under any restraint in respect to the measures of members of Government; if you thus deprive the people of the means of obtaining information of their conduct, you in fact render their right of electing nugatory; and this bill must be considered only as a weapon used by a party now in power, in order to perpetuate their authority and preserve their present places.

The gentleman from Connecticut had concluded his observations by stating that he could not conceive how gentlemen could day after day hear or read such abusive and seditious pieces and rest quietly on their pillows. He would give to that gentleman a piece of information that would diminish his astonishment. He had himself heard day after day the illiberal abuse poured from several quarters of this House against himself and his friends; he had heard the grossest and most abusive language from the lips of that gentleman; nay, he had heard the most seditious expressions falling from him; he had heard him say, that if gentlemen on this floor did not adopt certain measures, he knew that the people would soon come and compel them to act. And yet, he could assure that gentleman, that torrent of sedition and personal abuse had never deprived him of an hour's sleep.

The gentleman from South Carolina (Mr. HARPER) had taken a different ground. He had stated that he did not apprehend any serious mischief from the present licentiousness of the press until he had heard the speech of a member from New York (Mr. LIVINGSTON) inviting the people to resist a law of Congress. That gentleman had forgotten that the bill which he now meant to support, could suppress and punish only that licentiousness of which he declared he was not afraid, and could not reach speeches of members of Congress, which, by the Constitution, could not be noticed out of these walls. This was the first attack made upon a speech delivered in this House, but what, from the gentleman from South Carolina, he had, for some time expected; for, in his career, after having grossly attacked members first for writing circular letters, and then on account of their private correspondence, the next step must be to make their speeches the foundation of a sedition law. As to the speech itself, so far as he had heard the expressions alluded to, it was not an invitation to the people, or an opinion that the people should oppose the alien bill itself as unconstitutional; but merely a general position that they had a right to resist, and would resist unconstitutional and oppressive laws. He believed that doctrine to be strictly correct, and neither seditious or treasonable. The opposite doctrines of passive obedience and non-resistance had long been exploded. America had never received them. America had asserted the right of resisting unconstitutional laws, and the day we were celebrating yesterday (4th of July) is a monument of that right. When and how such a right should be exercised, was a different and delicate question. It is a question to be decided by motives of prudence and by principles of morality. It is a question which America had once decided in the affirmative. It is a right to which they may, perhaps, in the course of events be again obliged to resort. God forbid that we should ever see that day! But it is above all in the power of Government to avert such an evil by refraining from unconstitutional and arbitrary laws. Mr. G. added that he was one of those who had the most sincere and strong conviction impressed on his mind that the alien bill was unconstitutional. [The SPEAKER said, that was not the question.] Mr. G. said, that he was not going to make any remarks on that law, or any that could by any one be supposed to be out of order. He meant only to state that, notwithstanding that conviction, his opinion was that an appeal must be made to another tribunal, to the Judiciary in the first instance, on the subject of a supposed unconstitutional law; and that even where no redress could be obtained, he did not think that law alone, and in itself, sufficient to justify resistance and opposition even in those who thought it unconstitutional.

Mr. G. concluded by observing, that he had considered only the general object of the bill on the table, on a supposition that it might be modified so as to be rendered consonant with the Constitution. The object of the first section was to punish unlawful combinations, resistance to laws, and other crimes and misdemeanors, all of which were already punishable, and had in some instances actually been punished by the Courts of the United States. That section, therefore, is altogether useless. In order to prove the necessity of the second section, which went to impose restraints on the liberty of speech and of the press, it was at least necessary to prove the existence of a seditious disposition amongst the people. The supporters of the bill had been unable to bring a single fact before this House, in support of that position. So long as they were compelled to resort only to newspaper paragraphs and speeches on this floor, in order to show the absolute necessity of passing sedition laws, he thought it useless to investigate more deeply the principles of this bill, and he trusted the weakness of their arguments would afford a sufficient proof to this House of the weakness of their cause, and was sufficient to insure a rejection of the bill.

House of Representatives, July 10, 1798

Prosecution for sedition had a long history in England, where such cases fell under the English common law of libels. Although the accused received a jury trial, the function of the

---

Annals of Congress (5 Cong., 2 Sess., 1798), pp. 2156–2164.

jury was merely to decide the fact: whether the accused had spoken or written the words attributed to him. The judge decided the law, that is, whether his words constituted libel and passed sentence. The truth of the statements in question was immaterial to the determination of guilt; the greater the truth the greater the offense. In America the procedure in libel cases was irregular, differing from state to state, but it appears that juries ordinarily had some share in determining the law and that truth was generally admitted as a defense. Early in the House debate on the Sedition Bill a clause was inserted making truth admissible in defense, and on July 9 the House readily agreed by a vote of 67 to 15 to allow the jury to determine the law—whether "libel or no libel" had been committed. Hence the protection afforded to the accused, ultimately agreed to by the Senate, went beyond the common law. The Federalists held that the Sedition Act was therefore inoffensive, as it contained nothing not already practiced by state courts.

Republicans contended that federal courts had no jurisdiction over libel, whether committed against individuals or against officers or agencies of the government. Invoking strict construction doctrine, they argued that jurisdiction over libel cases was not mentioned in the constitution nor was it necessary to execute the functions of government. Moreover, the Sedition Act was in fact unconstitutional on other grounds since it violated the First Amendment. Supporters of the act countered with the argument that federal courts were not restricted to cases arising under federal law and the Constitution; they also had common law jurisdiction. English common law, they said, was the basis of American judicial systems. The founding fathers had it constantly in mind and surely intended it to be referred to in all cases that would otherwise be doubtful. In any event, the present legislation was justifiable under the Constitution. Any government had a right to protect itself, a right which preceded and superseded the Bill of Rights. The federal government could not be placed in the position of being dependent for its existence upon state courts.

The debate over the Sedition Act in and outside of Congress was notable in the history of civil liberties for its clarification of the meaning of the First Amendment. Americans always spoke proudly of the freedom of speech and of press which they enjoyed, a freedom conspicuously guaranteed by federal and state bills of rights. That it did exist in fact was evident from the unbridled journalism of the Federalist era. Yet almost no one subscribed before 1798 to the idea that unlimited criticism of the government was permissible. Even Jefferson and other Republican leaders, to say nothing of the Federalists, believed that deliberate falsehood and calumny should be punished. So far as any definition of freedom of the press prevailed, it was the English common law formula of the absence of prior restraint: journalists were free to publish without censorship but were liable to penalties for what they had published. Federalists underscored this doctrine in the debate on the Sedition Act. They argued further that since truth was accepted as a defense, the legitimate freedom of the press was untouched, only the abuse of that freedom was to be punished.

The exigencies of their position led some of the Republicans to reexamine the implications of the First Amendment. In a brilliant speech delivered on the last day of debate, John Nicholas pointed out that political criticism was by its nature a matter of opinion, not susceptible of verification, its truth or falsity in the mind of the beholder. The test of truth could not therefore distinguish between liberty and licentiousness

of the press. Gallatin, while advancing constitutional argu-
ments and criticizing the rationality of the bill, nearly got to
the point of articulating the modern doctrine that words are
punishable only for their substantive effects.

The Sedition Act passed the House by a vote of 44 to 41.

Mr. GALLATIN observed that the same kind of general answer to
all the objections against the bill, which had now fallen from
the gentleman from Connecticut, had already been used by
him on the first reading of the bill, when the criminality of
certain writings was not to depend on their being false and
malicious. The remarks of that gentleman were, however, as
little in point now, and no more applicable to the argument
urged against this bill, than they were before it had received
its present modifications. Was the bill, in its present shape, free
from Constitutional objections? Supposing it to be Constitutional, was it expedient? or, to use the words of the Constitution, was it necessary and proper, at present, to pass this
law? These were the two important questions which claimed
the attention of the House.

The gentleman from Massachusetts (Mr. OTIS) had attempted to prove the constitutionality of the bill by asserting,
in the first place, that the power to punish libels was originally
vested in Congress by the Constitution, and, in the next place,
that the amendment to the Constitution, which declares that
Congress shall not pass any law abridging the liberty of the
press, had not deprived them of the power originally given.
In order to establish his first position, the gentleman had
thought it sufficient to insist that the jurisdiction of the Courts
of the United States extended to the punishment of offences at
common law, that is to say, of offences not arising under the
statutes or laws of the Union—an assertion unfounded in itself,
and which, if proven, would not support the point he endeav-

ors to establish. That assertion was unfounded; for the judicial
authority of those courts is, by the Constitution, declared to
extend to cases of Admiralty, or affecting public Ministers; to
suits between States, citizens of different States, or foreigners,
and to cases arising under the Constitution, laws, and treaties,
made under the authority of that Constitution; excluding,
therefore, cases not arising under either—cases arising under
the common law. It was preposterous to suppose, with the
gentleman from Massachusetts, that, in cases arising under the
Constitution, were included offences at common law; for the
cases meant were only, either such as might arise from any
doubtful construction of the Constitution—for instance the
constitutionality of a law—or those arising immediately under
any specific power given or prohibition enjoined by the Constitution; such, for instance, as declaring a retrospective law
of any State to be null and void. Nor was that gentleman more
fortunate in his choice of arguments, when he thought he could
derive any proofs in support of the supposed jurisdiction of the
Federal Courts from the number of technical expressions in the
Constitution—such as writ of *habeas corpus, levying war*, &c.,
which, as he supposed, recognised the common law. He had
there confounded two very distinct ideas—the principles of
the common law, and the jurisdiction over cases arising under
it. That those principles were recognised in the cases where
the courts had jurisdiction, was not denied; but such a recognition could by no means extend the jurisdiction beyond the
specific cases defined by the Constitution. But, had that gentleman succeeded in proving the existence of the jurisdiction of
the Federal Courts over offences at common law, and more
particularly over libels, he would thereby have adduced the
strongest argument against the passing of this bill; for, if the
jurisdiction did exist, where was the necessity of now giving it?
If the judicial authority of the Federal Courts, by the Constitution, extended to the punishment of libels, it was unnecessary to pass this law, which, modified as it is, was in-

tended by its supporters for the sole purpose of enacting into
a law of the United States the common law of libels. The
gentleman from Massachusetts himself, by his efforts to obtain
this law, had shown that he did not believe that the courts
could act in the case of libels, without the assistance of a law;
and every gentleman who had spoken in favor of this bill had
explicitly declared, as his opinion, that the Federal Courts
had no jurisdiction whatever over offences at common law.
The fact was, that the gentleman from Massachusetts, although
he had at first stated the question correctly, by saying that it
was sufficient to prove that the power of passing this bill was
given by the Constitution, had afterwards altogether forgotten
his own position—the position which it was incumbent upon
him to prove—and had attempted to establish another point,
unconnected with the first. The question was not whether the
Courts of the United States had, without this law, the power
to punish libels, but whether, supposing they had not the
power, Congress had that of giving them this jurisdiction—
whether Congress were vested by the Constitution with the
authority of passing this bill?

For a proper discussion of that question, Mr. G. said, it
would be necessary for him to bring once more to the recollection of the House those Constitutional principles to which he
had already, on another occasion, adverted. The people of the
United States were not under the authority of a simple, or of
one, but under two distinct Governments—that of the different
States in which they respectively lived, and that of the Union.
The Government of the Union was not a consolidated one,
possessing general power; it was only a federal one, vested
with specific powers, defined by the Constitution; and though
it should seem that no one could, on reading that instrument,
mistake its principle, yet, for greater security, it had been provided, by an amendment which now made a part of the Constitution, that the power not delegated to the United States,
nor prohibited to the individual States, remained respectively

with the States, or with the people. Hence it was that Congress had no undefined general legislative powers, but that it became necessary for them, whenever they passed a law, to show from what article of that charter under which they acted—from what specific power vested in them by the Constitution—they derived the authority they claimed. In this instance, it must be shown that the Constitution has given them the power to pass a law for the punishment of libels. It would not be contended that any such power was specifically given, and it only remained to be examined whether it was included in any more general authority. It had been insisted that Congress had the power, generally, to provide for the punishment of any offences against Government. It is evident that such a power, if it did exist, would embrace the punishment of any offences whatever, or rather of any act, which, though not criminal in itself, might be obnoxious to the persons who happened to have Government in their hands; for any such act might by them, be called an offence against Government, and made criminal. But, so far from this being the case, it would be found that the Constitution had actually specified the cases in which Congress should have power either to define or to provide for the punishment of offences; and they were the following: piracies, felonies on the high sea, and offences against the law of nations, which they had a right to define and punish; counterfeiting the coin or public securities of the United States; treason, which they had a right to punish, but not to define, it being expressly defined by the Constitution itself; all offences that might be committed within the ten miles square, forts, arsenals, &c., over which the United States might, with the consent of a State, acquire exclusive jurisdiction; and, finally, opposition or offences against the laws or exercise of the Constitutional authority of any department—which offences Congress had a right to define and punish, by virtue of the clause of the Constitution which empowered them to pass all laws necessary and proper for carrying into execution any power vested by the Constitution in them, or in any department. Mr. G. then proceeded to enumerate the several offences defined by the two acts providing for the punishment of crimes against the United States, in order to show that Congress had heretofore strictly adhered to the specification of the Constitution, and never attempted to legislate in the manner proposed by this bill.

It must be evident, from that enumeration, that the only clause of the Constitution which can give a color to the authority now claimed, is that already quoted, which gives Congress authority to make all laws which shall be necessary and proper for carrying into execution the power vested by the Constitution in the Government of the United States, or in any department or officer thereof.

But the language here used was strict and precise; it gave not a vague power, arbitrarily, to create offences against Government, or to take cognizance of cases which fall under the exclusive jurisdiction of the State courts. In order to claim any authority under this clause, the supporters of this bill must show the specific power given to Congress or to the President, by some other part of the Constitution, which would be carried into effect by a law against libels. They must go further— they must show which of those Constitutional powers it was which could not be carried into effect, unless this law was passed. It was in that manner that the authority of Congress had heretofore been exercised; they had passed now penal laws, except such as arose from the necessity of carrying into effect some of the specific powers vested in them. Thus, as they had the exclusive power to establish post roads, they had made it penal to rob the mail; and as they were authorized to lay taxes, they had passed laws to punish frauds of revenue officers, or evasions of the revenue laws. But, until this bill was proposed, Congress had never attempted to define or punish offences generally; and the gentleman from Massachusetts was mistaken when he had stated that forgery was generally punishable by the laws of the United States. It was only in those specific cases defined by the Constitution, or which arose from some power heretofore exercised by Congress, that forgery came under the jurisdiction of the Federal Courts.

Mr. G. said that he had heretofore considered the Constitution as it originally stood, and that it must be evident that no law against libels could be passed by Congress, unless it was under color of carrying into effect some other distinct power vested in them. However improbable such an attempt might have appeared, the bill now under discussion justified the suspicions of those who, at the time of the adoption of the Constitution, had apprehended that the sense of that generally expressed clause might be distorted for that purpose. It was in order to remove these fears, that the amendment, which declares that Congress shall pass no law abridging the freedom of speech or the liberty of the press, was proposed and adopted —an amendment which was intended as an express exception to any supposed general power of *passing laws*, &c., vested in Congress by the other clause. The sense, in which he and his friends understood this amendment was that Congress could not pass any law to punish any real or supposed abuse of the press. The construction given to it by the supporters of the bill was, that it did not prevent them to punish what they called the licentiousness of the press, but merely forbade their laying any previous restraints upon it. It appeared to him preposterous to say, that to punish a certain act was not an abridgement of the liberty of doing that act. It appeared to him that it was an insulting evasion of the Constitution for gentlemen to say, "We claim no power to abridge the liberty of the press; *that,* you shall enjoy unrestrained. You may write and publish what you please, but if you publish anything against us, we will punish you for it. So long as we do not prevent, but only punish your writings, it is no abridgement of your liberty of writing and printing." Congress were by that amendment prohibited from passing any law abridging, &c.;

they were, therefore, prohibited from adding any restraint, either by previous restrictions, or by subsequent punishment, or by any alteration of the proper jurisdiction, or of the mode of trial, which did not exist before; in short, they were under an obligation of leaving that subject where they found it—of passing no law, either directly or indirectly, affecting that liberty.

In the next place, this amendment was introduced as an exception to some pre-existing power vested by the Constitution in Congress; so that, to render the construction given by the supporters of the bill admissible, it was necessary for them to prove, that, by virtue of some such pre-existing power, or in order to carry into effect some distinct power, Congress could have laid previous restraints upon the press—a suggestion which never was hinted, even by the most violent opponents of the Constitution, at the time of its adoption. The danger intended to be remedied was that which had been actually apprehended, and which might have some frail foundation in the general clause so often quoted. Finally, that construction was inconsistent with the amendment itself. That amendment provided against the passing of any law abridging either the liberty of the press or the freedom of speech; and a sound construction must be such as to be applicable to both. But that contended for, to wit, that the only prohibition was that of passing any law laying previous restraints upon either, was absurd, so far as it related to speech; for it pre-supposed that Congress, by the Constitution, as it originally stood, might have passed laws laying such restraints upon speech; and what these possibly could have been, he was altogether at a loss to conceive, unless gentlemen chose to assert that the Constitution had given Congress a power to seal the mouths or to cut the tongues of the citizens of the Union; and these, however, were the only means by which previous restraints could be laid on the freedom of speech. Was it not evident, that, as speech could not be restrained, but might be punished, a Constitutional clause forbidding any abridgment of the freedom of speech must necessarily mean, not that no laws should be passed laying previous restraints upon it, but that no punishment should by law be inflicted upon it? But, admit the construction given to the amendment by the supporters of this bill, still must they recur to the original provisions of the Constitution—still is it incumbent on them to show that this bill is *necessary*, in order to carry into operation some of the powers of Government. Government has existed for more than nine years without the assistance of this law. This law is not, then necessary at all times; indeed, it is intended to last for three years. Let, then, gentlemen prove that that necessity now exists which heretofore did not exist. It is an obligation laid upon them by the Constitution itself, evidently, to prove that an alteration has taken place in the situation of this country, which impels us to pass this law. And yet they are silent. Where is the House to find proofs of that wonderful, yet unknown change in our circumstances? Will they derive their information from the newspaper scraps with which they had been entertained, the other day, by a member from Connecticut? as if there was anything alarming or novel in paragraphs blaming or attacking certain measures or certain individuals of Government; as if the present Administration felt more afraid of newspaper abuse than former Administration, or than other men. Or is Congress to receive a conviction of that alteration from the plot which the gentleman from South Carolina (Mr. HARPER) had promised to unfold—a plot in which not one member on this floor did believe, when it was announced, and in which he suspected the gentleman himself had long since discovered he had been mistaken? Leaving, however, those ridiculous grounds of alarm, (and, ludicrous as it might appear to an indifferent hearer, they were the only ones that had yet been alleged in support of this bill,) Mr. G. would ask whether gentlemen did not believe themselves, that at no time had there been less to be apprehended from presses that circulated opinions in opposition to the measures of Government; that no reason could be adduced why this bill should pass, except that a party in the United States, feeling that they had more power, were not afraid of passing such a law, and would pass it, because they felt themselves so strong—so little in need of the assistance of that measure—that they expected to be supported by the people, even in that flagrant attack upon the Constitution? Would any of them dare to assert that the time when the Western insurrection took place, when it was thought *necessary* to call to arms fifteen thousand men, was not a more dangerous moment for Government, and did not more forcibly call forth a law punishing misrepresentations of the measures or motives of Government, than the present period?

The advocates of this measure must show to us its necessity for carrying into operation the powers vested in the President, or in either branch of the Legislature—who are its objects. They must prove that the President dare not, cannot, will not, execute the laws, unless the abuse poured upon him from certain presses is suppressed. If there be a majority of this House in favor of this law, are that majority ready to declare that that law is *necessary,* in order to enable them to execute the powers vested in them by the Constitution? Are they ready to say that they are prevented from voting according to the dictates of their conscience, for voting is the only power belonging to them, by newspaper paragraphs? Are they ready to say, that unless libels against them shall be punished; that unless they may obtain revenge from the insolence of the printers, they will not or dare not vote as they would otherwise do? But if they are ready to make those declarations; if they do believe this bill *necessary* in order to enable this House to do their duty, they must recollect that this House is composed of individuals, and that, according to their own doctrine, in order to insure a conscientious vote in the whole House, every individual, and not a majority of the House, ought to be equally sheltered by this law from the abuse of printers. Whilst, therefore, they support the bill in its present shape, do they not avow that the true object of the law is to enable one party to oppress the other; that they mean to have the power to punish printers who may publish against them, whilst their opponents will remain alone, and without redress, exposed to the abuse of Ministerial prints? Is it not their object to frighten and suppress all presses which they consider as contrary to their views; to prevent a free circulation of opinion; to suffer the people at large to hear only partial accounts, and but one side of the question; to delude and deceive them by partial information, and, through those means, to perpetuate themselves in power?

In vain did those gentlemen attempt to shelter themselves under the different pleas that this bill could only affect the authors of false publications, since any man might justify his writings by giving in evidence the truth of his assertions; and that it created no new offence, but only re-enacted what had always been the common law of libels.

It was true that, so far as related merely to facts, a man would be acquitted by proving that what he asserted was true. But the bill was intended to punish solely writings of a political nature, libels against the Government, the President, or either branch of the Legislature; and it was well known that writings, containing animadversions on public measures, almost always contained not only facts but opinions. And how could the truth of opinions be proven by evidence? If an individual thinking, as he himself did, that the present bill was unconstitutional, and that it had been intended, not for the public good, but solely for party purposes, should avow and publish his opinion, and if the Administration thought fit to prosecute him for that supposed individual offence, would a jury, composed of the friends of that Administration, hesitate much in declaring the opinion ungrounded, or, in other words, false and scandalous, and its publication malicious? And by what kind of argument or evidence, in the present temper of parties, could the accused convince them that his opinion was true?

As to the assertion that the bill, under its present modifications, was nothing more than the common law of libels, he would observe that no gentleman could be satisfied that the few lines, of which the bill consisted, contained the genuine and unadulterated principles of the law of libels—a law which had arisen from the precedents and judicial decisions of three centuries; a law which, like every other branch of the common law of England, had received different modifications in the different States, so as to be now dissimilar in every one. He had not critically examined the bill in that point of view; but he would just notice a mode of expression which, if strictly construed, would introduce a principle now unknown to the common law of libels. By the bill, every person who should write, print, utter, or publish, &c., was guilty; so that a person only writing what might be adjudged a libel, although he neither printed, published, read, or communicated his work to any one, and although he did not intend it for publication, might, like Algernon Sidney, be found guilty, under this act for the offence only of having thrown his ideas on paper.

But although there might be no change made by this bill in the law of libels, there was an all-important one made by the transfer of jurisdiction. Heretofore the cognizance of offences of this nature had exclusively belonged to the State courts, and the mode of trial was essentially altered by being had before the Federal courts. It was not only by being deprived of the benefits of a trial by a jury of their vicinage that the accused persons were put in a worse situation; the manner of selecting the jury was, in some States, in Pennsylvania, especially, very different in the Courts of the United States from what it was in the State courts. It was provided, by the act to establish the Judicial Courts of the United States, "that jurors, to serve for the Courts of the United States, shall be designated by lot, or otherwise, in each State, respectively, according to the mode of forming juries therein now practised, so far as the laws shall render such designation practicable, by the courts or marshal in the United States." Juries, in the New England States, were selected by the towns, or by lot, and under that act, they still were selected in the same manner to serve in the Federal Courts, without the interference of any federal officer. Gentlemen from those States were, therefore, very easy on account of this bill, as, in practice, it left their constituents in the same situation in which it found them. In case of a prosecution for a libel, an inhabitant of Massachusetts would be tried by a similar jury, whether the trial was had before the State or Federal court. But, in other States, where the juries were summoned by the sheriff, the case was far different. In Pennsylvania, if the prosecution was before the State court, the jury would be summoned by the sheriff, but if before the Federal court, the marshal, in that case would summon the jury. The difference in this case was immense; for the sheriff in Pennsylvania was elected by the people, and held his commission for three years, revocable only for misbehaviour. The marshal was appointed by the President of the United States, was removable from office at his pleasure, and sometimes held other offices under the Executive; for instance, the marshal of Pennsylvania, till within a few weeks, had been inspector of the revenue. The sheriff was the officer of the people, the marshal was the creature of the Executive. And, however immaterial this might be in ordinary suits or prosecutions, when the offences were, as under this bill altogether of a political nature; when the supposed crimes to be punished were a libel against the Administration, what security of a fair trial remained to a citizen, when the jury was liable to be packed by the Administration, when the same men were to be judges and parties.

After having given this short sketch of the features of this bill, Mr. G. said he had intended to make some general remarks on the nature of political libels, or of writings against the measures of the Administration, and on the propriety of interfering at all by law with them. The lateness of the hour prevented him. He would only observe that laws against writings of this kind had uniformly been one of the most powerful engines used by tyrants to prevent the diffusion of knowledge, to throw a veil on their folly or their crimes, to satisfy those mean passions which always denote little minds, and to perpetuate their own tyranny. The principles of the law of political libels were to be found in the rescripts of the worst Emperors of Rome, in the decisions of the Star Chamber. Princes of elevated minds, Governments actuated by pure motives, had ever despised the slanders of malice, and listened to the animadversions made on their conduct. They knew that the proper weapon to combat error was truth, and that to resort to coercion and punishments in order to suppress writings attacking their measures, was to confess that these could not be defended by any other means.

THE ELECTION OF 1800

18. LETTER TO

HENRY A. MUHLENBERG

May 8, 1848

According to the procedure established by the Constitution, Presidential electors cast two votes. The person receiving the highest number, if a majority of the whole number of electors

---

Writings, II, 662–665.

*appointed, became President, the next highest Vice-President.
If two men were tied and both received the vote of a majority of the electors, the choice between them fell to the
House of Representatives, in which each state could cast one
vote. To win, a candidate had to receive the endorsement of
a majority of all the states. The inadequacy of this procedure
was evident in the election of 1800, in which Jefferson and
Aaron Burr both had 73 votes, a majority of the total number
of electors, over John Adams, who had 65. Although Jefferson
was clearly the Republican candidate for President, Federalists decided to support Burr. Their object was to secure Burr's
election and thereby make him their creature or else to exact
concessions from Jefferson. If these tactics failed, some Federalists intended to prevent an election and authorize the
lame-duck Congress to name the next President. Republicans
were determined to prevent any such usurpation, by force if
necessary. But they were confident of victory and abstained
from provocative acts. Over the course of thirty-five ballots
the vote in the House of Representatives was eight states for
Jefferson, six for Burr, with two states equally divided. Before
the thirty-sixth ballot Federalist ranks were broken by James
A. Bayard's announcement that he was going to switch his
vote. Jefferson was elected by the vote of ten states. Later.
the electoral procedure was revised by the Twelfth Amendment.*

*Almost a half century later in recalling the tense events in
Washington in 1801, Gallatin made clear that he had coun-
selled his party against using force in the event of a Federalist
usurpation.*

Although I was at the time probably better acquainted with
all the circumstances attending Mr. Jefferson's election than

any other person, and I am now the only surviving witness, I could not, without bestowing more time than I can spare, give a satisfactory account of that ancient transaction. A few observations must suffice.

The only cause of real apprehension was that Congress should adjourn without making a decision, but without usurping any powers. It was in order to provide against that contingency that I prepared myself a plan which did meet with the approbation of our party. No appeal whatever to physical force was contemplated; nor did it contain a single particle of revolutionary spirit. In framing this plan, Mr. Jefferson had not been consulted; but it was communicated to him, and he fully approved it.

But it was threatened by some persons of the Federal party to provide by law that if no election should take place, the Executive power should be placed in the hands of some public officer. This was considered as a revolutionary act of usurpation, and would, I believe, have been put down by force if necessary. But there was not the slightest intention or suggestion to call a convention to reorganize the government and to amend the Constitution. That such a measure floated in the mind of Mr. Jefferson is clear from his letters of February 15 and 18, 1801, to Mr. Monroe and Mr. Madison. He may have wished for such measure, or thought that the Federalists might be frightened by the threat.

Although I was lodging in the same house with him, he never mentioned it to me; I did not hear it even suggested by any one. That Mr. Jefferson had ever thought of such plan was never known to me till after the publication of his correspondence; and I may aver that under no circumstance would that plan have been resorted to or approved by the Republican party. Anti-Federalism had long been dead; and the Republicans were the most sincere and zealous supporters of the Constitution. It was that which constituted their real strength.

I always thought that the threatened attempt to make a

President by law was impracticable. I do not believe that if a motion had been made to that effect there would have been twenty votes for it in the House. It was only intended to frighten us; but it produced an excitement out-of-doors, in which some of our members participated. It was threatened that if any man should be thus appointed President by law, and accept the office, he would instantaneously be put to death. It was rumored, and, though I did not know it from my own knowledge, I believe it was true, that a number of men from Maryland and Virginia, amounting, it was said, to fifteen hundred (a number undoubtedly greatly exaggerated), had determined to repair to Washington on the 4th of March for the purpose of putting to death the usurping, pretending President.

It was under those circumstances that it was deemed proper to communicate all the facts to Governor McKean, and to submit to him the propriety of having in readiness a body of militia, who might, if necessary, be in Washington on the 3d of March, for the purpose not of promoting but of preventing civil war and the shedding of a single drop of blood. No person could be better trusted on such a delicate subject than Governor McKean. For he was energetic, patriotic, and, at the same time, a most steady, stern, and fearless supporter of law and order. It appears from your communication that he must have consulted General Peter Muhlenberg on that subject. But subsequent circumstances which occurred about three weeks before the 4th of March rendered it altogether unnecessary to act upon the subject.

There was but one man whom I can positively assert to have been decidedly in favor of the attempt to make a President by law. This was General Henry Lee, of Virginia, who, as you know, was a desperate character and held in no public estimation. I fear, from the general tenor of his conduct, that Mr. Griswold, of Connecticut,—in other respects a very worthy man,—was so warm and infatuated a partisan that he might have run the risk of a civil war rather than to see Mr. Jefferson elected. Some weak and inconsiderate members of the House might have voted for the measure; but I could not designate any one.

On the day on which we began balloting for President, we knew positively that Mr. Baer, of Maryland, was determined to cast his vote for Mr. Jefferson rather than that there should be no election; and his vote was sufficient to give us that of Maryland and decide the election. I was certain, from personal intercourse with him, that Mr. Morris, of Vermont, would do the same, and thus give us also the vote of that State. There were others equally prepared, but not known to us at the time. Still, all those gentlemen, unwilling to break up their party, united in the attempt, by repeatedly voting for Mr. Burr, to frighten or induce some of us to vote for Mr. Burr rather than to have no election. This balloting was continued several days for another reason. The attempt was made to extort concessions and promises from Mr. Jefferson as the conditions on which he might be elected. One of our friends, who was very erroneously and improperly afraid of a defection on the part of some of our members, undertook to act as an intermediary, and, confounding his own opinions and wishes with those of Mr. Jefferson, reported the result in such a manner as gave subsequently occasion for very unfounded surmises.

It is due to the memory of James Bayard, of Delaware, to say that, although he was one of the principal and warmest leaders of the Federal party, and had a personal dislike for Mr. Jefferson, it was he who took the lead, and from pure patriotism directed all those movements of the sounder and wiser part of the Federal party which terminated in the peaceable election of Mr. Jefferson.

Mr. Jefferson's letter to Mr. Monroe, dated February 15, 1801, at the very moment when the attempts were making to obtain promises from him, proves decisively that he made no concessions whatever. But both this letter, that to Mr. Madison of the 18th of February, and some other of preceding dates afford an instance of that credulity so common to warm partisans, which makes them ascribe the worst motives, and occasionally acts of which they are altogether guiltless, to their opponents. There was not the slightest foundation for suspecting the fidelity of the post.

You may use such portions of this communication as you may think proper for the purpose of correcting or modifying what, in your life of General Peter Muhlenberg, you have to say on that subject. But I pray you to consider this communication, so far as I am concerned, as entirely confidential. My name must not be mentioned as your authority. I have enough to encounter in that which I think it my duty to write concerning the present or future state of the country, and I do not wish to be annoyed in my old age by discussions on past events, to which I attach, indeed, but little importance. When I am no more, you may do what you please with my letter. Permit me to add that, although I have not the pleasure of a personal acquaintance with you, there is, on my part, an hereditary friendship for all that bear the revered name of Muhlenberg.

PART FOUR

Secretary of the Treasury
1801–1813 (I)

Except for Jefferson himself, Gallatin as Secretary of the Treasury was the leading executor of the "revolution of 1800." As Hamiltonian financial measures were the arch of the Federalist system, so the antistatist program of the Republicans depended upon reforms in public finance. Gallatin's chief task was to achieve the utmost economy in government and pay off the national debt. No man could have been more fully committed to these goals, and he fought hard and successfully to achieve them. In other respects, however, his views were indicative of the divergence within his party, its drift away from pure doctrine, that was to be the chief feature of a quarter century of Republican rule.

REDUCTION OF THE PUBLIC DEBT

19. LETTER TO THOMAS JEFFERSON

November 16, 1801

Gallatin wrote to Jefferson in 1809: "I consider the fortunes of our Republic as depending in an eminent degree on the extinction of the public debt before we engage in any war. . . . If the debt should once more be swelled to formidable size . . . we shall be committed to the English career of debt, corruption, and rottenness, closing with revolution. The discharge of the debt, therefore, is vital to the destinies of our government."

A fundamental aim of the Republicans was to reverse the rising indebtedness that had occurred under the Federalists. Yet the Republicans were also pledged to eliminate the system of internal taxation. Gallatin addressed himself to this two-fold program.

. . . If we cannot with the probable amount of impost and sale of lands pay the debt at the rate proposed and support the establishments on the proposed plans, one of three things must be done: either to continue the internal taxes, or to reduce the expenditure still more, or to discharge the debt with less rapidity. The last recourse, to me, is the most objectionable, not only because I am firmly of opinion that, if the present Administration and Congress do not take the most effective measures for that object, the debt will be entailed on us and the ensuing generations, together with all the systems which support it, and which it supports; but also any sinking fund

---

Writings, I, 70–71. Marked "Received, Nov. 16, 1801."

operating in an increased ratio as it progresses, a very small deduction from an appropriation for that object would make a considerable difference in the ultimate term of redemption, which, provided we can, in some shape, manage the three per cents. without redeeming them at their nominal value, I think may be paid at fourteen or fifteen years.

On the other hand, if this Administration shall not reduce taxes, they never will be permanently reduced. To strike at the root of the evil and avert the danger of increasing taxes, encroaching government, temptations to offensive wars, &c., nothing can be more effectual than a repeal of *all* internal taxes, but let them all go, and not one remain on which sister taxes may be hereafter engrafted. I agree most fully with you that pretended tax-preparations, treasury-preparations, and army-preparations against contingent wars tend only to encourage wars. If the United States shall unavoidably be drawn into war, the people will submit to any necessary tax, and the system of internal taxation which, *then,* shall be thought best adapted to the then situation of the country may be created, instead of engrafted on the old or present plan; if there shall be no real necessity for them, their abolition by this Administration will most powerfully deter any other from reviving them. . . .

20. STATEMENT OF THE PUBLIC DEBT FROM JANUARY 1, 1791 TO JANUARY 1, 1810

At Gallatin's recommendation Congress discontinued direct property taxes and in 1802 repealed all internal taxes, in-

American State Papers, Finance. "Receipts and Public Debt." Communicated April 16, 1810 to the House of Representatives. 5 vols. (Washington, 1832–1859), II, 425.

Statement of the annual amount, and of the annual increase and decrease of the public debt, from 1st January, 1791, to 1st January, 1810.

	Amount of Public Debt on the first day of each year.				Amount of Public Debt annually incurred and reimbursed.		
1st of Jan. in the years	Gross amount of debt.	Payments made by the Treasury on account of subsequent years.	Amount of debt unprovided for.	Payments in each year on account of principal.	Amount of debt contracted.	Annual increase of debt.	Annual decrease of debt.
1791	75,463,476 52	293,502 31	75,169,974 21	3,324,842 86	5,089,291 00	1,764,448 14	—
1792	77,227,924 66	854,157 50	76,373,767 16	2,056,208 86	5,180,918 24	3,124,709 38	—
1793	80,352,634 04	2,764,636 11	77,587,997 93	3,189,932 63	1,264,703 36	—	1,925,229 27
1794	78,427,404 77	2,431,234 21	75,996,170 56	2,420,520 74	4,740,703 36	2,320,182 62	—
1795	80,747,587 39	2,597,649 56	78,149,937 83	2,949,415 32	5,964,000 00	3,014,584 68	—
1796	83,762,172 07	2,119,899 11	81,642,272 96	2,097,692 74	400,000 00	—	1,697,692 74
1797	82,064,479 33	1,130,455 79	80,934,023 54	2,835,950 21	—	—	2,835,950 21
1798	79,228,529 12	734,363 37	78,494,165 75	1,027,324 42	207,465 07	—	819,859 35
1799	78,408,669 77	1,008,760 42	77,399,909 35	1,144,075 42	5,711,700 00	4,567,624 58	—
1800	82,976,294 35	1,342,968 61	81,633,325 74	1,419,943 55	1,481,700 00	61,756 45	—
1801	83,038,050 80	1,037,883 44	82,000,167 36	2,325,418 55	—	—	2,325,418 55
1802	80,712,632 25	1,958,063 55	78,754,568 70	3,657,945 95	—	—	3,657,945 95
1803	77,054,686 30	2,322,763 45	74,731,922 85	5,627,565 42	15,000,000 00	9,372,434 58	—
1804	86,427,120 88	1,073,477 66	85,353,643 22	4,114,970 38	—	—	4,114,970 38
1805	82,312,150 50	1,778,091 85	80,534,058 65	6,588,879 84	—	—	6,588,879 84
1806	75,723,270 66	1,180,313 04	74,542,957 62	6,504,872 02	—	—	6,504,872 02
1807	69,218,398 64	1,486,753 02	67,731,645 62	4,022,080 67	—	—	4,022,080 67
1808	65,196,317 97	453,991 71	64,742,326 26	8,173,125 88	—	—	8,173,125 88
1809	57,023,192 09	290,812 28	56,732,379 81	3,850,889 77	—	—	3,850,889 77
1810	53,172,302 32	15,769 68	53,156,532 64	—	—	—	—

RECAPITULATION.

Debt on 1st January, 1791, - - - - - - - - - -	- - -	$75,463,476 52
Debt contracted from 1st January, 1791, to 1st January, 1801, -	30,040,481 03	
Deduct debt reimbursed during the same period, - - -	22,465,906 75	
Increase of debt in those ten years, - - -		7,574,574 28
Debt on 1st January, 1801, - - - - - - -		83,038,050 80
Debt reimbursed from 1st January, 1801, to 1st January, 1810, -	44,865,748 48	
Deduct debt contracted during the same period, - - -	15,000,000 00	
Decrease of debt in those nine years, - - - - -		29,865,748 48
Debt on 1st January, 1810, - - - - - - -		53,172,302 32
But as this sum of $53,172,302 32 includes the Louisiana stock, -		11,250,000 00
The old debt remaining due on the 1st January, 1810, is only -		41,922,302 32
And the old debt redeemed during the last nine years, amounts to -		41,115,748 48
Debt on 1st January, 1801, - - - - - - -		$83,038,050 80

cluding the excise on whiskey. An annual appropriation of $7,300,000, then nearly three-fourths of the government's revenue, was pledged to the discharge of the debt, which on this basis could have been paid off by 1814. Every effort was made to cut federal expenditures. Although not much could be done in reducing the civil service, Republicans found a congenial way of practicing economy by dismantling the Federalist military establishment. The expenses of the army and navy dropped from $6,000,000 to $1,600,000 a year, largely as a result of substituting gunboats for a high ocean navy.

Gallatin's economy drive was interrupted by the Tripolitan War and the purchase of Louisiana, both of which entailed considerable federal expenditures. Routine expenses increased somewhat with the growth of population, economic expansion, and the acquisition of new territory. By 1805 the annual budget was back to Federalist levels. The program of debt retirement was saved, however, by heavy increases in customs receipts arising from the trade expansion which the country enjoyed as a neutral in the renewed European war. Excluding $11,250,000 added by the Louisiana purchase, the debt was cut almost in half within nine years—from $83,000,000 in 1801 to $42,000,000 in 1810.

EXPANSION: THE LOUISIANA PURCHASE

In 1801 Spain ceded Louisiana to France. This vast and ill-defined territory between the Mississippi River and the Rocky Mountains included the strategic port of New Orleans on the east bank of the river. Jefferson was alarmed by the presence of such a strong power as France on the American frontier, and by the threat to American navigation on the Mississippi. Without much hope of success he endeavored to persuade

France to sell New Orleans and nearby areas. Napoleon, now emperor of France, decided to sell the entire province of Louisiana, including New Orleans. His price was $15,000,000.

21. LETTER TO THOMAS JEFFERSON

January 13, 1803

The purchase, concluded, May 2, 1803, was one of the greatest diplomatic coups in American history, but the New England Federalists objected to it, fearful that such a vast addition of territory would diminish the weight and importance of their section in the Union. On constitutional grounds they argued that the President had no right to make the purchase. Jefferson himself had misgivings as to its constitutionality. During the negotiations with France, up to that time confined to the area of New Orleans, Jefferson confided his doubts to Attorney General Levi Lincoln, who supplied a formula for evading the constitutional issue. His suggestion was to word the treaty in such a way as to denote merely an alteration of boundaries and to annex the new territory to an existing state or territory.

Gallatin scorned such sophistry. In an argument for implied powers that Alexander Hamilton might have written, he met the constitutional issue head on. Although Jefferson still persisted in his scruples, when the chance came to buy the whole of Louisiana, he was afraid that delay would lose the opportunity. He presented the treaty to the Senate without men-

Writings, I, 111–114.

*tioning the Constitution and it was ratified October 17 by a
vote of 24 to 7.*

. . . I have read Mr. Lincoln's observations, and cannot distinguish the difference between a power to acquire territory
for the United States and the power to extend by treaty the
territory of the United States; yet he contends that the first
is unconstitutional, supposes that we may acquire East Louisiana and West Florida by annexing them to the Mississippi Territory. Nor do I think his other idea, that of annexation to a
State, that, for instance, of East Florida to Georgia, as proposed by him, to stand on a better foundation. If the acquisition of territory is not warranted by the Constitution, it is
not more legal to acquire for one State than for the United
States; if the Legislature and Executive established by the
Constitution are not the proper organs for the acquirement
of new territory for the use of the Union, still less can they be
so for the acquirement of new territory for the use of one
State; if they have no power to acquire territory, it is because
the Constitution has confined its views to the then existing
territory of the Union, and *that* excludes a possibility of enlargement of one State as well as that of territory common to
the United States. As to the danger resulting from the exercise of such power, it is as great on his plan as on the other.
What could, on his construction, prevent the President and
the Senate by treaty annexing Cuba to Massachusetts, or
Bengal to Rhode Island, if ever the acquirement of colonies
shall become a favorite object with governments, and colonies shall be acquired?

But does any constitutional objection really exist?

The 3d Section of the 4th Article of the Constitution provides:

1st. That new States may be admitted by Congress into
this Union.

2d. That Congress shall have power to dispose of and make all needful rules and regulations respecting the territory or other property belonging to the United States.

Mr. Lincoln, in order to support his objections, is compelled to suppose, 1st, that the new States therein alluded to must be carved either out of other States, or out of the territory belonging to the United States; and, 2d, that the power given to Congress of making regulations respecting the territory belonging to the United States is expressly confined to the territory *then* belonging to the Union.

A general and perhaps sufficient answer is that the whole rests on a supposition, there being no words in the section which confine the authority given to Congress to those specific objects; whilst, on the contrary, the existence of the United States as a nation presupposes the power enjoyed by every nation of extending their territory by treaties, and the general power given to the President and Senate of making treaties designates the organs through which the acquisition may be made, whilst this section provides the proper authority (viz., Congress) for either admitting in the Union or governing as subjects the territory thus acquired. It may be further observed in relation to the power of admitting new States in the Union, that this section was substituted to the 11th Article of Confederation, which was in these words: "Canada acceding, &c., shall be admitted into, &c., but no other colony shall be admitted into the same, unless such admission be agreed to by nine (9) States." As the power was there explicitly given to nine (9) States, and as all the other powers given in the Articles of Confederation to nine (9) States were by the Constitution transferred to Congress, there is no reason to believe, as the words relative to the power of admission are, in the Constitution, general, that it was not the true intention of that Constitution to give the power generally and without restriction.

As to the other clause, that which gives the power of gov-

erning the territory of the United States, the limited construction of Mr. Lincoln is still less tenable; for if that power is
limited to the territory belonging to the United States at the
time when the Constitution was adopted, it would have precluded the United States from governing any territory acquired, since the adoption of the Constitution, by cession of
one of the States, which, however, has been done in the case
of the cessions of North Carolina and Georgia; and, as the
words "other property" follow, and must be embraced by the
same construction which will apply to the territory, it would
result from Mr. L.'s opinion, that the United States could not,
after the Constitution, either acquire or dispose of any personal property. To me it would appear:

1st. That the United States as a nation have an inherent
right to acquire territory.

2d. That whenever that acquisition is by treaty, the same
constituted authorities in whom the treaty-making power is
vested have a constitutional right to sanction the acquisition.

3d. That whenever the territory has been acquired, Congress have the power either of admitting into the Union as a
new State, or of annexing to a State with the consent of that
State, or of making regulations for the government of such
territory.

The only possible objection must be derived from the 12th
Amendment, which declares that powers not delegated to the
United States, nor prohibited by it to the States, are reserved
to the States or to the people. As the States are expressly prohibited from making treaties, it is evident that, if the power of
acquiring territory by treaty is not considered within the
meaning of the Amendment as delegated to the United States,
it must be reserved to the people. If that be the true construction of the Constitution, it substantially amounts to this: that
the United States are precluded from, and renounce altogether, the enlargement of territory, a provision sufficiently
important and singular to have deserved to be expressly en-

acted. Is it not a more natural construction to say that the power of acquiring territory is delegated to the United States by the several provisions which authorize the several branches of government to make war, to make treaties, and to govern the territory of the Union?

I must, however, confess that after all I do not feel myself perfectly satisfied; the subject must be thoroughly examined; and the above observations must be considered as hasty and incomplete.

22. LETTER TO THOMAS JEFFERSON

April 13, 1803

Four months before the purchase of Louisiana, Jefferson invited Gallatin's comments on a message to Congress proposing an expedition to explore the northern reaches of Louisiana and go on to the Pacific Coast. Although the United States did not then lay claim to the trans-Mississippi region and possession of Oregon was in dispute with several powers, Gallatin enthusiastically supported the idea. Plans for the Lewis and Clark expedition were laid before a secret session of Congress, January 3, 1803. In April Gallatin urged the President to go ahead with the scheme. The immediate purpose was to find a way to wrest the Rocky Mountain fur trade from the British, but in both Jefferson's and Gallatin's minds the ultimate object was to prepare the way for American settlement. Under Meriwether Lewis and William Clark—both were army officers

---

Writings, I, 120–122.

and Lewis had been Jefferson's private secretary—a party of
twenty-seven men ascended the Missouri River in 1804, crossed
the Rockies, followed the Columbia River to the Pacific Ocean
to return in 1806.

I perceive nothing in the enclosed which should, in my opinion, require alteration; perhaps something might be added.

The present aspect of affairs may ere long render it neces-sary that we should, by taking immediate possession, prevent G. B. [Great Britain] from doing the same. Hence a perfect knowledge of the posts, establishments, and force kept by Spain in Upper Louisiana, and also of the most proper station to occupy for the purpose of preventing effectually the occu-pying of any part of the Missouri country by G. B., seems important; with that view the present communications of the British with the Missouri, either from the Mississippi, or, which is still more in point, from the waters emptying in Lake Winnipeg and generally in Hudson Bay, should be well as-certained, as well as the mode in which a small but sufficient force could best be conveyed to the most proper point from whence to prevent any attempt from Lake Winnipeg. But, whatever may be the issue of the present difficulties, the fu-ture destinies of the Missouri country are of vast importance to the United States, it being perhaps the only large tract of country, and certainly the *first* which, lying out of the bound-aries of the Union, will be settled by the people of the United States. The precise extent, therefore, of the country drained by all the waters emptying into that river, and consequently the length and directions of all the principle branches, ought to be as far as practicable ascertained, as well as that particu-lar branch which may be followed for the purpose of exam-ining the communications with the Pacific Ocean. That tract of country is bounded on the north by the waters of Hudson's Bay, the extent of which southwardly is tolerably ascertained by Mackenzie and others; westwardly by the waters of the

Columbia and other rivers emptying into the Pacific, which it is the principal object of this voyage to explore; and southwardly, it is presumed, by the waters of Rio Norte. How far these extend northwardly and confine the waters of the Missouri it is important to know, as their position would generally determine the extent of territory watered by the Missouri. It is presumable, from analogy, that the waters of Hudson Bay, which interlock with the many northerly streams of the Missouri, are divided from them by elevated lands interspersed with lakes, but not by any regular chain of mountains. By the same analogy (for within the United States and known parts of North America the spring of every river north of 42° latitude issues from a lake, and south of 41° from a mountain), it is probable that the northern branches of the Rio Norte are separated from the southern streams of the Kansas and Missouri Rivers by a chain of mountains running westwardly till it unites with the chain which divides the waters of the Missouri and other rivers from those emptying into the Pacific. Hence it is presumable that the distance of that east and west chain from the Missouri will generally show the extent of country watered by this river. And although Capt. L. going westwardly towards his main object may not personally become acquainted with the country lying south of his track, yet so far as he may collect information on that subject, and also on the communications with the Rio Norte or other southern rivers, if any other, which is not probable, interlocks with the Missouri, it would be a desirable object. The great object to ascertain is whether from its extent and fertility that country is susceptible of a large population in the same manner as the corresponding tract on the Ohio. Besides the general opinion which may be formed of its fertility, some more specific instructions on the signs of the soil might be given, the two principal of which are the *prevailing* species of timber, whether oak, beech, pine, or barren, and the evenness or mountainous and rocky situation of the lands.

Those two circumstances do generally determine in America the quantity of soil fit for cultivation in any one large tract of country, for I presume there are no swamps in that part of the world. But several more signs might be added, to which the traveller should pay attention.

I think Capt. L. ought to take, on the Spanish side of the Illinois settlement, some person who had navigated the Missouri as high as possible, and it might not be amiss to try to winter with the traders *from that quarter* who go to the farthest tribes of Indians in the proper direction. A boat or canoe might be hired there (at the Illinois) to carry up to that spot a sufficient quantity of flour to enable him to winter there with comfort, so that his hands should be fresh and in good spirits in the spring.

23. LETTER TO THOMAS JEFFERSON

September 5, 1803

After the purchase of Louisiana was concluded Jefferson was uncertain whether France would go through with the bargain or whether Spain, which had protested vigorously and still occupied the province, would give it up. Gallatin advised taking no chances. With members of Congress and the War Department he worked out plans to take immediate possession by force if necessary. However, there was no cause for anxiety. On November 30, 1803 the Spanish governer of New Orleans

---

Writings, I, 152–153.

turned over his authority to the French governor, and twenty days later the province passed to the United States.

... Permit me to suggest the propriety of having everything in readiness to take possession of New Orleans, whether the prefect and Spanish officers shall be willing to give it up or not, the moment we shall have received the order to that effect from Mr. Pichon; this is recommended by the possible event of our delivering the stock on receiving only the order to take possession, and before actual possession shall have been obtained. The *disponible* regular force at Fort Adams, the militia of the Mississippi Territory, and the crews of the Kentucky boats and of American vessels from the Atlantic States then in New Orleans, will be sufficient against any force now in that place, provided that we may arm the boatmen and sailors, and provided that the French militia of Louisiana be disposed to be at least neutral.

Although I do not share in the alarm of our ministers, I think it wise to be as perfectly prepared as if it had a real ground, and that no time should be lost in having a supply of arms at Natchez; instructions given to Governor Claiborne; and Clark, if he can be trusted to that extent, informed by a safe communication of our intentions, with instructions to prepare the way with the inhabitants so as to meet no opposition from them.

The establishment of expresses both by Hawkins and Nashville if practicable, and at all events by the last route, seems also desirable. If there is any apprehension that that force may not ultimately be sufficient, such part of the militia of Kentucky and Tennessee as may be thought necessary might be ordered, under the Act of last session, to be in a state of readiness to float down the river on the arrival of an express from Claiborne applying for such aid.

If it shall be found necessary to take possession of New Orleans against the will of the possessors, there can be no doubt of the propriety of occupying at the same time that part of West Florida which we claim. But if New Orleans and West Louisiana shall be yielded without difficulty, the policy of occupying the rest of what we claim against the will of the Spanish officers is a subject which deserves serious consideration.

THE PUBLIC LANDS

As a Jeffersonian and a westerner, Gallatin hoped that the public domain beyond the Appalachians would be conveyed to settlers rather than to speculators. As a responsible statesman he regarded public lands as a source of income to be applied to broad national purposes. To encompass both these aims by legislation was not an easy task.

The price of land and the minimum size of tracts were interrelated factors in the formation of public land policy. Purchase by actual settlers was best promoted, at least before 1815, by selling small tracts at relatively high prices, near the level at which comparable lands sold in the area. This procedure made it difficult for speculators to buy and resell at higher figures. It was a policy calculated to people the land with yeoman farmers, and although this was a gradual process, it was one which in time would produce maximum returns to the government. The disadvantage was that it did not realize a quick income, moreover, it offered nothing to poor people who wanted to migrate but who could not afford to pay cash for land. Their plight opened a legitimate place for the speculator in schemes for land disposal. If enabled to buy large tracts at low prices, speculators were in a position to extend credit to settlers until they could bring their farms into production. Some people argued that there was no other practical method, but it meant the initial engrossment of public land by large operators and a small return to the government.

Under the first public land legislation, the Ordinance of 1785, land was sold in tracts of 640 acres at a minimum price of $1.00 an acre. Since depreciated public securities were accepted in payment, the actual price was less than twenty cents an acre. What effect the Ordinance of 1785 would have had on the disposal of the western domain is uncertain, for it was largely inoperative. Indian resistance hindered settlement by individuals, and Congress was in too much of a hurry to pay the national debt to wait for surveys. In 1787 the colonization of the West was turned over to organized companies by the grant of a million acres to the Ohio Company in 1787 at an actual price of about sixteen cents an acre.

Congress reconsidered land policy in 1796. A House committee reported a bill providing for disposal of land in minimum tracts of three square miles at a minimum price of $2.00 an acre, payable in hard money. Gallatin, who was a member of the House at that time, did not argue against the price, which he felt should be kept up, but against the size of tracts. He moved to sell half the land in 160 acre tracts. The proposal was adopted by the House but was rejected by the Senate. Gallatin also supported the idea of requiring purchasers to occupy the land. The act as finally adopted set the price at $2.00 and the minimum tract at 640 acres. As these terms were not competitive with land offered by private companies and state governments, very little was sold. In 1800 the first "frontiersman's bill" accommodated both speculators and settlers. The relatively high price of $2.00 was retained, but part of the land was to be sold in 640 acre tracts, part in 320 acre tracts. The outstanding feature of the act was the government's attempt to take the place of the speculator by allowing four years credit.

24. REPORT TO A COMMITTEE

OF CONGRESS

January 2, 1804

In 1803 a House committee considering public land policy put a number of questions to Gallatin: whether the land should be sold in smaller tracts, whether the price should be reduced, whether the credit system should be retained, whether pre-emption should be allowed, and how any such changes were likely to affect the revenue. Gallatin's reply showed a mature grasp of the issues. His recommendations were embodied in the committee's report, but overridden by Congress. Beyond reducing the minimum price to $1.64 an acre, the land act of 1804 retained the existing system, including the credit feature. Not until 1820 was credit discontinued, at which time the minimum price was set at $1.25 and the minimum tract at 80 acres.

In conformity with the request contained in your letter of the 1st ultimo, I have the honor to communicate such observations respecting the proposed alterations in the laws providing for the sale of public lands, as have been suggested by their operation.

Under the present system, the public lands north of the river Ohio, and east of the river Muskingum, are sold only

---

American State Papers, Public Lands. "Report on Public Land, January 2, 1804, to Joseph H. Nicholson." (7 vols., Washington, 1832–1860), I, 183–184.

in sections of one mile square, and containing six hundred and forty acres each. The other lands north of the Ohio, and above the mouth of Kentucky river, are sold one half in sections, and the other half in half sections, containing three hundred and twenty acres each. No provision has yet been made by law for the sale of the reserved sections which are interspersed through those lands, nor for that of the tracts lying below the mouth of Kentucky river, and lately purchased from the Indians, one of which is situated on the Wabash river, around St. Vincennes, and the other between the Mississippi and Ohio, above the confluence of those two rivers.

The price at which all the lands offered for sale may be purchased is two dollars per acre, payable in specie or in six per cent. stock, at par, and in four equal instalments; the first of which must be paid at the time, and the three others within two, three, and four years after the time of making the purchase. In every instance, except in the case of persons who had made contracts with Judge Symmes for lands lying between the two Miamies, interest at the rate of six per cent. a year is charged on the three last instalments, from the date of the purchase; and, in every case, a discount at the rate of eight per cent. a year is allowed for prompt payment.

The cash price of the lands is, therefore, only one dollar and eighty-four cents per acre, except for lands lying between the two Miamies, for which contracts had been made with Judge Symmes, which may be paid for at the rate of one dollar and sixty-four cents per acre. It follows from thence, that, if all the lands were sold on the same terms as the last mentioned, that is to say without charging interest until after the instalments had become due, it would operate a reduction on their cash price of twenty cents per acre.

The reasons which probably influenced the Legislature in fixing a price so much beyond what had been the usual terms on which vacant lands had theretofore been granted in the several States were, a wish to prevent monopolies and large speculations, and, at the same time, to secure a permanent revenue to the Union.

The first object has been fully obtained; and, although the proceeds of the sales have not been commensurate with the vast increase of population, more than nine hundred thousand acres have been sold in three years, on which near eight hundred thousand dollars have been received, and about eleven hundred thousand remain due by the purchasers.

It must, however, be observed that the price of public securities, at the time of passing those laws, would have reduced the real cash price of lands at about a dollar and a half per acre, and that the sales have been affected by the competition of lands held by individuals in the Connecticut reserve, in the military tracts, and in Kentucky, and which might generally be purchased for a less price than that set on the public lands.

A considerable reduction of the price might be considered as a waste of public property, and as promoting migration beyond its natural and necessary progress. It would certainly be injurious to private landholders, and, by throwing the lands into the hands of a few individuals, prevent that gradual and equal distribution of property which is the result of the present system. To reduce it only to what may be considered as the market price which actual settlers give for small tracts in similar situations, would only satisfy the demand for land created by the existing population, and, without promoting migrations or speculations on a large scale, would increase the receipts in the treasury; provided that reduction was connected with another measure which is considered as of first importance for the security of that branch of the revenue.

It has been observed that about eleven hundred thousand dollars are due to the United States on account of preceding sales. Great difficulties may attend the recovery of that debt, which is due by nearly two thousand individuals; and its daily increase may ultimately create an interest hostile to the general welfare of the Union. It appears extremely desirable, in every point of view, that lands should hereafter be sold without allowing any other credit than that of forty days, now given for the payment of the first instalment; and, as that provision might be considered injurious to that part of the community who are not able to make large payments, it would seem proper to connect it with a moderate reduction in the price, and with a permission to purchase smaller tracts than is now allowed by law.

Supposing that the lands which are now sold in entire sections should be offered for sale in half sections; that those which are now sold in half sections should be offered for sale in quarter sections; and that the price of entire and half sections should be reduced to one dollar and twenty-five cents, and that of quarter sections to one dollar and a half, per acre; it is believed that the benefits resulting from the present system would not be impaired, and that several important advantages would be obtained.

1. The price being still as high as that at which lands held by individuals in similar situations are generally sold, and higher than can be afforded for any other purpose than that of improving the land, or securing it for the use of the purchaser's family, monopolies and large speculations would be as effectually prevented as under the existing provisions.

2. The poorest individuals, as they cannot at present purchase less than three hundred and twenty acres, must, in order to become freeholders, be able to pay one hundred and sixty dollars, and become bound for four hundred and eighty more, payable within four years; and it is proper to observe that, if they have no other resources, it is almost impossible that they should, during the first four years of a new settlement, draw the means of payment from the produce of the land. By the proposed alteration, a man might, by the payment of two hundred and forty dollars, acquire a freehold of one hundred and sixty acres, without encumbering himself with any debt whatever. The difficulty of raising eighty dollars

more at first is unimportant, if it shall be admitted that the subsequent payments must at present be provided for from other resources than those arising from the land itself; and, in every other respect, the purchaser will evidently be placed in a much more eligible situation.

3. Whatever revenue may be derived from that source will be collected in the most simple manner, and will be completely secured. There will be no outstanding debts, and the interest of every new purchaser will become identified with that of the Union.

4. It has already been observed, that the sales have not, by any means, been commensurate with the demand for land and the increase of population; they have been limited, partly by the competition of other lands in the market, and partly by the existing means of payment. Under the system, altered as has been suggested, they would be limited only by the last clause, and be altogether regulated by the amount of circulating medium acquirable by the purchase[r]. It is evident, indeed, that it would be more easy to sell three hundred thousand acres at a dollar and a third, than two hundred thousand acres at two dollars per acre; and no doubt is entertained that the revenue would be not only secured, but also increased, by the proposed alterations.

The only difference to the United States will be, that they will transfer the property of a greater quantity of land for the same sum of money than they do at present. The estimated revenue of four hundred thousand dollars, derived from that source, is predicated on annual sales of two hundred thousand acres, at two dollars; or rather of about two hundred and twelve thousand acres, at one dollar and eighty-four cents per acre; two hundred and sixty-six thousand six hundred and sixty-six acres, at one dollar and a half, or three hundred and twenty thousand acres, at one dollar and twenty-five cents per acre, would produce an equal sum. It would, therefore, under the proposed alterations, cost annually to the United States about one hundred thousand acres more than at present, to raise a revenue equal to that which may be collected under the existing regulations. Compared with the quantity of land north of the Ohio and east of the Mississippi, not less, certainly, than one hundred and fifty millions of acres, the soil of which belongs to the United States, that difference is so trifling, and the effect which, in that respect, may result from the alteration, so distant, that neither of them seems to afford sufficient ground of objection.

A more serious difficulty will arise from former purchasers, who may complain that they should be left in a worse situation than those who shall purchase under the new arrangement. It is true that those persons have had the selection of the most eligible spots, in point of situation and of soil; yet, under all circumstances, and also in order to secure punctual payments, it might be expedient to release them from the payment of interest until after their instalments had become due. That provision which, it is believed, would be perfectly satisfactory, should be extended only in favor of those who shall discharge those instalments with punctuality, and who have not alienated the property. In the few cases where the purchasers have already completed their payments, certificates, receivable in payment for land, might be given to them for the sums which may have been charged for interest.

It is believed that the alterations which have been suggested will enable a great portion of the actual settlers to become purchasers; but the principle of granting them a right of pre-emption, exclusively of the abuses to which it is liable, appears irreconcilable with the idea of drawing a revenue from the sale of lands. Nor would the reduction of price, and especially the sale in smaller tracts, be an eligible measure, so far as respects the revenue, unless connected with a suppression of the credit which is now given to purchasers. . . .

INTERNAL IMPROVEMENTS

Jefferson never failed to qualify his states rights views when they conflicted with his conception of the public welfare.

Stimulated by the prosperity of the nation in 1805, he envisaged a program of internal development financed by federal funds. In his second inaugural address, he suggested that Treasury surpluses beyond the amounts necessary to discharge the public debt on schedule might be "applied in time of peace to rivers, canals, roads, arts, manufacturers, education, and other great objects. . . ." To reconcile such federal expenditures with strict construction doctrine, he proposed that they be proportionate in each state to its population, although he felt that in the end a constitutional amendment might be necessary.

Gallatin shared Jefferson's enthusiasm for internal improvements but not his cavils. In his opinion, such projects did not require a constitutional amendment, nor was it proper to apportion federal expenditures according to population since, as he pointed out, the benefits of river improvements, canals, and roads did not necessarily accrue to the states in which they were constructed.

25. REPORT ON ROADS AND CANALS

April 6, 1808

In 1807 with the public debt apparently on its way to extinction, Gallatin inspired a Senate resolution which requested him to submit plans for internal improvements. His report, long in preparation, was delivered in April 1808. Comparable

---

American State Papers, Miscellaneous, I, 724–725, 739–741.

in scope to Hamilton's Report on Manufacturers, *it set forth a
magnificent scheme for a transportation network tying all parts
of the nation together: an inland waterway along the East
coast from Massachusetts to Georgia, paralleled by a system
of turnpikes; four major highways across the mountains (in
addition to the Cumberland Road authorized in 1802) which
would link coastal rivers with branches of the Mississippi;
canals leading from the Hudson River to Lake Champlain and
west to Lake Ontario, and a canal around Niagara Falls; a
network of canals and roads in the West to give that section
an integrated transportation system. As some states would not
benefit as much as others, he proposed to compensate them
with federal appropriations for purely local projects.*

*The total cost of the program he estimated at $20,000,000,
which he thought could be met by an annual appropriation of
$2,000,000 over a ten year period. If peace continued, he held
out the hope that the surplus of federal revenues would support a continuing program.*

*The following selection presents the opening and closing
sections of his long, detailed report.*

The SECRETARY OF THE TREASURY, in obedience to the resolution of the Senate of the 2nd March 1807, respectfully submits
the following report on roads and canals:

The general utility of artificial roads and canals is at this
time so universally admitted, as hardly to require any additional proofs. It is sufficiently evident that, whenever the annual expense of transportation on a certain route, in its natural
state, exceeds the interest on the capital employed in improving the communication, and the annual expense of transportation (exclusively of the tolls,) by the improved route, the
difference is an annual additional income to the nation. Nor
does in that case the general result vary, although the tolls

may not have been fixed at a rate sufficient to pay to the under-takers the interest on the capital laid out. They, indeed, when that happens, lose; but the community is nevertheless bene-fited by the undertaking. The general gain is not confined to the difference between the expense of the transportation of those articles which had been formerly conveyed by that route, but many which were brought to market by other channels will then find a new and more advantageous direc-tion; and those which on account of their distance or weight could not be transported in any manner whatever, will ac-quire a value, and become a clear addition to the national wealth. Those and many other advantages have become so obvious, that in countries possessed of a large capital, where property is sufficiently secure to induce individuals to lay out that capital on permanent undertakings, and where a com-pact population creates an extensive commercial intercourse, within short distances, those improvements may often, in ordi-nary cases, be left to individual exertion, without any direct aid from Government.

There are, however, some circumstances, which, whilst they render the facility of communications throughout the United States an object of primary importance, naturally check the application of private capital and enterprise to improvements on a large scale.

The price of labor is not considered as a formidable ob-stacle, because whatever it may be, it equally affects the expense of transportation, which is saved by the improve-ment, and that of effecting the improvement itself. The want of practical knowledge is no longer felt; and the occasional influence of mistaken local interests, in sometimes thwarting or giving an improper direction to public improvements, arises from the nature of man, and is common to all countries. The great demand for capital in the United States, and the extent of territory compared with the population, are, it is believed, the true causes which prevent new undertakings, and render those already accomplished less profitable than had been expected.

1. Notwithstanding the great increase of capital during the last fifteen years, the objects for which it is required continue to be more numerous, and its application is generally more profitable than in Europe. A small portion therefore is applied to objects which offer only the prospect of remote and moderate profit. And it also happens that a less sum being subscribed at first than is actually requisite for completing the work, this proceeds slowly; the capital applied remains unproductive for a much longer time than was necessary, and the interest accruing during that period becomes, in fact, an injurious addition to the real expense of the undertaking.

2. The present population of the United States, compared with the extent of territory over which it is spread, does not, except in the vicinity of the seaports, admit that extensive commercial intercourse within short distances, which, in England and some other countries, forms the principal support of artificial roads and canals. With a few exceptions, canals particularly cannot, in America, be undertaken with a view solely to the intercourse between the two extremes of, and along the intermediate ground which they occupy. It is necessary, in order to be productive, that the canal should open a communication with a natural extensive navigation which will flow through that new channel. It follows that whenever that navigation requires to be improved, or when it might at some distance be connected by another canal to another navigation, the first canal will remain comparatively unproductive until the other improvements are effected, until the other canal is also completed. Thus the intended canal between the Chesapeake and Delaware, will be deprived of the additional benefit arising from the intercourse between New York and the Chesapeake, until an inland navigation shall

have been opened between the Delaware and New York. Thus the expensive canals completed around the falls of Potomac will become more and more productive in proportion to the improvement, first, of the navigation of the upper branches of the river, and then of its communication with the Western waters. Some works already executed are unprofitable; many more remain unattempted, because their ultimate productiveness depends on other improvements, too extensive or too distant to be embraced by the same individuals.

The General Government can alone remove these obstacles.

With resources amply sufficient for the completion of every practicable improvement, it will always supply the capital wanted for any work which it may undertake, as fast as the work itself can progress; avoiding thereby the ruinous loss of interest on a dormant capital, and reducing the real expense to its lowest rate.

With these resources, and embracing the whole Union, it will complete on any given line all the improvements, however distant, which may be necessary to render the whole productive, and eminently beneficial.

The early and efficient aid of the *Federal* Government is recommended by still more important considerations. The inconveniences, complaints, and perhaps dangers, which may result from a vast extent of territory, can not otherwise be radically removed or prevented than by opening speedy and easy communications through all its parts. Good roads and canals will shorten distances, facilitate commercial and personal intercourse, and unite, by a still more intimate community of interests, the most remote quarters of the United States. No other single operation, within the power of Government, can more effectually tend to strengthen and perpetuate that Union which secures external independence, domestic peace, and internal liberty.

With that view of the subject the facts respecting canals, which have been collected in pursuance of the resolution of the Senate, have been arranged under the following heads:

1. Great canals, from north to south, along the Atlantic seacoast.

2. Communications between the Atlantic and Western waters.

3. Communications between the Atlantic waters, and those of the great lakes, and river St. Lawrence.

4. Interior canals. . . .

RECAPITULATION AND RESOURCES.

The improvements which have been respectfully suggested as most important in order to facilitate the communication between the great geographical divisions of the United States, will now be recapitulated; and their expense compared with the resources applicable to that object.

I. From north to south, in a direction parallel to the seacoast.

    1. Canals opening an inland navigation for sea vessels from Massachusetts to North Carolina, being more than two-thirds of the Atlantic seacoast of the United States, and across all the principal capes, Cape Fear excepted, ... $3,000,000

    2. A great turnpike road from Maine to Georgia along the whole extent of the Atlantic seacoast, ... 4,800,000

                                         $7,800,000

II. From east to west, forming communications across the mountains between the Atlantic and western rivers.

    1. Improvement of the navigation of four great Atlantic rivers, including canals parallel to them, ... 1,500,000

    2. Four firstrate turnpike roads from those rivers across the mountains, to the four corresponding western rivers, ... 2,800,000

3. Canal around the falls of
   the Ohio, ...   300,000
4. Improvement of roads to Detroit,
   St. Louis, and
   New Orleans, ...   200,000
                                        ──────────
                                        4,800,000

III. In a northern and northwestwardly direction, forming
   inland navigations between the Atlantic seacoast, and
   the great lakes and the St. Lawrence.
   1. Inland navigation between the North river
      and Lake Champlain, . .   800,000
   2. Great inland navigation opened the whole way
      by canals from the North river
      to Lake Ontario, ...   2,200,000
   3. Canal around the falls and rapids of Niagara,
      opening a sloop navigation from Lake Ontario to
      the upper lakes as far as the
      extremities of Lake
      Michigan, ...   1,000,000
                                        ──────────
                                        4,000,000
                                        ──────────
   Making, together,   . . . $16,600,000
                                        ══════════

IV. The great geographical features of the country have been
solely adhered to in pointing out those lines of communication; and
these appear to embrace all the great interests of the Union, and
to be calculated to diffuse and increase the national wealth in a
very general way, by opening an intercourse between the remotest
extremes of the United States. Yet it must necessarily result from
an adherence to that principle, that those parts of the Atlantic
States through which the great western and northwest communications will be carried, must, in addition to the general advantages
in which they will participate, receive from those communications
greater local and immediate benefits than the Eastern and perhaps
Southern States. As the expense must be defrayed from the general
funds of the Union, justice, and, perhaps, policy not less than justice,
seems to require that a number of local improvements, sufficient to
equalize the advantages, should also be undertaken in those States,

parts of States, or districts which are less immediately interested in those inland communications. Arithmetical precision cannot, indeed, be attained in objects of that kind; nor would an apportionment of the moneys applied according to the population of each State be either just or practicable, since roads and particularly canals are often of greater utility to the States which they unite, than to those through which they pass. But a sufficient number of local improvements, consisting either of roads or canals may, without any material difficulty, be selected, so as to do substantial justice and give general satisfaction. Without pretending to suggest what would be the additional sum necessary for that object, it will, for the sake of round numbers,

be estimated at	$ 3,400,000
Which, added to the sum estimated for general improvements, ...	16,600,000
Would make an aggregate of	$20,000,000

An annual appropriation of two millions of dollars would accomplish all those great objects in ten years, and may, without inconvenience, be supplied in time of peace by the existing revenues and resources of the United States. This may be exemplified in several ways.

The annual appropriation, on account of the principal and interest of the public debt, has, during the last six years, amounted to eight millions of dollars. After the present year, or, at furthest, after the ensuing year, the sum which, on account of the irredeemable nature of the remaining debt, may be applied to that object cannot, in any one year, exceed four million six hundred thousand dollars; leaving, therefore, from that source alone, an annual surplus of three million four hundred thousand dollars applicable to any other object.

From the 1st January, 1801, to the 1st January, 1809, a period of eight years, the United States shall have discharged about thirty-four millions of the principal of the old debt, or deducting the Louisiana debt incurred during the same period and not yet discharged, about twenty-three millions of dollars. They may, with equal facility, apply, in a period of ten years, a sum of twenty millions of dollars to internal improvements.

The annual permanent revenue of the United States, calculated on a state of general peace, and on the most moderate estimate, was, in a report made to Congress on the 6th day of December, 1806, computed for the years 1809, 1815, at fourteen millions of dollars. The annual expenses on the peace establishment, and including the four million six hundred thousand dollars on account of the debt, and four hundred thousand dollars for contingencies, do not exceed eight millions and a half, leaving an annual surplus of five millions and a half of dollars. To provide for the protection and defence of the country is undoubtedly the object to which the resources of the United States must, in the first instance, be applied, and to the exclusion of all others, if the times shall require it. But it is believed that, in times of peace, and to such period only are these remarks applicable; the surplus will be amply sufficient to defray the expenses of all the preparatory measures of a permanent nature which prudence may suggest, and to pay the sum destined for internal improvements. Three millions annually applied during the same period of ten years, would arm every man in the United States, fill the public arsenals and magazines, erect every battery and fortification which could be manned, and even, if thought eligible, build a navy. That the whole surplus would be inadequate to the support of any considerable increase of the land or naval force kept in actual service in time of peace, will be readily admitted. But such a system is not contemplated; if ever adopted, the objects of this report must probably be abandoned; for it has not heretofore been found an easy task for any Government to indulge in that species of expense, which, leaving no trace behind it, adds nothing to the real strength of the country, and, at the same time, to provide for either its permanent defence or improvement.

It must not be omitted that the facility of communications constitutes, particularly in the United States, an important branch of national defence. Their extensive territory opposes a powerful obstacle to the progress of an enemy; but, on the other hand, the number of regular forces which may be raised, necessarily limited by the population, will, for many years, be inconsiderable when compared with that extent of territory. That defect cannot otherwise be supplied than by those great national improvements, which will afford the means of a rapid concentration of that regular force, and of a formidable body of militia on any given point.

Amongst the resources of the Union, there is one which, from its nature, seems more particularly applicable to internal improvements. Exclusively of Louisiana, the General Government possesses, in trust for the people of the United States, about one hundred millions of acres fit for cultivation, north of the river Ohio, and near fifty millions south of the State of Tennessee. For the disposition of these lands a plan has been adopted, calculated to enable every industrious citizen to become a freeholder, to secure indisputable titles to the purchasers, to obtain a national revenue, and, above all, to suppress monopoly. Its success has surpassed that of every former attempt, and exceeded the expectations of its authors. But a higher price than had usually been paid for waste lands by the first inhabitants of the frontier became an unavoidable ingredient of a system intended for general benefit, and was necessary, in order to prevent the public lands being engrossed by individuals possessing greater wealth, activity, and local advantages. It is believed that nothing could be more gratifying to the purchasers, and to the inhabitants of the Western States generally, or better calculated to remove popular objections, and to defeat insidious efforts, than the application of the proceeds of the sales to improvements conferring general advantages on the nation, and an immediate benefit on the purchasers and inhabitants themselves. It may be added, that the United States, considered merely as owners of the soil, are also deeply interested in the opening of those communications which must necessarily enhance the value of their property. Thus the opening an inland navigation from tide water to the great lakes, would immediately give to the great body of lands bordering on those lakes as great value as if they were situated at the distance of one hundred miles by land from the seacoast. And if the proceeds of the first ten millions of acres which may be sold were applied to such improvements, the United States would be amply repaid in the sale of the other ninety millions.

The annual appropriation of two millions of dollars drawn from the general revenues of the Union, which has been suggested, could operate to its full extent only in times of peace and under prosperous circumstances. The application of the proceeds of the sales of the public lands, might, perhaps, be made permanent until it had amounted to a certain sum, and until the most important improvements had been effected. The fund created by those improvements, the expense of which has been estimated at twenty millions of dollars, would afterwards become itself a perpetual resource for further improvements. Although some of those first communications should not become immediately productive; and although the same liberal policy, which dictated the measure, would consider them less as objects of revenue to Government, than of increased wealth and general convenience to the nation, yet they would all, sooner or later, acquire, as productive property, their par value. Whenever that had taken place in relation to any of them, the stock might be sold to individuals or companies, and the proceeds applied to a new improvement. And by persevering in that plan, a succession of improvements would be effected until every portion of the United States should enjoy all the advantages of inland navigation and improved roads, of which it was susceptible. To effect that great object, a disbursement of twenty millions of dollars, applied with more or less rapidity, according to the circumstances of the United States, would be amply sufficient.

The manner in which the public moneys may be applied to such objects remains to be considered.

It is evident that the United States cannot, under the constitution, open any road or canal, without the consent of the State through which such road or canal must pass. In order, therefore, to remove every impediment to a national plan of internal improvements, an amendment to the constitution was suggested by the Executive when the subject was recommended to the consideration of Congress. Until this be obtained, the assent of the States being necessary for each improvement, the modifications under which that assent may be given, will necessarily control the manner of applying the money. It may be, however, observed that in relation to the specific improvements which have been suggested, there is hardly any which is not either already authorized by the States respectively, or so immediately beneficial to them, as to render it highly probable that no material difficulty will be experienced in that respect.

The moneys may be applied in two different manners. The United States may, with the assent of the States, undertake some of the works at their sole expense, or they may subscribe a certain number of shares of the stock of companies incorporated for the purpose. Loans might also, in some instances, be made to such companies. The first mode would, perhaps, by effectually controlling local interests, give the most proper general direction to the work. Its details would probably be executed on a more economical plan by private companies. Both modes may, perhaps, be blended together so as to obtain the advantages pertaining to each. But the modifications of which the plan is susceptible must vary according to the nature of the work, and of the charters, and seem to belong to that class of details which are not the immediate subject of consideration.

At present the only work undertaken by the United States at their sole expense, and to which the assent of the States has been obtained, is the road from Cumberland to Brownsville; an appropriation may, for that purpose, be made at any time. In relation to all other works, the United States have nothing at this time in their power but to assist those already authorized, either by loans, or by becoming stockholders; and the last mode appears the most eligible. The only companies incorporated for effecting some of the improvements, considered in this report as of national and firstrate importance, which have applied for such assistance, are the Chesapeake and Delaware Canal, the Susquehannah Canal, and the Dismal Swamp companies; and authority might be given to subscribe a certain number of shares to each on condition that the plan of the work to be executed should be approved by the General Government. A subscription to the Ohio Canal, to the Pittsburg Road, and perhaps to some other objects not fully ascertained, is also practicable at this time. As an important basis of the general system, an immediate authority might also be given to take the surveys and levels of the routes of the most important roads and canals which are contemplated: a work always useful, and by which the practicability and expense of the undertakings would be ascertained with much more correctness than in this report. A moderate appropriation would be sufficient for those several objects.

In the selection of the objects submitted in obedience to the order of the Senate, as claiming, in the first instance, the aid of the General Government, general principles have been adhered to as best calculated to suppress every bias of partiality to particular objects. Yet some such bias, of which no individual is perfectly free, may, without being felt, have operated on this report. The National Legislature alone, embracing every local interest, and superior to every local consideration, is competent to the selection of such national objects. The materials contained in the papers, herewith transmitted, and the information to be derived from surveys taken under the authority of the General Government, will furnish the facts necessary for a correct decision. Two communications by Mr. B. H. Latrobe, and by Mr. Robert Fulton, (marked E and F,) are, in the mean while, respectfully referred to as containing much interesting practical information, connected with observations of a general nature on the subject.

MANUFACTURES

Gallatin delivered a comprehensive report on manufactures in April 1810. The report disclosed the progress made in a wide range of American industries, particularly in textile manufactures which had been recently stimulated by reduced imports consequent upon the Embargo and nonimportation laws. Gallatin estimated the annual product of American manufactures at more than $120,000,000.

The demand for protective tariffs was already a public issue. Although a free-trader in principle, Gallatin was not as confirmed in his views as he later became.

26. REPORT ON MANUFACTURES

April 19, 1810

Gallatin attributed the growth of American manufactures to general causes: the advantage of a large integrated domestic market, low taxes, abundant raw materials, and the absence

American State Papers, Finance, II, 425–431.

of monopolies or governmental restrictions. As incidental factors he acknowledged the effect of the Embargo, the extraordinary rate of capital accumulation in recent years, and the protection afforded by the existing revenue tariff. He was willing to concede the central proposition of what was later to be Henry Clay's American System, that industrialization would increase domestic markets for the nation's farmers and thus reduce dependence upon foreign trade. However, he dismissed the idea of a deliberate protectionist policy. Since he considered lack of investment capital the most serious obstacle to the progress of manufactures, he proposed that they be assisted by a government loan of $20,000,000. Such a suggestion, coming from a leading Jeffersonian might be considered singular, but the most remarkable feature of his plan was that he proposed to issue loans in the form of circulating notes, a system modeled on state land banks.

The Secretary of the Treasury, in obedience to the resolution of the House of Representatives, respectfully submits the following report, in part, on the subject of domestic manufactures:

The following manufactures are carried on to an extent which may be considered adequate to the consumption of the United States, the foreign articles annually imported being less in value than those of American manufacture belonging to the same general class, which are annually exported, viz:

Manufactures of wood, or of which wood is the principal material.

Leather, and manufactures of leather.

Soap, and tallow candles.

Spermaceti oil and candles.

Flaxseed oil.

Refined sugar.

Coarse earthen ware.

Snuff, chocolate, hair powder, and mustard.

The following branches are firmly established, supplying, in several instances, the greater, and, in all, a considerable, part of the consumption of the United States, viz:

Iron, and manufactures of iron.
Manufactures of cotton, wool, and flax.
Hats.
Paper, printing types, printed books, playing cards.
Spirituous and malt liquors.
Several manufactures of hemp.
Gunpowder.
Window glass.
Jewelry and clocks.
Several manufactures of lead.
Straw bonnets and hats.
Wax candles.

Progress has also been made in the following branches, viz:

Paints and colors, several chemical preparations and medicinal drugs, salt, manufactures of copper and brass, japanned and plated ware, calico printing, queens and other earthen and glass wares, &c.

Many articles, respecting which no information has been received, are undoubtedly omitted; and the substance of the information obtained, on the most important branches, is comprehended under the following heads:

Wood, and Manufactures of Wood.

All the branches of this manufacture are carried to a high degree of perfection, supply the whole demand of the United States, and consist principally of cabinet ware, and other household furniture, coaches and carriages, either for pleasure or transportation, and ship building.

The ships and vessels, above twenty tons burthen, built in the United States during the years 1801 to 1807, measured 774,922 tons, making, on an average, about 110,000 tons a year, and worth more than six millions of dollars. About two thirds were registered for the foreign trade, and the remainder licensed for the coasting trade and fisheries.

Of the other branches, no particular account can be given.

But the annual exportations of furniture and carriages amount to 170,000 dollars. The value of the whole, including ship building, cannot be less than twenty millions of dollars a year.

Under this head may also be mentioned pot and pearl ash, of which, besides supplying the internal demand, 7,400 tons are annually exported.

Leather, and Manufactures of Leather.

Tanneries are established in every part of the United States, some of them on a very large scale—the capital employed in a single establishment amounting to one hundred thousand dollars. A few hides are exported, and it is stated that one-third of those used in the great tanneries of the Atlantic States are imported from Spanish America. Some superior or particular kinds of English leather and morocco are still imported; but about 350,000 pounds* of American leather are annually exported. The bark is abundant and cheap; and it seems, by the annexed communication, marked A, that hides cost, in America, 5½ cents, and in England, seven cents a pound; that the bark used for tanning, costs, in England, nearly as much as the hides, and in America not one-tenth part of that sum. It is, at the same time, acknowledged, that much American leather is brought to market, of an inferior quality, and that better is generally made in the middle than in the Northern or Southern States. The tanneries of the State of Delaware employ, collectively, a capital of one hundred and twenty thousand dollars, and ninety workmen, and make, annually, one hundred thousand dollars' worth of leather. Those of Baltimore amount to twenty-two, seventeen of which have, together, a capital of 187,000 dollars, and tan, annually, 19,000 hides, and 25,000 calf skins.

Morocco is also made in several places, partly from imported

---

* Unless otherwise stated, the importations and exportations are in this report taken on the average of the years 1806 and 1807.

goat skins, and principally from sheep skins. And it may be proper here to add, that deer skins, which form an article of exportation, are dressed and manufactured in the United States, to the amount required for the consumption of the country.

The principal manufactures of leather are those of shoes and boots, harness and saddles. Some inconsiderable quantities of the two last articles are both imported and exported. The annual importation of foreign boots and shoes, amounts to 3,250 pair boots and 59,000 pair of shoes, principally kid and morocco. The annual exportation of the same articles, of American manufacture, to 8,500 pair of boots and 127,000 pair of shoes. The shoe manufactures of New Jersey are extensive. That of Lynn, in Massachusetts, makes 100,000 pair of women's shoes annually.

The value of all the articles annually manufactured in the United States, which are embraced under this head, (leather) may be estimated at twenty millions of dollars.

Soap, and Tallow Candles.

A great portion of the soap and candles used in the United States is a family manufacture. But there are also several establishments, on an extensive scale, in all the large cities, and several other places. Those of the village of Roxbury, near Boston, employ, alone, a capital of one hundred thousand dollars, and make, annually, 370,000 pounds candles, 380,000 pounds brown soap, and 50,000 pounds windsor and fancy soap, with a profit, it is said, of 15 per centum on the capital employed.

The annual importations of foreign manufacture, are, candles, 158,000 pounds, soap, 470,000 pounds.

The annual exportations of domestic manufacture, are, candles, 1,775,000 pounds, soap, 2,220,000 pounds.

The annual value manufactured in the United States, and including the quantity made in private families, for their own use, cannot be estimated at less than eight millions of dollars.

Spermaceti Oil and Candles.

The establishments for this manufacture are at Nantucket and New Bedford, in Massachusetts, and at Hudson, in New York. Besides supplying the whole of the domestic consumption, they furnished, annually, for exportation to foreign countries, 230,000 pounds of candles, and 44,000 gallons of oil. The whole quantity, annually manufactured, amounted to about 300,000 dollars. But the exclusion from foreign markets has lately affected the manufacture.

Refined Sugar.

The annual importations of foreign refined sugar amount, for the years 1803 to 1807, to 47,000 pounds.

The annual exportation of American refined sugar, amount, for the same years, to 150,000 pounds.

The then existing duty was, in the year 1801, collected on 3,827,000 pounds; and as the manufacture has kept pace with the increase of population, the quantity now annually made may be estimated at five millions of pounds, worth one million of dollars. The capital employed is stated at three millions and a half of dollars; and as the establishments have increased in number, some of them have declined in business. It is believed that, if a drawback, equivalent to the duty paid on the importation of the brown sugar used in the refined sugar exported, was again allowed, the foreign demand, particularly of Russia, would give a great extension to this branch. A special report has been made on that subject to the committee of commerce and manufactures.

COTTON, WOOL, AND FLAX.

I. *Spinning Mills and Manufacturing Establishments.*

The first cotton mill was erected in the State of Rhode Island, in the year 1791; another, in the same State, in the year 1795; and two more, in the State of Massachusetts, in the years 1803 and 1804. During the three succeeding years, ten more were erected or commenced, in Rhode Island, and one in Connecticut; making, altogether, fifteen mills erected before the year 1808, working, at that time, about eight thousand spindles, and producing about three hundred thousand pounds of yarn a year.

Returns have been received of eighty-seven mills, which were erected at the end of the year 1809; sixty-two of which (forty-eight, water, and fourteen, horse, mills) were in operation, and worked, at that time, thirty-one thousand spindles. The other twenty-five will all be in operation in the course of this year, and, together with the former ones, (almost all of which are increasing their machinery) will, by the estimate received, work more than eighty thousand spindles at the commencement of the year 1811.

The capital required to carry on the manufacture, on the best terms, is estimated at the rate of one hundred dollars for each spindle; including both the fixed capital applied to the purchase of the mill-seats, and to the construction of the mills and machinery, and that employed in wages, repairs, raw materials, goods on hand, and contingencies. But it is believed that no more than at the rate of sixty dollars for each spindle is generally actually employed. Forty-five pounds of cotton, worth about 20 cents a pound, are, on an average, annually used for each spindle; and these produce about thirty-six pounds of yarn, of different qualities, worth, on an average, one dollar and twelve and a half cents a pound. Eight hundred spindles employ forty persons, viz: five men and thirty-five women and children. On those data, the general results for the year 1811, are estimated in the following table:

Mills	Spindles	Capital employed	Cotton used	
No.	No.	Dollars	Pounds	Value
87	80,000	4,800,000	3,600,000	720,000

Yarn spun		Persons employed		
Pounds	Value	Men	Women & Children	Total
2,880,000	3,240,000	500	3,500	4,000

The increase of carding and spinning of cotton by machinery, in establishments for that purpose, and exclusively of that done in private families, has, therefore, been fourfold, during the two last years, and will have been tenfold in three years. The table B shews the situation and extent of those several mills, and that, although the greater number is in the vicinity of Providence, in Rhode Island, they are scattered and extending throughout all the States. Those situated within thirty miles of Providence, are exhibited in the table C, and the statement marked D gives the details of one of the establishments, as furnished by the proprietors.

The seventeen mills in the State of Rhode Island, included in the table C, which were in operation, and worked 14,290 spindles in the year 1809, are also stated to have used, during that year, 640,000 pounds of cotton, which produced 510,000 pounds of yarn; of which, 124,000 pounds were sold for thread and knitting; 200,000 pounds were used in manufactures attached to, or in the vicinity of, the mills; and the residue was either sold for wick, and for the use of family manufactures, or exported to other parts. Eleven hundred looms are said to be employed in weaving the yarn spun by those mills into goods, principally of the following descriptions, viz:

Bed ticking, sold at 55 to 90 cents per yard;

Stripes and checks, sold at 30 to 42 cents per yard;

Ginghams, sold at 40 to 50 cents per yard;

Cloth, for shirts and sheeting, sold at 35 to 75 cents per yard;

Counterpanes, at 8 dollars each.

Those several goods are already equal, in appearance, to the English imported articles of the same description, and superior in durability; and the *finishing* is still improving. The proportion of fine yarns is also increasing.

The same articles are manufactured in several other places, and particularly at Philadelphia, where are also made, from the same material, webbing and coach laces, (which articles have also excluded, or will soon exclude, similar foreign importations) table and other diaper cloth, jeans, vest patterns, cotton kerseymeres and blankets. The manufacture of fustians, cords, and velvet, has also been commenced in the interior and western parts of Pennsylvania, and in Kentucky.

Some of the mills, above mentioned, are also employed in carding and spinning wool, though not to a considerable amount. But almost the whole of that material is spun and wove in private families; and there are yet but few establishments for the manufacture of woollen cloths. Some information has, however, been received, respecting fourteen of these, as stated in table E, manufacturing, each, on an average, ten thousand yards of cloth a year, worth from one to ten dollars a yard. It is believed that there are others, from which no information has been obtained; and it is known that several establishments, on a smaller scale, exist in Philadelphia, Baltimore, and some other places. All those cloths, as well as those manufactured in private families, are generally superior in quality, though somewhat inferior in appearance, to imported cloths of the same price. The principal obstacle to the extension of the manufacture is the want of wool, which is still deficient, both in quality and quantity. But those defects are daily and rapidly lessened, by the introduction of sheep of the merino and other superior breeds; by the great demand for the article; and by the attention now every where paid by farmers to the increase and improvement of their flocks.

Manufacturing establishments, for spinning and weaving flax, are yet but few. In the State of New York, there is one, which employs a capital of 18,000 dollars, and twenty-six persons, and in which about ninety thousand pounds of flax are annually spun and wove, into canvass and other coarse linen. Information has been received respecting two, in the vicinity of Philadelphia, one of which produces, annually, 72,000 yards of canvass, made of flax and cotton; in the other, the flax is both hackled and spun by machinery; thirty looms are employed; and it is said that 500,000 yards of cotton bagging, sail cloth, and coarse linen, may be made annually.

Hosiery may also be considered as almost exclusively a household manufacture. That of Germantown has declined, and it does not appear to have been attempted on a large scale in other places. There are, however, some exceptions; and it is stated that the island of Martha's Vineyard exports, annually, nine thousand pair of stockings.

II. *Household Manufactures.*

But by far the greater part of the goods made of those materials, (cotton, flax, and wool,) are manufactured in private families, mostly for their own use, and partly for sale. They consist principally of coarse cloth, flannel, cotton stuffs, and stripes of every description, linen, and mixtures of wool with flax or cotton. The information received from every State, and from more than sixty different places, concurs in establishing the fact of an extraordinary increase, during the last two years, and in rendering it probable that about two-thirds of the clothing, including hosiery, and of the house and table linen, worn and used by the inhabitants of the United States, who do not reside in cities, is the product of family manufactures.

In the Eastern and Middle States, carding machines, worked by water, are every where established, and they are rapidly extending southwardly and westwardly. Jennies, other family spinning machines, and flying shuttles, are also introduced in many places; and as many fulling mills are erected as are required for finishing all the cloth which is woven in private families.

Difficult as it is to form an estimate, it is inferred, from a comparison of all the facts which have been communicated, with the population of the United States, (estimated at six millions of white and twelve hundred thousand black persons) that the value of all the goods made of cotton, wool, and flax, which are annually manufactured in the United States, exceeds forty millions of dollars.

The manufacture of cards and wire is intimately connected with this part of the subject. Whittemore's machine for making cards has completely excluded foreign importations of that article. It will appear, by the communication H, that the capital employed in that branch may be estimated at 200,000 dollars, and that the annual consumption amounted, till lately, to twenty thousand dozen pair of hand cards, and twenty thousand square feet of cards for machines, worth together about 200,000 dollars. The demand of last year was double that of 1808, and is still rapidly increasing. But the wire itself is altogether imported, and a very serious inconveniency might arise from any regulation which would check or prevent the exportation from foreign countries. It appears, however, by the communication I, that the manufacture may, and would be, immediately established, so as to supply the demand both for cards and other objects, provided the same duty was imposed on wire, now imported duty free, which is laid on other articles made of the same material. The whole amount of wire, annually used for cards, does not at present exceed twenty-five tons, worth about 40,000 dollars.

Hats.

The annual importations of foreign hats
    amount to -   -   -   -   - $350,000 00
The annual exportation of American hats to   100,000 00
The domestic manufacture is, therefore, nearly equal to the home consumption. The number made in the State of Massachusetts is estimated, by the hat company of Boston, at four times the number required for the consumption of the State; and from other information it would appear, that, in that State alone, the capital applied to that branch is near three millions of dollars, the number of persons employed about four thousand, and the number of hats annually made, 1,550,000; of which, 1,150,000 are fine hats, worth, on an average, four dollars each, and 400,000 felt hats, worth one dollar each. That the manufacture is still profitable, appears from a late establishment on Charles river, calculated to make, annually, 35,000 hats, at five dollars a piece, and to employ 150 workmen.

The quantity made in Rhode Island, is stated at 50,000, worth $5 each, exclusively of felt hats. Connecticut and New York make more than is necessary for their consumption; the largest establishment being that of Danbury, where 200 persons are employed, and to the amount of 130,000 dollars annually manufactured. In Vermont, the manufacture supplies the consumption. It is stated by the hatters of Philadelphia, that 92,000 hats, worth five dollars each, are annually made there, in addition to which, 50,000 *country* hats, worth three dollars each, are annually sold in the city. In various quarters, the scarcity of wool is complained of, as preventing the making of a sufficient quantity of coarse hats. From all the information which has been received, it is believed that the value of all the hats, annually made in the United States, is near ten millions of dollars.

Paper and Printing.

Some foreign paper is still imported, but the greater part of the consumption is of American manufacture; and it is believed that, if sufficient attention was every where paid to the preservation of rags, a quantity equal to the demand would be made in the United States. Paper mills are erected in every part of the Union. There are twenty one in the States of New Hampshire, Vermont, Rhode Island, and Delaware, alone, and ten in only five counties of the States of New York and Maryland. Eleven of those mills employ a capital of two hundred thousand dollars, and 180 workmen, and make, annually, 150,000 dollars' worth of paper.

Printing is carried on to an extent commensurate with the demand. Exclusively of the numerous newspapers, which alone form a considerable item in value, all the books for which there is an adequate number of purchasers, are printed in the United States. But sufficient data have not been obtained to form an estimate of the annual aggregate value of the paper made, and of the printing and book binding executed in the United States, other than what may be inferred from the population. The manufactures of hanging paper, and of playing cards, are also extensive; and that of printing types, of which there are two establishments, the principal at Philadelphia, and another at Baltimore, was fully adequate to the demand, but has lately been affected by the want of regulus of antimony.

Manufactures of Hemp.

The annual importations of foreign hemp, amounted to 6,200 tons. But the interruption of commerce has greatly promoted the cultivation of that article in Massachusetts, New

York, Kentucky, and several other places; and it is believed that a sufficient quantity will, in a short time, be produced in the United States.

The manufacture of ropes, cables, and cordage, of every description, may be considered as equal to the demand, the exportations of American manufacture, for 1806 and 1807, having exceeded the average of 6,500 quintals, and the importations from foreign ports, having fallen short of 4,200 ditto.

Exclusively of the rope walks in all the sea ports, there are fifteen in Kentucky alone, which consume about one thousand tons of hemp a year; and six new works were in a state of preparation for the present year.

The manufactures of sail duck, formerly established in Rhode Island, in Connecticut, and at Salem, have been abandoned or suspended, partly on account of the high price of hemp, and partly for want of capital. Some is still made; and the species of canvass, commonly called cotton bagging, is now manufactured, in various places, on an extensive scale. An establishment at Philadelphia, employs eight looms, and can make, annually, 17,000 yards of duck, or 45,000 yards of cotton bagging. There are thirteen manufactures in Kentucky, and two in West Tennessee. The five at or near Lexington, make annually 250,000 yards of duck and cotton bagging.

Spirituous and Malt Liquors.

The duty on licensed stills, amounted, in 1801, to $372,000, and, on account of omissions, might be estimated at $450,000. As the duty actually paid on the spirits distilled in those stills, did not, on an average, exceed five cents per gallon, the quantity of spirits distilled during that year, from grain and fruit, (exclusively of the large gin distilleries in cities) must have amounted to about 9,000,000 of gallons, and may, at present, the manufacturing having increased, at least, in the same ratio as the population, be estimated at twelve millions of gallons. To this must be added about three millions of gallons of gin and rum, distilled in cities; making an aggregate of fifteen millions of gallons.

The importations of foreign spirits, are, nevertheless, very considerable, having amounted, during the years 1806 and 1807, to 9,750,000 gallons a year, and yielding a net annual revenue to the United States, of $2,865,000.

The quantity of malt liquors made in the United States is nearly equal to their consumption.

The annual foreign importations amount
    only to   -   -   -   - 185,000 gallons.
And the annual exportations of American
    beer and *cider* to -   -   - 187,000 do.

But the amount actually made, cannot be correctly stated. It has been said, that the breweries of Philadelphia consumed, annually, 150,000 bushels of malt; and, exclusively of the numerous establishments on a smaller scale, dispersed throughout the country, extensive breweries are known to exist in New York and Baltimore.

From those data, the aggregate value of spirituous and malt liquors, annually made in the United States, cannot be estimated at less than ten millions of dollars.

Iron, and Manufactures of Iron.

The information received respecting that important branch is very imperfect. It is, however, well known, that iron ore abounds, and that numerous furnaces and forges are erected, throughout the United States. They supply a sufficient quantity of hollow ware, and of castings, of every description; but about 4,500 tons of bar iron are annually imported from Russia, and probably, an equal quantity from Sweden and England together. A vague estimate states the amount of bar iron annually used in the United States, at fifty thousand tons, which would leave about forty thousand for that of American manufacture. Although a great proportion of the ore found in Vermont, Pennsylvania, Maryland, and Virginia, be of a superior quality, and some of the iron manufactured there, equal to any imported, it is to be regretted, that, from the demand, and from want of proper attention in the manufacture, much inferior American iron is brought to market. On that account, the want of the ordinary supply of Russian iron has been felt in some of the slitting and rolling mills. But, whilst a reduction of the duty on Russian iron is asked from several quarters, it is generally stated that a high or prohibitory duty on English bar, slit, rolled, and sheet iron, would be beneficial; that which is usually imported on account of its cheapness, being made with pit coal, and of a very inferior quality.

The annual importations of sheet, slit, and hoop iron, amount to five hundred and sixty-five tons; and the quantity rolled and slit in the United States, is estimated at seven thousand tons. In the State of Massachusetts alone, are found thirteen rolling and slitting mills, in which about 3,500 tons of bar iron, principally from Russia, are annually rolled or slit. A portion is used for sheet iron and nail rods for wrought nails; but two-thirds of the whole quantity of bar iron flattened by machinery in the United States, is used in the manufacture of *cut nails*, which has now extended throughout the whole country, and, being altogether an American invention, substituting machinery to manual labor, deserves particular notice. The details on that subject will be found in the communications L and M; and it will be sufficient here to state, that the annual product of that branch alone, may be estimated at twelve hundred thousand dollars, and that, exclusively of the saving of fuel, the expense of manufacturing cut nails, is not one-third part of that of forging wrought nails. About two hundred and eighty tons are already annually exported, but the United States continue to import, annually, more than fifteen hundred tons of wrought nails and spikes. An increase of duty on these, and a drawback on the exportation of the cut nails is generally asked for.

A considerable quantity of blistered, and some refined steel, are made in America; but the foreign importations exceed 11,000 cwt. a year.

The manufactures of iron consist principally of agricultural implements, and of all the usual work performed by common blacksmiths. To these may be added anchors, shovels, and spades, axes, scythes, and other edge tools, saws, bits, and stirrups, and a great variety of the coarser articles of iron-mongery; but cutlery, and all the finer species of hardware, and of steel work, are almost altogether imported from Great Britain. Balls, shells, and cannon, of small caliber, are cast in several places; and three foundries for casting solid, those of the largest caliber, together with the proper machinery for boring and finishing them, are established at Cecil county, Maryland, near the city of Washington, and at Richmond, in Virginia; each of the two last may cast 300 pieces of artillery a year, and a great number of iron and brass cannon are made at that, near the seat of Government. Those of Philadelphia and near the Hudson river, are not now employed. It may be here added, that there are several iron foundries for casting every species of work wanted for machinery, and that steam engines are made at that of Philadelphia.

At the two public armories of Springfield and Harper's ferry, 19,000 muskets are annually made. About 20,000 more are made at several factories, of which the most perfect is said to be that near New Haven, and which, with the exception of that erected at Richmond by the State of Virginia, are all private establishments. These may, if wanted, be immediately enlarged, and do not include a number of gunsmiths employed in making rifles, and several other species of arms. Swords and pistols are also manufactured in several places.

Although it is not practicable to make a correct statement of the value of all the iron and manufactures of iron, annually made in the United States, it is believed to be from twelve to fifteen millions of dollars. The annual importations from all foreign countries, including bar iron, and every description of manufactures of iron or steel, are estimated at near four millions of dollars.

Copper and Brass.

Rich copper mines are found in New Jersey, in Virginia, and near lake Superior; but they are not now wrought. The principal manufactures of that material, are those of stills and other vessels; but the copper in sheets and bolts is almost universally imported, the only manufacture for that object, which is at Boston, not receiving sufficient encouragement, although a capital of $25,000 has been invested in a rolling mill and other apparatus. The true reason is, that those articles are imported free of duty; and the owners seem to be principally employed in casting bells and other articles.

Zinc has been lately discovered in Pennsylvania; and there are a few manufactures of metal buttons, and various brass wares.

Manufactures of Lead.

Lead is found in Virginia and some other places, but the richest mines of that metal are found in Upper Louisiana, and also, it is said, in the adjacent country, on the east side of the Mississippi. They are not yet wrought to the extent of which they are susceptible, and, after supplying the Western country, do not furnish more than two hundred tons annually to the Atlantic States.

The annual importations from foreign countries of red and white lead, amount to 1,150 tons.

And those of lead itself, and of all other manufactures of lead, to 1,225 tons.

The principal American manufactures are those of shot, and colors of lead. Of the first, there are two establishments on a large scale at Philadelphia, and another in Louisiana, which are more than sufficient to supply the whole demand, stated at six hundred tons a year. Five hundred and sixty tons of red and white lead, litharge, and some other preparations of that metal, are made in Philadelphia alone. A repeal of the duty of one cent. per pound on lead, and an equalization of that on the manufactures of lead, by charging them all with the two cents per pound laid on white and red lead, is asked by the manufacturers.

Various other paints and colors are also prepared in Philadelphia, and some other places.

Tin, japanned, plated Wares.

The manufacture of tin ware is very extensive, and Connecticut supplies the greater part of the United States with that article; but the sheets are always imported. The manufacture of plated ware, principally for coach makers and saddlers, employs at Philadelphia 73 workmen; and the amount annually made there, exceeds one hundred thousand dollars. There are other similar establishments at New York, Baltimore, Boston, and Charleston.

Gunpowder.

Saltpetre is found in Virginia, Kentucky, and some other of the Western States and Territories; but it is principally imported from the East Indies. The manufacture of gunpowder is nearly, and may at any moment be made altogether adequate to the consumption; the importation of foreign powder amounting only to 200,000 pounds, and the exportation of American powder to 100,000 pounds. The manufacture of Brandywine, which employs a capital of $75,000 and 36 workmen, and is considered as the most perfect, makes alone 225,000 lbs. annually, and might make 600,000 lbs. if there was a demand for it. Two others, near Baltimore, have a capital of $100,000, and make 450,000 lbs. of a quality said lately to be equal to any imported. There are several other powder mills in Pennsylvania and other places; but the total amount of gunpowder made in the United States, is not ascertained.

Earthen and Glass Ware.

A sufficient quantity of the coarser species of pottery is made every where; and information has been received of four manufactures of a finer kind lately established. One at Philadelphia, with a capital of $11,000, manufactures a species similar to that made in Staffordshire, in England, and the others, in Chester county, in Pennsylvania, in New Jersey, and on the Ohio, make various kinds of queensware.

Information has been obtained of ten glass manufactures, which employ about 140 glass blowers, and make annually twenty-seven thousand boxes of window glass, containing, each, 100 square feet of glass. That of Boston, makes crown glass equal to any imported: all the other make green or German glass, worth 15 per cent. less; that of Pittsburgh, uses coal, and all the others, wood for fuel.

The annual importations of foreign window glass, amount to 27,000 boxes; the extension of the domestic manufacture, which supplies precisely one half of the consumption, being prevented by the want of workmen.

Some of those manufactures, make also green bottles and other wares; and two works, employing together six glass blowers, have been lately erected at Pittsburgh, and make decanters, tumblers, and every other description of flint glass of a superior quality.

Chemical Preparations.

Copper is extracted, in large quantities, from pyrites in Vermont, New Jersey, and Tennessee. About 200,000 pounds of oil of vitriol and other acids, are annually manufactured in a single establishment at Philadelphia. Various other preparations and drugs, are also made there, and in some other places; and the annual amount exported, exceeds 30,000 dollars in value.

Salt.

The salt springs of Onondaga and Cayuga, in the State of New York, furnish about 300,000 bushels a year; and the quantity may be increased in proportion to the demand. Those of the Western States and Territories, supply about an equal quantity; that known by the name of the Wabash Saline, which belongs to the United States, making now 130,000 bushels. Valuable discoveries have also lately been made on the banks of the Kenhawa. But the annual importation of foreign salt amounts to more than three millions of bushels, and cannot be superseded by American salt, unless it be made along the sea coast. The works in the State of Massachusetts are declining, and cannot proceed, unless the duty on foreign salt should again be laid. It is necessary to shelter the works from the heavy summer rains by light roofs moving on rollers. This considerably increases the expense; and it appears that the erection of ten thousand superficial square feet, costs one thousand dollars, and that they produce only two hundred bushels a year. A more favorable result is anticipated on the coast of North Carolina, on account of the difference in the climate; and works covering 275,000 square feet have been lately erected there.

Miscellaneous.

Respecting the other manufactures enumerated in the former part of this report, no important or correct information has been received, except as relates to the two following:

Straw bonnets and hats are made with great success; and a small district in Rhode Island and Massachusetts, annually exports to other parts of the Union, to the amount of 250,000 dollars. See communication N.

Several attempts have been made to print calicoes; but it

does not seem that the manufacturers can, without additional duties, stand the competition of similar foreign articles. The difficulties under which they labor are stated in the petition of the calico printers of Philadelphia to Congress. A considerable capital has been vested in an establishment near Baltimore, which can print 12,000 yards a week and might be considerably extended, if the profits and the demand afforded sufficient encouragement.

From that imperfect sketch of American manufactures, it may, with certainty, be inferred that their annual product exceeds one hundred and twenty millions of dollars. And it is not improbable that the raw materials used, and the provisions and other articles consumed, by the manufacturers, create a home market for agricultural products not very inferior to that which arises from foreign demand. A result more favorable than might have been expected from a view of the natural causes which impede the introduction, and retard the progress of manufactures in the United States.

The most prominent of those causes are the abundance of land compared with the population, the high price of labor, and the want of a sufficient capital. The superior attractions of agricultural pursuits, the great extension of American commerce during the late European wars, and the continuance of habits after the causes which produced them have ceased to exist, may also be enumerated. Several of those obstacles have, however, been removed or lessened. The cheapness of provisions had always, to a certain extent, counterbalanced the high price of manual labor; and this is now, in many important branches, nearly superseded by the introduction of machinery; a great American capital has been acquired during the last twenty years; and the injurious violations of the neutral commerce of the United States, by forcing industry and capital into other channels, have broken inveterate habits, and given a general impulse, to which must be ascribed the great increase of manufactures during the two last years.

The revenue of the United States, being principally derived from duties on the importation of foreign merchandise, these have also operated as a premium in favor of American manufactures, whilst, on the other hand, the continuance of peace, and the frugality of Government, have rendered unnecessary any oppressive taxes, tending materially to enhance the price of labor, or impeding any species of industry.

No cause, indeed, has, perhaps, more promoted, in every respect, the general prosperity of the United States, than the absence of those systems of internal restrictions and monopoly which continue to disfigure the state of society in other countries. No law exists here, directly or indirectly, confining man to a particular occupation or place, or excluding any citizen from any branch, he may, at any time, think proper to pursue. Industry is, in every respect, perfectly free and unfettered; every species of trade, commerce, art, profession and manufacture, being equally opened to all, without requiring any previous regular apprenticeship, admission, or licence. Hence the progress of America has not been confined to the improvement of her agriculture, and to the rapid formation of new settlements and States in the wilderness; but her citizens have extended their commerce through every part of the globe, and carry on with complete success, even those branches for which a monopoly had heretofore been considered essentially necessary.

The same principle has also accelerated the introduction and progress of manufactures, and must ultimately give in that branch, as in all others, a decided superiority to the citizens of the United States over the inhabitants of countries oppressed by taxes, restrictions and monopolies. It is believed that, even at this time, the only powerful obstacle against which American manufactures have to struggle, arises from the vastly superior capital of the first manufacturing nation of Europe, which enables her merchants to give very long credits, to sell on small profits, and to make occasional sacrifices.

The information which has been obtained is not sufficient to submit, in conformity with the resolution of the House, the plan best calculated to protect and promote American manufactures. The most obvious means are bounties, increased duties on importation, and loans by Government.

Occasional premiums might be beneficial; but a general system of bounties is more applicable to articles exported than to those manufactured for home consumption.

The present system of duties may, in some respects, be equalized and improved, so as to protect some species of manufactures without effecting the revenue. But prohibitory duties are liable to the treble objection of destroying competition, of taxing the consumer, and of diverting capital and industry into channels generally less profitable to the nation than those which would have naturally been pursued by individual interest left to itself. A moderate increase will be less dangerous, and, if adopted, should be continued during a certain period; for the repeal of a duty once laid, materially injures those who have relied on its permanency, as has been exemplified in the salt manufacture.

Since, however, the comparative want of capital, is the principal obstacle to the introduction and advancement of manufactures in America, it seems that the most efficient, and most obvious remedy would consist in supplying that capital. For, although the extension of banks may give some assistance in that respect, their operation is limited to a few places, nor does it comport with the nature of those institutions to lend for periods as long as are requisite for the establishment of manufactures. The United States might create a circulating stock, bearing a low rate of interest, and lend it at par to manufacturers, on principles somewhat similar to that formerly adopted by the States of New York and Pennsylvania, in their *loan offices*. It is believed that a plan might be devised by which five millions of dollars a year, but not exceeding, in the whole, twenty millions, might be thus lent, without any material risk of ultimate loss, and without taxing or injuring any other part of the community.

THE BANK OF THE UNITED STATES

Gallatin never shared the agrarian prejudice against banks, nor the hostility of many of his Republican colleagues toward the Bank of the United States. He differed more with Jefferson on this issue, probably, than on any other. As Secretary of the Treasury, he worked closely with the Bank of the United States, which at his request founded branches in Washington and New Orleans for the convenience of the Treasury. From time to time he defended the Bank against Jefferson, who periodically resolved to abolish its "monopoly" by transferring government deposits to state banks. Once he ignored Jefferson's request that he draw up plans for an independent treasury system. He was keenly aware of the security and convenience which the Bank afforded to the government and its value as a source of loans in event of war.

27. REPORT ON THE BANK OF
THE UNITED STATES

March 3, 1809

During the later years of his administration of the Treasury the Bank became an acute political issue. Its charter, granted

---

in 1791, was to expire in 1811. At Gallatin's suggestion the Bank petitioned Congress for a renewal in April 1808. Waiting until after the national elections, Gallatin addressed the Senate in connection with the memorial assigned to him for a report. He reviewed the Bank's record, found it good, and strongly advocated renewal of the charter. Gallatin's position was that whatever its faults, particularly the fact that nearly three-fourths of its $10,000,000 capital was held by foreigners, they could be corrected by a new charter. Under the plan he offered, the capital was to be increased to $30,000,000 and the Bank obliged to lend as much as $18,000,000 to the government on demand, a sum equal to three-fifths of its capital. This would ensure a large credit in event of war, which was perennially on the horizon in these years. Gallatin also proposed changes in organization calculated to make the Bank a truly national institution and bring it more into line with Republican principles. States as well as individuals were to be shareholders and were to participate in the management. The new shares created by enlarging the capitalization were to be confined to American citizens and state governments; their holdings would overbalance shares held by foreigners. The national bank would truly be, as Hamilton intended, a bond of union.

The Secretary of the Treasury, to whom was referred the memorial of the stockholders of the Bank of the United States, praying for a renewal of their charter, which will expire on the 14th day of March, 1811, respectfully submits the following report:

The Bank of the United States was incorporated by act of March 2d, 1791, with a capital of ten millions of dollars, divided into 25,000 shares, of 400 dollars each. Two millions of dollars were subscribed by the United States, and paid in ten equal annual instalments. Of the eight millions of dollars subscribed by individuals, two millions were paid in specie and six millions in six per cent. stock of the United States. Two thousand four hundred and ninety-three of the shares belonging to Government were sold in the years 1796 and 1797, at an advance of 25 per cent.; two hundred and eighty-seven were sold in the year 1797, at an advance of 20 per cent., and the other two thousand two hundred and twenty shares in the year 1802, at an advance of 45 per cent.; making together, exclusively of the dividends, a profit of 671,860 dollars to the United States. The greater part of the six per cent. stock, originally paid by the stockholders, has since been sold by the bank: a portion has been redeemed by Government, by the operation of the annual reimbursement, and the bank retains, at present, only a sum of 2,231,598 dollars, in six per cent. stock.

About eighteen thousand shares of the bank stock are held by persons residing abroad, who are, by the charter, excluded from the right of voting. The stockholders resident within the United States, and who have the exclusive control over the institution, hold only seven thousand shares, or little more than one fourth part of its capital. They appoint annually twenty-five directors of the bank itself, which is established at Philadelphia; and those directors have the entire management of the discounts and other transactions of the institution in that city, and the general superintendence and appointment of the directors and cashiers of the offices of discount and deposite, established in other places. There are at present eight of those offices, viz: at Boston, New York, Baltimore, Norfolk, Charleston, Savannah, the city of Washington, and New Orleans. The two last were established at the request of the Secretary of the Treasury.

The profits of a bank arise from the interest received on the loans made, either to Government or to individuals; and they exceed six per cent., or the rate of interest at which the loans are made, because every bank lends, not only the whole of its capital, but, also, a portion of the moneys deposited for safe keeping in its vaults, either by Government or by individuals. For every sum of money thus deposited, the party making that deposite either receives the amount in bank notes, or obtains a credit on the books of the bank. In either case he has the same right, at any time, to withdraw his deposite; in the first case, on presentation and surrender of the bank notes; in the other case, by drawing on the bank for the amount. Bank notes and credits on the books of the bank, arise, therefore, equally from deposites, although the credits alone are, in common parlance, called deposites; and the aggregate of those credits, and of the bank notes issued, constitutes the circulating medium substituted by the banking operations to money; for payments from one individual to another are equally made by drafts on the bank, or by the delivery of bank notes. Experience has taught the directors what portion of the money thus deposited they may lend, or, in other words, how far they may, with safety, extend their discounts beyond the capital of the bank, and what amount of specie it is necessary they should keep in their vaults. The profits, and, therefore, the dividends of a bank, will increase in proportion as the directors will increase loans of the moneys deposited, and suffer the amount of specie on hand to diminish. Moderate dividends, when not produced by some particular cause, which checks the circulation of bank paper, are the best evidence of the safety of the institution, and of the wisdom of its direction.

The annexed table of all the dividends made by the Bank of the United States, since its establishment, shows that they have, on an average, been at the rate of $8\frac{3}{8}$ (precisely $8\frac{13}{34}$) per cent. a year, and proves, that the bank has not, in any considerable degree, used the public deposites for the purpose of extending its discounts.

From what has been premised, it appears that the property

of a bank in full operation consists of three general items, viz: 1st. outstanding debts, consisting principally of the notes payable at sixty days, which have been discounted at the bank; 2dly, specie in the vaults; 3dly, buildings necessary for the institution. On the other hand, the bank owes, 1st. to the stockholders, the amount of the capital stock originally subscribed, payable only in case of the dissolution of the institution; 2dly, to Government or individuals, the whole amount of moneys deposited, payable on demand, and including both the credits on the bank books, commonly called deposites, and the bank notes in circulation. The account is balanced by the amount of undivided profits and accruing discounts, which constitute the fund for defraying current expenses, for paying subsequent dividends, and for covering contingent losses.

The following statement of the situation of the Bank of the United States, including its branches, exhibits the true amount of public stock, which is still held by the institution, of the cost of its buildings, and lots of ground, and of the undivided surplus or contingent fund, subsequent to the dividend made in January last. But the amount of loans to individuals, or discounts, of specie in the vaults, and of moneys deposited, including both the credits on the bank books, commonly called deposites, and the bank notes in circulation, is taken on a medium; and, so far as relates, on the credit side of the account, to specie on hand, and, on the debit side, to deposites, is several millions of dollars less than it happens to be at this moment; both having been swelled much beyond the average by the embargo, and by the unusually large balance in the treasury, which is principally deposited in the bank. Some minor items, arising from accidental circumstances, are omitted, for the sake of perspicuity.

It sufficiently appears, from that general view, that the affairs of the Bank of the United States, considered as a moneyed institution, have been wisely and skilfully managed.

Cr.

I. Debts due to the bank, viz:

  1. Six per cent. stock of the United States, being the residue of that part of the original subscription paid in public stocks, which is still held by the bank, - - $ 2,230,000

  2. Loans to individuals, consisting chiefly of discounted notes, payable at sixty days, and, in some instances, of bonds and mortgages taken in order to secure doubtful debts, - - 15,000,000

  3. Due by banks incorporated by the States, - 800,000

    $18,030,000

II. Specie in the vaults, - 5,000,000

III. Cost of lots of ground and buildings erected, 480,000

  Total Credits, $23,510,000

Dr.

I. Capital stock of the bank, payable to the stockholders, whenever the institution may be dissolved, - $10,000,000

II. Moneys deposited, viz:

  1. Credits on the bank books, commonly called deposites, including the deposites both by Government and by individuals, - $ 8,500,000

  2. Bank notes in circulation, - 4,500,000

    13,000,000

  Total debtor, - $23,000,000

Balance, being the amount of undivided profits, commonly called the "contingent fund," and applicable to cover losses which may arise from bad debts or other contingencies, and to extra dividends, - $ 510,000

The advantages derived by Government from the bank, are nearly of the same nature with those obtained by individuals, who transact business with similar institutions, and may be reduced to the following heads:

1. *Safe-keeping of the public moneys.*—This applies not only to moneys already in the treasury, but, also, to those in the hands of the principal collectors, of the commissioners of loans, and of several other officers, and affords one of the best securities against delinquencies.

2. *Transmission of public moneys.*—As the collectors will always, in various quarters of the extensive territory of the Union, either exceed or fall short of the expenditures in the same places, a perpetual transmission of money, or purchases of remittances at the risk and expense of the United States, would become necessary, in order to meet those demands; but this is done by the bank, at its own risk and expense, for every place where one of its branches is established, which embraces all payments of any importance.

3. *Collection of the revenue.*—The punctuality of payments introduced by the banking system, and the facilities afforded by the bank to the importers indebted for revenue bonds, are amongst the causes which have enabled the United States to collect, with so great facility, and with so few losses, the large revenue derived from the impost.

4. *Loans.*—Although the prosperity of past years has enabled Government, during the present administration, to meet all the public demands without recurring to loans, the bank had, heretofore, been eminently useful in making the advances, which, under different circumstances, were necessary. There was a time, when, exclusively of the six per cent. stock held by the institution, as part of the original subscription, the loans obtained by Government from the bank, amounted to 6,200,000 dollars. And a similar disposition has been repeatedly evinced, whenever the aspect of public affairs has rendered it proper to ascertain whether new loans might, if wanted, be obtained.

The numerous banks now established, under the authority of the several States, might, it is true, afford considerable assistance to Government in its fiscal operations. There is none, however, which could effect the transmission of public moneys with the same facility, and to the same extent, as the Bank of the United States is enabled to do, through its several branches. The superior capital of that institution offers, also, a greater security against any possible losses, and greater resources in relation to loans. Nor is it eligible, that the General Government should, in respect to its own operations, be entirely dependent on institutions over which it has no control whatever. A National Bank, deriving its charter from the National Legislature, will, at all times, and under every emergency, feel stronger inducements, both from interest and from a sense of duty, to afford to the Union every assistance within its power.

The strongest objection against the renewal of the charter seems to arise from the great portion of the bank stock held by foreigners—not on account of any influence it gives them over the institution, since they have no vote—but of the high rate of interest payable by America to foreign countries, on the portion thus held. If the charter is not renewed, the principal of that portion, amounting to about 7,200,000 dollars, must, at once, be remitted abroad; but, if the charter is renewed, dividends, equal to an interest of about 8½ per cent. a year, must be annually remitted in the same manner. The renewal of the charter will, in that respect, operate, in a national point of view, as a foreign loan, bearing an interest of 8½ per cent. a year.

That inconvenience might, perhaps, be removed, by a modification in the charter, providing for the repayment of that portion of the principal by a new subscription to the same amount, in favor of citizens; but it does not, at all events, appear sufficient to outweigh the manifest public advantages derived from a renewal of the charter.

The conditions in favor of the public, on which this should be granted, are the next subject of consideration.

The nett profit annually derived by the stockholders, from a renewal of the charter, is equal to the difference between the annual dividends and the market rate of interest. Supposing this to continue at six per cent. during the period granted by the extension of the charter, and the dividends to be on an average at the rate of 8½ per cent., that profit will be 2½ per cent. a year. If the charter be extended twenty years, the value of the privilege will be equal to an annuity of 2½ per cent. on the capital, that is to say, 250,000 dollars, for twenty years; and such annuity being payable semi-annually, is worth almost 2,890,000 dollars. This, however, would be much more than any bank would give for a charter, as it would leave it nothing but the right of dividing at the rate of six per cent. a year, which the stockholders have without a charter. It is believed, that they would not be willing to give even half that sum for the extension; and that about 1,250,000 dollars may be considered as the maximum, which could be obtained, if it was thought eligible to sell the renewal of the charter for a fixed sum of money.

It is, however, presumed, that the decision on the conditions, which may be annexed to an extension of the charter, will be directed by considerations of a much greater importance than the payment of such sum into the treasury. The object will, undoubtedly, be to give to the institution all the public utility of which it is susceptible, and to derive from it permanent and solid advantages, rather than mere temporary aid. Under these impressions, the following suggestions are respectfully submitted:

    I. That the bank should pay interest to the United States, on the public deposites, whenever they shall exceed a certain sum, which might perhaps be fixed at about three millions of dollars.

    II. That the bank should be bound, whenever required, to

lend to the United States a sum not exceeding three-fifths of its capital, at a rate of interest not exceeding six per cent.; the amount of such loan or loans to be paid by the bank in instalments, not exceeding a certain sum, monthly, and to be reimbursed at the pleasure of Government.

III. That the capital stock of the bank should be increased to thirty millions of dollars, in the following manner, viz:

    1. Five millions of dollars to be subscribed by citizens of the United States, under such regulations as would make an equitable apportionment amongst the several States and territories.

    2. Fifteen millions to be subscribed by such States as may desire it, and under such equitable apportionment amongst the several States as may be provided by law; and a branch to be established in each subscribing State, if applied for by the State.

    3. The payments, either by individuals or States, to be either in specie or in public stock of the United States, at such rates as may be provided by law.

    4. The subscribing States to pay their subscription in ten annual instalments, or sooner if it suits their convenience, but to receive dividends in proportion only to the amount of subscription actually paid; and their shares of bank stock not to be transferable.

IV. That some share should be given in the direction to the General and State Governments, the General Government appointing a few directors in the general direction, and the Government of each subscribing State appointing a few directors in the direction of the branch established in such State.

The result of that plan would be, 1st., that the United States, receiving an interest on the public deposites, might, without inconvenience, accumulate, during years of peace and prosperity, a treasure sufficient to meet periods of war and calamity, and, thereby, avoid the necessity of adding, by increased taxes, to the distresses of such periods. Secondly, that they might rely on a loan of eighteen millions of dollars, on any sudden emergency. Thirdly, that the payment of the greater part of the proposed increase of capital, being made in ten annual instalments, that increase would be gradual, and not more rapid than may be required by the progressive state of the country. Fourthly, that the bank itself would form an additional bond of common interest and union, amongst the several States.

Dividends on United States' Bank Stock

No.			Rate per cent.	No.			Rate per cent.
1	July	1792	4	18	January	1801	6
2	January	1793	4	19	July	1801	4
3	July	1793	3⅝	20	January	1802	4½
4	January	1794	3⅞	21	July	1802	4½
5	July	1794	4	22	January	1803	4½
6	January	1795	4	23	July	1803	4
7	July	1795	4	24	January	1804	4½
8	January	1796	4	25	July	1804	4
9	July	1796	4	26	January	1805	4
10	January	1797	4	27	July	1805	4
11	July	1797	4	28	January	1806	4
12	January	1798	5	29	July	1806	4
13	July	1798	4	30	January	1807	6
14	January	1799	4	31	July	1807	4
15	July	1799	4	32	January	1808	4
16	January	1800	4	33	July	1808	4
17	July	1800	4	34	January	1809	4

28. LETTER TO WILLIAM H. CRAWFORD,

CHAIRMAN OF THE SENATE

January 30, 1811

Congress took no action until early in 1811 when the expiration of the Bank's charter was imminent. War was also imminent. Unsupported by President Madison, Gallatin fought hard against old Virginia Republicans who called the Bank a "British institution," also against middle state and New England banking interests which wanted to destroy the Bank of the United States' monopoly of federal deposits. After the House denied a recharter by a vote of 65 to 64 Gallatin appealed to the Senate. The vote was taken in the Senate on February 20, ending in a 17 to 17 tie which was broken by Vice-President George Clinton's negative. The recharter failed, leaving the government to face the War of 1812 with diminished resources.

Having already, in a report to the Senate, of 2d March, 1809, expressed my opinion in favor of a renewal of the charter of the Bank of the United States, an opinion which remains unchanged, I can only add a few explanatory remarks in answer to the inquiries of the committee, as stated in your letter of yesterday.

The banking system is now firmly established; and, in its

American State Papers, Finance, II, 481.

ramifications, extends to every part of the United States. Under that system, the assistance of banks appears to me necessary for the punctual collection of the revenue, and for the safe keeping and transmission of public moneys. That the punctuality of payments is principally due to banks, is a fact generally acknowledged. It is, to a certain degree, enforced by the refusal of credit at the custom house, so long as a former revenue bond, actually due, remains unpaid. But I think, nevertheless, that, in order to ensure that precision in the collection, on which depends a corresponding discharge of the public engagements, it would, if no use was made of banks, be found necessary to abolish, altogether, the credit now given on the payment of duties—a measure which would affect the commercial capital, and fall heavily on the consumers. That the public moneys are safer by being weekly deposited in banks, instead of accumulating in the hands of collectors, is self-evident. And their transmission, whenever this may be wanted, for the purpose of making payments in other places than those of collection, cannot, with any convenience, be effected, on a large scale, in an extensive country, except through the medium of banks, or of persons acting as bankers.

The question, therefore, is, whether a bank, incorporated by the United States, or a number of banks, incorporated by the several States, be most convenient for those purposes.

State banks may be used, and must, in case of a non-renewal of the charter, be used by the treasury. Preparatory arrangements have already been made to that effect; and it is believed that the ordinary business will be transacted, through their medium, with less convenience, and, in some respects, with perhaps less safety than at present, but without any insuperable difficulty. The difference, with respect to safety, results from the organization of the Bank of the United States, by which it is responsible for the money deposited in any of its branches, whilst each of the State banks, which may be employed, will be responsible only for the sums in its own hands. Thus, the Bank of the United States is now answerable for the moneys collected at New Orleans, and deposited there in its branch—a security which will be lost under a different arrangement. Nor will the United States have any other control over the manner in which the business of the banks may be conducted, than what may result from the power of withdrawing the public deposites; and they will lose that which a charter, or a dependence on the General Government for a charter, now gives over the Bank of the United States. The facility of obtaining such accommodations as may, at times be wanted, will, for the same reason, be lessened, and the national power will, to that extent, be impaired. It may be added, that, even for the ordinary business of receiving and transmitting public moneys, the use of a State bank may be forbidden by the State; and that loans to the United States are, by many of the charters, forbidden, without a special permission from the State.

As it is not perceived, on the other hand, that a single advantage will accrue to the public from the change, no reason presents itself, on the ground of expediency, why an untried system should be substituted to one under which the treasury business had so long been conducted with perfect security to the United States, and great convenience not only to the officers, but also to all those who have had payments of a public nature to make or to receive.

It does not seem necessary to advert to the particular objections made against the present charter, as these may easily be obviated by proper alterations. What has been called a National Bank, or, in other words, a new Bank of the United States, instead of the existing one, may be obtained by such alterations. The capital may be extended, and more equally distributed; new stockholders may be substituted to the foreigners, as had been suggested in the report of 2d March, 1809; and any other modifications which may be thought expedient may be introduced, without interrupting the operations of the institution now in force, and without disturbing all the commercial concerns of the country.

If, indeed, the Bank of the United States could be removed without affecting either its numerous debtors, the other moneyed institutions, or the circulation of the country, the ordinary fiscal operations of Government would not be materially deranged, and might be carried on by means of another general bank, or of State banks. But the transition will be attended with much individual, and probably with no inconsiderable public injury. It is impossible that an institution which circulates thirteen millions of dollars, and to whom the merchants owe fourteen, should terminate its operations, particularly in the present unfavorable state of the American commerce, and after the great losses lately experienced abroad, without giving a serious shock to commercial, banking, and national credit. It is not intended to overrate the extent of an evil which there are no certain data to appreciate. And, without expatiating on the fatal and unavoidable effects on individuals; without dwelling on the inconvenience of repaying, at this time, to Europe, a capital of seven millions; and without adverting to other possible dangers, of a more general nature, it appears sufficient to state that the same body of men who owe fourteen millions of dollars to the bank, owe, also, ten or twelve to the United States, on which the receipts into the treasury, for this year, altogether depend; and that, exclusively of absolute failures, it is improbable that both debts can be punctually paid at the same time. Nor must it be forgotten that the approaching non-importation will considerably lessen the efficiency of the provision, by which subsequent credits are refused to importers who have not discharged former revenue bonds. Upon the whole, a perfect conviction is felt that, in the critical situation of the country, new evils ought not to be superadded, and a perilous experiment be attempted, unless required by an imperious necessity.

In these hasty remarks, I have not adverted to the question

of constitutionality, which is not a subject of discussion for the Secretary of the Treasury. Permit me, however, for my own sake, simply to state, that the bank charter having, for a number of years, been acted upon, or acquiesced in, as if constitutional, by all the constituted authorities of the nation, and thinking, myself, the use of banks to be at present necessary for the exercise of the legitimate powers of the General Government, the continuation of a bank of the United States has not, in the view which I have been able to take of the subject, appeared to me to be unconstitutional.

PART FIVE

Secretary of the Treasury
1801–1813 (II)

The war in Europe, renewed in 1803, had by 1805 reached a stalemate. Napoleon was master of the Continent, but Britain controlled the sea. Since neither antagonist could strike directly at the other, they carried on the war with economic weapons, and both nations pursued their objectives by operating upon neutral commerce. The main victim was the United States.

For seven years the nation exhausted every resource short of war, often to its own injury, to protect its commerce and preserve its neutrality, but received nothing more than rebuffs and deception from the great powers. What unity the Republicans once possessed steadily eroded under the stress of events. Congress was demoralized by factions within the majority party and the disaffection of the Federalist minority. At length, supported by a newly elected group of "War Hawks," President Madison, in 1812, proposed a declaration of war against Britain as the only alternative. The proposal was adopted June 18 after long debate by a vote of 74 to 49 in the House and 19 to 13 in the Senate.

AMERICAN RIGHTS: THE LEOPARD-
CHESAPEAKE AFFAIR, 1807

*A particular grievance the United States had against Britain
was her impressment of American seamen. British cruisers
hovered about the American coast, stopping American merchant vessels and taking off British nationals found among
their crews. During the whole course of the European war
after 1793 an estimated 9,000 American citizens were seized
as "deserters" and forced into British service.*

*In the summer of 1807 the British warship, Leopard, hunt-
ing deserters from the British navy, opened fire upon the
American frigate, Chesapeake, outside Chesapeake Bay when
the American commander refused to permit search. The Chesapeake was unprepared to fight and surrendered after the loss
of three men killed and eighteen wounded. This humiliating
episode dramatized grievances against British impressments
and drove the United States to the verge of war.*

29. LETTER TO JOSEPH H. NICHOLSON

July 17, 1807

*Gallatin shared the nation's indignation. However important
to him were economy and discharging the national debt, they
were secondary to upholding national honor. Believing war
inevitable, he approached the banks in order to obtain loans.*

Writings, I, 338–340.

... With you, I believe that war is inevitable; and there can be but one opinion on the question whether the claims of the parties prior to the attack on the Chesapeake should be a subject of discussion. There were but two courses to be taken, —either to consider the attack as war, and retaliate immediately, or, on the supposition that that act might be that of an unauthorized officer, to ask simply, and without discussion, disavowal, satisfaction, and security against a recurrence of outrages. The result will, in my opinion, be the same, for Great Britain will not, I am confident, give either satisfaction or security; but the latter mode, which, as you may have perceived by the President's proclamation and his answer to military corps, has been adopted, was recommended not only by the nature of our Constitution, which does not make the President arbiter of war, but also by the practice of civilized nations; and the cases of Turk's Island, Falkland Islands, Nootka Sound, &c., are in point in that respect. Add to this that the dissatisfaction caused by that course operates only against the Administration, and that the other will produce an unanimity in support of the war which would not otherwise have existed. It will also make our cause completely popular with the Baltic powers, and may create new enemies to Britain in that quarter. Finally, four months were of importance to us, both by diminishing the losses of our merchants and for preparations of defence and attack.

I will, however, acknowledge that on that particular point I have not bestowed much thought, for, having considered from the first moment war as a necessary result, and the preliminaries appearing to me but matters of form, my faculties have been exclusively applied to the preparations necessary to meet the times; and although I am not very sanguine as to the brilliancy of our exploits, the field where we can act without a navy being very limited, and perfectly aware that a war in a great degree passive and consisting of privations will become very irksome to the people, I feel no apprehension of the ultimate result. We will be poorer, both as a nation and as a government, our debt and taxes will increase, and our progress in every respect be interrupted. But all those evils are not only not to be put in competition with the independence and honor of the nation; they are, moreover, temporary, and very few years of peace will obliterate their effects. Nor do I know whether the awakening of nobler feelings and habits than avarice and luxury might not be necessary to prevent our degenerating, like the Hollanders, into a nation of mere calculators. In fact, the greatest mischiefs which I apprehend from the war are the necessary increase of executive power and influence, the speculations of contractors and jobbers, and the introduction of permanent military and naval establishments.

Money we will want to carry on the war; our revenue will be cut up; new and internal taxes will be slow and not sufficiently productive; we must necessarily borrow. This is not pleasing particularly to me; but it must be done; for whilst we must avoid expenses for inefficient operations and waste, as far as is practicable, the expense, provided we can by any method whatever defray it, must never be an objection to any necessary measure of defence, or to any rational active operations against the enemy. We have about eight millions in the Treasury, and from a very rough estimate I think that we will want to borrow about ten millions annually whilst the war lasts; rather less, however, the first year, although it will be the most expensive. People will fight, but they never give their money for nothing. Patriotic gifts and loyalty loans cannot be depended upon; we must buy money at its market price, and in order to borrow cheaper it will be necessary to keep up the price of stocks by occasional purchases. All this is, of course, between ourselves. But as I think that our first loans must be obtained from the banks, and you are a bank director, I will thank you to sound the ground on that subject. With the Bank of the United States I will treat separately;

but the best course would perhaps [be] that the directors of all the other banks of Baltimore should consult together and see what in their opinion might be loaned. From the extent of banking capital there and the great diminution which will take place in commerce, and therefore in their business, I am confident they might lend one-half of their capital to government without any inconvenience either to the mercantile interest or to themselves. The periods both of their advance and of the reimbursement, as well as the manner of throwing the thing into form, would be a matter of detail. Will you consult with General Smith, who is connected with other banks, on that subject? I will write to him about it to-day or to-morrow. I mean to make similar informal overtures in the other seaports; and it would have a good effect both here and abroad to be able to state to Congress that resources are already prepared. The war may be of shorter continuance if the enemy receives an early impression that we are willing and able to hold out.

30. LETTER TO THOMAS JEFFERSON

July 25, 1807

On the assumption that war was imminent Gallatin drafted a long, hasty prospectus for defensive and offensive action, part of which is reproduced here. His plans for invading Canada exhibit a grasp of major strategy and a degree of energy sadly lacking in the prosecution of the war against Britain when it came in 1812. Gallatin, however, supposed

---

Writings, I, 340–350.

that the burden of military operations would fall on New England, whose disaffection in 1812 crippled the military effort. His confidence suggests that 1807 would have been a better time to fight Britain. It is noteworthy that he did not envisage any postponement of payments on the debt.

I enclose a list of our seaports, showing, by the respective amount of tonnage belonging to each, of their annual exports, and of their annual payments into the Treasury, their relative importance as to navigation, commerce, and revenue.

I wanted also to take a general view of all the measures for defence and attack which might become a proper subject of consideration at this time; because, however incorrect I might be in many respects, it was the best mode not to forget anything. But I have been so unwell and my head so muddy that I was unable to analyze the subject in a manner satisfactory to myself. Such as it is, I, however, enclose my memorandum, as it may at all events contain something which might otherwise have been omitted. . . .

Offensive operations may, in the first instance, be directed against Upper Canada, Lower Canada, New Brunswick, Nova Scotia, Bermuda, New Providence, Newfoundland.

Upper Canada—necessary to be taken in order to cover our northern frontier and to ruin the British fur-trade. Points of attack designated by nature,—Detroit and Niagara. Detroit may be approached:

1. Through the wilderness from Upper Miami or Scioto.
2. More easily by land and water from Connecticut settlements on Lake Erie. The provisions and magazines must necessarily be sent that way. Provisions will be supplied by Connecticut Reserve, and settlements on Ohio, Alleghany, Muskingum.

The force may be drawn, if first route, from Ohio and Kentucky; but if from Lake Erie, from Ohio and, perhaps, partly from Pennsylvania. Fifteen hundred men, in addition to Michigan militia, appear sufficient. Subsequent operations in that quarter will be:

Reduction of Fort Huron and Grand Portage, destroying fortifications, intercepting the fur returns in the spring.

Securing the country against the Indians and disaffected Canadians, by a small naval force on Lakes Michigan and Huron; a small, strong post at St. Mary's Fall. Strong detachments, say 500 each, at Detroit, Michilimackinac, and Chicago.

Niagara may be approached:

1. From Alleghany, by which route Western Pennsylvania militia may march.

2. From Genesee, by land and Lake Ontario, which is the route of provisions and magazines.

The force must be drawn from Upper Pennsylvania, on Alleghany and Susquehanna, and from western parts of New York.

Its extent must depend on the British force and temper of inhabitants.

Lower Canada must be taken as far down as Montreal, to cut up the communication with Indians and Upper Canada.

The taking of Quebec will better secure the object. At all events, it would be better to have the seat of war between Montreal and Quebec than predatory incursions at home.

Points of attack are, Kingston, at lower end of Lake Ontario.

Montreal and Point Sorel, by Champlain and St. John.

Quebec, by Kennebec, &c.

Kingston and adjoining country must be attacked by militia from the adjacent New York settlements, which will afford also the provisions. Will 500 men be sufficient? Montreal, the great point of attack, must of course be attacked by Lake Champlain, through which troops, provisions, artillery, and magazines will be transported.

The force to be drawn from New York can be but moderate,

as part of the militia of that State will be employed against Niagara and Kingston, and nothing can be taken from the city and its vicinity. But in the employment of militia, the distance from which they are taken becomes so important a point of expense, that a part must be taken from that State. Vermont, in the first place, and a portion of the nearest parts of New Hampshire, Massachusetts, and Connecticut, should supply the rest. If more are wanted, New Jersey and Pennsylvania must furnish it. The mass of New Hampshire, Massachusetts, and Rhode Island must be reserved for New Brunswick and Nova Scotia. From the States south of Pennsylvania I would draw nothing for the North, because they are too distant and not used to the climate; [besides] that none can be spared from the negro country, and they will be wanted for Norfolk, Charleston, and Savannah, and New Orleans.

The extent of the force must depend, for this winter, on the question whether Quebec can be attacked. Considering the lateness of the season when active operations can commence, I should think that if regular approaches are necessary, that place cannot be attacked before spring. If that opinion is correct, 4 or 5000 men might be sufficient to take and occupy the country as low down as Trois Rivières. Quebec may be approached by Kennebec or Montreal. But I think that an operation by the first route should be only for a feint, and to distract and divide the force of the enemy. The principal attack must be from Montreal. The British force does not exceed two regiments of regulars, but may be reinforced even this autumn, and will certainly be so early in the spring. Our operations should therefore commence against that place extremely early, which will require every preparation of artillery for a siege— provisions and magazines—to be made in winter, and moved as far down St. Lawrence as possible. Not less than 8000 men will be wanted to take and afterwards to defend the country. But I think that if we take Quebec, the fortifications should, on the land side, be levelled to the ground, depending on our troops to defend the country, and disabling the enemy from occupying so strong a place against us if they shall make an attempt to retake Canada. In that case, if they have no strong place, they must evacuate the country before winter, or run the risk of all being taken in winter. It is improbable, because it would be impolitic on their part, that they shall attempt to reconquer the country; and perhaps a less force may be sufficient on that account to defend it. A naval force calculated to defend the river above a given point should make a part of the system. It will also be necessary to consider what should be the point where to retreat and make a stand in case of disaster, and to provide accordingly—Quere, Point Sorel, or some point below it, which may defend the approaches both to Montreal and to Lake Champlain.

New Brunswick is important as leading us to Nova Scotia, and as cutting off the communication between that colony and Quebec. It can only be approached from Maine by land and water. Provisions must be taken from Portland and Kennebec by water. The eastern county of Maine cannot supply them. Some small armed vessels may be necessary. If the brigs in the Mediterranean come in time, they would answer. The British force consists of only a regiment of fencibles. Our force, if this winter's operations be limited to St. John's, which is only forty miles from our boundary, may be drawn entirely from Maine and New Hampshire.

Fort Cumberland on the isthmus is (I believe) 150 miles beyond St. John's River, intermediate country thinly inhabited, and bad roads. A considerable settlement in the vicinity of Fort Cumberland, both in New Brunswick and Nova Scotia. It would be important to make a lodgment there this winter. But it would require 4000 men to be secured, and all the provisions, artillery, magazines, must be transported by water. The reason why, if Nova Scotia is not attempted this winter, I think the occupation of New Brunswick, and particularly Cumberland, important is, that such position threatening Halifax will, even if we are unable to attack that place, compel the British to keep there all their land forces, and secure us against land attacks in our vulnerable southern points.

Nova Scotia is to us the most important colony to occupy, on account of Halifax, and the most difficult to take, on account of its peninsular situation, and of the difficulty and distance of land communication through the eastern part of Maine and New Brunswick. But so long as the British hold Halifax they will be able, by the superiority of their naval force, to blockade, during the greater part of the year, all our principal seaports, and particularly New York, including the Sound, Philadelphia, the Chesapeake, and Charleston. If we take it, the difficulty to refit and obtain refreshments will greatly diminish that evil, and enable us to draw some advantage from our small navy on our own coast. Add to this, that being compelled to keep a strong land force at Halifax, they will, whenever they may perceive that there is no immediate danger of attack from us, detach occasionally corps of 3 or 4000 men to co-operate with their fleet and make predatory descents in various parts.

Halifax is the point of attack, and may be approached, 1, by marching round via Cumberland, which will perhaps be the only practicable route, but, for reasons already mentioned, will prove a difficult route for provisions, artillery, &c.; 2, by landing at some of the harbors in the immediate vicinity of Halifax; which, considering the naval superiority of the British and the distance from our nearest port, appears not practicable; 3, by crossing Bay Fundy from the nearest seaport, and landing at Windsor in the Basin of Mines. The distance is short, and the passage may by watching a proper opportunity be effected. By this, the whole distance through the difficult parts of the march is avoided; and the port may be kept against naval attacks; for although you have 40 feet water, ships lie dry every tide; indeed, no large ship would venture there, and if she did would be destroyed. Windsor is the best settlement in the province, 40 miles from Halifax, and a good road; it lies also precisely on the road from Halifax (which forks there) to Cumberland and to Annapolis, each of which lies about 80 miles further,—the first northwest, the other southwest,—and are the two next best settlements. By landing at Windsor, the garrisons of those two places would be cut off, and Halifax reached in two or three days. It does not seem to me that it is more difficut or dangerous to cross Bay Fundy than to coast all around it, which must be done if the Cumberland road is taken. Of this, however, military men can alone judge, and by them, also, must be decided the question whether Halifax can be attempted this winter (which, for similar reasons to those stated in relation to Quebec, appears impracticable); and if not, whether a landing should be made this autumn at Windsor. In relation to those operations generally, it may be observed that two frigates as convoy either to Cumberland or Windsor might be risked. In that case, that from the Mediterranean and the Chesapeake might be used; the Chesapeake going whilst she can, first to New York, in order to conceal the object, and, at the moment of action, through the Sound, if necessary, to the eastward.

The force now at Halifax consists of two regiments of regulars and one fencible. But they may and undoubtedly will be reinforced this autumn and winter.

The force to be employed against Nova Scotia must necessarily be drawn principally from the New England States; and, whatever route be taken, 10 or 12,000 men seem necessary. A force not much inferior must be kept to defend it, and it will not be easy to supply it with provisions, &c. I should also think that the land fortifications should be destroyed, leaving only the forts and batteries which defend the harbor.

Bermuda and New Providence will be important, as affording stations to British privateers and affording refreshments to their fleet on our coast. I think they might both be taken by small armaments from the Southern States; Bermuda to be retained and garrisoned; the vessels and forts in Providence to be destroyed and the place evacuated. But whether the advantages be worth the expense and risk, particularly as relates to the permanent occupation of Bermuda, is a doubtful question.

Newfoundland.—It is true that a landing in summer would materially injure the fisheries for that year. But the British keep always for their protection a fleet of sufficient strength during that season. The object, being of a more remote nature, may be kept for future consideration. . . .

31. LETTER TO THOMAS JEFFERSON

October 21, 1807

Ordering British warships out of American waters, Jefferson instructed James Monroe, United States minister to London, to demand indemnities and renunciation of the right of impressment. To avoid an open break with Britain, however, Jefferson delayed calling a special session of Congress until war fever had abated. In October, preparing for the special session, he submitted to Gallatin the draft of a message he proposed to deliver. By this time Gallatin's indignation had subsided, and he well knew that the commercial centers of the nation shrank from the prospect of war. In any case, as a rational man, he preferred to negotiate. Taking exception to the bellicose temper of Jefferson's proposed message, he advised him to tone it down. Jefferson took his advice.

Writings, I, 358–361.

I have kept your message longer than usual, because my objections being less to details than to its general spirit, I was at a loss what alterations to submit to your consideration.

Instead of being written in the style of the proclamation, which has been almost universally approved at home and abroad, the message appears to me to be rather in the shape of a manifesto issued against Great Britain on the eve of a war, than such as the existing undecided state of affairs seems to require. It may either be construed into a belief that justice will be denied,—a result not to be anticipated in an official communication,—or it may be distorted into an eagerness of seeing matters brought to issue by an appeal to arms. Although it be almost certain that the expected answer will decide the question, yet unforeseen circumstances may protract its discussion; or the British government may, without acceding precisely to your ultimatum, take some new admissible ground which will require your sanction and delay the final arrangement. So long as any hope, however weak, remains of an honorable settlement, it is desirable that no act of the Executive may, by widening the breach, or unnecessarily hurting the pride of Britain, have a tendency to defeat it. Unless, therefore, some useful and important object can be obtained by the message in its present form, I would wish its general color and expression to be softened; nothing inserted but what is necessary for assisting Congress in their first deliberations, and to account for their early meeting; no recapitulation of former outrages further than as connected with the unratified treaty; no expression of a belief that war is highly probable, which seems either to presuppose absolute injustice on the part of Great Britain, or to acknowledge high pretensions on ours. For, unless some important object be in view, those may do harm, and cannot be productive of any substantial benefit. If the object be to urge Congress to make the necessary preparations for war, this may be attained by a direct and strong recommendation, founded not on the probability but on the uncertainty of the issue. If it be to incite them to a speedy declaration of war, this also seems premature, and may as effectually be done at its proper time when the answer of the British government will be communicated. It may be added that recommendations or incitements to war should not, under our Constitution, be given by the Executive without much caution; and, above all, that the precise manner and time of acting which Congress should adopt are subjects which have not yet been sufficiently examined. That the choice of the manner will not probably be left to us is true. That Great Britain will prefer actual war to any system of retaliation short of war which we might select, I do believe. Yet how far it may be proper to leave the choice to her deserves, at least, consideration. Public opinion abroad is to us highly valuable; at home it is indispensable. We will be universally justified in the eyes of the world, and unanimously supported by the nation, if the ground of war be England's refusal to disavow or to make satisfaction for the outrage on the Chesapeake. But I am confident that we will meet with a most formidable opposition should England do that and we should still declare war because she refuses to make the proposed arrangement respecting seamen. It is in that case that measures short of war may become proper, leaving to England, if she chooses, the odium of commencing an actual war. But although that policy may be questionable, and decisive measures, even under that contingency, be thought preferable, the question of time requires most serious consideration. Under an impression that this month would decide the question of war or peace, it was thought prudent to contemplate (rather than to prepare) immediate offensive operations. To strike a blow the moment war is begun is doubtless important; but it does not follow that war ought to be commenced at this very moment. So far as relates to Canada, it may as easily, and, considering the state of our preparations, I might say more easily be invaded and conquered in winter, or even early in the spring, than this autumn. European reinforcements cannot in the spring reach Montreal, much less Upper Canada, before they shall have been occupied by us. Quebec will certainly be reinforced before the season shall permit regular approaches. No advantage, therefore, will result in that respect from an immediate attack; no inconvenience from the declaration of war being somewhat delayed. In every other respect it is our interest that actual war should not be commenced by England this autumn; and as for the same reason it is her interest to commence it if she thinks it ultimately unavoidable, I wish not only that we may not declare it instantaneously, but that she and her government and her officers in America may, until the decision takes place, still consider the result as uncertain. The operations of war on the part of Great Britain will consist in the capture of our vessels, attacks on our most exposed seaports, and defense of Canada. On our part, unable either to protect our commerce or to meet their fleets, our offensive operations must, by sea, be confined to privateers; we must as far as practicable draw in those vessels we cannot defend; place our ports in a situation to repel mere naval aggressions; organize our militia for occasional defense; raise troops or volunteers for permanent garrisons or attack. Those essential preparations are in some points hardly commenced, in every respect incomplete; our China and East India trade to an immense amount yet out; no men raised; and, indeed, nothing more was practicable beyond a draft of militia; but whatever relates to its better selection or organization, or to the raising of regulars or volunteers, wanting the authorization of Congress, and requiring time for executing; the batteries contemplated at New York not yet commenced; not even a temporary rampart in any part of the city; and hardly a cannon mounted on Governor's Island. How far the works of the two other seaports, mentioned in the message as particularly exposed, have progressed, I do not know. Further appropriations stated to be necessary for the contemplated batteries of every other harbor. It seems essentially necessary that we should, if we are permitted, provide such rational and practicable means of defence as we think may be effected within a short time, before we precipitate the war. Is it not probable that England will, if she presumes that her answer may lead to a war, immediately despatch a few ships with contingent orders? And if Congress were to declare war in November, what would prevent their naval force here, even if not reinforced, to lay New York under contribution before winter? Great would be the disgrace attaching to such a disaster. The Executive would be particularly liable to censure for having urged immediate war whilst so unprepared against attack; nor need I say that as a prosperous Administration is almost invulnerable, adverse events will invariably destroy its popularity. Let it be added that, independently of immense loss to individuals, three millions at least of next year's revenue rest on bonds due by the merchants of that city.

In every view of the subject I feel strongly impressed with the propriety of preparing to the utmost for war, and carrying it with vigor, if it cannot be honorably avoided; but in the mean while persevering in that caution of language and action which may give us some more time and is best calculated to preserve the remaining chance of peace and most consistent with the general system of your Administration. . . .

THE EMBARGO

After the Leopard-Chesapeake *incident Jefferson persuaded Congress to adopt the Embargo as a substitute for war. It had long been a primary article of the Republican creed, at least among Virginia ideologues, that the advanced commercial and industrial nations of Europe were ultimately dependent upon American farmers for food and raw materials. A firm believer in this agrarian fundamentalism, Jefferson wanted to demon-*

*strate to history the ultimate power of the tillers of the soil.
The Embargo Act was passed December 22, 1807 at his in-
stigation. It prohibited the departure of any vessel to a foreign
port. Thus American vessels were to be protected from seizure
by removing them from the seas, and it was expected that
stoppage of American exports and imports would force Britain
and France to repeal their decrees against American commerce.*

32. LETTER TO THOMAS JEFFERSON

July 29, 1808

*In Cabinet discussions Gallatin opposed the Embargo as
ruinous, and if long continued worse than war. He had no
confidence that it would obtain concessions from Britain at
whom it was primarily aimed. Nevertheless, as the officer
chiefly concerned with its enforcement he tried his best to
make it work. His problems multiplied with each passing
month. Illicit trade sprang up along the coasts of the middle
states and New England, often with the connivance of local
authorities. Overland trade with Canada grew to major pro-
portions. By the spring of 1808 whole sections of the northern
border were in open defiance, necessitating the use of troops
and naval vessels. Gallatin saw clearly that such a colossal
interdiction of the normal pursuits of the country required the
assumption of abitrary, "dangerous," and "odious" powers by*

Writings, I, 396–399.

*the federal government. He took the position that he must be
given such powers in order to enforce the law, otherwise the
Embargo must be abandoned; but that if it was enforced and
failed to secure concessions from European powers within a
limited time, there was no recourse but war.*

I sent yesterday to the Secretary of the Navy, and he will
transmit to you, a letter from General Dearborn, and another from General Lincoln, showing the violations of the
embargo. As these are now effected by vessels which go off
without clearances, with intention either of putting their loads
on board of vessels at sea, chiefly British, or of sailing over
to Nova Scotia or the West Indies, the danger is much
greater from New York northwardly, principally from Massachusetts, than from either the Delaware, Chesapeake, or
North Carolina. This arises from the proximity of the Northern
seaports to the sea, which enables them to be at sea in two
hours from the time they leave the wharf, from the vicinity
of Nova Scotia, and from the number of British vessels hover-
ing for that purpose between that colony and Massachusetts.
There are some, also, in Long Island Sound, and amongst the
islands between Nantucket and Rhode Island. The Senate did,
by an amendment, confine to districts adjacent to foreign
territories the power of seizing deposits of provisions, &c.,
which the House had, on my suggestion, made general, and
which, connected with the authority of detaining vessels
ostensibly bound coastwise, would have given us much additional security. But now the collectors cannot seize any articles,
though placed in the most suspicious and remote places, nor
even on board of vessels remaining or apparently intended
to remain in harbor (Passamaquoddy and other districts
adjacent to foreign territories only excepted); and where they
have attempted it suits are commenced against them. Mr.
Gelston here, cautious as he is, has nerve and zeal, and has

made several doubtful seizures, for which he is sued. But we cannot expect that the collectors generally will risk all they are worth in doubtful cases; and it results that, until Congress meets, we must depend entirely on force for checking this manner of violating the law. I have requested Mr. Smith to send northwardly all the force that can be spared either in gunboats or cruising vessels; and I have, presuming on your approbation, which I now request, directed General Lincoln to sell the small cutter and to purchase and man one fitted for the present exigencies. I contemplate a similar arrangement for the New London and Portsmouth cutters, so as to obtain in all three good cruisers on that coast exclusively of the vessels belonging to the navy, and request you will authorize me to make that and any other similar alteration in the cutter establishment which may be wanted.

On the Lakes we are in no better situation. I have sent a blank commission for the collectorship of Sacket's Harbor, and new instructions to all the collectors, and will send a proper person, for whom I am now inquiring, to examine strictly the conduct of all those officers, give proper directions, inquire whether any further removals be necessary, and obtain the names of the infractors in order to institute suits. But want of efficiency in the law at first, and of energy in the collectors on Lake Ontario afterwards, have, together with avarice and the open encouragement by Federalists, organized opposition in that quarter to a degree which will probably baffle all our endeavors. Nothing but force on *land* (for there the collectors have the right to seize property on shore) will put a stop to the violations. As to judiciary redress there is very little hope. For, a few days ago, a Republican jury, notwithstanding the charge of Judge Sailly and the efforts of the attorney, have refused to find bills against the Canadians made prisoners after resistance on board one of the rafts which they were forcibly carrying away across the line on Lake Champlain.

The recruiting service cannot, scattered as it is throughout the United States, procure shortly many men for that quarter;

and it is not improbable that you will still be obliged to call out militia in that quarter.

With those difficulties we must struggle as well as we can this summer; but I am perfectly satisfied that if the embargo must be persisted in any longer, two principles must necessarily be adopted in order to make it sufficient: 1st, that not a single vessel shall be permitted to move without the special permission of the Executive; 2d, that the collectors be invested with the general power of seizing property anywhere, and taking the rudders or otherwise effectually preventing the departure of any vessel in harbor, though ostensibly intended to remain there; and that without being liable to personal suits. I am sensible that such arbitrary powers are equally dangerous and odious. But a restrictive measure of the nature of the embargo applied to a nation under such circumstances as the United States cannot be enforced without the assistance of means as strong as the measure itself. To that legal authority to prevent, seize, and detain must be added a sufficient physical force to carry it into effect; and although I believe that in our seaports little difficulty would be encountered, we must have a little army along the Lakes and British lines generally. With that result we should not perhaps be much astonished. For the Federalists having at least prevented the embargo from becoming a measure generally popular, and the people being distracted by the complexity of the subject, orders of council, decrees, embargoes, and wanting a single object which might rouse their patriotism and unite their passions and affections, selfishness has assumed the reins in several quarters, and the people are now there altogether against the law.

In such quarters the same thing happens which has taken place everywhere else, and even under the strongest governments under similar circumstances. The navy of Great Britain is hardly sufficient to prevent smuggling; and you recollect, doubtless, the army of *employés* and the sanguinary code of France,—hardly adequate to guard their land frontiers.

That in the present situation of the world every effort should be attempted to preserve the peace of this nation cannot be doubted. But if the criminal party-rage of Federalists and Tories shall have so far succeeded as to defeat our endeavors to obtain that object by the only measure that could possibly have effected it, we must submit and prepare for war. I am so much overwhelmed even here with business and interruptions, that I have not time to write correctly or even with sufficient perspicuity; but you will guess at my meaning where it is not sufficiently clear. I mean generally to express an opinion founded on the experience of this summer, that Congress must either invest the Executive with the most arbitrary powers and sufficient force to carry the embargo into effect, or give it up altogether. And in this last case I must confess that, unless a change takes place in the measures of the European powers, I see no alternative but war. But with whom? This is a tremendous question if tested only by policy; and so extraordinary is our situation that it is equally difficult to decide it on the ground of justice, the only one by which I wish the United States to be governed. At all events, I think it the duty of the Executive to contemplate that result as probable, and to be prepared accordingly.

33. LETTER TO WILLIAM B. GILES

November 24, 1808

Congress passed a number of acts to tighten the Embargo, culminating in the Force Act of January 9, 1809, which invested the government with arbitrary power beyond anything

Writings, I, 428–435.

the Federalists had attempted. The economic life of the country was put under the supervision of federal officers, who could seize any goods on land or sea and were absolved from legal liability for their actions. They inspected vessels loading or unloading goods in the coastal trade, and to ensure that vessels would not sail to a foreign port, required the owners to post bond of six times the value of ship and cargo. The volume of foodstuffs transported from state to state was regulated by the President, and entire communities considered untrustworthy were placed under restrictions.

The Force Bill was the product of Gallatin's recommendations to a Senate committee on November 24, 1808, presented in this letter to Senator William B. Giles.

Indisposition has prevented an earlier answer to your letter of the 14th instant.

For better preventing coasting vessels, regularly cleared, from violating the embargo, two measures appear necessary:

1. That the amount of the bond should be increased. 2. That neither capture, distress, nor any other accident should be admitted as a plea, or given in evidence on trial.

By the first regulation, the temptation of going to a foreign port, in hopes that the profit on the sale of the cargo will indemnify for the forfeiture of the penalty, will be done away. By the second, every expectation of escaping the payment of the penalty under fraudulent pretenses will be disappointed, and the power of remitting the penalties in the few cases of unavoidable accident which may occur will remain as heretofore, and, as in other cases, with the Treasury.

As the object of those two regulations will be to make the bond a sufficient and complete security, they will have a tendency to relieve, in a considerable degree, the coasting trade from the inconvenience resulting from detentions.

The sufficiency of the bond will, in many doubtful cases, remove the necessity of detaining vessels, or, what amounts to the same, of informing the owners that, unless they reduce the amount of their cargoes, they will be detained.

I would also submit the propriety of placing under the control of the President that power of detention vested in the collectors by the Act of the 25th of April last. That subject has been a constant source of complaint and difficulty. It has been the uniform practice, from the establishment of the government of the United States, to give positive instructions to the collectors respecting the execution of the laws, and which they were bound to obey, unless a different construction should be established by a legal decision. This, indeed, was essentially necessary, in order to secure an uniform construction and execution of the laws. But the provision now alluded to makes the detention to rest on the opinion of each collector, and this must necessarily produce a great diversity in the manner in which the power should be executed. All has been done that could be done to obviate that evil, and, the President being authorized to decide on the detentions when made, the opportunity was taken to inform the collectors of what, in his opinion, should be a proper cause of detention. This, however, could be given only as opinion, and operate as a recommendation, and not as an order. Nor does it appear practicable to establish uniformity and to prevent partiality, and either laxity or too great severity in practice, unless the power of prescribing general rules in that respect, by which the collectors will be bound to abide, be vested in the President.

I am aware that there is another mode of evasion by regular coasting vessels, which will not be prevented by either of the preceding provisions. Either whilst in port, or on their way down our rivers and bays, coasting vessels may receive articles not entered in their manifest, which they put on board other vessels, lying off the coast for that purpose.

But it is not perceived that any legal provision can prevent that infraction, nor that any other remedy can be found than the vigilance of the officers. Another general regulation will, however, be suggested, perhaps useful as a permanent measure, but which would, at all events, under existing circumstances, give additional security for the observance of the laws, and afford some relief to our own seamen, to wit, a prohibition to employ any aliens either as masters or part of the crew of any coasting vessel.

It is still more difficult to guard against violations by vessels departing without clearance, in open defiance of the laws. The following provisions, on mature consideration, appear the most efficient that can be devised against infractions, which it is the more necessary to repress, as they may be daily expected to increase, and threaten to prostrate the law and government itself:

1. To forbid expressly under pain of forfeiture (the penalty now being only implied) the lading of any vessel without the permission of the collector, and without the bond for a coasting voyage being previously given, authorizing the collectors to refuse permission unless the object be that of a lawful coasting or fishing voyage. The great number of vessels now laden and in a state of readiness to depart shows the necessity of this provision. If there be cases in which the indulgence of converting vessels into warehouses ought to be granted, there will be no hardship, where the intention is fair, to require a bond similar to that given for a coasting voyage. And the collectors should likewise, in such cases, be expressly authorized to take such efficient precautions as will put it out of the power of such vessels to sail without warning.

2. In order to prevent those fraudulent sales of vessels by which ostensible owners of no responsibility are substituted for those from whom penalties might be recovered, it is necessary to provide that those owners of vessels whose names appear on the register or license should continue to be reputed as such, and liable to the penalties, in case of infraction of the laws, until the register or license shall have been actually

surrendered, and new papers shall have been regularly granted by the collector to the purchaser. And, in every such case of purchase, a sufficient bond that the embargo shall not be infringed, to be previously required.

3. The power to seize unusual deposits, now vested in the collectors of districts adjacent to the territories of foreign nations, should, as was contemplated in the bill passed by the House of Representatives, be extended to all the districts. That this is an arbitrary power, which nothing but the un-remitted efforts in some places to evade the law can possibly justify, cannot be denied, and it should, like that of detention, be placed under the control of the President, and be executed only in conformity with such general rules as he would prescribe.

4. Exclusively of the assistance which may be derived from gunboats and from the armed vessels of the United States, it would be advisable to authorize the President to add ten or twelve cutters to the establishment. Fast sailing vessels, of easy draft of water, and requiring only from fifteen to thirty men each, are mostly wanted, and would, for the object contemplated, be as useful as the largest frigates.

5. It is with regret that the necessity of authorizing, on the application of the collector, an immediate call for the local physical force of the country must also be stated. But such partial acts of violence as have taken place in some of the seaports cannot be prevented by the circuitous manner in which the public force must now be brought out in support of the laws. And no doubt exists that the mass of the citizens, whether they approve or disapprove of the embargo, would, in every port, instantaneously suppress any such outrage, pro-vided they can be called upon to act in a legal manner.

Some other provisions appear also necessary for the purpose of carrying the laws more completely into effect along our land frontier:

1. The exportation of specie by land should be expressly prohibited.

2. The power of detaining deposits should be so expressed as to leave no doubt of the authority to detain wagons and other carriages laden and actually on their way to a foreign territory. Although I cannot perceive any reason for the distinction, it has been supposed, in one of the districts, that the law which authorized the detention of flour, beef, or potash deposited in a warehouse, did not extend to the case of their being deposited in a wagon, although evidently on its way to Canada.

3. The offence now punishable by law is that of exportation. This is not consummated till after the property has actually been carried beyond the lines, where, being in a foreign jurisdiction, it cannot be seized, so that forfeiture, which is the most efficient penalty, can never apply to exportations by land; and no bond being required, as in the case of vessels, the only remedy is the uncertain one of recovering penalties against apparent offenders, who either abscond or have no property. How far it may be practicable to make the act of preparing the means of exportation punishable, or to provide some other remedy, is submitted to the committee.

But it must also be observed that every degree of opposition to the laws which falls short of treason is now, with but few exceptions, an offence undefined and unprovided for by the laws of the United States; whence it follows that such offences remain unpunished when the State authorities do not interfere. The necessity of defining those offenses by law as misdemeanors, and of providing an adequate punishment, appears obvious.

I will beg leave here to add, that it does not appear necessary to continue any longer the indulgence granted to the British merchants to import, for the use of the Indians, articles of which the importation is generally prohibited by law, as that privilege is liable to great abuse, and affords just ground of dissatisfaction to American citizens. Whether it be advisable to continue the permission given to those Indian traders to export furs and peltries, is a question to be decided by political considerations.

The last branch of the subject to which I wish at present to call the attention of the committee relates to interruptions and certain injurious proceedings attempted under color of law.

1. Vexatious suits are brought against collectors, which not only perplex faithful officers, but have the effect of intimidating others, and prevent an energetic performance of their duties. The only provisions which have occurred to me on that subject are, to enable the collectors who may be sued always to remove the cause before a court of the United States; to make a certificate, issued by the proper authority, that there was reasonable cause of detention; protect them against damages in cases of detentions, in the same manner as is now provided in case of seizures; and to provide for the safe-keeping and restoring, when proper, and on security being given, the vessels and property which may be detained.

2. Attempts have in several instances been made to wrest from the collectors, by writs of replevin issued by State courts or officers, property detained or seized by said collectors, or which in any other manner is in their possession, in conformity with some law of the United States. It is evident that such attempts, if submitted to, would defeat not only the embargo, but also the revenue laws of the United States; that whenever property is, by virtue of a law of the United States, in possession of a collector, marshal, or any other of their officers, no process, in rem, which will take the property away, whether of replevin, attachment, or any other, can be legally issued by a State authority; and that the sheriff or other person executing the same must be considered as a mere trespasser, and be resisted accordingly. But there is no other way at present to resist such illegal process but actual force. And it appears necessary that another remedy should be afforded by providing a summary mode of superseding any such process through the interference of the courts and judges of the

United States, and by making it penal for any sheriff or other person to execute the same, or in any manner to attempt to take property which, by virtue of any law of the United States, is in the collector's possession.

3. In some instances where vessels and cargoes libelled for infractions of the embargo have been restored to the owners on their giving security for the appraised value, the valuations have been so low as to reduce the forfeiture to an inconsiderable sum, thereby defeating altogether the law. It is suggested that this might be prevented by a provision authorizing and directing the district judges to set aside, on motion of the district attorney, such valuations whenever, in their opinion, falling short of the true value.

On the subject of mandamus, I will only observe that, in the only instance which has taken place, the court, supposing they had jurisdiction, could not, from the manner in which the question was brought before them, have decided otherwise than they did; but that it is desirable that the question of jurisdiction, as it relates either to the courts in whom the power ought to be vested, or to the cases to which it should extend, should be precisely defined by law.

I have not, in this communication, taken into consideration the technical defects of the existing embargo laws, because prosecutions do not fall within my immediate cognizance, and I do not feel competent to the task of pointing out the necessary alterations. Measures have, however, been taken to procure on that subject, and from the proper sources, information, which will hereafter be laid before the committee.

To the remaining inquiry of the committee, whether the inconveniences of the present system may not in some degree be removed, I can only answer, generally, that a law which lays such extensive restrictions as the embargo cannot be carried into effect without imposing serious inconveniences, even on the domestic intercourse of the United States; and that these must necessarily be increased in proportion to the opposition and efforts to evade or violate the law. It has already been stated that provisions which will render the bond given by coasting vessels a complete security against violations by them will diminish the necessity and extent of more arbitrary restrictions. An authority to permit, on proper security being given, such vessels, when they arrive in port, to keep their cargoes on board, would afford some relief. And I think that the credit on duties accruing on the importation of certain articles which was allowed by the Act of the 10th March last, should be extended to all importations of the same articles made after the passing of the Act; those made in vessels which sailed under special permission only excepted. With respect to this last class of importations, as they were permitted by special indulgence, and as it is understood that it has been impossible in many cases to prevent its being abused, and as in almost all, the parties, having a species of exclusive privilege, have made sufficiently profitable voyages, the propriety, particularly in the existing situation of the revenue, of allowing them also the advantage of an extended credit on duties, is not perceived.

34. CAMPBELL'S REPORT

November 22, 1808

As the economic life of the country stagnated and custom receipts sank toward zero, Gallatin became convinced that continuing the Embargo was more injurious than war. Jefferson

Writings, I, 435–446.

still wanted to keep it going, but Pennsylvania and New York Republicans were beginning to revolt. In November Gallatin submitted a long report to a House committee headed by George W. Campbell in which he reviewed the diplomatic record and spelled out the choice between the Embargo, degrading submission to British and French edicts, or war with both countries. The point of the message was to steel Congress to a decision either to enforce the Embargo, with all its bitter consequences, or to face war. In February 1809 Congress repudiated Jefferson's leadership by repealing the Embargo, its termination to be effective March 4, the day Jefferson retired from office. Jefferson did not have the courage to use his veto.

The committee to whom, &c., report:

After a period of twenty-five years of peace, hardly interrupted by transient hostilities, and of prosperity unparalleled in the history of nations, the United States are, for the first time since the treaty which terminated the Revolutionary war, placed in a situation equally difficult, critical, and dangerous.

Those principles recognized by the civilized world, under the name of law of nations, which heretofore controlled belligerent powers, regulated the duties of neutrals, and protected their rights, are now avowedly disregarded or forgotten by Great Britain and France. Each of those two nations captures and condemns all American vessels trading with her enemy or her enemy's allies; and every European power having become a party in the contest, the whole of our commerce with Europe and European colonies becomes liable to capture by either the one or the other. If there be any nominal exception, it is made on a condition of tribute which only adds insult to the injury.

The only plea urged in justification of those hostilities is that of retaliation, grounded on a presumed acquiescence of the United States in previous aggressions of the other party. Waiving a discussion of the correctness of the principle of retaliation,—a principle doubtful in itself, and altogether inadmissible to the extent to which it has been carried, and when operating on the neutral rather than on the enemy,— it is altogether untrue that the United States have ever voluntarily acquiesced in the unlawful aggressions of either nation, omitted or delayed any measures calculated to obtain redress, or in any respect deviated from that strict impartiality to which they were bound by their neutrality.

France has alluded to the violations of the national flag and of the sovereignty of the United States in the instances of Pierce's murder, of the outrage on the Chesapeake, and of the destruction of the Impetuous. The measures taken to obtain redress in those cases are of public notoriety; and it may be added that, with the exception of the last, those aggressions on the sovereignty of the United States did not affect their neutrality, and gave no right to France either of complaint or interference.

Setting aside irregularities of less importance, and equally chargeable to both nations, such as the British order of June, 1803, and the decree of the French general, Ferrand, the principal violations by England of the neutral rights of America prior to the Berlin decree of November, 1806, and which, if acquiesced in, might have given grounds of complaint to France, are, the captures of American vessels laden with colonial produce, founded on a renewal of that pretended principle generally called "the Rule of 1756;" the impressment of American seamen, compelled thereby to become the auxiliaries of England against France, and proclamation or nominal blockades, particularly that of the coast from the river Elbe to Brest, notified in May, 1806.

It will not be asserted that the United States ever tamely

acquiesced in either of those pretensions. It will not be denied that, with respect to the two first, the most strenuous efforts were incessantly made to procure an alteration of the British system.

It is true that to the nominal proclamation blockades of England the United States had opposed only spirited and repeated remonstrances, and that these had not always been successful. But the measures which a neutral nation may be supposed bound to take against the infractions of its neutrality must always bear a certain proportion to the extent and nature of the injury received and to the means of opposition. It cannot certainly be pretended that a hasty resort to war should, in every such instance, have become the duty of America. Nor can the irregularities of England in declaring in a state of blockade a certain extent of coast, part of which was not, and the whole of which could not, even by her powerful navy, be actually invested and blockaded, be pleaded in justification of that decree by which France, without an efficient fleet, pretends to announce the blockade of the dominions of a power which has the incontestable command of the sea, and before no port of which she can station a single vessel.

The Milan decree of 1807 can still less rest for its defence on the supposed acquiescence of the United States in the British orders of the preceding month, since those orders, which have not certainly been acquiesced in, were not even known in America at the date of the decree. And it is proper here to add that the French have, particularly by the sequestration of certain vessels in their ports, and by burning our ships on the high seas, gone even beyond the tenor of their own extraordinary edicts.

The allegation of an acquiescence in the Berlin decree of November, 1806, by which alone the British government pretends to justify the orders of council, is equally unfounded. In the note on that subject addressed, on the 31st December,

1806, by the British government to the American ministers,
after having stated that they would not believe that the
enemy would ever seriously attempt to enforce such a system,
the following declaration is expressly made: "If, however, the
enemy should carry these threats into execution, and if neutral
nations, contrary to all expectation, should acquiesce in such
usurpations, his Majesty might probably be compelled, however reluctantly, to retaliate in his just defense," &c. The two
requisites necessary in the opinion of Great Britain to justify
retaliation are stated to be the execution of the decree, and
the acquiescence of neutral nations. Yet within eight days
after, and in the face of that declaration, without waiting
for ascertaining either of these facts, the retaliating British
order of January 7, 1807, was issued, which, contrary to the
acknowledged law of nations, subjected to capture vessels
of the United States sailing from the ports of one belligerent
to a port of another belligerent.

The United States, in the mean while, and without delay,
had taken the necessary steps to ascertain the manner in which
the French government intended to execute their decree.

That decree might be construed merely as a municipal law
forbidding the introduction of British merchandise and the
admission of vessels coming from England. Under that aspect,
and if confined to that object, the neutral rights of America
were not affected by its operation.

A belligerent may, without any infraction of neutral rights,
forbid the admission into his ports of any vessel coming from
the ports of his enemy. And France had undoubtedly the same
right to exclude from her dominions every species of British
merchandise which the United States have exercised in forbidding the importation of certain species. Great Britain might
be injured by such regulations; but America had no more
right to complain of that part of the decree than France had
to object to the American Non-Importation Act. So far, indeed,
as respects the United States, they were placed by the

municipal part of the decree in the same situation in relation to France in which they are placed in their intercourse with Great Britain by the permanent laws of that country. The French decree forbids American vessels to import British merchandise into France. The British Navigation Act forbids American vessels to import French merchandise into England. But that broad clause of the Berlin decree which declared the British Islands in a state of blockade, though not followed by regulations to that effect, still threatened an intended operation on the high seas. This, if carried into effect, would be a flagrant violation of the neutral rights of the United States, and, as such, they would be bound to oppose it. The minister of the United States at Paris immediately applied for explanations on that subject; and the French Minister of Marine, on the 24th December, 1806, seven days before the date of the above-mentioned note of the British government, stated in answer that the decree made no alteration in the regulations then observed in France with regard to neutral navigators, or to the commercial convention of the United States with France; that the declaration of the British Islands being in a state of blockade did not change the existing French laws concerning maritime captures; and that American vessels could not be taken at sea for the mere reason of their being going to or returning from an English port.

The execution of the decree comported for several months with those explanations; several vessels were arrested for having introduced articles of English growth or manufacture, and among them some which, being actually from England and laden with English colonial produce, had entered with forged papers as if coming from the United States. But no alteration of the first construction given by the French government took place until the month of September, 1807. The first condemnation on the principle that the decree subjected neutral vessels to capture on the high seas was that of the Horizon, on the 10th October following; prior to that time there could have been no acquiescence in a decree infringing the neutral rights of the United States, because till that time it was explained, and, what was more inportant, executed in such a manner as not to infringe those rights,—because till then no such infraction had taken place. The ministers of the United States at London, at the request of the British minister, communicated to him on the 18th October, 1807, the substance of the explanations received, and of the manner in which the decree was executed, for they were at that time ignorant of the change which had taken place.

It was on the 18th September, 1807, that a new construction of the decree took place, an instruction having on that day been transmitted to the council of prizes by the Minister of Justice, by which that court was informed that French armed vessels were authorized under that decree to seize, without exception, in neutral vessels, either English property or merchandise of English growth or manufacture. An immediate explanation having been asked from the French Minister of Foreign Relations, he confirmed, in his answer of 7th October, 1807, the determination of his government to adopt that construction. Its first application took place on the 10th of the same month, in the case of the Horizon, of which the minister of the United States was not informed until the month of November, and on the 12th of that month he presented a spirited remonstrance against that infraction of the neutral rights of the United States. He had in the mean while transmitted to America the instruction to the council of prizes of the 18th September. This was received on the   of December, and a copy of the decision in the case of the Horizon having at the same time reached government, the President, aware of the consequences which would follow that new state of things [and of the intentions of the British government to extend at all events what was called retaliating measures],[1]

---

[1] Omitted in the printed report.

communicated immediately to Congress the alterations of the
French decree, and recommended the embargo, which was
accordingly laid on the 22d December, 1807; at which time it
was well understood in this country that the British orders
of council of November preceding had been issued, although
they were not officially communicated to our government.

On the 11th November preceding, the British orders of
council had been issued, declaring that all the ports of France,
of her allies, and of any other country at war with England,
and all other ports of Europe from which, although not
at war with England, the British flag was excluded, should
thenceforth be considered as if the same were actually blockaded; that all trade in articles of the produce or manufacture
of the said countries should be deemed unlawful; and that
every vessel trading from or to the said countries, together
with all goods and merchandise on board, and also all articles
of the produce or manufacture of the said countries, should
be liable to capture and condemnation.

These orders cannot be defended on the ground of their
being intended as retaliating on account of the Berlin decree,
as construed and uniformly executed from its date to the 18th
September, 1807, its construction and execution having till
then infringed no neutral rights. For certainly the monstrous
doctrine will not be asserted even by the British government
that neutral nations are bound to resist not only the acts of
belligerent powers which violate their rights, but also those
municipal regulations which, however they may injure the
enemy, are lawful, and do not affect the legitimate rights of
the neutral. The only retaliation to be used in such cases
must be such as will operate on the enemy without infringing
the rights of the neutral. If solely intended as a retaliation on
the Berlin decree as executed prior to the month of September,
the British orders of council should have been confined to
forbidding the introduction into Great Britain of French or
enemy's merchandise, and the admission into British ports of

neutral vessels coming from a French or other enemy's port. Indeed, the ground of retaliation on account of any culpable acquiescence of neutrals in decrees violating their rights is abandoned by the very tenor of the orders, their operation being extended to those countries from which the British flag was excluded,—such as Austria,—although such countries were neither at war with Great Britain nor had passed any decree in any way affecting or connected with neutral rights.

Nor are the orders justifiable on the pretence of an acquiescence on the part of the United States in the French decree as construed and executed subsequent to the 18th September, 1807, when it became an evident infraction of their rights, and such as they were bound to oppose. For their minister at Paris immediately made the necessary remonstrances, and the orders were issued not only without having ascertained whether the United States would acquiesce in the injurious alteration of the French decree, but more than one month before that alteration was known in America. It may even be asserted that the alteration was not known in England when the orders of council were issued, the instruction of the 18th September, 1807, which gave the new and injurious construction, not having been promulgated in France, and its first publication having been made in December, 1807, and by the American government itself.

The British orders of council are therefore unjustifiable on the principle of retaliation, even giving to that principle all the latitude which has ever been avowedly contended for. They are in open violation of the solemn declaration made by the British ministers in December, 1806, that retaliation on the part of Great Britain would depend on the execution of an unlawful decree and on the acquiescence of neutral nations in such infraction of their rights. And they were also issued notwithstanding the official communication made by the ministers of the United States that the French decree was construed and executed so as not to infringe their neutral rights, and without any previous notice or intimation denying the correctness of that statement. The Berlin decree as expounded and executed subsequent to the 18th September, 1807, and the British orders of council of the 11th November ensuing, are therefore, as they affect the United States, contemporaneous aggressions of the belligerent powers, equally unprovoked and equally indefensible on the presumed ground of acquiescence. These, together with the Milan decree of December, 1807, which filled the measure, would, on the principle of self-defence, have justified immediate hostilities against both nations on the part of the United States. They thought it more eligible in the first instance, by withdrawing their vessels from the ocean, to avoid war, at least for a season, and at the same time to snatch their immense and defenceless commerce from impending destruction.

Another appeal has in the mean time been made, under the authority vested in the President for that purpose, to the justice and true interest of France and England. The propositions made by the United States and the arguments urged by their ministers are before Congress. By these the very pretext of the illegal edicts was removed; and it is evident that a revocation by either nation on the ground on which it was asked, either must have produced what both pretended to have in view, a restoration of the freedom of commerce and of the acknowledged principles of the law of nations, or, in case of refusal by the other belligerent, would have carried into effect in the most efficient manner the ostensible object of the edicts and made the United States a party in the war against him. The effort has been ineffectual. The propositions have been actually rejected by one of the belligerent powers, and remain unanswered by the other. In that state of things, what course ought the United States to pursue? Your committee can perceive no other alternative but abject and degrading submission, war with both nations, or a continuance and enforcement of the present suspension of commerce. The first cannot require any discussion. But the pressure of the embargo, so sensibly felt, and the calamities inseparable from a state of war, naturally create a wish that some middle course might be discovered which should avoid the evils of both and not be inconsistent with national honor and independence. That illusion must be dissipated, and it is necessary that the people of the United States should fully understand the situation in which they are placed.

There is no other alternative but war with both nations or a continuance of the present system. For war with one of the belligerents only would be submission to the edicts and will of the other; and a repeal, in whole or in part, of the embargo must necessarily be war or submission.

A general repeal without arming would be submission to both nations. A general repeal and arming of our merchant vessels would be war with both, and war of the worst kind, suffering the enemy to plunder us without retaliation upon them.

A partial repeal must, from the situation of Europe, necessarily be actual submission to one of the aggressors and war with the other.

The last position is the only one on which there can be any doubt, and it will be most satisfactorily demonstrated by selecting amongst the several modifications which might be suggested that which may on first view appear the least exceptionable; a proposition to repeal the embargo so far only as relates to those powers which have not passed or do not execute any decrees injurious to the neutral rights of the United States.

It is said that the adoption of that proposition would restore our commerce with the native powers of Asia and Africa, and with Spain, Portugal, Sweden, and Russia. Let this be taken for granted, although, the precise line of conduct now pursued by most of those nations in relation to the United States is not correctly ascertained. So far as relates to any advantages which would result from that measure if confined to its ostensible object, it will be sufficient to observe that the exports of articles of the domestic produce of the United States during the year ending the 30th September, 1807, amounted to $48,700,000, and that the portion exported to the countries above enumerated falls short of $7,000,000,—an amount too inconsiderable, when compared with the bulk of our exports, to deserve attention, even if a question affecting the independence of the nation was to be decided by considerations of immediate profit.

But the true effect of the proposition would be to open an indirect trade with Great Britain, which, through St. Bartholomew and Havana, Lisbon, Cadiz, or Gottenburg, would receive, at prices reduced by glutted markets and for want of competition, all the provisions, naval stores, raw materials for her manufactures, and other articles, which she may want. Whether she would be satisfied with that favorable state of things, or whether, considering that boon as a pledge of unqualified submission, she would, according to the tenor of her orders, interrupt our scanty commerce with Russia, and occasionally, under some new pretext, capture, rather than purchase, the cargoes intended for her own use, is equally uncertain and unimportant. Nor can it be doubted that a measure which would supply exclusively one of the belligerents would be war with the other. Considered merely as a question of profit, it would be much more eligible at once to raise the embargo in relation to Great Britain, as we would then at least have the advantages of a direct market with the consumer. But the proposition can only be defended on the ground that France is the only aggressor, and that having no just reason to complain of England, it is our duty to submit to her orders. On that inadmissible supposition it would not only be more candid, but also a more dignified as well as a more advantageous course, openly to join England and to make war against France. The object would be clearly understood, an ally would be obtained, and the meanness of submission might be better palliated.

It appears unnecessary to pursue any further the examination of propositions which the difficult situation of the United States could alone have suggested, and which will prove more inadmissible or impracticable as the subject is more thoroughly investigated. The alternative is painful; it is between a continued suspension of commerce, and war with both England and France. But the choice must ultimately be made between the two, and it is important that we should be prepared for either the one or the other.

The aggressions of England and France collectively, affecting almost the whole of our commerce, and persisted in notwithstanding repeated remonstrances, explanations, and propositions the most candid and unexceptionable, are to all intents and purposes a maritime war waged by both nations against the United States. It cannot be denied that the ultimate and only effectual mode of resisting that warfare, if persisted in, is war. A permanent suspension of commerce, after repeated and unavailing efforts to obtain peace, would not properly be resistance; it would be withdrawing from the contest and abandoning our indisputable right freely to navigate the ocean. The present unsettled state of the world, the extraordinary situation in which the United States are placed, and the necessity, if war be resorted to, of making it at the same time against both nations, and these the two most powerful of the world, are the principal causes of hesitation. There would be none in resorting to that remedy, however calamitous, if a selection could be made on any principle of justice or without a sacrifice of national independence.

On a question of such difficulty, involving the most important interests of the Union, and which has not perhaps till lately been sufficiently considered, your committee think the

House alone competent to pronounce a decisive opinion; and they have in this report confined themselves to an exposition of the subject and to such introductory resolutions as will be equally applicable to either alternative. The first of these, being merely declaratory of a determination not to submit to foreign aggressions, may perhaps at a first view appear superfluous. It is, however, believed by the committee that a pledge by the representatives of the nation that they will not abandon its essential rights will not at this critical moment be unacceptable. The misapprehensions which seem to have existed, and the misrepresentations which have been circulated respecting the state of our foreign relations, render also such declarations expedient; and it may not be useless that every foreign nation should understand that its aggressions never will be justified or encouraged by any description of American citizens. For the question for every citizen now is, whether he will rally round the government of his choice or enlist under foreign banners;—whether he will be for his country or against his country.

The committee respectfully submit the following resolutions:

1. Resolved, That the United States cannot, without a sacrifice of their rights, honor, and independence, submit to the late edicts of Great Britain and France.

2. Resolved, That it is expedient to prohibit by law the admission into the ports of the United States of all public or private armed or unarmed ships or vessels belonging to Great Britain or France, or to any other of the belligerent powers having in force orders or decrees violating the lawful commerce and neutral rights of the United States; and also the importation of any goods, wares, or merchandise the growth, produce, or manufacture of the dominions of any of the said powers, or imported from any place in the possession of either.

3. Resolved, That measures ought to be immediately taken for placing the country in a more complete state of defence.

*FACTIONAL POLITICS AND THE
APPROACH OF WAR*

35. LETTER TO THOMAS JEFFERSON

November 8, 1809

*As guardian of the economy program, Gallatin exerted a
restraining influence over the other executive departments.
This aroused the resentment of Secretary of the Navy Robert
Smith, who was personally incompetent but had powerful
political connections through his brother, Samuel Smith, a
wealthy Maryland merchant and prominent Republican. In
1809 the Smith faction bitterly attacked Gallatin for exposing
irregularities that had occurred in the Navy department. On a
visit to Jefferson, then retired to Monticello, Gallatin expressed
deep concern about the ambitions of the pronavy group and
about the factionalism that was disrupting the Republican
Party. The following letter is his reply to Jefferson's consola-
tory note.*

I perused your affectionate letter of the 11th ult. with lively
sensations of pleasure, excited by that additional evidence
of your continued kindness and partiality. To have acquired
and preserved your friendship and confidence is more than

sufficient to console me for some late personal mortifications, though I will not affect to conceal that these, coming from an unexpected quarter, and being, as I thought, unmerited, wounded my feelings more deeply than I had at first been aware of. [Had I listened only to those feelings, I would have resigned and probably taken this winter a seat in Congress, which, as a personal object, would have been much more pleasing than my present situation, and also better calculated to regain the ground which, to my surprise, I found I had lost, at least in one of the branches of the Legislature. After mature consideration, I relinquished the idea, at least for that time, in a great degree on account of my personal attachment to Mr. Madison, which is of old standing. I am sure reciprocal, and strengthened from greater intimacy; and also because I mistrusted my own judgment, and doubted whether I was not more useful where I was than I could be as a member of Congress. All this passed in my mind before the last session, and the communication which I made to you at Monticello arose from subsequent circumstances.][1]

Yet I can assure you that I will not listen to those feelings in forming a final determination on the subject on which I conversed with you at Monticello. The gratitude and duty I owe to the country which has received me and honored me beyond my deserts, the deep interest I feel in its future welfare and prosperity, the confidence placed by Mr. Madison in me, my personal and sincere attachment for him, the desire of honorably acquiring some share of reputation, every public and private motive, would induce me not to abandon my post, if I am permitted to retain it, and if my remaining in office can be of public utility. But in both respects I have strong apprehensions, to which I alluded in our conversation. It has seemed to me from various circumstances that those who thought they had injured were disposed to destroy, and that

---

[1] Omitted in the draft as sent.

they were sufficiently skilful and formidable to effect their object. As I may not, however, perhaps see their actions with an unprejudiced eye, nothing but irresistible evidence, both of the intention and success, will make me yield to that consideration. But if that ground which you have so forcibly presented to my view is deserted; if those principles which we have uniformly asserted and which were successfully supported during your Administration are no longer adhered to, you must agree with me that to continue in the Treasury would be neither useful to the public nor honorable to myself.

The reduction of the public debt was certainly the principal object in bringing me into office, and our success in that respect has been due both to the joint and continued efforts of the several branches of government and to the prosperous situation of the country. I am sensible that the work cannot progress under adverse circumstances. If the United States shall be forced into a state of actual war, all the resources of the country must be called forth to make it efficient, and new loans will undoubtedly be wanted. But whilst peace is preserved, the revenue will, at all events, be sufficient to pay the interest and to defray necessary expenses. I do not ask that in the present situation of our foreign relations the debt be reduced, but only that it shall not be increased so long as we are not at war. I do not pretend to step out of my own sphere and to control the internal management of other Departments. But it seems to me that as Secretary of the Treasury I may ask that, whilst peace continues, the aggregate of the expenditure of those Departments be kept within bounds such as will preserve the equilibrium between the national revenue and expenditure without recurrence to loans. I cannot, my dear sir, consent to act the part of a mere financier, to become a contriver of taxes, a dealer of loans, a seeker of resources for the purpose of supporting useless baubles, of increasing the number of idle and dissipated members of the community, of fattening contractors, pursers, and agents, and of introducing in all its ramifications that system of patronage, corruption, and rottenness which you so justly execrate. I thought I owed it to candor and friendship to communicate as I did to Mr. Madison and to yourself my fears of a tendency in that direction, arising from the quarter and causes which I pointed out, and the effect such a result must have on my conduct. I earnestly wish that my apprehensions may have been groundless, and it is a question which facts, and particularly the approaching session of Congress, will decide. No efforts shall be wanted on my part in support of our old principles. But, whatever the result may be, I never can forget either your eminent services to the United States nor how much I owe to you for having permitted me to take a subordinate part in your labors.

36. LETTER TO JAMES MADISON

March 1811

Gallatin was the target and eventually the victim of political attacks inspired partly by the desire to discredit President Madison, but Gallatin's identification with the Embargo and his open championship of the Bank of the United States added to his enemies. In 1809 he had expected Madison to appoint him Secretary of State, a post for which he was well-fitted, but the Samuel Smith faction in Congress managed to secure the appointment of Robert Smith. Gallatin stayed on at the Treasury. After he was defeated on the Bank recharter bill, he declared to Madison, in effect, that he would resign unless the incompetent and conniving Robert Smith was discharged from the Cabinet.

James Monroe became Secretary of State in April 1811.

I have long and seriously reflected on the present state of things and on my personal situation. This has for some time been sufficiently unpleasant, and nothing but a sense of public duty and attachment to yourself could have induced me to retain it to this day. But I am convinced that in neither respect can I be any longer useful under existing circumstances.

In a government organized like that of the United States, a government not too strong for effecting its principal object, —the protection of national rights against foreign aggressions, and particularly under circumstances as adverse and embarrassing as those under which the United States are now placed, —it appears to me that not only capacity and talents in the Administration, but also a perfect heartfelt cordiality amongst its members, are essentially necessary to command the public confidence and to produce the requisite union of views and action between the several branches of government. In at least one of these points your present Administration is defective, and the effects, already sensibly felt, become every day more extensive and fatal. New subdivisions and personal factions, equally hostile to yourself and to the general welfare, daily acquire additional strength. Measures of vital importance have been and are defeated; every operation, even of the most simple and ordinary nature, is prevented or impeded; the embarrassments of government, great as from foreign causes they already are, are unnecessarily increased; public confidence in the public councils and in the Executive is impaired, and every day seems to increase every one of these evils. Such state of things cannot last; a radical and speedy remedy has become absolutely necessary. What that ought to be, what change would best promote the success of your Administration and the welfare of the United States, is not for me to say. I can only judge for myself, and I clearly perceive that my continuing a member of the present Administration is no longer of any public utility, invigorates the opposition against yourself, and must necessarily be attended with an increased loss of reputation to myself. Under these impressions, not without reluctance, and after having, perhaps, hesitated too long in hopes of a favorable change, I beg leave to tender you my resignation, to take place at such day, within a reasonable time, as you will think most consistent with the public service. I hope that I hardly need add any expressions of my respect and sincere personal attachment to you, of the regret I will feel on leaving you at this critical time, and the grateful sense I ever will retain of your kindness to me.

37. LETTER TO THOMAS JEFFERSON

March 10, 1812

As the war spirit mounted in Congress, Gallatin repeatedly spelled out the Treasury's lack of resources to support a major conflict and stated the kind of taxes that would be necessary. He advocated levying taxes immediately in order to accumulate funds in advance. His warnings were ignored. As a substitute for taxation Congress in March 1812 authorized him to launch a public loan of $11,000,000. Gallatin foresaw difficul-

Writings, I, 517.

*ties. Although he thought the war avoidable under other cir-
cumstances, he could see no way out and merely hoped that
the country would be united.*

. . . You have seen from your retreat that our hopes and
endeavors to preserve peace during the present European contest have at last been frustrated. I am satisfied that domestic
faction has prevented that happy result. But I hope nevertheless that our internal enemies and the ambitious intriguers
who still attempt to disunite will ultimately be equally disappointed. I rely with great confidence on the good sense of
the great mass of the people to support their own government
in an unavoidable war, and to check the disordinate ambition
of individuals. The discoveries made by Henry will have a
salutary effect in annihilating the spirit of the Essex junto, and
even on the new focus of opposition at Albany. Pennsylvania
never was more firm or united. The South and the West cannot be shaken. With respect to the war, it is my wish, and it
will be my endeavor, so far as I may have any agency, that
the evils inseparable from it should, as far as practicable, be
limited to its duration, and that at its end the United States
may be burdened with the smallest possible quantity of debt,
perpetual taxation, military establishments, and other corrupting or anti-republican habits or institutions.

Accept the assurances of my sincere and unalterable attachment and respect.

PART SIX

Diplomat: The Treaty of Ghent and Postwar Readjustment 1814–1816

THE TREATY OF GHENT

Gallatin remained in the Treasury for nearly a year after the declaration of war on June 18, 1812 trying to avert national insolvency. At a critical juncture in April 1813 three personal friends, David Parrish, Stephen Girard, and John Jacob Astor purchased $9,100,000 in federal bonds, thus filling out a stalled federal loan of $16,000,000. With the pressure on the Treasury temporarily relieved, Gallatin asked Madison to send him on a diplomatic mission along with James A. Bayard, to join John Quincy Adams at the court of Czar Alexander, who had proposed Russian mediation in the Anglo-American conflict. Since the mission was expected to be short, Gallatin did not resign his position as Secretary of the Treasury. At St. Petersburgh some months later he learned that his enemies had been at work and that the Senate had refused to confirm his appointment, holding it incompatible with his Treasury post. Since the Russian mission was no longer important, as Britain had proposed direct negotiation, Gallatin went to London. He

shortly received word that Madison having found another Sec-
retary of the Treasury, had named him to the distinguished
commission that opened negotiations with British representa-
tives at Ghent in August 1814. Besides Gallatin, the commis-
sion included John Quincy Adams, Henry Clay, James A.
Bayard, and Jonathan Russell.

The negotiations began under the most unfavorable aus-
pices. At the time the United States declared war, British re-
sources had been committed to her struggle against Napoleon.
It seemed then that nothing could prevent the United States
from taking Canada. However, the extraordinary ineptitude of
the American war effort lost the moment of opportunity.
Napoleon's armies were driven from Spain and destroyed in
Russia. He abdicated on April 6, 1814. Thenceforth, Britain
was free to deploy her forces in America, and the United States
fought, not with any real prospect of victory, but to escape
defeat and loss of territory.

38. LETTER TO WILLIAM H. CRAWFORD

April 21, 1814

After his arrival in London Gallatin realized how slight were
the chances of making peace on reasonable terms. He therefore
wrote to Crawford, American minister to France, asking him
to solicit the good offices of Czar Alexander in behalf of the
United States.

Writings, I, 602–604.

Mr. Bayard and myself left St. Petersburg on the 25th January, remained four weeks at Amsterdam, and arrived here on the 9th instant. I could not write you sooner, there having been no communication with Paris from Holland, and Mr. Poletica, who is the bearer of this, having offered the first safe opportunity for a confidential letter.

Messrs. Clay and Russell, who are jointly with Messrs. Adams and Bayard appointed to open a direct negotiation for peace with Great Britain, arrived at Gottenburg on the 12th instant, after a passage of forty-six days; but, as they had not reached the town when the last packet sailed, we have not yet received any letter from them, or any American news brought by the vessel in which they came.

There is a newspaper report of Norfolk, under date of 12th February, stating that G. W. Campbell was made Secretary of the Treasury, Rush Attorney-General, and that I had been nominated fifth commissioner to treat of peace with England. My stay in Europe will of course depend on the official account which Messrs. Clay and Russell will have brought. You are sufficiently aware of the critical situation in which the restoration of a general European peace has placed our affairs. The numerous English forces in France, Italy, Holland, and Portugal ready for immediate service, and for which there is no further employment in Europe, afford to this government the means of sending both to Canada and to the United States a very formidable army, which we are not prepared to meet with any regular, well-organized force; and they will also turn against us as much of their superabundant naval forces as they may think adequate to any object they have in view. In the prosecution of the war the Ministry would be supported by the general voice of the nation. In the intoxication of an unexpected success, which they ascribe to themselves, the English people eagerly wish that their pride may be fully gratified by what they call the "punishment of America." They do not even suspect that we had any just cause of war, and ascribe it solely to a premeditated concert with Bonaparte at a time when we thought him triumphant and their cause desperate. That such opinions should be almost universally entertained here by the great body of the people is not at all astonishing. To produce such an effect, and thereby render the American war popular, the Ministerial papers have had nothing more to do than to transcribe American Federal speeches and newspapers. If Pickering, Quincy, Strong, Hanson, &c., have not brought a majority of the American people to their side, they have at least fully succeeded here, and had no difficulty in convincing all that part of the English community which derives its information from political journals that we had no cause of complaint, and acted only as allies of Bonaparte. I understand that the members of the Cabinet do not participate in that opinion, but it will certainly require an effort on their part against popular feeling to make peace with America. It must be added that even there (in the Cabinet) a belief is said to be entertained that a continuance of the war would produce a separation of the Union, and perhaps a return of the New England States to the mother-country. The multitude of persons in the army and navy, or connected with the war, where attached to the governing party, and whom peace will throw out of employment, will also press on government; and although it is probable that the immense military and naval establishments of this country will be so far reduced as to enable government to dispense with the most unpopular war taxes, a prosecution of the war against the United States would afford a convenient pretence for preserving a much more considerable standing force than is necessary and would otherwise be allowed by Parliament. It may, on the whole, be reasonably inferred that the ministers will be neither disposed to make the least concession (for doing us justice on any point would receive that name) in order to obtain peace, nor at all displeased in case of failure of the negotiations.

The only external check to those dispositions can be found in the friendly interposition of the Emperor Alexander, not as a mediator, but as a common friend, pressing on this government the propriety of an accommodation, and expressing his strong wishes for a general restoration of peace to the civilized world. I do not know whether your situation affords you means of approaching him, and can only state my opinion of the great importance that an early opportunity should be taken by you, or any other person you may think fitted for the object, to call his attention to the situation in which we are left, and to the great weight which his opinion in favor of peace on liberal conditions, strongly expressed to this government, must necessarily have at this time. Of his friendly disposition for the United States there is no doubt; but we may be forgotten; and it is necessary that he should be apprised of the hostile spirit which prevails here, and which, if not balanced by some other cause, may even carry ministers beyond their own wishes and views. It should also be stated that our government having accepted one year ago the Emperor's mediation, and not having supposed that, considering the political connection between him and Great Britain, she could reject that offer, no other provision was made on our part to obtain peace until our government was apprised in January last of the rejection of the mediation by England. Thus was a delay of a year produced, and the opening of our negotiations unfortunately prevented till after England is at peace with the rest of the world; a circumstance which, although it does not give us a positive right to claim the Emperor's interference, affords sufficient ground to present the subject to his consideration. I entreat you to lose no time in taking such steps as may be in your power in that respect, and to write to me whatever you may think important for the success of the mission should be known to us. The only modes of safe conveyance which I would recommend would be private American opportunities, or through the channel of the Russian Secretary of State, or of Mr. Poletica, directing to me under cover of "Count Lieven, Ambassador Extraordinary of H. I. M. the Emperor of all the Russias, London." . . .

39. GALLATIN AND JAMES BAYARD

TO JAMES MONROE

May 6, 1814

With the European war at an end, neutral rights were no longer a pressing issue, and most American war aims had no more than a theoretical significance. The only remaining positive goal of major consequence to the United States was to secure British renunciation of the right to impress seamen on American vessels. Gallatin and Bayard warned Madison, however, that in view of American military reverses and popular enthusiasm in Britain for continuing the war, the ministry would probably not concede anything on this or indeed any other point. The next month Madison changed the instructions of the peace commissioners, authorizing them to postpone or even waive discussion of impressments. Thus the principal American demand was compromised.

It is much to be apprehended that the great and unexpected events which have so entirely changed the state of affairs in Europe may have a serious effect on the nature and aspect of the war carried on by Great Britain against the United States, as well as on the proposed negotiations for peace. A convention has already been signed between France and the allies for the suspension of hostilities and for the restoration of prisoners. It is said and believed that the articles of a definitive treaty of peace between all the European powers have been chiefly agreed upon, and the treaty is expected to be concluded in a few weeks. This state of things, and the security derived by Great Britain from the restoration of the Bourbons on the throne of France and from the expulsion of Bonaparte to Elba, put at the disposition of this government the whole of their force heretofore employed against France. It might also be inconvenient here to reduce suddenly the army and navy to a peace establishment, and there can be no doubt that if the war continues, as great a portion of that disposable force as will be competent to the objects of the British government will be employed in America.

The complete success obtained by this country in their European contest has excited the greatest popular exultation, and this has been attended with a strong expression of resentment against the United States. Extravagant projects and hopes of success are entertained. The restriction of our commerce and fisheries is said to have been the subject of petitions to the Ministry; the curtailment of our northern boundary and an exclusive right to navigate the Lakes are suggested; and even a division of the Union is expected from a continuance of the war. The popular feeling is evidently strongly in favor of the prosecution of the war against us. This sentiment is universal, and so powerful that it will be difficult for ministers to control it should they be disposed to peace. Having no direct intercourse with any member of the Cabinet, our information as to its disposition or views is necessarily imperfect and uncertain. There is, however, no reason to doubt that peace may be had; but it seems certain that whatever modifications in the practice of impressment may be obtained, the point itself will not be conceded. On this subject the opposition and the whole nation support the Ministry. It is true that the restoration of peace in Europe has for the present reduced the conflicting rights and pretensions of the two countries on that subject to little more than questions of abstract rights, which might at this moment remain undecided without material prejudice to the interest of either party; but we have reason to believe that the Ministry is more disposed to an arrangement of the subject with a view to prevent what is called the abuses of the practice than to pass it over in silence. We think that we may at all events distinctly state that for our government the alternative only remains either to resolve on a vigorous prosecution of the war under an expectation of probable success, or to forego for the present the assertion of our rights on what was the principal remaining object of the war.

No persons have as yet been appointed on the part of this government to conduct the negotiation at Gottenburg. Having received an intimation that an official communication would be expected of the appointment of commissioners on our part and of their arrival in Europe before an appointment would be made by this government, we despatched a messenger to Gottenburg to Messrs. Clay and Russell, who we expect will enable us, in the course of a few days, to make the official notification which is suggested to be required. As soon as there is a probability of our being shortly followed by the British commissioners, we shall not fail to repair to the rendezvous agreed upon.

Conceiving that the negotiation could be conducted with more facility and despatch in Holland than at Gottenburg, and presuming that if the neutrality of Holland had been known in America when the place was fixed upon it would have been preferred, we have undertaken to recommend to Messrs. Clay and Russell, if our powers leave us a discretion on the subject, to transfer the seat of negotiation to Amsterdam or the Hague, which we are allowed to say would meet with the concurrence of this government. The good dispositions of the Prince of Orange towards our country are marked by his prompt appointment of a minister to our government, and we have reason to believe that he would freely contribute any friendly offices in his power to the re-establishment of peace.

We are also of opinion that under existing circumstances England would in every point of view be at present preferable for the seat of negotiation to any other place. These circumstances may, however, vary, and we beg leave to suggest the propriety of authorizing the commissioners of the United States to remove those negotiations to any place which in their judgment may appear most proper for insuring their successful issue.

40. LETTER TO JAMES MONROE

June 13, 1814

Gallatin anticipated the course that the negotiations would take. He advised Monroe that the United States could hope to obtain no more than the status quo ante bellum *and a postponement of issues to later discussion, but that the British, expecting military victories to enhance their bargaining position, would pile demand upon demand as the price of peace. Only America's determination and ability to continue the war would change Britain's attitude.*

The armament fitted against America will enable the British, besides providing for Canada, to land at least 15 to 20,000

men on the Atlantic coast. Whether the Ministry be nevertheless disposed for peace a few weeks will determine. It may
be intended to continue the war for the purpose of effecting
a separation of the Union, or with a view of promoting the
election of a President of the Federal party, or in the hope of
imposing conditions which will curtail the territory, the fisheries, and diminish the commerce of the United States; but
even with the intention of a speedy and equal peace, the pride
and vindictive passions of the nation would be highly gratified
by what they would consider a glorious termination of the war,
by an expedition that may console them for the mortification
of naval defeats, retrieve the disgrace of the campaign in the
Chesapeake, and cripple the naval and commercial resources,
as well as the growing manufactures, of the United States.
To use their own language, they mean to inflict on America
a chastisement that will teach her that war is not to be declared against Great Britain with impunity. This is a very
general sentiment in the nation, and that such are the opinions
and intentions of the Ministry was strongly impressed on the
mind of——by a late conversation he had with Lord Castle-
reagh. Admiral Warren also told to Levett Harris, with whom
he was intimate at St. Petersburg, that he was sorry to say that
the instructions given to his successor on the American station
were very different from those under which he had acted, and
that he apprehended that very serious injury would be inflicted
on America. Knowing the species of warfare practised under
him, and that he was blamed for the inefficiency and not on
account of the nature of his operations, you may infer what
is now intended. Without pretending to correct information
respecting their plan of campaign, I think it probable that
Washington and New York are the places the capture of
which would most gratify the enemy, and that Norfolk, Baltimore, and the collected manufacturing establishments of the
Brandywine and Rhode Island are also in danger. The ostensible object everywhere will be the destruction of the public

naval magazines and arsenals, and of all the shipping, whether public or private; but heavy contributions, plunder, and whatever marks a predatory warfare must be expected, unless the ultimate object be to sever the Union, demand a cession of territory, &c., in which case the permanent occupation of New York or some other important tenable point will probably be attempted instead of mere destruction. Whatever may be the object and duration of the war, America must rely on her resources alone. From Europe no assistance can, for some time, be expected. British pride begins, indeed, to produce its usual effect. Seeds of dissension are not wanting. Russia and England may, at the approaching Congress of Vienna, be at variance on important subjects, particularly as relates to the aggrandizement of Austria. But questions of maritime rights are not yet attended to, and America is generally overlooked by the European sovereigns or viewed with suspicion. Above all, there is nowhere any navy in existence; and years of peace must elapse before the means of resisting with effect the sea power of Great Britain can again be created. In a word, Europe wants peace, and neither will nor can at this time make war against Great Britain. The friendly disposition of the Emperor of Russia, and a just view of the subject, make him sincerely desirous that peace should be restored to the United States. He may use his endeavors for that purpose; beyond that he will not go, and in that it is not probable he will succeed. I have also the most perfect conviction that, under the existing unpropitious circumstances of the world, America cannot, by a continuance of the war, compel Great Britain to yield any of the maritime points in dispute, and particularly to agree to any satisfactory arrangement on the subject of impressment, and that the most favorable terms of peace that can be expected are the status ante bellum, and a postponement of the questions of blockade, impressment, and all other points which in time of European peace are not particularly injurious; but, with firmness and perseverance, those terms, though perhaps unattainable at this moment, will ultimately be obtained, provided you can stand the shock of this campaign, and provided the people will remain and show themselves united; this nation and government will be tired of a war without object, and which must become unpopular when the passions of the day will have subsided and the country sees clearly that America asks nothing from Great Britain. It is desirable that the negotiations of Ghent, if not productive of immediate peace, should at least afford satisfactory proof of this last point. I might have adduced several facts and collateral circumstances in support of the opinions contained in this letter, but you know I would not risk them on light grounds. You may rest assured of the general hostile spirit of this nation and of its wish to inflict serious injury on the United States; that no assistance can be expected from Europe; and that no better terms of peace will be obtained than the status ante bellum, &c., as above stated. I am less positive, though I fear not mistaken, with respect to the views of the Ministry, to the object of the armament, to the failure of the Emperor's interference, and to the consequent improbability of peace, even on those terms, before the conclusion of this year's campaign.

41. LETTER TO JAMES MONROE

August 20, 1814

Conversations began at Ghent August 8, 1814. As they proceeded the American commissioners were appalled by the extent of British demands. While conceding nothing, the

Writings, I, 637–640.

British insisted upon conditions that would have reduced the United States to quasi-colonial status: the creation of an Indian buffer state in the Northwest out of American territory, naval control of the Great Lakes, rectification of the Canadian boundary to allow British access to and navigation of the Mississippi River, and revocation of American fishing rights in Canadian waters unless Britain received an equivalent. The American envoys dispatched this information to Madison August 18. The next day, upon Gallatin's inquiry, the British commissioners declared that the Indian buffer state was a sine qua non *of any treaty.*

On August 20 Gallatin informed Monroe of Britain's territorial ambitions in the West and predicted an assault upon New Orleans.

The negotiations at this place will have the result which I have anticipated. In one respect, however, I had been mistaken. I had supposed, whilst in England, that the British Ministry in continuing the war yielded to the popular sentiment, and were only desirous of giving some éclat to the termination of hostilities, and by predatory attacks of inflicting gratuitous injury on the United States. It appears now certain that they have more serious and dangerous objects in view. On these I will not dwell, as they are sufficiently explained by our public despatches, and will only observe that the capture of Moose Island, and the manner of taking possession, accord with the general scope of their demands here. But I beg leave to advert to the effect which those views, now fully disclosed, may have on the manner of conducting the war.

The British will naturally attempt the conquest of what they wish to acquire by the peace. They will make great efforts in Canada with respect to the possession of Lakes Ontario and Erie, for the recapture of Detroit, and for the support of the Indians, so as to derive from the *status quo* some claim to what they already demand. And your attention will be naturally drawn to that quarter, and, amongst other objects, to a vigorous prosecution of the Indian war, which, by a total expulsion of the adjacent tribes, or by compelling them to make peace, will remove every pretext for what is now made a *sine qua non,* and, indeed, afford an opportunity to Great Britain to desist (without retracting) from that preliminary. It is not improbable that their warfare on our Atlantic shore will be on a smaller scale than I had conjectured, and may be confined to desultory attacks made successively on several points, for the purpose principally of distracting our defensive measures and of diverting a considerable part of our force from the points of real and serious attack. It appears to me most likely that their true and immediate object is New Orleans. They well know that it is our most distant and weakest point, and that if captured it could not be retaken without great difficulty. If successful in other quarters, there is no possession which, as a sugar colony, as a port in the Gulf of Mexico, and as commanding all our Western country both in a political and in a commercial view, they would be more desirious of holding. If less successful in Canada than they expect, New Orleans would be made a set-off, and its restitution to depend on our compliance with their demands in the North.

You will also perceive that they would hardly have any other object in view when they gave in their official note the formal intimation that if we did not now sign a treaty, Great Britain would not be precluded from the right of varying her demands according to the state of the war at the time of resuming the negotiations.

Finally, the expedition ready to sail under Lord Hill in the beginning of September cannot, it seems, considering the season of the year, have any other object but Louisiana. It is evidently too late for Canada, and even for all our Northern coast. There is no apparent utility for them in an attack on Charleston or Georgia, and immense advantages to be derived from the conquest of New Orleans. It is not impossible that this last object may be connected with Florida, the cession of which by Spain to England is possible.

It is now evident that Great Britain intends to strengthen and aggrandize herself in North America. Knowing that that object would be fully disclosed by her proposals, and that these were inadmissible, it is not uncandid to suppose that her object in protracting the negotiations has been to delay their rupture to the very moment when her expedition under General Hill would be ready and must sail, in order to prevent, as far as practicable, our taking early alarm and making sufficient preparations to repel the attack.

It is highly probable that our struggle will be longer and more arduous than I had anticipated. I believe the other views I had given you respecting Europe to be correct. We cannot expect assistance from any quarter on our own account. An earlier renewal of war here than had been conjectured is not impossible, and would operate in our favor. It is an event which we cannot in any respect control, and of which, without relying on it, we must be ready to take advantage whenever it may happen.

Mr. Dallas is the bearer of our despatches. I have told him that I expected government would pay his expenses from this place to the Helder, and those of his passage and provisions on board the John Adams. He will accordingly state and transmit his account to you.

I do not expect that we can be detained more than two or three weeks longer, for the purpose either of closing the negotiation, of taking every other necessary step connected with it, and of making all the arrangements for our departure. In the hope of having the pleasure of seeing you again very soon, I have, &c.

I do not know to what the British commissioners allude in their note of yesterday, when they say that their government has forborne to press certain points on which they had a right to insist, unless it be to a recognition of their assumed right of impressment.

42. LETTER TO JAMES MONROE

December 25, 1814

Early in November the British ministry suddenly decided to drop its demands and make peace on reasonable terms. Great power rivalries at the Congress of Vienna portended a renewal of European war, suggesting the wisdom of keeping British forces near at hand. Depressed British manufactures clamored for the reopening of American markets. A continuation of war posed financial difficulties for the government; the treasury was depleted, the national debt had risen to a colossal figure, and an increase in the land tax was certain to have grave political consequences. Basically, however, as Gallatin had predicted, Britain's change of front was dictated by military reverses in America that dispelled any idea of easy conquest. The naval victories of Captain Oliver Hazard Perry on Lake Erie in November 1813 and of Captain Thomas Macdonough on Lake Champlain in September 1814 had given the United States control of the invasion routes from Canada. Macdonough's

Writings, I, 645–647.

victory had compelled the retreat of a strong British force under General George Prevost which was preparing to invade the United States along the Lake Champlain-Hudson River route. In England, Lord Wellington, when asked to take command in America, informed the ministry that military prospects indicated a long and dubious war, and that present achievements did not justify demands for territorial cessions.

On November 12 the British commissioners under instructions from their home government agreed to waive all the major points except those relative to the fisheries and the navigation of the Mississippi. Their position on these issues was that the treaty of 1783 had lapsed with the outbreak of war and that therefore the American right to fish in Canadian waters guaranteed by that treaty did not exist and could not be renewed except in return for an equivalent concession by the United States. The concession they had in mind was a boundary adjustment in the northwest to permit direct access to the Mississippi River from Canada, along with the right to navigate the river. This gambit created a rift in the American delegation. Henry Clay, the westerner, would not countenance British access to the Mississippi, whereas John Quincy Adams was determined to preserve New England's fisheries. Divided internally, the committee studied various alternatives but at length agreed to a compromise sponsored by Gallatin—to omit reference both to the fisheries and the Mississippi, leaving these topics to later negotiation. The British accepted this proposal on December 23, and the treaty was signed the next day. Ownership of certain islands in Passamaquoddy Bay was to be submitted to arbitration. Otherwise, disputed issues were passed over in silence: boundaries, fisheries, impressments, spoliation claims, and neutral rights.

The treaty of peace we signed yesterday with the British ministers is, in my opinion, as favorable as could be expected under existing circumstances, so far as they were known to us. The attitude taken by the State of Massachusetts, and the appearances in some of the neighboring States, had a most unfavorable effect. Of the probable result of the congress at Vienna we had no correct information. The views of all the European powers were precisely known from day to day to the British Ministry. From neither of them did we in any shape receive any intimation of their intentions, of the general prospect of Europe, or of the interest they took in our contest with Great Britain. I have some reason to believe that all of them were desirous that it might continue. They did not intend to assist us; they appeared indifferent about our difficulties; but they rejoiced at anything which might occupy and eventually weaken our enemy. The manner in which the campaign has terminated, the evidence afforded by its events of our ability to resist alone the now very formidable military power of England, and our having been able, without any foreign assistance, and after she had made such an effort, to obtain peace on equal terms, will raise our character and consequence in Europe. This, joined with the naval victories and the belief that we alone can fight the English on their element, will make us to be courted as much as we have been neglected by foreign governments. As to the people of Europe, public opinion was most decidedly in our favor. I anticipate a settlement with Spain on our own terms, and the immediate chastisement of the Algerines. Permit me to suggest the propriety of despatching a squadron for that purpose without losing a single moment. I have little to add to our public despatch on the subject of the terms of the treaty. I really think that there is nothing but nominal in the Indian article as adopted. With respect to precedents, you will find two, though neither is altogether in point, viz.: the article of the Treaty of Utrecht, and the latter part of the article of our treaty with Spain. You know that there was no alternative between breaking off the negotiations and accepting the article, and that we accepted it only as provisional and subject to your approbation or rejection. The exception of Moose Island from the general restoration of territory is the only point on which it is possible that we might have obtained an alteration if we had adhered to our opposition to it. The British government had long fluctuated on the question of peace: a favorable account from Vienna, the report of some success in the Gulf of Mexico, or any other incident, *might* produce a change in their disposition; they had already, after the question had been referred to them, declared that they could not consent to a relinquishment of that point. We thought it too hazardous to risk the peace on the question of the temporary possession of that small island, since the question of title was fully reserved, and it was therefore no cession of territory. On the subject of the fisheries within the jurisdiction of Great Britain, we have certainly done all that could be done. If, according to the construction of the treaty of 1783, which we assumed, the right was not abrogated by the war, it remains entire, since we most explicitly refused to renounce it directly or indirectly. In that case it is only an unsettled subject of difference between the two countries. If the right must be considered as abrogated by the war, we cannot regain it without an equivalent. We had none to give but the recognition of their right to navigate the Mississippi, and we offered it on this last supposition. This right is also lost to them, and in a general point of view we have certainly lost nothing. But we have done all that was practicable in support of the right to those fisheries, 1, by the ground we assumed respecting the construction of the treaty of 1783; 2, by the offer to recognize the British right to the navigation of the Mississippi; 3, by refusing to accept from Great Britain both her implied renunciation to the right of that navigation and the convenient boundary of 49 degrees for the whole extent of our and her territories west of the Lake of the Woods, rather than to make an implied renunciation on our own part to the right of America to those particular fisheries. I believe that Great Britain is very desirous of obtaining the northern part of Maine, say from about 47 north latitude to the northern extremity of that district as claimed by us. They hope that the river which empties into Bay des Chaleurs, in the Gulf of St. Lawrence, has its source so far west as to intervene between the head-waters of the river St. John and those of the streams emptying into the river St. Lawrence: so that the line north from the source of the river St. Croix will first strike the heights of land which divide the waters emptying into the Atlantic Ocean (river St. John's) from those emptying into the Gulf of St. Lawrence (River des Chaleurs), and afterwards the heights of land which divide the waters emptying into the Gulf of St. Lawrence (River des Chaleurs) from those emptying into the river St. Lawrence; but that the said line never can, in the words of the treaty, strike any spot of land actually dividing the waters emptying into the Atlantic Ocean from those which fall into the river St. Lawrence. Such will be the foundation of their disputing our claim to the northern part of that territory; but, feeling that it is not very solid, I am apt to think that they will be disposed to offer the whole of Passamaquoddy Bay and the disputed fisheries as an equivalent for this portion of northern territory, which they want in order to connect New Brunswick and Quebec. This may account for their tenacity with respect to the temporary possession of Moose Island, and for their refusing to accept the recognition of their right to the navigation of the Mississippi, provided they recognized ours to the fisheries. That northern territory is of no importance to us, and belongs to the United States, and not to Massachusetts, which has not the shadow of a claim to any land north of 45 to the eastward of the Penobscot River, as you may easily convince yourself of by recurring to her charters.

43. LETTER TO MATTHEW LYON

May 7, 1816

Gallatin's considered reflections upon the War of 1812 might have been written almost word for word by the Federalists about the quasi-war with France in 1798.

. . . The war has been productive of evil and good, but I think the good preponderates. Independent of the loss of lives, and of the losses in property by individuals, the war has laid the foundation of permanent taxes and military establishments, which the Republicans had deemed unfavorable to the happiness and free institutions of the country. But under our former system we were becoming too selfish, too much attached exclusively to the acquisition of wealth, above all, too much confined in our political feelings to local and State objects. The war has renewed and reinstated the national feelings and character which the Revolution had given, and which were daily lessened. The people have now more general objects of attachment with which their pride and political opinions are connected. They are more Americans; they feel and act more as a nation; and I hope that the permanency of the Union is thereby better secured. . . .

THE RESUMPTION OF SPECIE PAYMENT

During the War of 1812 the government had issued nearly $37,000,000 in Treasury notes and legal tender notes. To this

---

Writings, I, 700.

unredeemed currency was added a proliferation of state bank notes, increasing from $45,000,000 in 1812 to $100,000,000 in 1817. Little of this currency was convertible into specie. Except in New England state banks had suspended specie payments in September 1814, and two months later the federal government had followed. The large quantities of irredeemable and depreciated paper in circulation had caused inflation and encouraged wild speculation.

As a corrective measure Congress in 1816 charted the second Bank of the United States, along lines, it may be noted, very different from Gallatin's recommendations in 1811. When the Bank had been in existence less than six months, Congress attempted to force a general resumption of specie payments by declaring that after February 20, 1817 the federal government would accept nothing but specie or paper redeemable in specie. This resumption policy, which conformed with Gallatin's views, forced the Bank of the United States to require specie payment from state banks. Although mismanagement of the Bank was a factor, the premature resumption of specie payments contributed to the Panic of 1819.

44. LETTER TO THOMAS JEFFERSON

November 27, 1815

Contemplating Napoleon's return from Elba (March 1, 1815), the Battle of Waterloo, and the Bourbon restoration, Gallatin voiced his final disenchantment with the French Revolution.

Writings, I, 666–668.

With respect to the internal affairs of the United States, his most immediate concern was the monetary problem. His remedy was the immediate resumption of specie payment, lest the country become addicted to an irredeemable currency.

On my return from Washington I found your welcome letter of October 16, which my friends here, daily expecting my return, had kept instead of forwarding it.

Our opinion of Bonaparte is precisely the same. In that La Fayette's and every friend of rational liberty in France did coincide. The return of that man was generally considered by them as a curse. Notwithstanding the blunders and rooted prejudices of the Bourbons, the alienation of the army and the absolute want of physical force had made them, upon the whole, harmless, and as soon as the termination of the congress at Vienna and the dissolution of the coalition would have left France independent of foreign interference, they must in the course of things either have been overset or have governed according to public opinion. After Bonaparte's restoration, it was hoped by some that his weakness would compel him to pursue a similar course; others, placing confidence in the declarations of the allies, hoped to get rid both of him and of the Bourbons. All saw the necessity of defending the country against foreign invasion, but the fatal catastrophe was not, to its full extent, anticipated by any. I call it a catastrophe with an eye only to the present; for, exhausted, degraded, and oppressed as France now is, I do not despair of her ultimate success in establishing her independence and a free form of government. The people are too enlightened to submit long to any but a military despotism. What has lately passed was a scene in the drama, perhaps necessary to effect a radical cure of that love of conquest which had corrupted the nation and made the French oppressors abroad and slaves at home. As to independence, we have the recent instance of Prussia, which, with far inferior population, resources, or intellect, arose in two years from almost annihilation to the rank of a preponderating power. But, to return to Bonaparte, I lament to see our Republican editors so much dazzled by extraordinary actions or carried away by natural aversion to our only dangerous enemy as to take up the cause of that despot and conqueror, and to represent him as the champion of liberty, who has been her most mortal enemy, whose hatred to republican systems was founded on the most unbounded selfishness and on the most hearty contempt for mankind. I really wish that you would permit me to publish, or rather that you would publish, your opinion on that subject. This might have a tendency to correct those which are daily published, and which do injury to our cause at home, to our country abroad.

Under different circumstances, without having any wish for a foreign mission or a residence in France, I might have accepted the appointment of minister there. But, satisfied that nothing can at this moment be effected in that country, and it being very reluctant to my feelings to be on a mission to a degraded monarch and to a nation under the yoke of foreign armies, I thought that I might, without any breach of public duty or of private gratitude, consult my own convenience, and I have accordingly officially informed our government that I declined altogether the appointment.

On the lamentable state to which the banks have reduced the circulating medium of the country there ought to be but one opinion. Yet I fear with you that there will be no legislative effectual interference. The remedy becomes also more difficult every day it is delayed. Specie, for which there is no use but for exportation, is hoarded up or exported. The number of borrowers and of pretended lenders, equally interested in continuing and extending the present system at the expense of the community, daily increases. What might have been done last

April with perfect facility cannot now be effected without causing much clamor and some distress, and if delayed much longer will not be done at all, and will place us in a situation similar to that of Great Britain. I have no patience on that subject. The war has been successfully and honorably terminated; a debt of no more than 80 millions incurred, which, as we had paid more than 40 during your Administration and till the war began, makes that debt only 40 millions or 50 per cent. more than it was in March, 1801; and Louisiana paid for, and an incipient navy created in the bargain; our population increased in the same, and our resources in a much greater proportion; our revenue greater than ever; and yet we are guilty of a continued breach of faith towards our creditors, our soldiers, our seamen, our civil officers; public credit, heretofore supported simply by common honesty, declining at home and abroad; private credit placed on a still more uncertain basis; the value of property and the nature of every person's engagements equally uncertain; a baseless currency varying every fifty miles and fluctuating everywhere,—all this done, or at least continued, contrary to common sense and to common integrity, not only without necessity or law, but in the face of positive laws and of the provisions of the Constitution itself. Yet a majority of the Republican papers already leans to that system. The seat of government is the worst focus of the evil, there not being less than 14 banks already organized in the District of Columbia, and some more preparing. The language of several of the bank directors is similar to that of Peter to his brothers in the Tale of the Tub. They insist that their bread (God grant it was even bread!) is good, substantial mutton, that their rags are true solid silver; and some of them do already damn to all eternity every unbeliever. I have, however, some hope that the magnitude of the evil will produce a corrective, and I cannot help thinking that the Treasury will now be so rich that its will would alone be sufficient to prostrate at once that paper fabric. I have also indulged, with more warmth than is usual to me, in a political effusion; but I have been so long wedded to the national credit and integrity, that any stain which attaches to them touches me in a very tender point.

THE TARIFF OF 1816

In 1816 nascent American manufactures were in danger of being overwhelmed by British imports, creating an emergency that in some degree overrode ideological cavils or sectional interests. Gallatin was never doctrinaire on this or on any other question, but even Jefferson had qualified the old Republican creed. Jefferson wrote in 1816: "We have experienced what we did not then believe, that there exists both profligacy and power enough to exclude us from the field of interchange with other nations; that to be independent for the comforts of life we must fabricate them ourselves. We must now place the manufacturer by the side of the agriculturalist."[1]

45. LETTER TO T. R. GOLD

March 19, 1816

Gallatin had no objections to the tariff of 1816 except to warn that excessive duties would encourage smuggling.

---

[1] Jefferson to Benjamin Austin, Jan. 9, 1816. Andrew A. Lipscomb, ed., *The Writings of Thomas Jefferson* (20 vols., The Thomas Jefferson Memorial Association, Washington, 1905), XIV, 387–393.

Writings, I, 689–691.

I am this moment honored with your note of this day. The information you have received that I was concerned with Mr. Astor in the importing business is altogether erroneous. I never have been, nor am at present, either directly or indirectly, connected with that gentleman in any business whatever. I am not engaged and do not intend to engage in any commercial pursuits. However unimportant or erroneous my opinions may be on the subject, they are at least wholly disinterested; yet the length of time I spent in the Treasury may have produced some bias on my mind, and the danger of infractions of the revenue laws probably strikes me more forcibly than it does other persons.

From various considerations I have been induced to wish that there should be a total prohibition of the importation of East India cotton goods, so far at least as relates to those of coarse fabric. That opinion I expressed to Mr. Thomas Morris in New York, and is, I presume, that to which you allude. It has been communicated to others, and is not changed.

With respect to the proposed tariff, I do not perceive, as it relates to the consumer, that it can be very material to him whether his share of the public burdens is raised on the cloth he wears or on the sugar and coffee he consumes. There appears, therefore, in that respect, no objection to a modification of the duties which shall afford encouragement to domestic manufactures. The limit to high duties is the danger of smuggling on that large scale which will defeat the object in view. What that limit is must be matter of opinion. No man can assert positively the precise point to which you may go with safety and beyond which it would be dangerous to raise the duty. I may, however, state as a fact that prior to the adoption of our restrictive measures a duty of 17½ per cent. was raised on a considerable portion of the goods paying duties ad valorem, without any sensible or dangerous evasions of the duties having taken place. I do at the same time most sincerely believe that the highest rates of duties proposed by the Secretary of the Treasury, as applicable to the finer species of goods, would fill the country with smuggled merchandise, and would prove equally injurious to the fair trader and to the manufacturer himself. The revenue may be protected against considerable illicit importations by sea; but the great danger arises from the vicinity of New Brunswick and from our very extensive northern land frontier. To what extent smuggling is carried on under similar circumstances in Europe is well known, and the habits and skill acquired here during the restrictive system cannot be overlooked. I must repeat that what may be thought the highest safe rate of duty is only a matter of opinion until it has been tested by experience. I give mine with diffidence, but think that with coarse cotton and woollen goods, which may, I presume, be discriminated, and with the exception of other bulky articles, such as hardware, &c., it would be dangerous at present to go beyond 20, or at most 25 per cent. If I was either a manufacturer or a legislator, I had rather begin with 20 per cent., with a view to a gradual subsequent increase if justified by the experiment. An absolute prohibition of East India cotton goods can be carried into effect with much more facility than very high duties, because in the first case the goods which are easily distinguished may be seized anywhere and at any time, whilst in the other they are almost entirely beyond the reach of seizure the moment they have passed our boundary-line. The experience of England with respect to French silks and even to laces is decisive on that point. I may add that the measure would also have the double effect of assisting in resuming specie payments, and demonstrate to the British government that we do not consider the permission to trade with their East India possessions as conferring any valuable privilege on us.

PART SEVEN

Financial Oracle:
The Bank War, 1830–1832

After its organization in 1816, the second Bank of the United States was at first mismanaged by its president, William Jones. Reforms were achieved under Langdon Cheves, elected president in 1819, and with the advent of Nicholas Biddle in 1823, the Bank entered upon a period of rapid growth and prosperity. While expanding all phases of its operations, it carried out the central banking functions expected of it by giving the country a uniform currency in the form of its circulating notes and by restraining the speculative proclivities of state banks, particularly in the West and Southwest. Nevertheless, it incurred a great deal of hostility. Westerners never forgot its role in the Panic of 1819 when its contractions of loans started an avalanche of bankruptcies. Its current restraints upon the note issues of western banks generated resentment on the part of western banking interests, farmers, and land speculators. Its monopoly of government deposits and the country-wide organization that allowed it virtually to preempt intersectional transfer of funds aroused the envy of eastern bankers. Hard money doctrinaires speaking for eastern laborers declared its operations a factor in causing business cycles and unemployment.

To residual Jeffersonians and leveling democrats it repre-
sented a corrupt union of government and private interest.

Andrew Jackson upon assuming the Presidency revived
doubts, presumably settled years before, about its constitu-
tionality, thus drawing the Bank into party politics. In 1830
Jackson and Biddle privately agreed to defer renewal of its
charter, due to expire in 1836, until after the 1832 election.
But Biddle, convinced of Jackson's inveterate hostility to the
Bank, yielded to the importunities of Jackson's political foes,
Henry Clay and Daniel Webster, who were seeking an issue
for the forthcoming campaign. Plans were made to introduce
a recharter bill into Congress.

46. LETTER TO ROBERT WALSH, JR.

April 27, 1830

In April 1830 Robert Walsh, Jr., editor of the American Quarterly Review, *who at Biddle's behest was printing material*
favorable to the Bank, solicited an article from Gallatin.
Gallatin returned a preliminary sketch of his views and asked
for statistical information, which Biddle eventually supplied, to
assist his writing the article. It was first published in the De-
cember issue of the Review, *then published in expanded form*
as a pamphlet.

It is doubtful whether I will have time to prepare in season
such an article in relation to currency as you desire, and still

more so whether I can write anything on that subject worthy of the public and corresponding with your views. So much has been written on that question, that it does not seem to me that anything new can be advanced in support of what are admitted by almost all enlightened and disinterested men to be correct principles. The only points at all dubious, at least in my opinion, are those of *local currencies,* or what is commonly called "country notes," and of the simultaneous circulation of gold and silver. Was it practicable, the following outline would appear to me preferable to any other, as combining safety, convenience, and facilities sufficient to promote industry and prudent enterprise.

1. No other but the Bank of the United States, nor any individuals, associations, or corporations, to be permitted to issue any bank-note, bills of credit, or paper in the nature of currency; but all such banks or bankers to be left, without restriction or special tax, at liberty to pursue in other respects their proper occupation, viz., to receive deposits, to discount notes, and to deal in bills of exchange or bullion; thereby assimilating them to the bankers of London and to all those of the Continent of Europe, neither of whom issues a single shilling of paper currency.

2. The Bank of the United States to issue no notes of a denomination under 100 dollars (a restriction the same as that of the Bank of France), those of a lower denomination excepted, which may be made redeemable at any of its offices where presented.

3. Gold and silver United States coins to circulate either on the new British plan of issuing silver at 10 or 15 per cent. above its intrinsic value, but not to be a legal tender for sums above ten dollars, or simultaneously for all purposes, but rating gold at its true value, which may be done so near the ratio of gold to silver (about 15.6 to 1) as to obviate every practical objection.

4. All foreign coins to be excluded; copper coins to remain

as now, but not to be a legal tender for more than 50 cents.

You may perceive that I am an ultra-bullionist, which it is right you should know. But I am perfectly sensible that Congress will not attempt to prohibit the issue of notes by State banks; that we have no other security against their over-issues but State laws, which some States will not enact, and the Bank of the United States; that our reliance for a sound currency and, therefore, for a just performance of contracts rests on that institution; and that, in order to enable it to check and counteract the evil tendency of the local currencies, it must be permitted to issue notes of a smaller denomination than would otherwise be eligible. The principal object at this time is to preserve what we have, rather than to aim at what cannot be obtained. But I know too well, from sad experience, how difficult it is, without the aid of party, to carry any measure, however useful, which is opposed from sectional or interested views. And yet, though aware of the unavailing effect of argument under such circumstances, I would be disposed to contribute my mite if I thought I could add anything to what has been done by others. It is also so long since my mind was made up on the subject, that I have not lately collected any facts. The evidence reported by the committees of both Houses of Parliament previous to the resuming of specie payments in Great Britain is the last document of any importance which I read with attention. A correct statement of the amount and nature of our currency is an indispensable preliminary to any essay on the subject. The ordinary returns of the Bank of the United States and of the several State banks, of the latest dates that can be obtained, not in the aggregate for each State, but showing the situation of each bank, would be sufficient, as I am familiar with those returns. The cashiers of the several offices of the Bank of the United States might with ease procure most of them. If you can obtain these for me, I will try to write, with the understanding that, if prevented or not satisfied myself, I will put my notes in your hands to be used as you may think proper.

47. LETTER TO NICHOLAS BIDDLE

August 14, 1830

While preparing his article Gallatin corresponded with Biddle. In view of the catastrophe that later overtook the Bank, Gallatin's admonitions to the financier are of interest. He felt that the ability of the Bank to sustain the convertibility of its own note issues and those of the state banks could not be assured without increasing the supply of hard money in the country. To this end he proposed altering the ratio between gold and silver established by the American coinage system. In 1792 the United States had instituted a bimetallic standard that provided for the coinage of silver and gold bullion at the rate of fifteen to one. This ratio soon ceased to represent the actual value of the two metals relative to one another. Silver became cheaper in the market and was therefore overvalued in coinage; gold was correspondingly undervalued. Hence gold was not presented for coinage, and gold coins, actually worth more than their face value for their metal content, were melted down and passed out of circulation. The coinage of silver was stopped by President Jefferson. Until the mid-1830's, therefore, the currency consisted almost exclusively of bank notes. Gal-

---

latin's suggestion was that instead of expanding the volume of United States Bank notes of small denominations, gold coinage should be encouraged by correcting the ratio between gold and silver. This would afford a supply of hard money to back all bank notes.

Gallatin understood better than Biddle the potential opposition to the Bank's recharter and suggested ways of forestalling it. Since the Bank made a profit out of the country's circulating medium, he advised Biddle that he could well expect that the Bank would have to make a large payment to the government as a condition of recharter. He also proposed reducing the Bank's discount on bills of exchange, giving up the practice of selling the Bank's bills at a premium, and making Bank of the United States notes uniformly receivable at all branches. All this was intended to mollify opposition. As a final hint he suggested that Biddle might concede that country banks had a legitimate and valuable function in the national economy.

Your answers to my several inquiries have in most instances corroborated my previous opinions, and on several points thrown new light and indeed opened new views of the subject. There is but one of any importance on which I apprehend that we do not altogether agree. I think that you are too sanguine in your expectation of the ability of the Bank of the United States to sustain, under the pressure of any very difficult crisis, specie payments throughout the United States. You have managed the affairs of that institution with so much ability and success that the error, if it is one, is very natural. My own opinion is that, in the use of any paper currency, what we gain in the cheapness of the instrument we lose in security, and that, in order to combine the undeniable utility of paper with real security under adverse as well as favorable circumstances, there is no other remedy than a permanent increase of

the *circulating* metallic currency and a corresponding diminution of the paper. And for that purpose the most simple and
efficient mode is the suppression of notes of inferior denomination. To this the government of Great Britain has gradually
been led by experience, and it has persevered against a most
powerful opposition on the part of the country banks and all
their ramifications. The result is that, on a circulation of about
58 millions sterling, they have about 28 millions in bank-notes,
22 in gold, and 8 in silver. They must necessarily give up their
indefensible silver currency and substitute one corresponding
with its intrinsic value, and time may suggest further improvements. With us, it seems from a first rough estimate that
our currency is less than 90 millions of dollars, of which about
60 in bank-notes, 20 in silver in the vaults of the banks (but
this portion is not in fact a part of the circulation, which, if
the estimate is correct, amounts actually to only 70 millions),
and less than 10 in silver circulating amongst the community.
You very justly observe that, if the Bank of the United States
was to withdraw its 5-dollar notes, the deficiency would be
filled, not by gold, but by the notes of other banks,—an objection which Congress may not have the will, but has the
undeniable constitutional power, to obviate by the imposition
of a stamp duty. But permit me to remark that, however analogous in other respects, there is in this point of view a most
essential difference between United States $5 and British £5
notes, since the admission of the first excludes, whilst the
suppression of all those under £5 brings in the circulation gold
coins or an equal value in silver, according to the mint regulations and circumstances of the country. You will at once
perceive why I have been anxious that gold, by being rated
at our mint at nearly its real value, *might* become part of the
circulating medium; and that, whilst allowing even in prosperous times the necessity of the Bank of the United States to
maintain a sound currency, I would wish, if practicable, such
further restrictions on the issue of paper generally as would

enable that institution at all times *and under any direction* to perform that office, and to afford complete security against the recurrence of a baneful and demoralizing inconvertible paper currency. The most skilfully administered bank can only be prepared to meet ordinary commercial fluctuations. But when a real and severe crisis occurs, you are perfectly aware that moral causes may increase the pressure to an extent that will baffle every calculation, for the very reason that those causes are beyond the reach of calculation. On the other hand, the example of France, under the united pressure of a double invasion, a failure of crops, large indemnities to foreign countries,—a vast portion of which was paid by the exportation of specie,—an unsettled government, and wild stock speculations, is decisive to prove with what facility a crisis is met with an abundant circulating metallic currency. We were, Mr. Baring and myself, spectators of the crisis, of which I could only see the external appearances and results, whilst he was behind the scenes and deeply interested in the event. We conferred often on the subject, and came to the same conclusions. He has ever since been an advocate in England of the simultaneous use of the two metals for the sole purpose of enlarging the basis of the metallic currency; and I beg leave to refer to his evidence before the House of Lords in March, 1819, particularly in reference to the *fact* that the Bank of France, in a situation nearly as critical as that of the Bank of England in February, 1797, was preserved by the supply afforded "through all the various small channels of circulation" of a country "every part of the circulation of which is saturated with specie." As far as I can yet judge, the amount of the State banks' notes now in circulation does not materially differ from what it was in 1819, whilst yours have increased from less than 3½ to near 18 millions. That increase is no more than what was wanted, that is to say, from about 45 to 60 millions, which corresponds with our increase of population; and in a country which is not in a retrograde situation the mass of exchanges and sales of commodities will, and the currency, all other things being equal, should, increase nearly in the same ratio as the population. Viewing, therefore, the currency not partially, but as a whole, your circulation has rather checked the increase than taken the place of the notes of the State banks, operating of course both ways where those banks were quite rotten. But we must expect that a corresponding gradual increase of currency will be wanted, amounting, at the same ratio, to 20 millions additional at the end of the next ten years. Now your circulation is already in the ratio of more than 50 per cent. to the amount of your capital, which exceeds the ratio not only of the Massachusetts, Rhode Island, and good city banks, but that of all the State banks taken together, this not being much above 40 per cent. Though probably practicable, and not inconsistent with the generally admitted banking principles, would it be prudent to increase your circulation much beyond its present amount? Keeping always in view ultimate security and the possibility of an extraordinary crisis, would it not be a safer course, if practicable, to supply that gradual want of an addition to the existing currency by an enlargement of the metallic currency, rather than by an increase of notes of any description?

Deeply impressed with what I consider a fundamental principle, I must necessarily advert to it whenever I treat the subject. But it does not follow that it would be proper to present it precisely in the same manner as when addressing you in confidence. The first duty is to preserve the anchor of safety to which we are now moored; and in every plan of reform it is but common wisdom to propose only that which there is a chance to obtain. Yet, and although I have heretofore always abstained from any allusion to the constitutional powers of Congress in reference to State banks, I do not know whether it may not now be proper to act on the offensive. The suggestion of a stamp duty, the animadversions on the guarantee of bank-notes by a State, and thorough exposure of the country banking system, are all of that character. How far and where it may be prudent to conciliate or necessary to attack I have not sufficiently examined, and must remain for the moment subject to further consideration. But I wish to call your early attention to the imminent danger there is that the renewal of the charter may not be obtained on any terms, and to the absolute necessity of the sacrifices which will, at all events, be requisite in order to succeed.

In 1810 the weight of the Administration was in favor of a renewal, Mr. Madison having made his opinion known that he considered the question as settled by precedent, and myself an open and strenuous advocate. We had the powerful support of Mr. Crawford in the Senate, and no formidable opponent in either House but Mr. Clay, a majority of political friends in both Houses, and almost all the Federal votes on that question, with no other untoward circumstance but the *personal* opposition to Mr. Madison or myself of the Clintons, the Maryland Smiths, Leib, and Giles; the banking system had not yet penetrated through the country, extending its ramifications through every hamlet, and the opposition due to the jealousy or selfishness of rival institutions was confined to a few cities; yet the question was lost. Now opposition arising from interested motives pervades the whole country; in this State, for instance, amidst the unintelligible commixture and distinction of parties, the country banking interest is all-powerful on all questions connected with that subject; with a sect of politicians throughout the Union "State rights" has become a watchword; worst of all, the President has prematurely and gratuitously declared himself and given the signal of attack to his adherents; and all these, with the exception of a few friends of Mr. Calhoun, are ready to obey. I believe that all the three enlightened members of Congress for this city are of the number. The result of my personal observations last winter at Washington was unfavorable; even Mr. Ingham, a friend to the institution, seemed to me to despair, and Mr. Van Buren's safety fund is at least a proof that his views of the banking system are not correct. Against all this we have only the experimental knowledge of what would be the result of uncontrolled State banks; and, taking in consideration all the circumstances of the case, I am clearly of opinion that, if the charter is renewed, it will not be on such terms as the bank might wish, but on the conditions which Congress may be pleased to impose, and which the bank will be compelled to accept. It was a mistake on the part of the agent of the former bank, Mr. Hollingsworth, to believe, when the discussion took place, that he could treat with Congress on equal terms. And I may add that the high dividends, extensive circulation, and flourishing situation of the bank will afford additional motives or arguments for imposing harder conditions. One of the most obvious arguments will be derived from the practice adopted by the States to tax their banks. If Massachusetts imposes one, and New York, including the safety fund, more than one, per cent. annually on the capital, why should the Bank of the United States, enjoying greater advantages, be exempted? I do believe a tax to that amount, or an equivalent, to be the minimum which will be required; and if the bank can, when paying no tax, divide 7 per cent., it will be clearly its interest to submit to the condition rather than to dissolve itself.

It must, indeed, be acknowledged that, independent of the value of the privilege to trade without incurring any greater risk than the amount of capital paid in, and setting aside the advantages derived from private and public deposits, there is a solid foundation for the claim on the part of the public to participate at least in the profits derived from the issues of a paper currency. No change may be said to be produced that affects the community by the substitution of convertible and not depreciated paper to gold and silver. In both cases the community loses (each individual in proportion to his share of it) the interest on the total amount of the circulation, and may be considered as paying an annual tax to that amount (which, being received, in the case of a metallic currency, by nobody, is a dead loss to the country); and as, in the case of such non-depreciated paper currency, the amount of the whole currency in circulation cannot be materially increased, the tax remains the same. But in this case the proceeds of that tax, or at least a considerable portion, instead of being lost to everybody, are actually received by those who have the privilege of issuing the paper; and this is in fact the principal advantage arising from the substitution of paper for gold and silver, a privilege in which there is a common, universal feeling, founded, as I think, in justice, that the community or the government has a right to participate. To what amount must be investigated; but I would think it consistent with the soundest policy at once to acknowledge the justice of the claim, and that an equivalent must be given for it. One of the advantages is that of meeting the argument that government has a right and ought to issue the paper. Admitting the principle, you have only to show that not only the object is attained in a cheaper, safer, and more efficient manner through the instrumentality of the bank, but that, in reality, government may through it also receive without risk or trouble as much profit as if issuing itself the paper.

Whether a direct tax on capital or dividends, or an equivalent by a moderate interest on public deposits, a participation in the dividends when exceeding a certain rate, or some other mode, would be preferable, should be subjects of early consideration, in order that the public mind may be prepared before the day of Congressional discussion. What I would prefer, as conferring more real benefit to the community than any payment in money, would be a reduction from 6 to 5 per cent. in the rate at which bills are discounted; but this may not be practicable; and banking left to private individuals has certainly that advantage over our system, that the rate at which they lend, varying with circumstances, always adapts itself to the state of commerce and of the money market. Here, and on the plan of an inflexible rate of discounting bills, when there is less demand for capital, banks must either lay on their oars, as your branch did at Boston at the time you mentioned, or discount doubtful paper; and when the demand becomes great they must reject good paper, or discount more than prudence would dictate. The private banker in London and everywhere on the Continent of Europe discounts, according to the plenty or scarcity of money (as it is called), at the rate of 3 or as high as 8 per cent. I have seen instances of both cases, the usury laws in the last being evaded by purchasing accommodation bills of exchange, instead of discounting notes; but this is a digression. When I alluded to the transactions in bills of exchange as perhaps affording means to give a popular equivalent, you will, I am persuaded, do me the justice to believe that I was quite aware that the principle was wrong, since it would only be transferring the legitimate profits of those operations from those who transacted them to another class of individuals who had not the slightest claim to them. And as relates to government, there is no branch of the business of which it has less reason to complain, its own part of it being done gratuitously, which is tantamount to a participation in the profits. Under whatever forms effected, the gratuitous transmission of the public moneys cannot be considered but as a purchase at par of Treasury drafts by the bank, or of bank drafts by the Treasury, to any amount, at any time, and from and on any places which may suit the convenience of the Treasury, without regard to that of the bank, or to the state of the market. (A comparative view of the amount thus transmitted for a longer period than that annexed to Mr. McDuffie's report, and of the inland exchange purchased by the bank, which I already have, might be useful; but you have not given me a corresponding statement of the drafts sold by the bank and offices on each other and of the profits thereon.) I was therefore induced to suggest the subject: 1st, because the analogous provision of making the bank and branches' notes payable everywhere is and always was the most popular measure within my knowledge which could be adopted, although I have always shown to the many country gentlemen who asked for it that, as an obligation, it was impossible to require it; 2d, because, having requested the President to explain to me what he meant by his assertion that the bank had failed in establishing an uniform currency, I understood his allusion to have been either to the bank and branches not receiving always other branches' notes as cash, or to their not purchasing individual bills or selling their own drafts at par. I rather think that their refusing thus to give drafts at par was what he particularly complained of; and I attempted, though without much success, to show that par of exchange and uniform currency were two very distinct things. Now, if you reflect on the time when your charter expires, you will perceive that it may become *necessary,* by some modification and sacrifice, to remove that objection, however unfounded it may appear to both of us.

I have thought it useful to call your attention to those two important points, viz., the propriety of enlarging the *circulating* metallic currency, and the necessity of being prepared for such modifications of the charter as will give to the government a greater participation in the profits of the bank and render it in some respects more popular. There is a third point on which I do not feel myself sufficiently informed: it is the real utility of country banks to the districts in which they are situated. I have only general and vague notions on that subject. That the local currencies they issue are anomalous and insecure I am satisfied; but independent of the selfish motives of speculators in those institutions, there is a general feeling even now in their favor, which must have its foundation in some real utility. It is fully admitted that in Scotland, and strongly asserted that in England, they have contributed to promote industry and the general prosperity. To distinguish in that case between use and abuse is important, and to me difficult. It would be equally unjust and bad policy to deny, indeed, not to state, the real advantages which, under proper restraints, may attend those banks even in districts almost purely agricultural. As far as applied, and in proportion to the commercial transactions in country produce, manufactures, &c., of the district, there is no intrinsic difficulty. This seems to me to lie in the question, whether and how far bank loans may be safely made to mere farmers on the security of their real estate. The Scotch banks do it constantly. But can a line be drawn founded on any principle? To state those with sufficient precision, in a way which may indeed show where the abuse lies, would be candid and conciliatory; and I will thank you if you can assist me in that respect, either from your own knowledge or by referring me to others, or even to any work worth consulting.

I have received the returns of the cashiers from which the general statement of banks was prepared, but have as yet only given them a cursory examination. The charter of the State Bank of Alabama is in point; we want that of the State Bank of South Carolina and Tennessee. Of the last there is only an extract in your Nashville cashier's letter, which is not sufficiently intelligible. (He says also that he has forwarded to Mr. McIlvain a report of the bank committee at the last session of the Legislature, showing the situation of the bank, which has been very loosely managed; and this report is not amongst the papers forwarded to me.) The State of South Carolina is stated in a note to be the sole owner of the bank of that name; the charter should therefore be examined.

Since writing this, I have read the printed "Reports of the Banks of Georgia," transmitted by you to me as above. There is no doubt that the Central Bank of that State is only an annex of the Treasury. Copy of its charter is wanted. This becomes very serious; four States erecting their Treasury into banks in whose names they emit bills of credit. Have the goodness to extend the inquiry as to that point to Louisiana, Mississippi, and North Carolina.

I am going for health and relaxation to Newport, and may be absent a fortnight. On my return I will again address you. You need not in the mean while write to me.

48. LETTER TO ROBERT POTTER

December 3, 1830

Gallatin wrote to an opponent of the Bank of the United States and a member of Congress, who had mistakenly taken him for a kindred soul to explain why he supported the Bank despite his bullionist views. His reason was that excessive note issues by state banks were the greatest immediate evil. Although he felt that Congress had undoubted authority to suppress state bank notes, he was sure Congress would not do so, and that the only practical means of achieving a sound currency was a central bank.

I duly received your letter of 19th June last, and was a little startled by the request to aid you in your intended attack on the Bank of the United States, as I thought you could not have been unacquainted with the fact that I had openly and officially advocated the renewal of the charter of the former bank, and that, although there were many opponents on constitutional grounds, the question would not have then been lost had it not been for the hostility of a portion of the Republican party either to Mr. Madison or to myself. Mr. Crawford was our principal support in defence of the renewal; and, without entering into details, it is known to all that the Clinton party was extremely dissatisfied with the preference given to Mr. Madison to the exclusion of Governor Clinton, and that De Witt was in 1812 the candidate of the opposition. This has nothing to do with the present question, but may explain why the tenor of your letter surprised me. But this was not the cause of the delay in answering your queries; and, although I was not ready to do it before this time, I ought to have acknowledged the receipt of your letter, and pray you to excuse the omission.

I had engaged in researches respecting the metallic currency of the United States, which led to a conviction that the circulation of gold coins ought not to be prevented, as it now is by our mint regulations, and that they ought to be rated according to their real market value as compared with silver. I could hardly avoid in the discussion some allusion to our paper currency, but had not properly investigated a subject of which I had lost sight since 1816, when I went to France. I received simultaneously your letter and one from Mr. Walsh requesting that I would prepare an article for his Review in relation to the reports of the two committees of the last session of Congress. It was impossible to answer without writing a book, and, having some leisure and no sufficient conception of the labor the scattered materials would require in order to an analysis and condensed form, I unwittingly promised to furnish the article. It has cost me three months of tedious labor, and, as it would not have been written but for your letter, I must ask your permission to inflict on you the task of reading it, and have accordingly written to the editor to send you a copy. I had not time to revise all the calculations myself, and the person I employed made several mistakes. Although there is none that can affect the argument, I have always felt conscientious with respect to facts, and particularly statements of numbers which readers have no means to verify, and I am now employed in revising and correcting those myself, with a view to a publication in a pamphlet form, which I will transmit to you when published.

You are quite right in believing that I would feel very averse to any interference or connection with the party politics of the day; and you will easily perceive from the general tenor of my essay that I am no friend either to *our* banking system generally or to a paper currency of any kind. Had I my choice, I would prefer a pure metallic currency and private banking-houses, as in London and on the Continent of Europe, who might with perfect freedom receive money on deposit, discount notes, and deal in exchange, but not issue bank-notes or in any respect interfere with the currency; and I would wish that government should neither restrain them in other respects nor grant them any privilege whatever. But I am equally averse to any issues of paper money by government, and still more so to its converting the Treasury into a banking, trading company. This I think the very worst plan, in every view of the subject, that could be devised, and the remedy worse than any evils, great as they are, that may flow not only from the existing system, but from letting again the State banks run wild and suspend their payments. I have viewed the subject with a single eye to a sound currency, which to provide for appears to me a constitutional and a moral duty. Independent of every temporary party consideration, there are questions of right and wrong, of what is just or unjust, which must be settled on that principle alone. Such is the question of currency. With a debased coinage or a fluctuating depreciated paper you subvert every private and public engagement, impair the performance of every contract, make invariably the ignorant and the weak dupes of the shrewd and wary, and demoralize the whole community. What are the means to prevent this under existing circumstances? Can Congress subvert the whole of the deep-rooted banking system, sustained as it is by almost every State in the Union, and revert at this day to a metallic currency? I have no doubt of the constitutional power in that respect, and have suggested the means; but I feel equally certain that the power will not be exercised. And in that case I will congratulate you and the country if you can discover any safe means of attaining the object otherwise than through a bank of the United States organized on principles in substance similar to those of the existing institution. Certain it is that none has as yet been suggested, and, perceiving no other myself, my conclusions are in favor of the renewal of the charter. For my arguments in support of the constitutionality of the measure I must refer you to the article in the Review. With me they are conclusive, and I have no doubt on the subject; but of that all are competent to judge, and provided I shall have succeeded in bringing the *facts* fairly and correctly before the public, I will be satisfied that it has been a useful task. I may be allowed to add that I am no otherwise concerned in the Bank of the United States than as owner of ten shares, and that from it or any other bank I have never asked or received any favor whatever, not having even had a single note discounted in the whole course of my life.

49. LETTER TO NICHOLAS BIDDLE

December 8, 1830

Gallatin was careful to afford no ground for any accusation that he had a pecuniary interest in supporting the Bank of the United States. He declined Biddle's offer of payment for his article supporting renewal of the charter.

Writings, II, 443–444.

Yours of 6th instant is received. I would not in ordinary cases feel the slightest reluctance to receive compensation for my labor. This would indeed be convenient at this time, as I must withdraw to the country unless I can make some addition to my income. But the article on banks and currency makes an exception. On this I had made up my mind from the beginning. I did not write, and would not have written, and do not wish it to be supposed that I have written, for the Bank of the United States; and I necessarily must accordingly decline any compensation. So far as I am concerned, I did write, on Mr. Walsh's invitation, on a subject of great importance, and am quite satisfied provided the bank will at its expense print and publish my corrected copy. I am confident that a moment's reflection will satisfy you that my decision is correct as respects myself, public utility, or the bank itself. Under existing circumstances, he who happens to have drawn conclusions favorable to the renewal of the charter must have no personal interest for having come to that result, if he wishes to produce any effect.

50. CONSIDERATIONS ON THE CURRENCY AND BANKING SYSTEM OF THE UNITED STATES

1831

In the opening section of this treatise, not reproduced here, Gallatin related the history of the currency question. In his

---

Considerations on the Currency and Banking System of the United States (Philadelphia: Carey and Lea, 1831). This essay was first printed as an article in the *American Quarterly Review,* December 1830. The extract that follows is taken from *Writings,* III, 319–346.

view the Constitution had prohibited both Congress and the states from making anything but gold or silver a legal tender. The clear intent had been to establish safeguards against the dangers of paper money. But the establishment of state banks revived paper money in another form. The evil was not fully appreciated until the bank collapse of 1814 and the suspension of specie payments. The second Bank of the United States was then instituted to curb state banks, stabilize the currency, and bring about a resumption of specie payment. It had fulfilled its purpose. The question now before the country was whether to renew its charter.

Delivering a lecture on first principles, Gallatin pointed out that an addition to the money supply would not, as the proponents of state banks supposed, increase either the capital or the purchasing power of the country. Nor could the currency be kept stable unless convertible on demand into gold or silver. Under existing circumstances a powerful central bank was the best means of regulating state banks. And to enlarge the supply of hard money and thereby to afford a specie foundation for bank notes, Gallatin proposed that notes of small denomination be suppressed and that the ratio of silver to gold in coinage be set at 15.6 to 1.

Gallatin was forced to concede something to the inflationist argument. Referring to his own early experiences on the Pennsylvania frontier and to the use of land banks in colonial times, he acknowledged the need for credit facilities in a new country and admitted that western Pennsylvania might have experienced a more rapid economic development if bank credit had been more available. Unless state banks were strictly regulated, however, he felt that their contribution to economic growth was overshadowed by their destructive effects.

In the selection given below, Gallatin defended the con-

stitutionality of the Bank of the United States and advanced a liberal construction argument in support of Congressional power over money and banking. Discarding the idea of a federal paper currency, which he felt should be reserved for critical emergencies, he spelled out the advantages offered by the Bank of the United States.

. . . The constitutional powers of Congress on the subject are the next and principal object of inquiry.

We have already adverted to the provisions of the Constitution, which declare that no State shall either coin money, emit bills of credit, make anything but gold and silver coins a tender in payment of debts, or pass any law impairing the obligation of contracts, and which vest in Congress the exclusive power to coin money and to regulate the value thereof, and of foreign coin. It was obviously the object of the Constitution to consolidate the United States into one nation, so far as regarded all their relations with foreign countries, and that the internal powers of the general government should be applied only to objects necessary for that purpose, or to those few which were deemed essential to the prosperity of the country and to the general convenience of the people of the several States. Amongst the objects thus selected were the power to regulate commerce among the several States, and the control over the monetary system of the country.

This last-mentioned power is, and has ever been, one of primary importance. It is for want of such general power that Germany has has always been inundated with coins often debased, and varying from state to state in standard and denomination; the same defect was found in the former United Provinces of the Netherlands; and the banks of deposit of Hamburg and Amsterdam were originally established for the purpose of correcting that evil. Even under the Articles of Confederation, Congress had already the sole and exclusive right and power of regulating the alloy and value of coins struck by their own authority, or by that of the respective States. It was on a most deliberate view of the subject that the same powers were confirmed and enlarged by the Constitution, and the individual States excluded from any participation which might interfere with the controlling power of the general government. With the exception of those which are connected with the foreign relations of the United States, either in war or in peace, there are no powers more expressly and exclusively vested in Congress of a less disputable nature, or of greater general utility, than those on the subject of currency. Arbitrary governments have, at various times, in order to defraud their creditors, debased the coin whilst they preserved its denomination, and thus subverted the standard of value by which the payment of public and private debts and the performance of contracts ought to have been regulated. This flagrant mode of violating public faith has been long proscribed by public opinion. Governments have, in modern times, substituted for the same purpose issues of paper money, gradually increasing in amount and decreasing in value. It was to guard against those evils that the provisions in the Constitution on that subject were intended, and it is the duty, not less than the right, of the United States to carry them into effect.

The first paragraph of the eighth section of the first article provides that Congress shall have power "to lay and collect taxes, duties, imposts, and excises, to pay the debts and provide for the common defence and general welfare of the United States; but all duties, imposts, and excises shall be uniform throughout the United States."

It has sometimes been vaguely asserted, though, as we believe, never seriously contended, that the words "to provide for the common defence and general welfare" were intended and might be construed as a distinct and specific power given to Congress, or, in other words, that that body was thereby invested with a sweeping power to embrace within its jurisdiction any object whatever which it might deem conducive to the general welfare of the United States. This doctrine is obviously untenable, subversive of every barrier in the Constitution which guards the rights of the States or of the people, expressly contradicted by the tenth amendment, which provides that the powers not delegated to the United States by the Constitution, nor prohibited by it to the States, are reserved to the States respectively or to the people, and tantamount to an assertion that there is no Constitution and that Congress is omnipotent. Mr. Jefferson stigmatizes this construction as "a grammatical quibble which has countenanced the general government in a claim of universal power. For (he adds) in the phrase to lay taxes *to pay the debts and provide for the general welfare,* it is a mere question of syntax whether the two last infinitives are governed by the first, or are distinct and co-ordinate powers; a question unequivocally decided by the exact definition of powers immediately following."

The words "to provide for the common defence and general welfare of the United States" are as obligatory as any other part of the Constitution; they cannot be expunged, and must be so construed as to be effective. Mr. Jefferson did not deny this, which is indeed undeniable; and he only contended that the words did not convey a distinct power but were governed by the preceding infinitive; that is to say, that this clause in the Constitution, instead of giving to Congress the three distinct powers, 1st, to lay taxes, &c.; 2dly, to pay the debts; 3dly, to provide for the common defence and general welfare of the United States, gave only that "to lay and collect taxes, duties, imposts, and excises *in order* to pay the debts and provide for the common defence and general welfare of the United States." He states the question as one of syntax, susceptible of only two constructions; one which would give, as a distinct, a sweeping power inconsistent with the spirit and other express provisions of the Constitution, and which he accordingly rejects; the other, which he adopts, and which admits, but confines the application of the words "to provide for the general welfare" to the only power given by that clause, viz., that of laying taxes, duties, &c.

This appears to have been the construction universally given to that clause of the Constitution by its framers and contemporaneous expounders. Mr. Hamilton, though widely differing in another respect from Mr. Jefferson in his construction of this clause, agrees with him in limiting the application of the words "to provide for the general welfare" to the express power given by the first sentence of the clause. In his report on manufactures, he contends for the power of Congress to allow bounties for their encouragement, and, after having stated the three qualifications of the power to lay taxes, viz., 1st, that duties, imposts, and excises should be uniform throughout the United States; 2d, that no direct tax should be laid unless in proportion to the census; 3d, that no duty should be laid on exports; he argues on the constitutional question in the following words:

"These three qualifications excepted, the power to raise money is plenary and indefinite, and the objects to which it may be appropriated are no less comprehensive than the payment of the public debts and the providing for the common defence and general welfare. The terms 'general welfare' were doubtless intended to signify more than was expressed or imported in those which preceded; otherwise numerous exigencies, incident to the affairs of a nation, would have been left without a provision. The phrase is as comprehensive as any that could have been used, because it was not fit that the constitutional authority of the Union to appropriate its revenues should have been restricted within narrower limits than the 'general welfare,' and because this necessarily embraces a vast variety of particulars, which are susceptible neither of specification nor of definition.

"It is, therefore, of necessity left to the discretion of the national Legislature to pronounce upon the objects which concern the general welfare, and for which, under that description, an appropriation of money is requisite and proper. And there seems to be no room for a doubt that whatever concerns the general interests of learning, of agriculture, of manufactures, and of commerce are within the sphere of the national councils, as far as regards an application of money.

"The only qualification of the generality of the phrase in question which seems to be admissible is this, that the object to which an appropriation of money is to be made be general and not local; its operation extending, in fact, or by possibility, throughout the Union, and not being confined to a particular spot.

"No objection ought to arise to this construction from the supposition that it would imply a power to do whatever else should appear to Congress conducive to the general welfare. A power to appropriate money with this latitude, which is granted, too, in express terms, would not carry a power to any other thing not authorized in the Constitution, either expressly or by fair implication."

Mr. Hamilton insisted that the power to *lay and collect* taxes and duties implied that of *appropriating* the money thus raised to any object which Congress might deem conducive to "the general welfare." But he confines throughout the application of those words to the power given, as he understood it, by the first sentence of the clause. Mr. Jefferson, who agreed with him in that respect, denied altogether that the power to lay taxes implied that of applying the money thus raised to objects conducive to the general welfare. It cannot be objected to this construction, which is the most literal, that the words "for the general welfare" are thereby rendered of no effect. For there are several cases in which the laying a tax or duty does alone effect the object in view, without the aid of an appropriation or of any other distinct act of the Legislature. On that point, however, and on that alone, they differed.

But it is foreign to the object now under consideration, and we do not mean to discuss it. All that is necessary for us is that, as admitted by both, the power *to lay duties and taxes* is vested in Congress, and may be exercised to provide (or in order to provide) for the general welfare of the United States, without any other limitation than the three qualifications specified by the Constitution, and above stated.

It has, indeed, been lately contended by some distinguished citizens that the words "general welfare" referred only to the powers expressly vested in Congress by the Constitution, or, in other words, that the power to lay duties and taxes could not be exercised but for the purpose of carrying into effect some of those specific powers. It seems to us that this, if intended, would have been distinctly expressed, instead of using the words "general welfare." And, although it is undeniable that a constructive power cannot be legitimately claimed unless necessary and proper for carrying into execution or fairly implied in a power expressly delegated, we do not perceive why it should be necessary in order to justify the exercise of a power expressly given that it should be exercised in reference to another similar power. But we do not mean to discuss this question, which is also foreign to our object. Allowing, for the sake of argument, the validity of the objection, it does not apply to cases where the object in reference to which the duty or tax is laid is clearly embraced within the powers of the general government. Although, because the power to protect manufactures is not expressly vested in Congress, that to lay taxes in order to effect that object should be denied, the power of laying a tax or duty for the purpose of carrying into effect an express provision of the Constitution would still be undeniable.

Congress has the power to lay stamp duties on notes, on bank-notes, and on any description of bank-notes. That power has already been exercised, and the duties may be laid to such an amount and in such a manner as may be necessary

to effect the object intended. This object is not merely to provide generally for the general welfare, but to carry into effect,
in conformity with the last paragraph of the eighth section of
the first article, those several and express provisions of the
Constitution which vest in Congress exclusively the control
over the monetary system of the United States, and more particularly those which imply the necessity of a uniform currency. The exercise of the power for that object is free of any
constitutional objection, provided the duties thus laid shall
be uniform and applied to the Bank of the United States as
well as to the State banks. The act of laying and collecting the
duties, which is expressly granted, is alone efficient to effect
the object. As no appropriation of money is wanted for that
purpose, the exercise of power which is required is purely that
of laying duties, and it is not liable to the objection that to
assert that the authority to lay taxes implies that of appropriating the proceeds is a forced construction. It is equally free
of any objection derived from any presumed meaning of the
words "general welfare," since the power to lay duties will
in this instance be exercised in order to carry into effect several expressed provisions of the Constitution having the same
object in view. Congress may, if it deems it proper, lay a
stamp duty on small notes, which will put an end to their
circulation. It may lay such a duty on all bank-notes as would
convert all the banks into banks of discount and deposit only,
annihilate the paper currency, and render a bank of the
United States unnecessary in reference to that object. But if
this last measure should be deemed pernicious, or prove impracticable, Congress must resort to other and milder means
of regulating the currency of the country. The Bank of the
United States, as has already been shown, was established for
that express purpose.

An act incorporating a bank is not an act either to raise or
appropriate money. The power to establish the bank cannot
in any way be founded on that clause of the Constitution

which has reference to the general welfare of the United States. It is sanctioned exclusively by that clause which gives to Congress power to make all laws which shall be necessary and proper for carrying into execution any of the powers vested in the government of the United States. And the first object of inquiry is the meaning of the words "necessary and proper" in that clause.

We are aware that it has at times been suggested that the word "necessary," in its strict sense, means "that without which the specific power cannot be carried into effect," and ought to be so construed. If appeal be made to verbal criticism, it may answered that, if such was the meaning of the word "necessary" in that sentence, the word "proper" would not have been added, since that which is necessary in that strict sense is of necessity proper. This last expression must, therefore, be taken in connection with the first; and since it was contemplated that what was called necessary might be proper or improper, the words "laws necessary and proper" do not appear to have been intended in that most limited sense, which implies absolute impossibility of effecting the object without the law, but to mean such laws as are fairly intended and highly useful and important for that purpose. We believe this to be the fair and to have been the uniform construction of the Constitution, and that indeed without which it could not have been carried into effect. In order to prove that this has ever been deemed the natural and clear construction, we will not resort to the establishment of light-houses, or to other numerous precedents, the authority of which may be disputed. We will appeal to the most general and important law of the United States, such as it was enacted from the first organization of the government under the Constitution, and to a provision in it which, under its various other modifications, has uninterruptedly and without any constitutional objection remained in force to this day.

The laws to lay and collect duties on imports require, and

have always required, a variety of oaths, and particularly that of the importers and consignees, with respect to the correctness of the invoices of goods imported, both as to quantity and as to cost or value. Yet this provision, however, useful and important, is not so absolutely necessary, in that strict sense of the word, as that the laws could not possibly be carried into effect without it. There are countries, France, for example, where those duties are efficiently collected without the assistance of similar oaths. This may be done at least as effectually by an appraisement of the merchandise as by resorting to the oaths of the parties. In point of fact, there has always been a discretionary power to appraise, which has lately been enlarged. Since it is on that provision and not on the oath that the ultimate reliance for the faithful collection of the duties is placed, those duties might be collected without the assistance of oaths, by substituting in every instance an appraisement or valuation. Oaths are not, therefore, necessary for the collection of duties, in that strict sense which is contended for; they are not that without which the duties could not be collected. The observation indeed applies to various other provisions of the revenue laws. Any one who will give them a perusal will find several implying powers not specially vested in Congress, the necessity of which was not absolute, and without which the object of the law might still have been effected. The oaths and various other provisions have been resorted to as means only highly useful, important, and proper, but not as being of *absolute* necessity for carrying the law into effect.[1]

Whenever it becomes the duty of Congress to carry into effect any of the powers expressly defined by the constitution, it will generally be found that there are several means to

---

[1] The opinion of the Supreme Court in the case of McCulloch *vs.* State of Maryland had not been seen by the writer of this essay when it was committed to the press, and the important inference drawn from the use of the words "absolutely necessary," in another clause of the Constitution, had escaped his notice.

effect the object. In that case, and whenever there is an option, each of the means proposed ought not to be successively
objected to as not being strictly necessary because other
means might be resorted to, since this mode of arguing would
defeat the object intended, and prevent the passage of any
law for carrying into effect the power which it was the duty of
Congress to execute. If every provision of a revenue law was
successively opposed on that ground, no efficient revenue law
could be passed. In the present case it is proposed to resort
either to a stamp duty or to a bank of the United States in
order to regulate the currency. Unless some other equally efficient mode can be suggested, this important object will be
defeated, if both means are successively rejected as not strictly
necessary. But, on the other hand, the means proposed for
carrying into effect any special or expressed power vested in
Congress should be highly useful and important, having clearly
and bona fide that object in view which is the avowed purpose, and not be intended, under color of executing a certain
special power, for the purpose of effecting another object.

It was on this ground that the former Bank of the United
States was at first opposed. That bank had not been proposed
for the express purpose of regulating the currency, but as incident to the powers of regulating commerce, of collecting the
revenue, of the safe-keeping of public moneys, and, generally,
of carrying on the operations of the Treasury. There had been
at that time but three banks established in the United States;
their operations were confined within a very narrow sphere;
there had been no experience in the United States of the utility
of a bank in assisting the operations of government, but that
which, during a short time, had been afforded by the Bank of
North America, incorporated, in the first instance, by Congress,
under the Articles of Confederation. The Bank of the United
States was considered by its opponents as not being intended
for the purpose alleged, but as having for its object the consoli-
dation of a moneyed aristocracy, and to further the views at

that time ascribed to a certain party and to its presumed leader. And the fears then excited respecting that object, and the supposed influence of the bank in promoting it, though long since dissipated, have left recollections and impressions which may still have some effect on public opinion in relation to the constitutional question.

Experience, however, has since confirmed the great utility and importance of a bank of the United States in its connection with the Treasury. The first great advantage derived from it consists in the safe-keeping of the public moneys, securing, in the first instance, the immediate payment of those received by the principal collectors and affording a constant check on all their transactions, and afterwards rendering a defalcation in the moneys once paid, and whilst nominally in the Treasury, absolutely impossible. The next and not less important benefit is to be found in the perfect facility with which all the public payments are made by checks or Treasury drafts, payable at any place where the bank has an office; all those who have demands against government are paid in the place most convenient to them, and the public moneys are transferred through our extensive territory, at a moment's warning, without any risk or expense, to the places most remote from those of collection, and wherever public exigencies may require. From the year 1791 to this day the operations of the Treasury have, without interruption, been carried on through the medium of banks; during the years 1811 to 1816, through the State banks; before and since, through the Bank of the United States. Every individual who has been at the head of that Department, and, as we believe, every officer connected with it, has been made sensible of the great difficulties that must be encountered without the assistance of those institutions, and of the comparative ease and great additional security to the public with which their public duties are performed through the means of the banks. To insist that the operations of the Treasury may be carried on with equal facility and safety through the aid of the State banks without the interposition of a bank of the United States, would be contrary to fact and experience. That great assistance was received from the State banks, while there was no other, has always been freely and cheerfully acknowledged. But it is impossible, in the nature of things, that the necessary concert could be made to exist between thirty different institutions; and in some instances heavy pecuniary losses, well known at the seat of government, have been experienced. To admit, however, that State banks are necessary for that purpose, is to give up the question. To admit that banks are indispensable for carrying into effect the legitimate operations of government, is to admit that Congress has the power to establish a bank. The general government is not made by the Constitution to depend for carrying into effect powers vested in it on the uncertain aid of institutions created by other authorities and which are not at all under its control. It is expressly authorized to carry those powers into effect by its own means, by passing the laws necessary and proper for that purpose, and in this instance by establishing its own bank, instead of being obliged to resort to those which derive their existence from another source and are under the exclusive control of the different States by which they have been established.

It must at the same time be acknowledged that, inasmuch as the revenue may be collected and the public moneys may be kept in public chests and transferred to distant places without the assistance of banks, and as all this was once done in the United States, and continues to be done in several countries, without any public bank, it cannot be asserted that those institutions are absolutely necessary for those purposes, if we take the word "necessary" in that strict sense which has been alluded to. All this may be done, though with a greater risk and in a more inconvenient and expensive manner. Public chests might be established, and public receivers, or subtreasurers, might be appointed, in the same places where there are now offices of the Bank of the United States, and specie might be transported from place to place, as the public service required it, or inland bills of exchange purchased from individuals.[1] The superior security and convenience afforded by the bank in the fiscal operations of government may not be considered as sufficient to make its establishment constitutional, in the opinion of those who construe the word "necessary" in that strict sense.

But it is far from being on that ground alone that the question of constitutionality is now placed. It was not at all anticipated, at the time when the former Bank of the United States was first proposed, and when constitutional objections were raised against it, that bank-notes issued by multiplied State banks, gradually superseding the use of gold and silver, would become the general currency of the country. The effect of the few banks then existing had not been felt beyond the three cities where they had been established. The States were forbidden by the Constitution to issue bills of credit; bank-notes are bills of credit to all intents and purposes, and the State could not do through others what it was not authorized to do itself; but the bank-notes, not being issued on the credit of the States, nor guaranteed by them, were not considered as being, under the Constitution, bills of credit emitted by the States. Subsequent events have shown that the notes of State banks, pervading the whole country, might produce the very effect

---

[1] With the exception of the power of receiving private deposits, the object of which provision is not perceived, this is precisely the species of national bank which has been suggested in the President's last message. The question whether the purchase of drafts would, as we think, be a charge on the Treasury, or prove, as seems to be expected, a source of profit, is one of secondary importance. It is sufficient to observe that the issues of the State banks could not, nor indeed is it anticipated in the message that they would, be checked by this plan. It would not, therefore, effect the great object contemplated by the Constitution, to carry which into effect is enjoined by that instrument, and for which we principally contend, viz, that of securing a sound and *uniform* currency.

which the Constitution had intended to prevent by prohibiting the emission of bills of credit by any State. The injustice to individuals, the embarrassments of government, the depreciation of the currency, its want of uniformity, the moral necessity imposed on the community either to receive that unsound currency or to suspend every payment, purchase, sale, or other transaction incident to the wants of society, all the evils which followed the suspension of specie payments have been as great, if not greater, than those which might have been inflicted by a paper currency issued under the authority of any State. We have already adverted to the several provisions of the Constitution which gave to Congress the right and imposed on it the duty of provide a remedy; but there is one which deserves special consideration.

Whatever consequences may have attended the suspension of specie payments in Great Britain, there still remained one currency which regulated all the others. All the country bankers were compelled to pay their own notes, if not in specie at least in notes of the Bank of England. These notes were, as a standard of value, substituted for gold; and if the currency of the country was depreciated and fluctuating in value from time to time, it was at the same time uniform throughout the country. There was but one currency for the whole, and every variation in its value was uniform as to places, and at the same moment operated in the same manner everywhere. But the currency of the United States, or, to speak more correctly, of the several States, varied, during the suspension of specie payments, not only from time to time, but at the same time from State to State, and in the same State from place to place. in New England, where those payments were not discontinued, the currency was equal in value to specie; it was at the same time at a discount of seven per cent. in New York and Charleston, of fifteen in Philadelphia, of twenty and twenty-five in Baltimore and Washington, with every other possible variation in other places and States.

The currency of the United States, in which the public and private debts were paid and the public revenue collected, not only was generally depreciated, but was also defective in respect to uniformity. Independent of all the other clauses in the Constitution which relate to that subject, it is specially provided, 1st, that all duties, imposts, and excises shall be uniform throughout the United States; 2d, that representative and direct taxes shall be apportioned among the several States according to their respective numbers, to be determined by the rule therein specified; and that no capitation or other direct tax shall be laid, unless in proportion to the enumeration. Both these provisions were violated whilst the suspension of specie payments continued. It is clear that after the quota of the direct tax of each State had been determined according to the rule prescribed by the Constitution, it was substantially changed by being collected in currencies differing in value in the several States. It is not less clear that the clause which prescribes a uniformity of duties, imposts, and excises was equally violated by collecting every description of indirect duties and taxes in currencies of different value. The only remedy existing at that time was the permission to pay direct and indirect taxes in Treasury notes. But those notes did not pervade every part of the country in the same manner as bank-notes; they were of too high denomination to be used in the payment of almost any internal tax; they were liable also to vary in value in the different States; and they could operate as a remedy only as long as their depreciation was greater than that of the most depreciated notes in circulation.

We will now ask whether, independent of every other consideration, Congress was not authorized and bound to pass the laws necessary and proper for carrying into effect with good faith those provisions of the Constitution? and whether that could or can be done in any other manner than either by reverting to a purely metallic, or by substituting a uniform paper currency to that which had proved so essentially defective in that respect, and which, from its not being subject to one and the same control, is, and forever will be, liable to that defect? The uniformity of duties and taxes of every description, whether internal or external, direct or indirect, is an essential and fundamental principle of the Constitution. It is self-evident that that uniformity cannot be carried into effect without a corresponding uniformity of currency. Without laws to this effect, it is absolutely impossible that the taxes and duties should be uniform, as the Constitution prescribes; such laws are therefore necessary and proper, in the most strict sense of the words. There are but two means of effecting the object, a metallic or a uniform paper currency. Congress has the option of either; and either of the two which may appear the most eligible will be strictly constitutional, because strictly necessary and proper for carrying into effect the object. If a currency exclusively metallic is preferred, the object will be attained by laying prohibitory stamp duties on bank-notes of every description and without exception. If it is deemed more eligible under existing circumstances, instead of subverting the whole banking system of the United States, and depriving the community of the accommodations which bank loans afford, to resort to less harsh means; recourse must be had to such as will insure a currency sound and uniform itself, and at the same time check and regulate that which will continue to constitute the greater part of the currency of the country.

Both those advantages were anticipated in the establishment of the Bank of the United States, and it appears to us that the bank fulfills both those conditions. As respects the past, it is a matter of fact that specie payments were restored and have been maintained through the instrumentality of that institution. It gives a complete guarantee that under any circumstances its notes will preserve the same uniformity which they now possess. Placed under the control of the general government, relying for its existence on the correctness, prudence, and skill with which it shall be administered, perpetually watched and occasionally checked by both the Treasury Department and rival institutions, and without a monopoly, yet with a capital and resources adequate to the object for which it was established, the bank also affords the strongest security which can be given with respect to paper not only for its ultimate solvency, but also for the uninterrupted soundness of its currency. The statements we have given of its progressive and present situation show how far those expectations have heretofore been realized.

Those statements also show that the Bank of the United States, wherever its operations have been extended, has effectually checked excessive issues on the part of the State banks, if not in every instance, certainly in the aggregate. They had been reduced, before the year 1820, from sixty-six to less than forty millions. At that time those of the Bank of the United States fell short of four millions. The increased amount required by the increase of population and wealth during the ten ensuing years has been supplied in a much greater proportion by that bank than by those of the States. With a treble capital, they have added little more than eight millions to their issues. Those of the Bank of the United States were nominally twelve, in reality about eleven, millions greater in November, 1829, than in November, 1819. The whole amount of the paper currency has during those ten years increased about forty-five, and that portion which is issued by the State banks only twenty-two and a half per cent. We have, indeed, a proof, not very acceptable, perhaps, to the bank, but conclusive of the fact, that it has performed the office required of it in that respect. The general complaints on the part of many of the State banks, that they are checked and controlled in their operations by the Bank of the United States, that, to use a common expression, it operates as a screw, is the best evidence that its general operation is such as had been intended. It was for that very purpose that the bank was established. We are not, however, aware that a single solvent bank has been injured by that of the United States, though many have undoubtedly been restrained in the extent of their operations much more than was desirable to them. This is certainly inconvenient to some of the banks, but in its general effects is a public benefit to the community.

The best way to judge whether, in performing that unpopular duty, the Bank of the United States has checked the operations of the State banks more than was necessary, and has abused, in order to enrich itself at their expense, the power which was given for another purpose, is to compare their respective situations in the aggregate. In order to avoid any erroneous inference, we will put out of question those banks of which we could only make an estimate, and compare with that of the United States those only of which we have actual returns.

The profit of banks beyond the interest on their own capital consists in that which they receive on the difference between the aggregate of their deposits and notes in circulation and the amount of specie in their vaults. We have given the aggregate situation for the end of the year 1829 of 281 banks, with a capital of 95,003,557 dollars, the deposits and circulating notes of which amounted together to $71,706,033
from which deducting the specie in their vaults, 11,989,643
leaves for the said difference $59,716,390
or 62.8 per cent. on their capital.

The notes in circulation of the Bank of the United States (adding one million for its drafts in circulation) amounted, in November, 1829, to $14,042,984, and together with the deposits to $28,827,793
from which deducting the specie in its vaults, 7,175,274
leaves for the difference $21,652,519
or 61.8 on its capital.

It is clear that those State banks, taken in the aggregate, have no just reason to complain, since that of the United States imposes no greater restraints on them than on itself. It will also be perceived that it had in specie more than one-fifth part of the aggregate of its notes in circulation and deposits, whilst the State banks had little more than one-sixth; and the Bank of the United States had in addition a fund of about one million of dollars in Europe. The difference would have been more striking had we taken a view of the situation of all the State banks, including those on estimate; for the difference between the aggregate of their notes and deposits and their specie is 67¼ on their capital.

This view of the subject applies to the present time, when the Bank of the United States has surmounted the difficulties which it had in its origin to encounter, and has reached a high degree of prosperity. It did not go into operation till the commencement of the year 1817, and such were the losses which it first experienced that its dividends during the first six years of its existence fell short of 3½ per cent. a year. The dividend has since gradually increased from 5 to 7 per cent.; but the average during the thirteen years and a half ending on the 1st of July, 1830, has been but 4⁸⁸⁄₁₀₀ per cent. a year. An annual dividend of about 9 per cent. during the residue of the time to which the charter is limited would be necessary in order that the stockholders should then have received, on an average, 6 per cent. a year on their capital. The dividends of the State banks vary too much, and our returns are too imperfect in that respect, to enable us to estimate the average; but it has certainly far exceeded that of the Bank of the United States.

The manner in which the bank checks the issues of the State banks is equally simple and obvious. It consists in receiving the notes of all those which are solvent and requiring payment from time to time, without suffering the balance due by any to become too large. Those notes on hand, taking the average of the three and a half last years, amount always to about a million and a half of dollars; and the balances due by the banks in account current (deducting balances due to some) to about nine hundred thousand. We think that we may say that on this operation, which requires particular attention and vigilance and must be carried on with great firmness and due forbearance, depends almost exclusively the stability of the currency of the country.

The President of the United States has expressed the opinion that the bank had failed in the great end of establishing a uniform and sound currency, and has suggested the expediency of establishing "a national bank, founded upon the credit of the government and its revenues." He has clearly seen that the uniformity of the currency was a fundamental principle derived from the Constitution, and that this, unless the United States reverted to a purely metallic currency, could not be effected without the aid of a national bank. But it appears to us that the objection of want of uniformity, which may be supported in one sense, though not in the constitutional sense, of the word, applies generally to a paper currency, and not particularly to that which is issued by the Bank of the United States. And although we are clearly of opinion that the United States at large are entitled to the pecuniary profit arising from the substitution of a paper for a metallic currency, we are not less convinced that this object cannot be attained in a more eligible way and more free of objections than through the medium of a national bank constituted on the same principles as that now existing. On both those topics we will make but few observations, those branches of the subject having been nearly exhausted in their report by the committee of the House of Representatives.

It has already been observed that the substitution of paper to gold and silver is a national benefit, in as far as it brings into activity an additional circulating capital equal to the difference between the amount of paper and that of the reserve in specie necessary to sustain the par value of that paper. But it is clear that the community derives no other immediate benefit from the substitution than the accommodations which the banks are thereby enabled to afford, and for which the borrowers pay the usual rate of interest. The immediate profit derived from the paper currency is received exclusively by the banks,—about three-fourths by the State banks, and one-fourth by that of the United States. So far as relates to profit, it is only to that one-fourth part of the whole that the measures of the general government are intended to apply. Several of the States, by levying a tax on the capital or on the dividends of their own banks, receive the public share of those profits. Other States have resorted to the mode suggested by the President, and have established banks of the State exclusively founded on its resources and revenue.

The proposition has not been suggested to resort to a third, though the most simple, mode: that of issuing, without the aid of machinery of any bank whatever, a government paper payable on demand in specie. We unite in considering it altogether inadmissible. Government may put its paper in circulation by lending it, like banks, to individuals; and this is, in fact, the proposition which has been suggested. But unless this mode is adopted, to issue paper in any other way is to borrow money; and the United States at this time wish to discharge and not to contract a debt. Nor would such a paper, without a mixture of banking operations, control in the least the issues of State banks and assist in establishing a general sound currency.

The general objections to a paper issued by government have already been stated at large. Yet it must be admitted that there may be times when every other consideration must yield to the superior necessity of saving or defending the country. If there ever was a time or a cause which justified a resort to that measure, it was the war of the independence. It would be doing gross injustice to the authors of the Revolution and founders of that independence to confound them with those governments which, from ambitious views, have, without necessity, inflicted that calamity on their subjects. The old

Congress, as the name purports, were only an assembly of plenipotentiaries delegated by the several colonies or States. They could only recommend, and had not the power to lay taxes; the country was comparatively poor; extraordinary exertions were necessary to resist the formidable power of Great Britain; those exertions were made, and absorbed all the local resources; the paper money carried the United States through the most arduous and perilous stages of the war; and, though operating as a most unequal tax, it cannot be denied that it saved the country. Mr. Jefferson was strongly impressed with the recollection of those portentous times when, in the latter end of the year 1814, he suggested the propriety of a gradual issue by government of two hundred millions of dollars in paper. He had, from the inperfect data in his possession, greatly overrated the amount of paper currency which could be sustained at par; and he had, on the other hand, underrated the great expenses of the war. Yet we doubt whether, in the state to which the banks and the currency had been reduced, much greater issues of Treasury notes, or other paper not convertible at will into specie, would not have become necessary if the war had been of much longer continuance. It is to be hoped that a similar state of things will not again occur; but, at all events, the issue of a government paper ought to be kept in reserve for the extraordinary exigencies.

The proposition then recurs to issue a paper currency payable on demand in specie through the medium of a bank founded on the revenue of the United States; or, in other words, to convert the general government or its Treasury Department into a banking institution. The experiment has been made in four of the States, and may have succeeded on a smaller scale, and where all the agents are personally known to government and are not merely in name but in reality under its immediate superintendence. But if thirty-five millions of dollars are to be placed at the disposal of three hundred bank directors selected by the government of the United States and living in twenty-five different States or Territories, with the authority to contract debts in behalf of the public to an equal amount and to lend the whole to individuals at their discretion, we must inquire how and over whom that enormous power will be exercised. However they may have differed with respect to removals from office, the various Administrations, with some exceptions commanded by the public interest, have all preferred, in appointing to office, their friends to their opponents; and in making the selections at a distance there is not perhaps, out of ten officers who are appointed, one who is personally known either to the President or to any of the heads of the Departments. It is morally impossible that the direction of the branches of the proposed bank should not fall into the hands of men generally selected from political considerations, often of a local nature. Without salary or any personal interest in the concern intrusted to their care, they would also be altogether irresponsible. The duties of the other officers of government may always be, and always are, defined by law; for any wilful official misconduct, for any act of oppression towards individuals, they may be prosecuted and punished. But the power vested in a bank director is in its nature discretionary, and error of judgment may always be pleaded for having improperly granted or withdrawn an accommodation. The exercise of that arbitrary power over the property and private concerns of individuals would be so odious that, if the attempt was made, we are confident that it would not be long tolerated. Considered as a source of profit, which is its only recommendation, it is equally obvious that the plan could not succeed; that whenever there was a temporary pressure and what is called a want of money, the debtors would ask and obtain relief, and that the same measure of indulgence would gradually be extended to every quarter of the Union. It seems indeed self-evident that a government constituted like that of the United States cannot by itself manage and control a banking system spread over their extensive territory; and we know, on the other hand, that the same object may be attained through the means of a bank governed and controlled as that of the United States. It may be added that, if an objection is raised against that institution because the power to incorporate a bank is not expressly granted by the Constitution, it appears to be equally applicable to the plan that has been suggested; since there is no clause in that instrument that expressly authorizes the government of the United States to discount the notes of individuals or to become a trading company.

The United States are, however, justly entitled to participate in the advantages which the bank derives from its charter, by being permitted to issue paper and to extend its operations over the whole country; and that institution must also be allowed, in addition to the usual interest on its capital, a reasonable profit, since it incurs all the risks and is liable for all the losses incident to those operations. The government receives already a portion of the profits in the shape of those services which are rendered here gratuitously, and form in England no inconsiderable part of the benefit allowed to the bank. But for the residue we would prefer to a bonus either a moderate interest on the public deposits or a participation in the dividends when exceeding a certain rate. There can be no doubt that, independent of perfect security, the United States would in that way derive greater pecuniary advantages than from any bank managed by its own officers.

In order to attain perfect uniformity, the value of a paper currency should in the United States be always the same as that of the gold and silver coins of which it takes the place. It is impossible to fulfill that condition better than by making that currency payable on demand in specie and at par. This cannot be done but at certain places designated for that purpose. The holder of a bank-note cannot at any other place give such note in payment of a debt, or exchange it for specie, without the consent of another party. Strictly speaking, it is not, therefore, at any other place of the same value with specie.

This is equally true of any bank-note or convertible paper in any other country. A note of the Bank of England, being only payable in London, will not be of the same value with gold or silver in Scotland, Ireland, or even at Liverpool, unless the exchange between those places respectively and London should be at par. This defect is inherent to every species of paper currency, even when payable on demand. There were three hundred and twenty-nine State banks and twenty-two offices of the Bank of the United States in operation on the 1st of January, 1830. We had, therefore, three hundred and fifty-one distinct currencies, all convertible into specie, but each at different places. A note of the Bank of the United States or of the Bank of North America, both payable at Philadelphia, was no more exchangeable for gold or silver at Bedford, in Pennsylvania, than at Cincinnati; the only difference consisting in the greater distance from the place of payment, which renders a fluctuation in the rate of exchange more probable. When, therefore, it is objected as a want of uniformity that the notes issued by the Bank of the United States and its several offices are not indiscriminately made payable at every one of those places, the objection does not go far enough. In order to attain perfect uniformity, or to render those notes everywhere precisely equal in value to specie, they should be made payable at every town or village in the United States. But although it may be admitted that the notes of the Bank of the United States now consist nominally of twenty-four currencies, each payable at a distinct place, they still fulfil the condition of uniformity required by the Constitution; and the defect complained of is not peculiar to them, but would equally attach to any other possible species of bank-notes or paper currency.

Those notes, wherever made payable, are, by the charter, receivable in all payments to the United States; and as the bank is obliged, without any allowance on account of difference of exchange, to transfer the public funds from place to place within the United States, any loss arising from that cause falls on the institution. For that purpose, therefore, all the notes issued by the bank constitute but one uniform currency, with which all the duties, taxes, imposts, and excises may be paid. Not only the condition of uniformity imposed by the Constitution is strictly fulfilled, but by far the greater part of the notes which may happen to circulate out of the States in which they are made payable is also absorbed by that operation. The objection is reduced to the simple fact that individuals who may still hold such notes cannot always exchange them at par at a place distant from that where they are payable. In answer to this it must, in the first place, be observed that notes are never found in that situation but by the act of the parties themselves. The banks and its officers never issue or make payments in notes payable at another place than that of issue but at the request of individuals whose convenience it may suit to apply for such notes. Through whatever channel a man residing in New Orleans may have come in possession of ten thousand dollars in notes payable at Charleston, it has always been with his own consent, and never by the act of the bank. When this objection is made, what in fact is complained of is, that the bank will not, or cannot, transfer the funds of individuals, as well as those of the public, from place to place gratuitously,—an operation which has no connection with the uniformity of currency. Supposing there were no bank-notes in circulation and there was no other but a uniform metallic currency, the man who had taken a cargo of flour from Louisville to New Orleans must, in order to transfer the proceeds back to Louisville, either have purchased a bill of exchange or transported the specie. This he may still do since the institution of the bank; and he has no more right to ask from the office at New Orleans to give him in exchange for the specie bank-notes payable at Louisville, than to require that it should pay the freight of his flour from Louisville to New Orleans.

But supposing there was any weight in the objection, it is inherent to the nature of a paper which cannot, in that respect, be made better than a metallic currency. If A contracts to pay a certain sum to B, it must be at a certain specified place. He cannot engage to do it at five or six different places at the option of B, since it would compel him to provide funds at all those different places, and therefore to five or six times the amount of his debt. It is true that the Bank of the United States has, through its extensive dealings in exchange, facilities to give accommodations in that respect which no individual can have. But it is its interest to extend, as far as is safe and practicable, the circulation of its notes, and one of the best means to effect that object is to pay everywhere their notes, wherever issued, whenever that is practicable. The five-dollar notes are already made thus payable; and, in reality, payment of notes of every denomination, wherever made payable, is rarely refused at any of the offices. The bank may be safely relied on for giving the greatest possible extension to a species of accommodation which it is its interest to give; but the condition can never be made obligatory either on that institution or on any other bank, by whatever name designated or on whatever principle constituted, without endangering its safety. It is obvious that no bank which has branches can have funds at every place sufficient to meet a sudden demand for the payment of a large amount of notes payable elsewhere which may fortuitously or designedly have accumulated at some one place. Even supposing this to be practicable, the condition imposed must necessarily occasion an additional expense, much greater than the benefit derived from it; and if this was done through the means of a bank founded on the public revenue, it would be a tax laid on the community for the advantage of a few individuals.

A similar objection has been made with respect to the dealings in domestic exchange of the bank. These consist of two correlative but distinct operations. The bank purchases at

Philadelphia and at every one of its offices bills of exchange payable at different dates and on all parts of the United States where there are such offices, and the bank and its offices sell their drafts on each other payable at sight. The amount of both has been progressively increasing to the great convenience of the public. That of bills of exchange was 29,335,254 and that of bank drafts 24,384,232 dollars, during the year 1829. In the same year the transfers of public moneys which are effected by Treasury drafts, analogous to bills of exchange at sight, have amounted to 9,066,000 dollars. The three items together make a total of 62,785,486 dollars transmitted by the bank in one year through the medium of bills and drafts, which are thus substituted to the transportation of specie to the same amount. The purchase of bills of exchange is an operation similar, as relates to interest, to the discounting of notes. The interest accruing from the time of purchase or discount to that when they become due is equally allowed in both cases. Deducting this, the gross profit on the purchase of bills, arising from the rate of exchange at which they were purchased, amounted, in the year 1829, to 227,224 dollars, or less than three-fourths per cent. The premiums on the sale of bank drafts amounted to 42,826 dollars; but to this must be added the interest accruing on the drafts actually in circulation, and which, estimating, as before stated, the time during which, on an average, they remain so, at fifteen days, amounts to near sixty-one thousand dollars. The profit on those drafts is therefore near one hundred and four thousand dollars, or about three sevenths per cent. The interest lost by the bank on the Treasury drafts is from fifteen to twenty thousand dollars, and the charges for transportation of specie, postage, and incidental expenses amounted, in the year 1829, to 49,847 dollars. The net profit of the bank on the aggregate of those transactions is, therefore, about two hundred and sixty-four thousand dollars, or a fraction more than two-fifths per cent. on the whole amount.

There is not, it is believed, a single country where the community is, in that respect, served with less risk or expense. It is obvious that no one will sell his bills to the bank unless that institution purchases them at a higher or at least as high rate as any other person, and that no one will purchase its drafts unless they are as cheap as any others at market or are considered safer. There is no other ground of complaint, unless it be that the bank can afford to purchase bills dearer and to sell its drafts cheaper than anybody else. This is certainly a public benefit, and the only consideration which has been urged with some degree of plausibility is, that one of the reasons which enables the bank to obtain a higher price for its drafts is the greater degree of security which they offer, whilst at the same time its peculiar situation would enable it to sell them cheaper than other persons. Without admitting the validity of this observation or denying that the current rate of exchange ought to regulate the price of those drafts, we would wish that they might be sold at par whenever it happens that the operation, from the situation of its funds, is in no degree inconvenient to the bank. Government receives its full share of the profits on those operations. As its business is done gratuitously, it not only saves the interest, as above stated, but also the premium which it would otherwise have to pay on the sale of its drafts. This, calculated at the same rate as for other bills of exchange, would amount to more than seventy, and together with the interest to about ninety, thousand dollars a year.

We have also heard complaints made against the purchase of foreign bills by the bank at the South, and the sale of their own bills on Europe at the East. That this may interfere with the business of capitalists who deal in exchange is true; but the principal public consideration seems to be whether the bank confers a benefit on the Southern planters or merchants by entering into competition for the purchase of their bills, and on the public by offering for sale cheaper or safer means of making remittances abroad. Another great advantage is found in the facility thereby afforded to the bank of having a fund in England on which it receives interest, and which, on an emergency, answers the same purpose as specie. That branch of business, either for the year 1829 or for the average of that and the two preceding years, amounted to 3,580,000 dollars.

The principal advantages derived from the Bank of the United States, which no State bank and, as it appears to us, no bank established on different principles could afford, are, therefore, first and principally, securing with certainty a uniform and, as far as paper can, a sound currency; secondly, the complete security and great facility it affords to government in its fiscal operations; thirdly, the great convenience and benefit accruing to the community from its extensive transactions in domestic bills of exchange and inland drafts. We have not adverted to the aid which may be expected from that institution in time of war, and which should, we think, be confined to two objects:

First. The experience of the last war has sufficiently proved that an efficient revenue must be provided before or immediately after that event takes place. Resort must be had for that purpose to a system of internal taxation not engrafted on taxes previously existing, but which must be at once created. The utmost diligence and skill cannot render such new taxes productive before twelve or eighteen months. The estimated amount must be anticipated, and advances to that extent, including at least the estimated proceeds of one year of all the additional taxes laid during the war, may justly be expected from the Bank of the United States.

Secondly. It will also be expected that it will powerfully assist in raising the necessary loans, not by taking up on its own account any sum beyond what may be entirely convenient and consistent with the safety and primary object of the institution, but by affording facilities to the money-lenders. Those who in the first instance subscribe to a public loan do not intend to keep the whole, but expect to distribute it gradually with a reasonable profit. The greatest inducement in order to obtain loans on moderate terms consists in the probability that, if that distribution proceeds slower than had been anticipated, the subscribers will not be compelled, in order to pay their instalments, to sell the stock, and, by glutting the market, to sell it at a loss; and the assistance expected from the bank is to advance, on a deposit of the scrip, after the two first instalments have been paid, such portions of each succeeding payment as may enable the subscribers to hold the stock a reasonable length of time. As this operation may be renewed annually, on each successive loan, whilst the war continues, the aid afforded in that manner is far more useful than large direct advances to government, which always cripple the resources and may endanger the safety of a bank.

PART EIGHT

The Free Trader:
The Tariff Controversy, 1832

During his early career as delegate of Pennsylvania to the House of Representatives, Gallatin did not publicize his views on tariff protection. After he became Secretary of the Treasury he indicated that he was in principle a free trader in his report on manufactures delivered in 1810. But he was not so intractable as to object to the Tariff of 1816. Apparently, the successive tariff increases that followed were too much, for he took sides in the tariff controversy that led to South Carolina's nullification in 1832 and the compromise tariff of 1833. In 1831 he headed a New York delegation to a free trade convention held at Philadelphia.

51. MEMORIAL OF THE COMMITTEE

APPOINTED BY THE FREE TRADE

CONVENTION

1832

Southern delegates had a majority in the convention and took the position that a protective tariff was unconstitutional. Gallatin defended the constitutionality even of the tariff of 1828, but held it to be unjust, fair neither to the North or the South. As chairman of a committee appointed by the convention, he drafted a memorial to Congress, which was printed as a government document and in 1832 published in pamphlet form. A free trade tract, it was, according to Gallatin's biographer, Raymond Walters, the "first statesmanlike challenge" to the principles of Henry Clay's American System. Gallatin's anti-slavery views did not prevent his full endorsement of the southern contention that protective tariffs had impaired that section's economic growth. The compromise tariff of 1833 was in general accord with his position.

The opening and concluding sections of the memorial are reproduced here.

Memorial of the Committee appointed by the "Free Trade Convention" held in Philadelphia in September and October, 1831, to prepare and present a memorial to Congress remonstrating against the existing tariff of duties. New York: William A. Mercein, 1832.

MEMORIAL.

To the Honorable the Senate and House of Representatives
of the United States, in Congress assembled,

THE Memorial of the Committee appointed for that purpose, by the "FREE TRADE CONVENTION," held at Philadelphia, in September and October, 1831. Respectfully shows:—

That a Convention of Delegates, appointed by public meetings in various States in the Union, for the purpose of cooperating by Constitutional and legal measures, in procuring the repeal of the restrictive system, was held at Philadelphia, on the 30th September, 1831, and continued in Session, till the 7th October, ensuing: when a Committee, consisting of one member from each State, represented in the Convention, was appointed for the purpose of preparing a memorial to Congress, setting forth the evils of the existing Tariff of duties, and asking such a modification of the same, as will be consistent with the purposes of revenue, and equal in its operation on the different parts of the United States, and on the various interests of the same.

Acting under that appointment, your Memorialists respectfully pray:

1st. That the duties be so reduced, as to leave, after the extinguishment of the public debt, only that amount of revenue which may be necessary to meet the ordinary exigencies of Government.

2ndly. That, allowing a reasonable time, for a gradual reduction of the existing exaggerated duties on some articles, the duties on all the imported articles not free of duty, be ultimately equalized, so as that the duty on any such article shall not vary materially from the general average rate of all the duties together, or in other words, from a uniform duty ad valorem on all imported articles subject to duty.

3dly. That wines, teas, coffee and similar articles, be not added to the list of those now free of duty, but, may on the contrary, be subject to duties corresponding, in proportion to their respective value, with those laid on other imported articles subject to duty.

It is hoped that no essential difference of opinion exists respecting the general reduction of the revenue.

So soon after the organization of the existing Government of the United States, as a sufficient revenue had been provided, and the first difficulties which they had to encounter, had been surmounted, Congress adopted the most efficient measures for the reimbursement of the debt necessarily incurred in asserting and securing the national independence. An annual appropriation of eight millions of dollars, founded on a real excess of revenue beyond the current expenditures, had in ten years reduced the debt from ninety seven millions of dollars (including therein the fifteen paid for Louisiana) to forty five millions; when the prospect of extinguishing the whole within six years was frustrated by the late war with Great Britain. After the restoration of peace, the whole of the public debt, including arrears afterwards paid or funded, and the subsequent payment of the Florida claims, exceeded on the first of January 1816 one hundred and twenty millions. Congress, without delay, raised the annual appropriation for the debt to ten millions of dollars, and provided a revenue sufficient, not only for the payment of that sum, and for discharging the current expenses of Government, but also for the gradual increase of all the means of defence by land and by sea, to the providing of which the former revenue was inadequate. At the end of sixteen years, during which the same measures have been unremittingly pursued, the public debt is accordingly reduced nominally to little more than twenty four, in fact to less than seventeen millions of dollars, an equivalent for the difference being found in the Bank Shares, the property of the United States, which have been paid for, during the same period. The revenue which will be actually received and that which will

accrue in the course of the year 1832, will be sufficient to re-
imburse the whole of the 24 millions still due. And, even without recurring to the Bank Shares owned by the United States,
the existing duties may be reduced near twelve millions of
dollars from the first of January 1832.

The people of the United States have constantly sustained
their representatives in the measures necessary for the attain-
ment of that great object. They have for more than thirty years,
cheerfully submitted to the burthens laid for that special purpose; and they are thus enabled to transmit, free of any encum-
brance, to the growing generation, the glorious inheritance
received from their fathers. But they have a right to expect,
that the burthens will cease with the occasion for which they
were laid, and that the intended reduction will be made in
good faith, without reserve, and to the full extent of the sum
which is no longer wanted.

The payments for the public debt have, during the ten years,
1821–1830, exceeded the annual appropriation of the ten millions. Including the payment of the Florida claims, the average
annual payments, during the first five years, exceeded eleven
millions; and they have during the last five years amounted
to near eleven millions, four hundred thousand dollars.

The average annual amount of all the other expenses of
Government, deducting the repayment to the claimants of the
sum paid by Great Britain, into the Treasury, for claims under
the first article of the treaty of Ghent, has been for the whole
ten years, about eleven millions, six hundred thousand dollars,
viz: for the first five years, less than ten millions and a half,
and for the last five years more that twelve millions and a half.
Two years only, those expenses have exceeded thirteen millions; in 1826, by about sixty thousand, and, in 1830, by two
hundred and thirty thousand dollars. A net revenue of thirteen
millions is therefore sufficient to meet, after the extinguishment of the debt, all the exigencies of Government, according
to the present scale of expenditure.

It is strictly just, that all classes of citizens and every section of the country, should share in the benefits arising from the reduction of the public burthens. That reduction ought to apply as well to the revenue arising from the public lands, as to the duties on importation. Your Memorialists do not pretend to suggest what, in their opinion, would be a proper reduction on each branch; but they had concluded that at all events, the necessary sum to be drawn from the impost, would fall short of thirteen millions. A different disposition of the public lands has been suggested by the Secretary of the Treasury. Unprepared for that proposal, and ignorant of the views on that subject, entertained by those in whose behalf your Memorialists now apply to your honorable body, they will abstain from giving an opinion on that question; and, in order to meet any plan which may be adopted in that respect, they will argue as if the whole revenue was to be exclusively drawn from duties on importations. But they beg leave earnestly to remonstrate against any attempt to provide a permanent revenue of fifteen millions, or exceeding the present rate of expenditure for other objects than the public debt.

A revenue derived from the same rate of duties on importation, will in the United States gradually increase, though in a much slower ratio than the population. The average annual gross revenue on merchandise, amounted, during the years 1821–1825, to 20.250.000 dollars, and during the years 1826–1830 to 23.130.900, showing an increase of about 14 per cent, within five years. But as the rate of duties was altered by the Tariffs of 1824 and 1828, a more correct criterion of the increase may perhaps be found in the comparative value of the domestic exports, with which the importations are paid, and which during the same period, have increased about six per cent, or at the rate of about one per cent a year. Moderate duties will also, as they always do, produce a greater proportionate revenue than when raised to an extravagant rate. The saving alone in the expenses of collection would defray within a short time, all the expense necessary for building Custom houses, and giving adequate salaries to the officers who may not be sufficiently remunerated. For to the Tariff of 1828, and to its system of minimums alone, can be ascribed the great increase in the expenses of collection, between the years 1828 and 1830. The gross revenue on customs, amounted in 1828, to 25.846.000, and those expenses to 869.000 dollars: the gross revenue of 1830, to 23.720.000, and the expenses to 1.024.000 dollars, or to 4.31 instead of 3.36 per cent. on the revenue.

The revolutionary pensions will also be gradually diminished; and, considering the great increase of the current expenditure during the last five years, a well founded hope is entertained that this may be lessened, without any injury to the public service, by a strict adherence to the specific appropriations made by law, improved order and regularity in the superintendance of every branch of expenditure, constant vigilance in checking abuses, and a proper discrimination between just and unfounded claims.

Your Memorialists wish it to be distinctly understood, that they ask only for a wise and skilful economy, and not for a retrenchment of any of the expenses necessary for the defence of the country, or for any object calculated to promote its prosperity, which is embraced by the legitimate powers of the General Government. They will only observe, that the average annual amount of expenses of the years 1829–1830, for all objects other than the public debt, falls short of thirteen millions, out of which the annual average expenditure for the progress and accumulation of the means of defence, including the increase of the Navy, fortifications, ordnance, and materials, has amounted to one million five hundred and seventy-five thousand dollars; and that for internal improvements of every description, and in every quarter, to one million two hundred and seventy-five thousand dollars. It is obvious that the expense under the first head, is from its nature definite, and that, after the intended fortifications and public ships shall have been completed, and the necessary stock of arms, ordnance, and every species of materials, either for the land or sea service been provided, the expense will be reduced to that of repairs and keeping up the stock. If, in the mean while, the existing annual appropriations for those great objects, should be deemed inadequate, if an earlier completion of any, or all of them be desirable, an additional revenue for that purpose can only be wanted for a short time, and will be supplied by the surplus arising from a gradual, instead of an immediate reduction of the high existing duties.

For the clearer understanding of the object they have in view and of the effect of the measures, which they solicit, on the several interests of the country, it is necessary in the first instance to form at least an approximate estimate of the average rate of duty, which, if levied equally on all the imports now subject to duty, would produce a net annual revenue of 13 millions, equivalent to a gross revenue, including the expenses of collection, of about 13.600,000 dollars.

The average annual value of foreign merchandise subject to duty consumed in the United States, during the six years 1825–1830, is according to the official "Statements of the Commerce and Navigation," 54.664.000 dollars. The re-exportations of foreign articles paying specific duties are however over-rated in those statements, probably from having been in most cases estimated at *long prices,* that is to say including the duty, by a sum amounting to about one million six hundred and fifty thousand dollars a year. And the articles paying duties ad valorem, which are imported from Great Britain and Ireland, being valued at the rate of four and sixpence st. per dollar, are under-rated by a sum amounting, after deducting the re-exportations, to about one million three hundred and forty-five thousand dollars a year. The actual annual consumption for those six years may therefore be estimated at about fifty seven millions and a half. As there are goods not entitled to drawback, exported to an amount of eight or nine hundred thousand dollars a year, on which the duty is paid, although they are not consumed in the United States, an average duty of twenty-five per cent. will commonly produce two hundred thousand dollars more than the estimate. Judging from analogy, the imports will, with the growth of the country, continue also gradually though slowly to increase. The estimate of the gross revenue at thirteen millions and a half, and of the value of imported articles paying duty, at fifty seven millions and a half, will therefore produce a net revenue exceeding thirteen millions: and that estimate gives for the required average, or uniform duty ad valorem, near twenty three and a half per cent. actual, or less than twenty-one and an half per cent. nominal duty. For it will be recollected, that on account of the addition to the prime cost of ten or twenty per cent. according to the place whence imported, a nominal duty of twenty per cent. is, in fact, one of twenty-four per cent. on goods imported from countries beyond the Cape of Good Hope, and of twenty-two per cent. on Goods imported from other places.

According to the same premises, the average duty required, to produce a net revenue of thirteen millions, would amount to near twenty-seven per cent. if wines, teas, coffee, cocoa, spices and fruits were exempted from duty. A net revenue of fifteen millions, would require in that case an average duty of thirty-one per cent. and of twenty-seven per cent. if those articles were subject to the same duty as every other import. The present average duty calculated on the average revenue derived from customs during the same period of six years, will be found to exceed forty per cent.

As a difference of three or four per cent. in the rate of an average duty, or of the aggregate of duties, would, on near sixty millions of taxed imports, produce a difference of two millions in the revenue, the attention of Congress will, under any modification of the tariff that may be adopted, be necessarily drawn to that subject. A thorough investigation will lead to much more correct results than those which are now presented. But this rough estimate is sufficient for our principal purpose. An error of even five per cent. in the rate, becomes almost unimportant, when contending against duties of fifty and more than one hundred per cent.

Your Memorialists are aware that, even for the purposes of revenue, a strict adherence, in every instance, to a uniform rate of duty would be attended with great inconvenience. There is propriety in taxing articles of luxury, in preference to those more generally used by the less wealthy classes of society. Yet it is found necessary to lessen the duty on watches, jewellry, thread-lace and other articles, which from their great value in a small bulk, may with facility be fraudulently imported. Considerations of a higher nature, may render a great reduction of the duties on spirits improper. An exception has always been admitted with respect to articles necessary for the defence of the country. When asking for a uniform duty, which, whether specific or laid ad valorem, shall not exceed the rate of twenty to twenty-five per cent. as sufficient for the purposes of the revenue, your Memorialists submit the proposition as a general principle. But whilst admitting that duties, not exceeding in the aggregate the amount thus required, may be arranged as the necessary exceptions to the general rule shall require, they contend, that any considerable variation from the average rate, for the purpose of favoring special branches, is injurious to American industry; attended with certain national loss; unequal and oppressive in its operation, both with regard to the several classes of society and to the several sections of the country.

We are not called upon to discuss the abstract question, whether another mode of taxation would be more eligible than the impost, or whether an unrestrained intercourse between all nations, free of the payment of any duties on imports, would be best calculated to promote the industry and prosperity of all. On that subject, the experience of forty years is conclusive so far as relates to the United States. The people prefer, in time of peace, duties raised on the importation of foreign merchandise to any internal tax, direct or indirect. Whether for good or for evil, that system affords an encouragement to domestic manufactures not less efficient for being incidental. Duties on imports, amounting perhaps on an average to about twenty-five per cent. on the value, appear necessary for the support of Government. Although they may to that extent, by diverting national industry from its natural channels, render it less productive; although they may, to that extent, lay a tax on the consumers, in addition to that which is paid to Government; although they operate unequally on different sections of the country; all your Memorialists ask is, that the evil shall not be aggravated by an inequality in the rates of duty. The question then at issue, is simply, whether the amount wanted, shall be so raised as to fall equally upon all the consumers, or in other words on the community, and so as to encourage equally every branch of industry, or, whether certain branches shall receive special protection by high, and sometimes, prohibitory duties.

Whether taxes are laid on income or on consumption, it is equally the duty of a Government founded in justice, to lay them equally on all, in proportion as the case may be, to the income or to the consumption. Were there no taxes of the latter description, every part of the country and every class of society would be left at liberty to supply its wants on the cheapest terms, and to pursue that branch of industry for which each was best fitted. If a tax, equivalent to an average duty of twenty-five per cent, (or at any other rate,) on all foreign commodities, becomes necessary for the support of Government, and is laid at an equal and uniform rate on all such commodities, all the sections of the country, classes of society and individuals, are left as far as is practicable, in the same relative situation as before. But any law materially varying the rate on any of the taxed articles, will in some respect change that relative situation, and to an extent proportionate to the change, render the burthen of the tax unequal. An alteration which thus deranges the natural order of things, should at least be productive of an adequate and indispensable advantage to the community. Higher duties on luxuries, than on articles generally and in some cases exclusively used by the less wealthy classes of society, are justified by the propriety of laying a heavier burden on those who are the best able to bear it. The domestic manufacture of a sufficient stock of arms by Government or by contract, at a much higher price than they could be procured abroad, may be necessary, in order to secure at all times a supply of those indispensable means of defence. Raw materials are admitted free of duty, because they are not, in that state, immediate objects of consumption, but necessary for the production of commodities to which the national industry may be advantageously applied. The presumed advantages of the restrictive system should be equally palpable and clearly demonstrated: the burthen of the proof lies altogether on its advocates.

Let it however be recollected that even the general benefit arising to the country at large, may not always be a sufficient justification of great and important deviations from an equal and uniform system of taxation. A government, which acknowledges the principle that no individual can be divested of his property for public purposes without indemnity, cannot claim the right to do that indirectly, which it is forbidden to do directly. A system calculated to lay permanent burthens, greatly unequal and oppressive, on some classes of society, or on a particular section of the country, would be radically unjust and altogether indefensible, even though it might be attended with some advantages to the community considered as a whole. But whether such advantages are in fact realized, whether, on any supposition, they ever can produce a profit equal to the actual national loss arising even from the indispensable duty of twenty to twenty-five per cent. must be first examined.

It is self evident, that the industry of a country is most profitably employed, or, in other words, that a country acquires the greatest wealth and its general prosperity is most advanced, in proportion as its capital and labor are most productive.

It is not less obvious, that if a given amount of capital and labor produces in the same time a less quantity of a certain commodity, than could have been purchased with that quantity of another article, which might have been produced, in the same time by the same amount of capital and labor, there has been a misapplication of such capital and labor, and a national loss equal to the difference between the quantity produced, and that which might have been purchased with the proceeds of the same capital and labor otherwise applied.

If the price, at which a commodity can be afforded by the person who undertakes to produce it, is higher than that at which it may be or might have been purchased from others, the difference of price is the measure of the national loss incurred by his misapplication of capital and labor to the production of that commodity.

With one thousand bushels of wheat worth one dollar a bushel, one thousand yards of cloth of a certain quality may be purchased. If the capital and labor employed, or which might be employed, in producing the thousand bushels of wheat, do, when applied to the production of similar cloth, produce in the same time one thousand yards, there is neither comparative gain or loss in that application of capital and labor. But, if thus applied it produces only eight hundred yards, there is an actual national loss of two hundred yards, equal to two hundred dollars, or to two hundred bushels of wheat; since the same labor and capital, if applied to the production of wheat, would have produced one thousand bushels, with which one thousand yards of the cloth might have been purchased.

There is not the slightest difference in the result, whether the cloth which might have been thus purchased at one dollar a yard, was manufactured in the same district where the unfortunate new undertaker resided, or whether it was imported, either from another district of the same country, or from a foreign country. In either case, it is again self evident that the national loss is precisely the same.

If the new manufacturer, (making a reasonable profit,) can afford to sell his cloth at one dollar a yard, it is a proof that there has been no misapplication of capital and labor, and neither comparative gain or loss in having produced cloth instead of wheat. But if he cannot afford without loss to sell the cloth for less than one dollar and twenty-five cents a yard, if he cannot; (making a reasonable profit) afford to sell eight hundred yards for less than one thousand dollars, it is certain that the same capital and labor, which might have been applied in producing one thousand bushels of wheat, with which one thousand yards of the cloth might have purchased, has within the same time produced but eight hundred yards; and that a national loss equivalent to two hundred dollars, or to two hundred bushels of wheat has been incurred by this misapplication of the national industry.

The difference between the price, at which a manufacturer can afford to sell the whole amount of the commodities produced by him in one year, and that at which the same quantity of the same articles may be or might have been purchased from others, is therefore equal to the annual national profit or loss, resulting from his application of capital and labor to that, instead of any other branch of industry.

When the new manufacturer has to compete with others of the same country, or if there is no duty on imports, with foreign manufacturers; as it is impossible for him to sell cloth of the same quality at a higher price, than it can be obtained from others, the loss must necessarily fall on him. This is not the less a public loss on that account. On whomsoever this may fall, a diminution of the quantity or exchangeable value of the commodities, which, with the same capital and labor, otherwise applied, might have been produced, is so much retrenched from what would otherwise have been an accumulation of capital or national wealth.

Although there may be occasional rash undertakings, it is also an indisputable truth, that the immense majority, even of this most enterprizing nation, pursues only such branches of industry as are attended with profit. The losing manufacturer, having discovered his error, would not, if let alone, persevere in ruining himself; and such abortive attempts, abandoned in time, would, on the whole, produce but a comparatively small loss to the community. It happens quite otherwise, when, from any peculiar circumstances, the Legislature is unfortunately induced to interfere in the pursuits of industry, instead of confining its care to that of providing, by wise laws, for the security and equal protection of the personal rights and property of every individual.

If the competition is with foreign merchandise, and the Legislature lays on this, a duty of twenty-five per cent. ad valorem, the importer cannot afford the cloth, which he previously sold at one dollar, for a price less than one dollar and twenty-five cents a yard. The manufacturer at home is thus enabled to sell his at the same price, and by obtaining one thousand dollars, for the eight hundred yards, to receive the same reasonable profit, as at the time may generally be derived from the application of capital and labor to similar pursuits. Since the duty in this instance, is not prohibitory, the cloth of that quality, which is wanted for the consumption of the country, will be supplied in part by the foreign importers, and partly by the home manufacturers. On the whole amount, whether foreign or domestic, the consumer will be obliged, so long as there is no general reduction of price, to pay twenty-five per cent. more than formerly. The amount of the additional price, thus paid for the foreign cloth, being paid by the importer into the treasury, is only an additional tax, which, as it relieves from the payment of some other tax otherwise necessary, cannot be considered as an actual loss to the community. The additional price paid on the domestic cloth, is equally a burthen on the consumer, but being paid not to Government, but to the manufacturer, is an actual national loss. The same loss is incurred in the manufacture of the cloth, as if the duty had not been laid, and its only effect is to transfer that loss from the manufacturer to the consumer.

The duty may not always be laid, so as to be nearly equal to the difference between the price, at which the domestic manufacture can be afforded, and that at which a similar foreign article might have been previously purchased.

If the duty is much less than that difference, it is only a fiscal measure, and does not enable the manufacturer to carry on his business. All the cloth, of the quality on which the duty is laid, will still be imported from abroad; but the additional price, at which it is sold, is only a tax on the consumer, and being paid to the Government, does not amount to a national loss.

If the duty is much greater than that difference, as the domestic article can be manufactured at a price less than the aggregate of the duty and of the price, at which the same foreign article might have been purchased previous to the duty, the price will probably be reduced by domestic competition to that; at which it can be manufactured and afforded with the ordinary rate of profit. The duty becomes then prohibitory; the whole amount consumed is of domestic manufacture; the consumer still pays the whole amount of difference between the price at which the manufacture can be afforded, and that at which the similar foreign article might have been previously purchased; and as no portion is paid into the public treasury, the whole of that amount is a public loss.

In every case the difference between the former price and that at which the domestic manufacture can be sold with a reasonable profit, is, to the whole extent of that manufacture, a loss to the community. That difference is equal, or nearly equal, on each yard of cloth, to the duty laid on a yard of the similar foreign article, whenever that duty is not too high to prevent partial foreign importations: it is less per yard than the duty, when this is higher than is necessary for the encouragement of the domestic manufacture and becomes prohibitory; but, in this case, the whole amount consumed being of domestic manufacture, the aggregate public loss is greater than when the duty admitted of foreign competition.

It may be urged, that these evils are compensated by extraneous advantages, which may accrue to the country from the establishment of manufactures, and as those cannot be indefinite, they should be compared with the national loss, which necessarily flows from the restrictive system. It may also be asserted, that the price, at which the domestic manufacture may be afforded, will be lessened by domestic competition, so as that it may not ultimately exceed that at which similar foreign articles might have been previously purchased; and that assertion deserves serious attention. But it cannot be denied, that until the price is thus reduced, or unless there are extraneous advantages, which compensate the difference between the former and the new artificial price, that difference is in the first instance a national loss arising from what is for the time a misapplication of capital and labor. For, in order to disprove that position, it would be necessary to show, that there is in the country a surplus amount of capital and labor, which cannot be more profitably employed.

That there is a sufficient amount of capital and labor applicable to manufactures, without withdrawing any that was previously actually employed in agriculture, commerce or mechanical pursuits, is generally true. For though there may be in certain parts of the country, instances of that kind, yet, considered as a whole, there is not, notwithstanding the numerous recent manufacturing establishments, any diminution in the agriculture, foreign commerce, or domestic exports of the country. Nor is it necessary, in order to explain this state of things, to recur either to an imaginary dormant capital, or to a pretended creation of capital by Banks or by legislative acts.

The five periodical enumerations of the inhabitants of the

United States show a uniform and not yet diminished increase of population, at the rate of near three per cent. a year. That population, which eighteen months ago, amounted, according to the census, to twelve millions eight hundred and fifty six thousand, exceeds at this time thirteen millions four hundred thousand souls. The increase is already at the rate of near four hundred thousand a year. Every year adds one hundred and fifty thousand able bodied men to the labor of the country. The whole of that population is most enterprizing and intelligent, and a great majority engaged in active and profitable pursuits, and continuing to make large annual additions to the capital of the country. Their energy and skill more than compensate the losses arising from an erroneous course of policy, notwithstanding which, and not through which, the prosperity of the country is rapidly increasing. This additional capital, and this additional labor are annually applied, the greater part to agriculture, the necessary portion to commerce, the residue to mechnical arts and manufacturing industry.

But the whole of that additional capital and labor would, if there were no legislative interference, be employed in remunerating pursuits, and it is not true that any portion must necessarily be applied to those particular branches, which, if not sustained by artificial means, could not, it is asserted, be carried on at all. The duty which enables the manufacturer of commodities of that description, to sell his eight hundred yards of cloth for one thousand instead of eight hundred dollars, does not enable him to produce one thousand yards with the same capital and labor. In order to show, that this difference, of two hundred yards or dollars, is not, in the first instance, a national loss, it must be demonstrated, that the capital and labor thus employed could not have been more advantageously applied in any other branch open to American industry, at the very time, when, if applied to any unprotected branch whatever no such loss was experienced.

A state of Society may indeed exist, where owing either to

a superabundant population, to over taxation, to a great inequality in the distribution of wealth, or in the means of acquiring it, or to any other natural or artificial cause, a portion of an industrious population may occasionally, or at all times, be in actual want of employment. Of a country thus situated, it may be said that it contains a capability of labor beyond that actually put forth. The symptoms of such a state of things are sufficiently visible; workmen discharged or with reduced wages, asking employment and food, and poor rates given to able bodied men, as a supplement to their insufficient salary. We may understand how, in that case, a new manufacture, some new channels opened to the national industry would, by giving employment to the laborer, bring into action an additional amount of labor.

There may also be countries, favored with a more genial climate, where the wants being few, and the absolutely necessary means of subsistence earned with less labor, long continued misgovernment has created deeply rooted habits of indolence. And such countries may also be said to have a dormant power of labor, which a free and wise government might stimulate and put in motion.

The situation in the United States is the very reverse in both respects. The existing rates of wages stimulate industry with a greater force, than in any other country; and, as a natural consequence, there is not, on the face of the globe, a nation incumbered with less indolence or idleness, a population more active, industrious, and we believe, more productive. This will continue "so long as the cheapness of unimproved land shall offer a certain employment to labor, and so long as the constitution, remains free as it is." If the restrictionists can find a more powerful cause, some more efficient means to stimulate labor and render American industry more productive and profitable, it will be a great and glorious discovery. For if it may perhaps be admitted, that the national progress in acquiring wealth may be tested by the general rate of profits,

there can be no doubt, and the most conspicuous illustration
of the fact is found in the situation of the United States compared with that of every other country, that the greatest mass
of comfort and happiness is always found, where the remuner-
ation is the highest. Should this prove to be one of the obstacles to the establishment of some manufactures, we nevertheless pray that it may long so continue.

It is impossible that the state of the country should have
been such, as that its capital and labor could not have been
more advantageously applied than to branches of industry,
which left to themselves, were attended with actual loss, without a corresponding great and sensible diminution in the demand for capital and the wages of labor; neither of which has
been felt. So long as those wages suffer no diminution, and so
long as the persons employed in commercial, and even agricultural pursuits, continue to borrow large capitals at the rate
of six per cent. a year, it is a clear proof, that those pursuits
afford profits at least equal to that rate of interest, and that
an application of capital and labor to the production of objects,
on which, if not artificially protected, a loss is experienced, is
not at all necessary.

That by multiplying in any country the channels of domestic
industry, a greater scope is given to its application, a market,
more diversified and less liable to be glutted, procured to its
products, and a larger field opened to every species of skill and
talent, is indubitably true. But to direct that industry to unprofitable pursuits, which cannot be sustained without exaggerated duties paid by the consumer and a corresponding
national loss, does not open new channels of productive industry, but only diverts it from profitable to unprofitable
pursuits to the community. It is truly remarkable, that the
advocates of the restrictive system who deny this obvious
truth, should pretend to consider your Memorialists as wild
theorists, when there cannot be a plainer matter of fact, than
that if a man is obliged to pay two dollars more for his coat, his

plough, or the implements of his trade, it is a loss to him which he must pay out of the proceeds of his industry, and that the aggregate of those individual losses is an actual national loss.

It is well known to your honorable body, that the tariff system is believed to be unconstitutional, by a numerous and respectable portion of the American people, including probably a majority of the citizens of the Southern States. Your Memorialists do not all unite in that opinion; but they assert, that the system is at variance with that spirit of justice and mutual concession, in which the Constitution was conceived and adopted, and that it operates unequally and unjustly upon those parts of the United States, which supply the greater portion of the National exports, and are less adapted to the introduction of manufacturing establishments.

The restrictive system lessens the amount of the foreign products which would otherwise be imported. It has therefore an immediate tendency to lessen the ever corresponding amount of exports. The avowed declarations of those who are benefited by it, and their general proscription of the trade with foreign nations, announce that such is their object. Retaliations, however unwise, may be provoked by a hostile course of legislation. It cannot be doubted, that a great diminution of the exportations will be the necessary consequence of persevering in that system, to the manifest and great injury of those States, which export most, and have no other resources than those exports.

The inhabited part of the United States embraces a territory, more extensive, and differing more in climate, than the whole of Western Europe. A necessary and great difference must arise between the branches of industry, to which the several portions of that territory are respectively best adapted. This difference is still more increased by that in the nature of the population. The Southern States have always confined themselves almost exclusively to the cultivation of the rich products of their climate. This is the only advantage they enjoy, and they owe it to nature. As they make but few, they consume a much greater proportion of manufactured articles, imported from other States, or other countries. That system therefore, which enhances, beyond measure, the price of those objects of necessary consumption, operates most unequally and unjustly upon them. They are forbidden to supply themselves, on the cheapest terms consistent with the revenue necessary for the exigencies of Government. As the greatest consumers, they must not only pay a greater share of the duties requisite to defray the necessary national expenditure, but they are compelled to pay the enhanced price occasioned by the protecting system. That system cannot be extended to them. They find in it no indemnity, no compensation, for the injury which it inflicts upon them. They have not, they cannot, in self defence, erect manufacturing establishments. The nature of their population forbids it. Whether from colour, or situation, is immaterial; the great mass of the working population, of the Southern States, is inferior in activity, skill and intelligence, to that of the other sections of the Union. Where such important and indelible differences do exist, each part should be permitted to enjoy its natural advantages: and that legislation is unjust, unequal and oppressive, which attempts to confer doubtful benefits on the one, at the expense of the other.

It is idle to say, that the Southern States find a compensation, in the general advantages, in the increased wealth resulting to the Union from the protecting system. The fallacy, of those pretended advantages, has been sufficiently exposed. But admitting their reality, they are, according to the doctrines even of the restrictionists, derived from the losses sustained by the consumers of the South. The duties on the iron, the woollen manufactures, the sugar, the salt, and all the other privileged articles which they consume, give no additional activity, or employment, to their labour. The amount of their products remains the same, and their value may be lessened; they pay more and receive nothing. In order that they might be placed on an equal footing with their fellow citizens, in order to enable them to erect manufactures, they stand in more need of a tariff against those of the Eastern States, than the Eastern States against those of England. From that weapon of self defence, they deprived themselves, in adopting the Constitution of the United States. It cannot be deemed consistent with justice and that spirit of mutual concession in which the Constitution was conceived and adopted, to convert that complete freedom of internal trade, secured by it to the several States, into a weapon of oppression upon those which, from uncontrollable circumstances, cannot compete with others in particular branches of industry. Is there any substantial difference between the British Government forbidding its American Colonies to trade with other nations, and to purchase any but British manufactures; and the adoption of that pretended American system, which compels one section of the Union to resort exclusively to another section, for its necessary supply of manufactured articles?

Your Memorialists are aware, that it may be urged, that whilst the exports of the Southern States have been increasing without interruption, those of the Middle and Northern States, though fluctuating in value, have for forty years been nearly stationary as to quantity. Whenever the demand for the articles of food, which constitute by far the greater part of those exports, ceased to increase in the same ratio as the population, it became not only useful, but absolutely necessary, to apply to new objects a portion of the industry of those States. They must, otherwise, have grown daily poorer and been deprived of the comforts which they had till then enjoyed. The Southern States might be asked, in that spirit of concession and compromise to which they appeal, not to oppose a course of legislation, intended to encourage the establishment of manufactures, which has become a matter of necessity in those parts of the Union, less favored by nature than themselves.

The facts are admitted, and the Southern States did not wait for that appeal. The compromise took place, the concession was made, from the time they consented, that the whole, or nearly the whole, of the public revenue should be raised by duties on imports. Unable to compete with others in manufactures, it was clearly their interest to purchase those they wanted, whenever they might be obtained on the cheapest terms, and that a part at least of the revenue should be derived from other sources. They voluntarily yielded the point, and submitted cheerfully to duties, amounting, on an average, to 40 per cent. whilst they were wanted to discharge the public debt. That object could not have been effected, without resorting to direct taxation, had not the foreign trade supplied the means. The taxed imports, which have paid the debt, have been purchased with the national exports; and of these, the oppressed States have supplied two thirds. Now that the object has been accomplished; after the manufacturing districts have during forty years enjoyed the incidental but not less efficient benefits of that mode of taxation, when the Southern States acquiesce in the continuance of the same system, on a scale proportionate to the exigencies of government: is it just, is it equitable, to aggravate instead of lightening, the burthen? and can this additional sacrifice be expected from them?

But no special protection, beyond the ordinary revenue duties, has been, or is, necessary for the introduction of the manufactures, required by the wants of the country. The annual average value of the imported merchandize, paying duties ad valorem, in the years 1798–1801, amounted, after deducting those exported with benefit of draw-back, to 33.-747.000 dollars. Deducting about 950.000 dollars, on account of articles exported, that were not entitled to draw-back, and of the fruits, spices and some other minor items, not then charged with specific duties, the residue amounting to 32.-800,000 dollars, is the value of the foreign manufactured commodities, annually consumed, at that time. The annual average value of the imported goods, paying duties ad valorem, during the years 1821–1826, taken from the annual statements of commerce, amounted after deducting the re-exportations, to 32.910.000 dollars. To this must be added, first 2.700.000 dollars, being the value of the iron and manufactured articles, which then paid duties ad valorem, and now pay specific duties; secondly, 7.00.000 dollars, being the difference between the present value of the cotton goods now imported, and that of the same quantity in the years 1799–1801. The increase therefore during that period of twenty-three years, amounts to about 10.600.000 dollars, or to less than thirty-three per cent. and that of the domestic exports will be found to have been thirty-five and a half per cent. During the same period, the population of the United States has more than doubled.

It will not be denied, that the people of the United States were at least as well supplied, in the year 1824, as in the year 1801, with clothing, furniture and every species of manufactured commodities. A population, twice as great, in order to be equally well supplied, required twice the amount of such articles. And since the value of foreign goods of that description, consumed in the United States in 1824, amounted only to 42.600.000, instead of 65.600.000 dollars, the difference must necessarily have been supplied by domestic manufactures. Not only those, which were established in 1801, must have increased in a ratio equal to the increase of population, but by a further quantity amounting to 23.000.000 dollars. The annual amount of foreign manufactures had during that period, and prior to the tariff of 1824 and 1828, been lessened more than one-third, in proportion to the population.

The actual increase of the domestic manufactures cannot be precisely ascertained, since the actual amount in 1801 is not known; but the limits of that increase may be correctly estimated. From the imperfect data obtained in the year 1810, it appears certain, that the amount, in the year 1801, did not exceed one hundred, or fall short of sixty millions of dollars. The domestic manufactures formed, therefore, from two-thirds to three-fourths of the total amount of the manufactured commodities consumed. The total amount consumed in the years 1821–1824 exceeded 265.000.000, according to the first supposition; and 185.000.000, according to the second. Deducting, in both cases, the amount of foreign goods, annually consumed in those years and amounting to 42.600.000 dollars, the increase of domestic manufactures would have been, in twenty-three years, 123 per cent. in the first case, and 138 per cent. in the second. We have a moral certainty, that it was within those limits; and that the amount of foreign manufactures was, in 1824, from one-fifth to one-sixth; whilst it was, in 1801, from one-third to one-fourth of the whole amount of manufactured commodities consumed.

Proceeding in the same manner, it will appear, that without any such special protection, as that of the tariffs of 1824 and 1828, the total value of the manufactures consumed in the United States, in the year 1847 will probably be 450.000.000, of which the domestic manufactures will form seven-eighths, and foreign merchandise no more than one-eighth part. In all probability, the increase of domestic manufactures will be greater in proportion, during that period of twenty-three years, than during the next preceding; since there will be more skill and experience, a more dense population, and a greater proportionate capital.

The principle is indisputable, and if there is some error in the numbers, it will no otherwise affect the result, than that it may take place a few years sooner or later. But that result, with a population so active and intelligent, is certain. The question is only one of time; and admitting for the sake of argument, that the protecting system has a tendency to accelerate the establishment of manufactures in general, all that can be gained by it is, that the same necessary result may be obtained a few years earlier.

A uniform and moderate duty does not derange the natural order of things; and, instead of sustaining, by artificial means, certain manufactures, for which the country may not be prepared, at the expense of the community, and particularly of the poorer classes, to the detriment of other manufactures, and to the great injury of some parts of the country, it will encourage and successively promote, the various branches of industry best adapted to that state of Society, and to the circumstances of the different parts of the Union. A maximum duty of twenty-five per cent. added to the charges on importation, will give to the manufactures that may require it, an actual protection of thirty-five per cent. An efficient system, that will prevent frauds, and, as far as practicable, check irregular importations on foreign account, will insure to the manufacturer the legal protection to its full extent; and, given in a true spirit of compromise and conciliation, it will have that stability, indispensable to him, on which he never can rely under the present system.

Your Memorialists beg leave here to observe, that whilst they have considered a duty of twenty-five per cent. as the highest that should, in any case, be allowed, they have not pretended to assert, that the average duty, required for the exigencies of Government, should be twenty-per cent. on the value. If they have adopted that rate in their calculations, it has been only in order to meet any determination, that may be taken by your Honorable body on the amount of the revenue, which should be provided, and any difference of opinions respecting the probable amount of importations, and the consequent productiveness of any given per centage. In their own opinion, the average duty actually required would fall far short of twenty per cent.

After having given the fullest consideration to this important subject, your Memorialists have not been able to perceive any other objection to the immediate adoption of the plan, which they have respectfully suggested, than that which arises from vested interests. These are entitled to respect only because they do exist; and not on account of any presumed legislative pledge, which no Legislature could give, and which, if so intended, your Memorialists altogether deny to be, in any degree, binding upon subsequent Legislatures. Your Memorialists have accordingly been instructed to express the willingness of those, in whose behalf they address your Honorable body, to acquiesce in such an interposition of the legislative power, as shall be prospective in its operation; thereby avoiding any sudden revulsion, which might operate with undue severity on the manufacturing interest, but leading to the desired result, with the least possible injury to the interests, which have grown up under the existing system of protective duties.

Your Memorialists trust, that the temporary and doubtful advantages ascribed to the tariff system, and which may perhaps accrue to some particular districts, will not be permitted to outweigh considerations of a far more important character. It may justly be expected, from the patriotism of those who calculate upon such local advantages, that they will not insist on what is manifestly unjust, and persevere in a course, which disturbs the peace of the country, and alienates the affections of a numerous portion of their fellow citizens.

Let it be recollected, that the system is in itself an infraction of an essential part of the liberty of the citizen. The necessity must be urgent and palpable, which authorizes any government to interfere in the private pursuits of individuals; to forbid them to do that which in itself is not criminal, and which every one would most certainly do, if not forbidden. Every individual, in every community, without exception, will purchase whatever he may want on the cheapest terms within his reach. The most enthusiastic restrictionist, the manufacturer, most clamorous for special protection, will, each individually, pursue the same course, and prefer any foreign commodity, or material, to that of domestic origin, if the first is cheaper, and the law does not forbid him. All men ever have acted, and continue, under any system, to act on the same principle. It is impossible, that they should universally act in that manner, unless it was evidently their interest so to do. The advocates of the tariff system affirm, that what is true of all men, individually, is untrue, when applied to them collectively. We cannot consider the adherence of enlightened nations to regulations of that description, but as the last relic of that system of general restrictions and monopolies, which had its origin in barbarous times. If the corn laws are the most odious of those protecting monopolies, it is because they enhance the price of that, which is still more essentially necessary than sugar, salt, clothing or fuel; and we may safely predict, that their repeal will be the first result of an improved representation of the people.

Your Memorialists are fully aware, that acquiescence in the will of the majority is the indispensable condition of a representative government. The true problem to be solved in the United States, is not, whether the people can govern themselves, of which not the slightest doubt can be entertained; but whether that government can be successfully applied to an extensive territory, embracing interests, which must occasionally be in collision with each other; whether majorities, formed by combinations of sectional interests, will be so governed by a sense of justice and a spirit of conciliation, as not to oppress those parts of the country, whose rights, though they may be a minority, ought nevertheless to be respected. The permanence of the Union, and the destinies of this great and happy nation, have been intrusted to your Honorable body; and with an humble hope, that your deliberations may be enlightened by Him, to whom the United States are indebted for all the blessings they enjoy, your Memorialists as in duty bound, will ever pray, &c.

PART NINE

Elder Statesman:

The Sectional Controversy, 1846–1847

"FIFTY-FOUR FORTY OR FIGHT"

The Democratic Party won the momentous election of 1844 on an expansionist program that featured "the re-annexation of Texas and the re-occupation of Oregon." A subsidiary slogan, "fifty-four forty or fight," denoted the intent to assert American claims to the whole of Oregon northward to the fifty-fourth parallel. Oregon was still under joint occupation with Britain according to the treaty of 1818, an arrangement which had been satisfactory to the United States until Americans began going into the region in the 1840's. In previous negotiations over Oregon, Britain and the United States had never been far from agreement on a division of the territory. The United States had repeatedly suggested a line at the forty-ninth parallel, the British had held out for the Columbia River; hence the dispute centered on an area comprising about two-thirds of the present state of Washington. This area, was important because it included Puget Sound, which had the best ocean port facilities north of San Francisco.

Although nearly all the Americans in Oregon had settled south of the Columbia and none had penetrated beyond the

441

forty-ninth parallel, the Democratic Presidential candidate, James K. Polk, declared that he would terminate the joint occupation treaty and take possession of an undetermined part of Oregon as a matter of right. He repeated this statement in his inaugural address. Nevertheless, he showed willingness to compromise. In July 1845 he proposed the forty-ninth parallel; however the British minister at Washington refused to negotiate on this basis. Polk then took a bellicose tone, recommending to Congress that the treaty be repudiated and steps taken to occupy the whole territory. After much debate Congress in April 1846 authorized him to give Britain the required year's notice that the joint occupation treaty was at an end.

52. THE OREGON QUESTION

1846

Gallatin believed that if the United States took possession of Oregon, Britain would declare war. In 1846 he published a series of articles in the Washington National Intelligencer which was published as a pamphlet the same year. The pamphlet fortified widespread opposition to the administration's policy. However, Gallatin's efforts and those of other publicists had less effect in ending the crisis than the determination of the British ministry to avoid war. Disregarding the bellicose utterances of Democratic leaders, the ministry

---

The Oregon Question with an Appendix on War Expenses (New York: Bartlett and Welford, 1846). The following excerpt is taken from Writings, III, 514–522, 533–536.

gave up the line of the Columbia and offered the forty-ninth parallel. After obtaining the sanction of the Senate, Polk accepted.

The first two sections of Gallatin's essay, omitted here, were devoted to proving that neither Britain nor the United States had an incontestable claim to Oregon by right of discovery, exploration, or settlement. Continuing his argument against unilateral action by the United States, Gallatin declared that the inevitable war would not only be unnecessary but destructive. If the present arrangement was merely allowed to stand, Oregon would soon be populated by American emigrants. A new republic would arise on the Pacific coast friendly to the United States or susceptible of incorporation as another American state.

NUMBER III.

Beyond the naked assertion of an absolute right to the whole territory, so little in the shape of argument has been adduced, and so much warmth has been exhibited in the discussion of the subject, that it cannot be doubted that the question has now become on both sides one of feeling rather than of right. This in America grows out of the fact that in this contest with a European nation the contested territory is in America and not in Europe. It is identical with the premature official annunciation that the United States could not acquiesce in the establishment of any new colony in North America by any European nation. This sentiment was already general at the time when it was first publicly declared, and now that it has been almost universally avowed, there can be no impropriety in any private citizen to say, as I now do, that I share in that feeling to its full extent. For the Americans Oregon is or will be home; for England it is but an outpost, which may afford means of annoyance rather than be a source of real power. In America all have the same ultimate object in view; we differ only with respect to the means by which it may be attained.

Two circumstances have had a tendency to nourish and excite these feelings. The British fur companies, from their position, from their monopolizing character, from their natural influence upon the Indians, and from that, much greater than might have been expected, which they have constantly had upon the British government in its negotiations with the United States, have for sixty years been a perpetual source of annoyance and collisions. The vested interests of the Hudson Bay Company are at this moment the greatest obstacle to an amicable arrangement. It is at the same time due to justice to say that, as far as is known, that company has acted in Oregon in conformity with the terms of the convention, and that its officers have uniformly treated the Americans, whether visitors or emigrants, not only courteously, but with great kindness.

If the British colonies on the continent of America were an independent country, or were they placed in their commercial relations, at least with the United States, on the same footing as the British possessions in Europe, these relations would be regulated by the reciprocal interests and wants of the parties immediately concerned. Great Britain has an undoubted right to persist in her colonial policy; but the result has been extremely vexatious, and to the United States injurious. All this is true. But feelings do not confer a right, and the indulgence of excited feelings is neither virtue nor wisdom.

The Western States have no greater apparent immediate interest in the acquisition of Oregon than the States bordering on the Atlantic. These stand in greater need of an outlet for their surplus emigrating population, and to them exclusively will for the present the benefit accrue of ports on the Pacific for the protection of the numerous American ships employed in the fisheries and commerce of that ocean. It is true that in case of war the inhabitants of the Western States will not, if a naval superiority shall be obtained on the upper Lakes, feel those immediate calamities of war to which the country along the sea-shore is necessarily exposed; but no section of the United States will be more deeply affected by the impossibility of finding during the war a market for the immense surplus of its agricultural products. It must also be remembered that a direct tax has heretofore been found as productive as the aggregate of all the other internal taxes levied by the general government; that, in case of war, it must necessarily be imposed; and that, as it must, in conformity with the Constitution, be levied in proportion to the respective population of the several States, it will be much more oppressive on those which have not yet accumulated a large amount of circulating or personal capital. The greater degree of excitement which prevails in the West is due to other and more powerful causes than a regard for self-interest.

Bordering through the whole of their northern frontier on the British possessions, the Western people have always been personally exposed to the annoyances and collisions already alluded to; and it may be that the hope of getting rid of these by the conquest of Canada has some influence upon their conduct. Independent of this, the indomitable energy of this nation has been and is nowhere displayed so forcibly as in the new States and settlements. It was necessarily directed towards the acquisition of land and the cultivation of the soil. In that respect it has performed prodigies. Three millions of cultivators of the soil are now found between the Lakes and the Ohio, where, little more than fifty years before, save only three or four half Indian French settlements, there was not a single white inhabitant. Nothing now seems impossible to those men; they have not even been sobered by fresh experience. Attempting to do at once, and without an adequate capital, that which should have been delayed five-and-twenty years, and might have then been successfully accomplished, some of those States have had the mortification to find themselves unable to pay the interest on the debt they had contracted, and obliged to try to compound with their creditors. Nevertheless, undiminished activity and locomotion are still the ruling principles; the Western people leap over time and distance; ahead they must go; it is their mission. May God speed them, and may they thus quietly take possession of the entire contested territory!

All this was as well known to the British government as to ourselves. A public and official declaration by the President of the United States was unnecessary and at least premature. Mr. Rush's correspondence of 1824 bears witness of its unfortunate effect on the negotiations of that year. These feelings had gradually subsided. But whatever may be the cause, the fact that an extraordinary excitement on this subject has manifested itself and does now exist on both sides cannot be denied. Time is absolutely necessary in order that this should subside. Any precipitate step now taken by either government would be attended with the most fatal consequences. That which, if done some years ago, might have been harmless, would now be highly dangerous, and should at least be postponed for the present.

The first incipient step recommended by the Executive is to give the notice that the convention of 1827 shall expire at the end of one year. This measure at this time, and connected with the avowed intention of assuming exclusive sovereignty over the whole territory, becomes a question of peace or war.

The conventions of 1818 and 1827, whilst reserving the rights of both parties, allowed the freedom of trade and navigation throughout the whole territory to remain common to both; and the citizens or subjects of both powers were permitted to occupy any part of it. The inconveniences of that temporary arrangement were well understood at the time. The British fur companies had established factories on the banks, and even south of the river Columbia, within the limits of that portion of the country which the United States had, whenever the subject was discussed, claimed as belonging exclusively to them. The conditions of the agreement were nominally reciprocal; but though they did not give, yet they did in fact leave the British company in the exclusive possession of the fur-trade. This could not be prevented otherwise than by resorting to actual force; the United States were not then either ready or disposed to run the risks of a war for that object; and it was thought more eligible that the British traders should remain on the territory of the United States by virtue of a compact and with their consent than in defiance of their authority. It is but very lately that the Americans have begun to migrate to that remote country; a greater number will certainly follow; and they have under the convention a perfect right to occupy and make settlements in any part of the territory they may think proper, with the sole exception of the spots actually occupied by the British company.

What is, then, the object in view in giving the notice at this time? This has been declared without reserve by the President: "At the end of the year's notice, should Congress think it proper to make provision for giving that notice, we shall have reached a period when the national rights in Oregon must either be abandoned or firmly maintained. That they cannot be abandoned without a sacrifice of both national honor and interests, is too clear to admit of doubt." And it must be recollected that this candid avowal has been accompanied by the declaration that "our title to the whole Oregon territory had been asserted and, as was believed, maintained by irrefragable facts and arguments." Nothing can be more plain and explicit. The exclusive right of the United States to absolute sovereignty over the whole territory must be asserted and maintained.

It may not be necessary for that purpose to drive away the British fur company, nor to prevent the migration into Oregon of British emigrants coming from the British dominions. The company may, if deemed expedient, be permitted to trade as heretofore with the Indians. British emigrants may be treated in the same manner as the other sixty or eighty thousand who already arrive yearly in the United States. They may, at their option, be naturalized or remain on the same footing as foreigners in other parts of the Union. In this case they will enjoy no political rights; they will not be permitted to own American vessels and to sail under the American flag; the permission to own real property seems, so long as Oregon remains a territory, to depend on the will of Congress. Thus far collision may be avoided.

But no foreign jurisdiction can be permitted from the moment when the sovereignty of the United States over the whole territory shall be asserted and maintained. To this all those who reside in the territory must submit. After having taken the decisive step of giving the notice, the United States cannot, as the President justly states, abandon the right of sovereignty without a sacrifice of national honor.

It had been expressly agreed by the convention that nothing contained in it should affect the claims of either party to the territory. The all-important question of sovereignty remained therefore in abeyance. Negotiations for a division of the territory have failed; the question of sovereignty remains undecided, as it was prior to the convention. If the United States exercise the reserved right to put an end to the convention, and if, from the time when it shall have expired, they peremptorily assume the right of sovereignty over the whole, it cannot be doubted that Great Britain will at once resist. She will adhere to the principle she had asserted prior to the Nootka convention, and has ever since maintained, that actual occupancy can alone give a right to the country. She will not permit the jurisdiction of the United States to be extended over her subjects; she will oppose the removal, arrest, or exercise of any other legal process against her justices of the peace, against any other officers who directly or indirectly act under her authority, against any of her subjects; and she will continue to exercise her jurisdiction over all of them throughout the whole territory. Whatever either power asserts must be maintained; military occupation and war must necessarily ensue.

A portion of the people, both in the West and elsewhere, see clearly that such must be the consequence of giving the notice. Such men openly avow their opinions, prefer war to a longer continuation of the present state of things, are ready to meet all the dangers and calamities of the impending conflict, and to adopt at once all the measures which may insure success. With them the discussion brings at once the question to its true issue: Is war necessary for the object they have in view? Or may it not be attained by peaceable means? It is a question of war or peace, and it is fairly laid before the nation.

But many respectable men appear to entertain hopes that peace may still be preserved after the United States shall have assumed, or attempted to assume, exclusive sovereignty. The reverse appears to me so clear, so obvious, so inevitable, that I really cannot understand on what grounds these hopes are founded.

Is it thought that the President will not, after the assent of Congress has been obtained (and whether immediately or at the end of this session is quite immaterial), give the notice which he has asked Congress to authorize? Or is it supposed that a change in the form which, in order to avoid responsibility, would give him a discretionary power, could lead to a different result, or be anything else but a transfer by Congress to the Executive of the power to declare war?

Can it be presumed that when, after the expiration of the term of notice, the convention shall have been abrogated, the President will not assert and maintain the sovereignty claimed by the United States? I have not the honor of a personal acquaintance with him; I respect in him the first magistrate of the nation; and he is universally represented as of irreproachable character, sincere, and patriotic. Every citizen has a right to differ with him in opinion; no one has that of supposing that he says one thing and means another. I feel an intimate conviction of his entire sincerity.

Is it possible that any one who does not labor under a singular illusion can believe that England will yield to threats and defiance that which she has refused to concede to our arguments? Reverse the case: Suppose for a moment that Great Britain was the aggressor and had given the notice, declaring at the same time that at the expiration of the year she would assume exclusive sovereignty over the whole country and oppose the exercise of any whatever by the United States, is there any American, even amongst those who set the least value on the Oregon territory and are most sincerely desirous of preserving peace, who would not at once declare that such pretension on the part of Great Britain was outrageous and must be resisted?

It is not certainly the interest of Great Britain to wage war against the United States, and it may be fairly presumed that the British government has no such wish. But England is, as well as the United States, a great, powerful, sensitive, and proud nation. Every effusion of the British press which displays hostility to the United States produces an analogous sentiment and adds new fuel to excitement in America. A moment's reflection will enable us to judge of the inevitable effect of an offensive and threatening act emanating from our government; an act which throws in the face of the world the gauntlet of defiance to Great Britain. Her claims and views, as laid down in her statement of December, 1826, remove every doubt respecting the steps she will take. "Great Britain claims no exclusive sovereignty over any portion of that territory. Her present claim not in respect to any part, but to the whole, is limited to a right of joint occupancy in common with other States, leaving the right of exclusive dominion in abeyance. . . . The pretensions of Great Britain tend to the mere maintenance of her own rights, *in resistance to the ex-*

clusive character of the pretensions of the United States. . . .
These rights embrace the right to navigate the waters of those
countries, *the right to settle in and over any part of them*, and
the right freely to trade with the inhabitants and occupiers of
the same. It is fully *admitted* that the *United States possess
the same rights*. But beyond these rights they possess none.
To the interests and establishments which British industry
and enterprise have created Great Britain owes protection.
That protection will be given, both as regards settlement and
freedom of trade and navigation, with every attention not to
infringe the co-ordinate rights of the United States."

Thus, the United States declare that they give notice of the
abrogation of the convention, with the avowed determination
of asserting their assumed right of absolute and *exclusive
sovereignty* over the whole territory of Oregon. And Great
Britain has explicitly declared that her pretensions were *in
resistance* to the *exclusive* character of those of the United
States; and that protection will be given, both as regards
settlement and freedom of trade and navigation, to the interests and establishments which British industry and enterprise
have created.

How war can be avoided if both powers persist in their conflicting determinations is incomprehensible. Under such circumstances negotiation is morally impossible during the year
following the notice. To give that notice with the avowed determination to assume exclusive sovereignty at the end of the
year is a decisive, most probably an irretrievable, step. "After
that period the United States cannot abandon their right of
sovereignty without a sacrifice of national honor."

The question of sovereignty has never been decided. Simply
to give notice of the abrogation of the convention would leave
the question in the same situation,—it would remain in abeyance. But when the President has recommended that the notice
should be given with the avowed object of assuming exclusive
sovereignty, an Act of Congress in compliance with his recom-

mendation necessarily implies an approbation of the object for which it is given. If the notice should be given, the only way to avoid that implication and its fatal consequences is to insert in it an explicit declaration that the sovereignty shall not be assumed. But then why give the notice at all? A postponement is far preferable, unless some other advantage shall be obtained by the abrogation of the convention. This must be examined, and it is necessary to inquire whether any and what measures may be adopted without any violation of the convention that will preserve the rights and strengthen the position of the United States.

NUMBER IV.

[*In the fourth section, Gallatin proposed that instead of bringing affairs to a crisis by abrogating the joint occupation agreement, the United States should strengthen its hold on Oregon by encouraging emigration, building forts along the route, improving the road, sponsoring a company to aid settlers, protect land titles in Oregon, and negotiate with Britain to establish organs of local government in the territory. As Oregon became populated by Americans, it would fall to the United States—ED.*]

NUMBER V.

. . . It has been attempted in these papers to prove:

1. That neither of the two powers has an absolute and indisputable right to the whole contested territory; that each may recede from its extreme pretensions without impairing national honor or wounding national pride; and that the way is therefore still open for a renewal of negotiations.

2. That the avowed object of the United States in giving notice of the abrogation of the convention is the determination

to assert and maintain their assumed right of absolute and exclusive sovereignty over the whole territory; that Great Britain is fully committed on that point, and has constantly and explicitly declared that such an attempt would be resisted and the British interests in that quarter be protected; and that war is therefore the unavoidable consequence of such a decisive step,—a war not only necessarily calamitous and expensive, but in its character aggressive, not justifiable by the magnitude and importance of its object, and of which the chances are uncertain.

3. That the inconveniences of the present state of things may in a great degree be avoided; that, if no war should ensue, they will be the same, if not greater, without than under a convention; that not a single object can be gained by giving the notice at this time, unless it be to do something not permitted by the present convention, and therefore provoking resistance and productive of war. If a single other advantage can be gained by giving the notice, let it be stated.

4. That it has been fully admitted by Great Britain that, whether under or without a convention, the United States have the same rights as herself to trade, to navigate, and to occupy and make settlements in and over every part of the territory; and that, if this state of things be not disturbed, natural causes must necessarily give the whole territory to the United States.

Under these circumstances, it is only asked that the subject may be postponed for the present; that government should not commit itself by any premature act or declaration; that, instead of increasing the irritation and excitement which exist on both sides, time be given for mutual reflection and for the subdual or subsidence of angry and violent feelings. Then, and then only, can the deliberate opinion of the American people on this momentous question be truly ascertained. It is not perceived how the postponement for the present and for a time can in any shape or in the slightest degree injure the United States.

It is certainly true that England is very powerful, and has

often abused her power, in no case in a more outrageous manner than by the impressment of seamen, whether American, English, or other foreigners, sailing under and protected by the American flag. I am not aware that there has ever been any powerful nation, even in modern times and professing Christianity, which has not occasionally abused its power. The United States, who always appealed to justice during their early youth, seem, as their strength and power increase, to give symptoms of a similar disposition. Instead of useless and dangerous recriminations, might not the two nations, by their united efforts, promote a great object, and worthy of their elevated situation?

With the single exception of the territory of Oregon, which extends from 42° to 54° 40/ north latitude, all the American shores of the Pacific Ocean, from Cape Horn to Behring's Straits, are occupied; on the north by the factories of the Russian Fur Company; southwardly by semi-civilized states, a mixture of Europeans of Spanish descent and of native Indians, who, notwithstanding the efforts of enlightened, intelligent, and liberal men, have heretofore failed in the attempt to establish governments founded on law, that might insure liberty, preserve order, and protect persons and property. It is in Oregon alone that we may hope to see a portion of the western shores of America occupied and inhabited by an active and enlightened nation, which may exercise a moral influence over her less favored neighbors, and extend to them the benefits of a more advanced civilization. It is on that account that the wish has been expressed that the Oregon territory may not be divided. The United States and England are the only powers who lay any claim to that country, the only nations which may and must inhabit it. It is not, fortunately, in the power of either government to prevent this taking place; but it depends upon them whether they shall unite in promoting the object, or whether they shall bring on both countries the calamities of an useless war, which may retard, but not prevent, the ultimate result. It matters but little whether the inhabitants shall come from England or from the United States. It would seem that more importance might be attached to the fact that within a period of fifteen years near one million of souls are now added to the population of the United States by migrations from the dominions of Great Britain; yet, since permitted by both powers, they may be presumed to be beneficial to both. The emigrants to Oregon, whether Americans or English, will be united together by the community of language and literature, of the principles of law, and of all the fundamental elements of a similar civilization.

The establishment of a kindred and friendly power on the north-west coast of America is all that England can expect, all perhaps that the United States ought to desire. It seems almost incredible that, whilst the object may be attained by simply not impeding the effect of natural causes, two kindred nations, having such powerful motives to remain at peace, and standing at the head of European and American civilization, should in this enlightened age give to the world the scandalous spectacle, perhaps not unwelcome to some of the beholders, of an unnatural and an unnecessary war; that they should apply all their faculties and exhaust their resources in inflicting, each on the other, every injury in their power, and for what purpose? The certain consequence, independent of all the direct calamities and miseries of war, will be a mutual increase of debt and taxation, and the ultimate fate of Oregon will be the same as if the war had not taken place.

TEXAS AND THE MEXICAN WAR

Gallatin opposed the annexation of Texas, regarding it as an attempt to extend slavery and to add more slave territory to the Union by war with Mexico. As his stand on the tariff indicated, Gallatin was not doctrinaire on sectional issues; he favored concessions to the South for the sake of preserving the Union. But he would not accept propagation of the southern interest by aggressive war. Late in 1846 as General Winfield Scott's troops were advancing into Mexico City, he published an indictment of the administration's policy. The pamphlet must be read in the context of growing popular sentiment for the annexation of the whole of Mexico. Northern Whigs and antislavery elements had opposed the Mexican War as leading to expansion of slave territory, but opinion began to change rapidly in the North and Northwest as it became evident that much of Mexico was unsuited to slavery. The annexation of part or all of Mexico appeared to some as the way of getting the better of the slave power. It also appealed to expansionist sentiment founded on the idea of America's "Manifest Destiny" to extend its beneficent and democratic institutions over the whole of North America. The movement was cut short by the early, and to many the premature, negotiation of the Treaty of Guadalupe Hidalgo and its ratification by the Senate on March 10, 1848.

53. PEACE WITH MEXICO

1847

Gallatin, in this pamphlet, heaped scorn upon the white man's burden argument that justified annexation as conferring the benefits of higher civilization upon the backward Mexicans. He reviewed the course of events leading to the conflict with

---

Peace with Mexico (New York: Bartlett & Welford, 1847), reprinted in *Writings*, III, 557–591.

Mexico, documenting his view that this was an unjust war, deliberately provoked, the first to sully the honor of the United States. Since the aggression could not now be undone, he pleaded at least for a just peace with minimal annexations of territory. Recalling the idealism of America's early years, he reminded his readers that the strength of a republic is in its virtue not its power. "Your mission was to be a model for all other governments and for all other less-favored nations, to adhere to the most elevated principles of political morality, to apply all your faculties to the gradual improvement of your own institutions and social state, and by your example to exert a moral influence most beneficial to mankind at large."

Gallatin was never more eloquent than in this work written three years before his death.

I.—THE LAW OF NATIONS.

IT seems certain that Mexico must ultimately submit to such terms of peace as the United States shall dictate. An heterogeneous population of seven millions, with very limited resources and no credit, distracted by internal dissensions and by the ambition of its chiefs, a prey by turns to anarchy and to military usurpers, occupying among the nations of the civilized world, either physically or mentally, whether in political education, social state, or any other respect, but an inferior position, cannot contend successfully with an energetic, intelligent, enlightened, and united nation of twenty millions, possessed of unlimited resources and credit, and enjoying all the benefits of a regular, strong, and free government. All this was anticipated; but the extraordinary successes of the Americans have exceeded the most sanguine expectations. All the advanced posts of the enemy, New Mexico, California, the line of the lower Rio Norte, and all the seaports which it was deemed necessary to occupy, have been subdued. And a small force, apparently incompetent to the object, has penetrated near three hundred miles into the interior, and is now in quiet possession of the far-famed metropolis of the Mexican dominions. The superior skill and talents of our distinguished generals and the unparalleled bravery of our troops have surmounted all obstacles. By whomsoever commanded on either side, however strong the positions and fortifications of the Mexicans, and with a tremendous numerical superiority, there has not been a single engagement in which they have not been completely defeated. The most remarkable and unexpected feature of that warfare is that volunteers, wholly undisciplined in every sense of the word, have vied in devotedness and bravery with the regular forces, and have proved themselves in every instance superior in the open field to the best regular forces of Mexico. These forces are now annihilated or dispersed, and the Mexicans are reduced to a petty warfare of guerrillas, which, however annoying, cannot be productive of any important results.

It is true that these splendid successes have been purchased at a price far exceeding their value. It is true that neither the glory of these military deeds nor the ultimate utility of our conquests can compensate the lamentable loss of the many thousand valuable lives sacrificed in the field, of the still greater number who have met with an obscure death or been disabled by disease and fatigue. It is true that their relatives, their parents, their wives and children find no consolation for the misery inflicted upon them in the still greater losses experienced by the Mexicans. But if, disregarding private calamities and all the evils of a general nature, the necessary consequences of this war, we revert solely to the relative position of the two countries, the impotence of the Mexicans and their total inability to continue the war with any appearance of success are still manifest.

The question then occurs, What are the terms which the

United States have a right to impose on Mexico? All agree that it must be an "honorable peace;" but the true meaning of this word must in the first place be ascertained.

The notion that anything can be truly honorable which is contrary to justice will, as an abstract proposition, be repudiated by every citizen of the United States. Will any one dare to assert that a peace can be honorable which does not conform with justice?

There is no difficulty in discovering the principles by which the relations between civilized and Christian nations should be regulated and the reciprocal duties which they owe to each other. These principles, these duties, have long since been proclaimed, and the true law of nations is nothing else than the conformity to the sublime precepts of the gospel morality, precepts equally applicable to the relations between man and man and to the intercourse between nation and nation. "Thou shalt love thy neighbor as thyself." "Love your enemies." "As you would that men should do to you, do ye also to them likewise." The sanctity of these commands is acknowledged, without a single exception, by every denomination of Christians, or of men professing to be such. The skeptical philosopher admits and admires the precept. To this holy rule we should inflexibly adhere when dictating the terms of peace. The United States, though they have the power, have no right to impose terms inconsistent with justice. It would be a shameful dereliction of principle on the part of those who were averse to the annexation of Texas to countenance any attempt to claim an acquisition of territory or other advantage on account of the success of our arms.

But in judging the acts of our government, it must be admitted that statesmen think a conformity to those usages which constitute the law of nations not as it should be, but as it is practically, sufficient to justify their conduct. And by that inferior standard those acts and our duties in relation to Mexico will be tested.

II.—INDEMNITIES TO CITIZENS OF
THE UNITED STATES.

The United States had, and continue to have, an indubitable right to demand a full indemnity for any wrongs inflicted on our citizens by the government of Mexico in violation of treaties or of the acknowledged law of nations. The negotiations for satisfying those just demands had been interrupted by the annexation of Texas. When an attempt was subsequently made to renew them, it was, therefore, just and proper that both subjects should be discussed at the same time; and it is now absolutely necessary that those just claims should be fully provided for in any treaty of peace that may be concluded, and that the payment should be secured against any possible contingency. I take it for granted that no claims have been, or shall be, sustained by our government but such as are founded on treaties or the acknowledged law of nations.

Whenever a nation becomes involved in war, the manifestoes and every other public act issued for the purpose of justifying its conduct always embrace every ground of complaint which can possibly be alleged. But admitting that the refusal to satisfy the claims for indemnity of our citizens might have been a just cause of war, it is most certain that those claims were not the cause of that in which we are now involved.

It may be proper, in the first place, to observe that the refusal of doing justice in cases of this kind, or the long delays in providing for them, have not generally produced actual war. Almost always long-protracted negotiations have been alone resorted to. This has been strikingly the case with the United States. The claims of Great Britain for British debts secured by the treaty of 1783 were not settled and paid till the year 1803; and it was only subsequent to that year that the claims of the United States for depredations committed in 1793 were satisfied. The very plain question of slaves carried away by the British forces in 1815, in open violation of the treaty of 1814, was not settled and the indemnity paid till the year 1826. The claims against France for depredations committed in the years 1806 to 1813 were not settled and paid for till the year 1834. In all those cases peace was preserved by patience and forbearance.

With respect to the Mexican indemnities, the subject had been laid more than once before Congress, not without suggestions that strong measures should be resorted to. But Congress, in whom alone is vested the power of declaring war, uniformly declined doing it.

A convention was entered into on the 11th of April, 1839, between the United States and Mexico, by virtue of which a joint commission was appointed for the examination and settlement of those claims. The powers of the commissioners terminated, according to the convention, in February, 1842. The total amount of the American claims presented to the commission amounted to 6,291,605 dollars. Of these, 2,026,140 dollars were allowed by the commission; a further sum of 928,628 dollars was allowed by the commissioners of the United States, rejected by the Mexican commissioners, and left undecided by the umpire, and claims amounting to 3,336,837 dollars had not been examined.

A new convention dated January 30, 1843, granted to the Mexicans a further delay for the payment of the claims which had been admitted, by virtue of which the interest due to the claimants was made payable on the 30th April, 1843, and the principal of the awards and the interest accruing thereon was stipulated to be paid in five years, in twenty equal instalments every three months. The claimants received the interest due on the 30th April, 1843, and the three first instalments. The agent of the United States having, under peculiar circumstances, given a receipt for the instalments due in April and July, 1844, before they had been actually paid by Mexico, the payment has been assumed by the United States, and discharged to the claimants.

A third convention was concluded at Mexico on the 20th November, 1843, by the plenipotentiaries of the two governments, by which provision was made for ascertaining and paying the claims on which no final decision had been made. In January, 1844, this convention was ratified by the Senate of the United States with two amendments, which were referred to the government of Mexico, but respecting which no answer has ever been made. On the 12th of April, 1844, a treaty was concluded by the President with Texas for the annexation of that republic to the United States. This treaty, though not ratified by the Senate, placed the two countries in a new position and arrested for a while all negotiations. It was only on the 1st of March, 1845, that Congress passed a joint resolution for the annexation.

It appears most clearly that the United States are justly entitled to a full indemnity for the injuries done to their citizens; that, before the annexation of Texas, there was every prospect of securing that indemnity; and that those injuries, even if they had been a just cause for war, were in no shape whatever the cause of that in which we are now involved.

Are the United States justly entitled to indemnity for any other cause? This question cannot be otherwise solved than by an inquiry into the facts, and ascertaining by whom and how the war was provoked.

III.—ANNEXATION OF TEXAS.

At the time when the annexation of Texas took place, Texas had been recognized as an independent power, both by the United States and by several of the principal European powers; but its independence had not been recognized by Mexico, and the two contending parties continued to be at war. Under those circumstances there is not the slightest doubt that the annexation of Texas was tantamount to a declaration of war against Mexico. Nothing can be more clear and undeniable than that, whenever two nations are at war, if a third power shall enter into a treaty of alliance, offensive and defensive, with either of the belligerents, and if such treaty is not contingent, and is to take effect immediately and pending the war, such treaty is a declaration of war against the other party. The causes of the war between the two belligerents do not alter the fact. Supposing that the third party, the interfering power, should have concluded the treaty of alliance with that belligerent who was clearly engaged in a most just war, the treaty would not be the less a declaration of war against the other belligerent.

If Great Britain and France were at war, and the United States were to enter into such a treaty with either, can there be the slightest doubt that this would be actual war against the other party? that it would be considered as such, and that it must have been intended for that purpose? If at this moment either France or England were to make such a treaty with Mexico, thereby binding themselves to defend and protect it with all their forces against any other power whatever, would not the United States instantaneously view such a treaty as a declaration of war, and act accordingly?

But the annexation of Texas by the United States was even more than a treaty of offensive and defensive alliance. It embraced all the conditions and all the duties growing out of the alliance; and it imposed them forever. From the moment when Texas had been annexed the United States became bound to protect and defend her, so far as her legitimate boundaries extended, against any invasion or attack on the part of Mexico; and they have uniformly acted accordingly.

There is no impartial publicist that will not acknowledge the indubitable truth of these positions; it appears to me impossible that they should be seriously denied by a single person.

It appears that Mexico was at that time disposed to acknowledge the independence of Texas, but on the express condition that it should not be annexed to the United States; and it has been suggested that this was done under the influence of some European powers. Whether this last assertion be true or not is not known to me. But the condition was remarkable and offensive.

Under an apprehension that Texas might be tempted to accept the terms proposed, the government of the United States may have deemed it expedient to defeat the plan, by offering that annexation which had been formerly declined when the government of Texas was anxious for it.

It may be admitted that, whether independent or annexed to the United States, Texas must be a slave-holding State so long as slavery shall continue to exist in North America. Its whole population, with hardly any exception, consisted of citizens of the United States. Both for that reason, and on account of its geographical position, it was much more natural that Texas should be a member of the United States than of the Mexican Confederation. Viewed purely as a question of expediency, the annexation might be considered as beneficial to both parties. But expediency is not justice. Mexico and Texas had a perfect right to adjust their differences and make peace on any terms they might deem proper. The anxiety to prevent this result indicated a previous disposition ultimately to occupy Texas; and when the annexation was accomplished, when it was seen that the United States had appropriated to themselves all the advantages resulting from the American settlements in Texas, and from their subsequent insurrection, the purity of the motives of our government became open to suspicion.

Setting aside the justice of the proceeding, it is true that it had been anticipated by those who took an active part in the annexation that the weakness of Mexico would compel it to yield, or at least induce her not to resort to actual war. This was verified by the fact; and had government remained in the hands with whom the plan originated, war might probably have been avoided. But when no longer in power, they could neither regulate the impulse they had given nor control the reckless spirits they had evoked.

Mexico, sensible of her weakness, declined war, and only resorted to a suspension of diplomatic intercourse; but a profound sense of the injury inflicted by the United States has ever since rankled in their minds. It will be found through all their diplomatic correspondence, through all their manifestoes, that the Mexicans, even to this day, perpetually recur to this never-forgotten offensive measure. And on the other hand, the subsequent Administration of our government seems to have altogether forgotten this primary act of injustice, and in their negotiations to have acted as if this was only an accomplished fact and had been a matter of course.

IV.—NEGOTIATIONS AND WAR.

In September, 1845, the President of the United States directed their consul at Mexico to ascertain from the Mexican government whether it would receive an *envoy* from the United States, intrusted with full power to adjust all the questions in dispute between the two governments.

The answer of Mr. De la Pena y Pena, Minister of the Foreign Relations of Mexico, was, "That although the Mexican nation was deeply injured by the United States through the acts committed by them in the department of Texas, which belongs to his nation, his government was disposed to receive the *commissioner* of the United States who might come to the capital with full powers from his government to settle the present dispute in a peaceful, reasonable, and honorable manner;" thus giving a new proof that, even in the midst of its injuries and of its firm decision to exact adequate reparation for them, the government of Mexico does not reply with contumely to the measures of reason and peace to which it was invited by its adversary.

The Mexican minister at the same time intimated that the previous recall of the whole naval force of the United States then lying in sight of the port of Vera Cruz was indispensable; and this was accordingly done by our government.

But it is essential to observe that whilst Mr. Black had, according to his instructions, inquired whether the Mexican government would receive an *envoy* from the United States with full power to adjust all the questions in dispute between the two governments, the Mexican minister had answered that his government was disposed to receive the *commissioner* of the United States who might come will full powers to settle the present dispute in a peaceful, reasonable, and honorable manner.

Mr. Slidell was, in November following, appointed envoy extraordinary and minister plenipotentiary of the United States of America near the government of the Mexican republic; and he arrived in Mexico on the sixth of December.

Mr. Herrera, the President of Mexico, was undoubtedly disposed to settle the disputes between the two countries. But, taking advantage of the irritation of the mass of the people, his political opponents were attempting to overset him for having made, as they said, unworthy concessions. The arrival of Mr. Slidell disturbed him extremely; and Mr. Pena y Pena declared to Mr. Black that his appearance in the capital at this time might prove destructive to the government, and thus defeat the whole affair. Under these circumstances General Herrera complained, without any foundation, that Mr. Slidell had come sooner than had been understood; he resorted to several frivolous objections against the tenor of his powers; and he intimated that the difficulties respecting Texas must be adjusted before any other subject of discussion should be taken into consideration.

But the main question was whether Mexico should receive Mr. Slidell in the character of envoy extraordinary and minister plenipotentiary, to reside in the republic. It was insisted by the Mexican government that it had only agreed to receive a commissioner, to treat on the questions which had arisen from the events in Texas; and that until this was done the suspended diplomatic intercourse could not be restored and a residing minister plenipotentiary be admitted.

Why our government should have insisted that the intended negotiation should be carried on by a residing envoy extraordinary and minister plenipotentiary is altogether unintelligible. The questions at issue might have been discussed and settled as easily, fully, and satisfactorily by commissioners appointed for that special purpose as by residing ministers or envoys. It is well known that whenever diplomatic relations have been superseded by war, treaties of peace are always negotiated by commissioners appointed for that special purpose, who are personally amply protected by the law of nations, but who are never received as resident ministers till after the peace has restored the ordinary diplomatic intercourse. Thus, the treaty of peace of 1783, between France and England, was negotiated and concluded at Paris by British commissioners, whom it would have been deemed absurd to admit as resident envoys or ministers before peace had been made.

The only distinction which can possibly be made between the two cases is that there was not as yet actual war between Mexico and the United States. But the annexation of Texas was no ordinary occurrence. It was a most clear act of unprovoked aggression; a deep and most offensive injury; in fact, a declaration of war, if Mexico had accepted it as such. In lieu of this, that country had only resorted to a suspension of the ordinary diplomatic relations. It would seem as if our government had considered this as an act of unparalleled audacity, which Mexico must be compelled to retract before any negotiations for the arrangement of existing difficulties could take place; as an insult to the government and to the nation, which must compel it to assert its just rights and *to avenge its injured honor.*

General Herrera was not mistaken in his anticipations. His government was overset in the latter end of the month of December, 1845, and fell into the hands of those who had denounced him for having listened to overtures of an arrangement of the difficulties between the two nations.

When Mexico felt its inability to contend with the United States, and, instead of considering the annexation of Texas to be, as it really was, tantamount to a declaration of war, only suspended the ordinary diplomatic relations between the two countries, its government, if directed by wise counsels and not impeded by popular irritation, should at once, since it had already agreed to recognize the independence of Texas, have entered into a negotiation with the United States. At that time there would have been no intrinsic difficulty in making a final arrangement founded on an unconditional recognition of the independence of Texas within its legitimate boundaries. Popular feeling and the ambition of contending military leaders prevented that peaceable termination of those unfortunate dissensions.

Yet, when Mexico refused to receive Mr. Slidell as an envoy extraordinary and minister plenipotentiary, the United States should have remembered that we had been the aggressors, that we had committed an act acknowledged, as well by the practical law of nations as by common sense and common justice, to be tantamount to a declaration of war; and they should have waited with patience till the feelings excited by our own conduct had subsided.

General Taylor had been instructed by the War Department as early as May 28, 1845, to cause the forces under his command to be put into a position where they might most promptly and efficiently act in defence of Texas in the event that it should become necessary or proper to employ them for that purpose. By subsequent instructions, and after the people of Texas had accepted the proposition of annexation, he was directed to select and occupy a position adapted to repel

invasion as near the boundary-line—the Rio Grande—as prudence would dictate; and that, with this view, a part of his
forces at least should be west of the river Nueces. It was certainly the duty of the President to protect Texas against invasion from the moment it had been annexed to the United
States; and as that republic was in actual possession of Corpus
Christi, which was the position selected by General Taylor,
there was nothing in the position he had taken indicative of
any danger of actual hostilities.

But our government seems to have considered the refusal, on
the part of Mexico, to receive Mr. Slidell as a resident envoy
of the United States as necessarily leading to war. The Secretary of State, in his letter to Mr. Slidell of January 28, 1846,
says: "Should the Mexican government finally refuse to receive
you, the cup of forbearance will then have been exhausted.
Nothing can remain but to take the redress of the injuries to
our citizens and the insults to our government into our own
hands." And again: "Should the Mexican government finally
refuse to receive you, then demand passports from the proper
authority and return to the United States. It will then become
the duty of the President to submit the whole case to Congress,
and call upon the nation to assert its just rights and avenge
its injured honor."

With the same object in view, the Secretary of War did, by
his letter dated January 13, 1846, instruct General Taylor, "to
advance and occupy, with the troops under his command,
positions on or near the east bank of the Rio del Norte. . . .
It is presumed Point Isabel will be considered by you an
eligible position. This point, or some one near it, and points
opposite Matamoras and Mier, and in the vicinity of Laredo,
are suggested for your consideration. . . . Should you attempt
to exercise the right, which the United States have in common
with Mexico, to the free navigation of this river, it is probable
that Mexico would interpose resistance. You will not attempt
to enforce this right without further instructions. . . . It is not

designed, in our present relations with Mexico, that you should treat her as an enemy; but should she assume that character by a declaration of war, or any open act of hostility towards us, you will not act merely on the defensive if your relative means enable you to do otherwise."

The Administration was therefore of opinion that this military occupation of the territory in question was not an act of hostility towards Mexico or treating her as an enemy. Now, I do aver, without fear of contradiction, than whenever a territory claimed by two powers is, and has been for a length of time, in the possession of one of them, if the other should invade and take possession of it by a military force, such an act is an open act of hostility according to the acknowledged and practical law of nations. In this case the law of nations only recognizes a clear and positive fact.

The sequel is well known. General Taylor, with his troops, left Corpus Christi, March 8 to 11, 1846, and entered the desert which separates that place from the vicinity of the del Norte. On the 21st he was encamped three miles south of the Arroyo, or Little Colorado, having by the route he took marched 135 miles, and being nearly north of Matamoras, about thirty miles distant. He had on the 19th met a party of irregular Mexican cavalry, who informed him that they had peremptory orders, if he passed the river, to fire upon his troops, and that it would be considered a declaration of war. The river was, however, crossed without a single shot having been fired. In a proclamation issued on the 12th, General Mejia, who commanded the forces of the department of Tamaulipas, asserts that the limits of Texas are certain and recognized, and never had extended beyond the river Nueces, that the Cabinet of the United States coveted the regions on the left bank of the Rio Bravo, and that the American army was now advancing to take possession of a large part of Tamaulipas. On the 24th March General Taylor reached a point on the route from Matamoras to Point Isabel, eighteen miles from the former, and ten from the latter place, where a deputation sent him a formal protest of the prefect of the northern district of the department of Tamaulipas, declaring, in behalf of the citizens of the district, that they never will consent to separate themselves from the Mexican republic and to unite themselves with the United States. On the 12th of April the Mexican general, Ampudia, required General Taylor to break up his camp within twenty-four hours, and to retire to the other bank of the Nueces River, and notified him that, if he insisted in remaining upon the soil of the department of Tamaulipas, it would clearly result that arms alone must decide the question; in which case he declared that the Mexicans would accept the war to which they had been provoked. On the 24th of April, General Arista arrived in Matamoras, and on the same day informed General Taylor that he considered hostilities commenced, and would prosecute them. On the same day a party of sixty-three American dragoons, who had been sent some distance up the left bank of the river, became engaged with a very large force of the enemy, and after a short affair, in which about sixteen were killed or wounded, were surrounded and compelled to surrender. These facts were laid before Congress by the President in his message of the 11th of May.

V.—THE CLAIM OF TEXAS TO THE RIO DEL NORTE AS ITS BOUNDARY EXAMINED.

From what precedes it appears that the government of the United States considered the refusal of Mexico to receive a resident envoy or minister as a sufficient cause for war, and the Rio del Norte as the legitimate boundary of Texas. The first opinion is now of no importance; but the question of boundary, which was the immediate cause of hostilities, has to this day been the greatest impediment to the restoration of peace. I feel satisfied that if this was settled there would be no insuperable difficulty in arranging other pretensions.

The United States claim no other portion of the Mexican dominions unless it be by right of conquest. The tract of country between the Rio Nueces and the del Norte is the only one which has been claimed by both parties as respectively belonging either to Texas or to Mexico. As regards every other part of the Mexican possessions, the United States never had claimed any portion of it. The iniquity of acquiring any portion of it, otherwise than by fair compact freely consented to by Mexico, is self-evident. It is in every respect most important to examine the grounds on which the claim of the United States to the only territory claimed by both nations is founded. It is the main question at issue.

The republic of Texas did, by an Act of December, 1836, declare the Rio del Norte to be its boundary. It will not be seriously contended that a nation has a right, by a law of its own, to determine what is or shall be the boundary between it and another country. The Act was nothing more than the expression of the wishes or pretensions of the government. Its only practical effect was that emanating from its Congress, or legislative body, it made it imperative on the Executive not to conclude any peace with Mexico unless that boundary was agreed to. As regards right, the Act of Texas is a perfect nullity. We want the arguments and documents by which the claim is sustained.

On a first view the pretension is truly startling. There is no exception; the Rio Norte from its source to its mouth is declared to be the rightful boundary of Texas. That river has its source within the department, province, or state of New Mexico, which it traverses through its whole length from north to south, dividing it into two unequal parts. The largest and most populous, including Santa Fé, the capital, lies on the left bank of the river, and is therefore embraced within the claim of Texas. Now, this province of New Mexico was first visited and occupied by the Spaniards, under Vasquez Coronado, in the years 1540 to 1542. It was at that time voluntarily evacuated, subsequently revisited, and some settlements made about the year 1583; finally conquered in 1595 by the Spaniards under the command of Onate. An insurrection of the Indians drove away the Spaniards in the year 1680. They re-entered it the ensuing year, and after a long resistance reconquered it. This was an internal conflict with the aborigines; but as related to foreign powers, the sovereignty of the Spaniards over the territory was never called in question; and it was in express terms made the western boundary of Louisiana in the royal charter of the French government.

The conquest of the province by Onate took place five-and-twenty years prior to the landing of the Pilgrims in New England, and twelve years before any permanent settlement had been made in North America on the shores of the Atlantic by either England, France, Holland, Sweden, or any other power but that in Florida by Spain herself.

I have in vain sought for any document emanating from the republic or state of Texas for the purpose of sustaining its claim either to New Mexico or to the country bordering on the lower portion of the del Norte. The only official papers within my reach, in which the claim of Texas is sustained, are the President's messages of May 11 and December 3, 1846, and these refer only to the country bordering on the lower part of the del Norte. The portion of the message of May 11, 1846, relating to that subject is as follows: "Meantime, Texas, by the final action of our Congress, had become an integral part of our Union. The Congress of Texas, by its Act of December 19, 1836, had declared the Rio del Norte to be the boundary of that republic. Its jurisdiction had been extended and exercised beyond the Nueces. The country between that river and the del Norte had been represented in the Congress and in the convention of Texas, had thus taken part in the act of annexation itself, and is now included within one of our Congressional districts. Our own Congress had, moreover, with great unanimity, by the Act approved December 31, 1845, recognized the country beyond the Nueces as a part of our territory by including it within our own revenue system, and a revenue officer, to reside within that district, has been appointed by and with the advice and consent of the Senate It became, therefore, of urgent necessity to provide for the defence of that portion of our country. Accordingly, on the 13th of January last, instructions were issued to the general in command of these troops to occupy the left bank of the del Norte. . . .

"The movement of the troops to the del Norte was made by the commanding general under positive instructions to abstain from all aggressive acts towards Mexico or Mexican citizens, and to regard the relations between that republic and the United States as peaceful, unless she should declare war or commit acts of hostility indicative of a state of war. He was specially directed to protect private property and respect personal rights."

In his annual message of December 8, 1846, the President states that Texas, as ceded to the United States by France in 1803, has been always claimed as extending west to the Rio Grande; that this fact is established by declarations of our government during Mr. Jefferson's and Mr. Monroe's administrations; and that the Texas which was ceded to Spain by the Florida Treaty of 1819 embraced all the country now claimed by the State of Texas between the Nueces and the Rio Grande.

He then repeats the Acts of Texas with reference to their boundaries; stating that "during a period of more than nine years, which intervened between the adoption of her constitution and her annexation as one of the States of our Union, Texas asserted and exercised many acts of sovereignty and jurisdiction over the territory and inhabitants west of the Nueces; such as organizing and defining limits of counties extending to the Rio Grande; establishing courts of justice and extending her judicial system over the territory; establishing also a custom-house, post-offices, a land office, &c."

The President designates by the name of *Texas* the cession of Louisiana by France to the United States, and he again calls the territory ceded to Spain by the Florida Treaty of 1819 *the Texas.* He intimates that the claim of the United States to the territory between the Sabine and the Rio Norte was derived from the boundaries of Texas, and that by claiming as far west as this river, the United States did recognize that it was the boundary of *the Texas.* I really do not understand what is meant by this assertion.

The United States claimed the Rio Norte as being the legitimate boundary of *Louisiana,* and not of Texas. Neither they nor France had ever been in possession of the country beyond the Sabine. Spain had always held possession, and had divided the territory into provinces as she pleased. One of these was called Texas, and its boundaries had been designated and altered at her will. With these the United States had no concern. If their claim could be sustained, it must be by proving that Louisiana extended of right thus far. This had no connection with the boundaries which Spain might have assigned to her province of Texas. These might have extended beyond the Rio del Norte; or have been east of the Rio Nueces. There is not the slightest connection between the legitimate boundaries of Louisiana and those of the Spanish province of Texas. The presumed identity is a mere supposition.

It is not necessary to discuss the soundness of the pretensions to the Rio Norte asserted by Mr. Jefferson and Mr. Monroe, since they were yielded in exchange of Florida and some other objects by the treaty of 1819,—a treaty extremely popular at the time, and the execution of which was pressed with great zeal and perseverance.

Whenever ultimately ceded to Mexico, that republic fixed its boundaries as it thought proper. Texas and Cohahuila were declared to form a state, and the Rio Nueces was made the boundary of Texas. When Texas declared itself independent, it was the insurrection of only part of a state; for Cohahuila remained united to Mexico. But the Rio Nueces was the boundary between the department of Texas and the state of Tamaulipas. The whole contested territory lies within the limits of Tamaulipas, which never was, under the Mexican government, connected in any shape with Texas.

The question now under consideration is only that between the United States and Mexico, and in that view of the subject it is quite immaterial whether the acts of the United States emanated from Congress or from the Executive. No act of either recognizing the country beyond the Nueces as a part of the territory of the United States can be alleged against Mexico as a proof of their right to the country thus claimed. Any such act is only an assertion, a declaration, but not an argument sustaining the right. It is, however, proper to observe here that the port of delivery west of the Nueces, erected by the Act of Congress "To establish a collection district in the State of Texas," was at Corpus Christi, a place which was in the actual possession of that State.

It must also be premised that, in the joint resolution for the annexation of Texas, the question of the boundary between it and Mexico was expressly reserved, as one which should be settled by treaty between the United States and Mexico.

The only arguments in the President's message which sustain the right of Texas to territory beyond the Nueces are contained in those passages in which it is asserted that the jurisdiction of Texas had been extended and exercised beyond the Nueces; that the country between that river and the del Norte had been represented in the Congress and convention of Texas, had taken part in the annexation itself, and was now included within one of our Congressional districts.

But it is not stated in the President's message how far beyond the Nueces the jurisdiction of Texas had been extended, nor what part of the country between that river and the del

Norte had been represented in the Congress and convention of Texas, and was then included within one of our Congressional districts.

Now the actual jurisdiction beyond the Nueces never extended farther than the adjacent settlement of San Patricio, consisting of about twenty families. That small district, though beyond the Nueces, was contiguous to, and in the actual possession of, Texas. On this account it might be rightfully included within the limits which we were bound to protect against Mexican invasion.

But what was the country between this small settlement of San Patricio, or between Corpus Christi and the Rio del Norte, over which it might be supposed from the message that the jurisdiction of Texas had been extended, so as to be included within one of our Congressional districts? Here, again, Texas had erected that small settlement into a county called San Patricio, and declared that this county extended to the Rio del Norte. This, like all other declaratory acts of the same kind, was only an assertion, not affecting the question of right. The State of Texas might with equal propriety have declared that their boundary extended to the Sierra Madre or to the Pacific. The true question of right to any territory beyond the Mexican limits of the department of Texas depends on the facts, By whom was the territory in question actually inhabited and occupied? and had the inhabitants united with Texas in the insurrection against Mexico?

The whole country beyond the settlement of San Patricio and Corpus Christi till within a few miles of the del Norte is a perfect desert, one hundred and sixty miles wide by the route pursued by General Taylor, as stated by himself, and near one hundred and twenty miles in a straight line.

The only settled part of it is along the left bank of the del Norte, and but a few miles in breadth. This belt was settled, inhabited, and occupied exclusively by Mexicans. It included the town of Laredo, and Mexico had a custom-house at Brazos, north of the mouth of the river. Till occupied by the American arms it had ever been, and was at the time when invaded by General Taylor, a part of the department of Tamaulipas, and subject to the jurisdiction of the prefect of the northern district of that department.

In the course of the war between Mexico and Texas, incursions had been occasionally made by each party into the territories of the other. A Mexican officer had once or twice obtained temporary occupation of San Antonio, within the limits of Texas; and the Texans had on one occasion taken Laredo itself, and more than once had carried their arms not only to the left bank of the del Norte, but even beyond that river. In both cases the aggressive parties had been repulsed and expelled. The last Texan expedition of that kind took place in December, 1842, and terminated in their defeat at Mier.

That the country adjacent to the left bank of the river was exclusively in the possession of the Mexicans was well known to our government.

When General Taylor marched to the del Norte, he issued an order (No. 30), translated into the Spanish, ordering all under his command to observe with the most scrupulous respect the rights of all the inhabitants who might be found in peaceful prosecution of their respective occupations, as well on the left as on the right side of the Rio Grande. No interference, he adds, will be allowed with the civil rights or religious privileges of the inhabitants.

In June, 1845, General Taylor had been directed to select and occupy, on or near the Rio Grande del Norte, such a site as would be best adapted to repel invasion and to protect our western border. But, on the 8th of July following, the Secretary of War (Mr. Marcy) addressed the following letter to him:

"This Department is informed that Mexico has some military establishments on the east side of the Rio Grande, which are, and for some time have been, in the actual occupancy of her troops. In carrying out the instructions heretofore received you will be careful to avoid any acts of aggression unless an actual state of war should exist. The Mexican forces at the posts in their possession, and which have been so, will not be disturbed as long as the relations of peace between the United States and Mexico continue."

On the 30th of July, 1845, the Secretary again addresses General Taylor as follows: "You are expected to occupy, protect, and defend the territory of Texas, to the extent that it has been occupied by the people of Texas. The Rio Grande is claimed to be the boundary between the two countries, and up to this boundary you are to extend your protection, only *excepting* any posts on the eastern side thereof which are in the actual occupancy of Mexican forces or *Mexican settlements*, over which the republic of Texas did not exercise jurisdiction at the period of annexation, or shortly before that event. It is expected, in selecting the establishment for your troops, you will approach as near the boundary-line—the Rio Grande—as prudence will dictate. With this view, the President desires that your position, for a part of your forces at least, should be west of the river Nueces."

The Mexican settlements thus excepted are not those over which Texas did not claim jurisdiction, but those on the east bank of the Rio Grande over which Texas did not *exercise* jurisdiction at the period mentioned. The President had no authority to give up the boundary claimed by Texas; but it is clear that at that time, when war was not contemplated, the Administration was of opinion that, till the question was definitely settled, the occupancy by the Mexicans of the territory adjacent the left bank of the del Norte ought not to be disturbed. Neither the subsequent refusal by Mexico to receive a residing envoy nor the successes of the American arms have affected the question of right. The claim of Texas, whether to New Mexico or to the lower portion of the Rio Norte, was identically the same, as invalid and groundless in one case as in the other. Why a distinction has been made by the Executive has not been stated. The fact is that he has established a temporary government for New Mexico as a country conquered, and without any regard to the claim of Texas; whilst, on the other hand, he has permitted that State to extend its jurisdiction over the country lying on the left bank of the del Norte, which, like New Mexico, had been conquered by the arms of the United States. Not a shadow of proof has been adduced to sustain the pretensions of Texas to that district; and justice imperiously requires that it should, by the treaty of peace, be restored to Mexico.

It so happens that the boundary which may be traced in conformity with this principle is a natural one, and that, as a measure of expediency, none more eligible could have been devised. A desert of one hundred and twenty miles separates the most southwesterly Texan settlements of Corpus Christi and San Patricio from those of the Mexicans on the left bank of the del Norte, than which no boundary could be devised better calculated to prevent collisions hereafter between the two nations. It will be sufficient for that purpose to draw a nominal line through the desert, leaving all the waters that empty into the Rio Norte to Mexico, and all those that empty into the Rio Nueces to Texas, together with such other provisions respecting fortifications and military posts as may be necessary for the preservation of peace.

The line of the Rio Norte is one from which Mexico would be perpetually threatened, and from which their adjacent town on the eastern bank may be bombarded. Such an intolerable nuisance would perpetuate most hostile feelings. With such a narrow river as the Rio del Norte, and with a joint right of navigation, repeated collisions would be unavoidable.

Among these, when there was nothing but a fordable river to cross, slaves would perpetually escape from Texas; and where would be the remedy? Are the United States prepared to impose by a treaty on Mexico, where slavery is unknown, the obligation to surrender fugitive slaves?

Mexico is greatly the weaker power, and requires a boundary which will give her as much security as is practicable. It is not required, either for the preservation of peace or for any other legitimate purpose, that the United States should occupy a threatening position. It cannot be rationally supposed that Mexico will ever make an aggressive war against them; and even in such case the desert would protect them against an invasion. If a war should ever again take place between the two countries, the overwhelming superiority of the navy of the United States will enable them to carry on their operations wherever they please. They would, within a month, reoccupy the left bank of the Rio Norte, and within a short time effect a landing and carry the war to any quarter they pleased.

Must the war be still prosecuted for an object of no intrinsic value, to which the United States have no legitimate right, which justice requires them to yield, and which even expediency does not require?

VI.—RECAPITULATION.

It is an indisputable fact that the annexation of Texas, then at war with Mexico, was tantamount to a declaration of war, and that the comparative weakness of Mexico alone prevented its government from considering it as such.

Under these circumstances, it was evidently the duty of the United States to use every means to soothe and conciliate the Mexicans, and to wait with patience for an unconditional recognition of the independence of Texas, till the feelings excited by our aggression had subsided.

It has been shown that after Mexico had resorted, as a substitute for war, to the harmless suspension of the ordinary diplomatic intercourse, the attempt to make it retract that measure, before any negotiations for the restoration of harmony between the two countries should be entered into, was neither countenanced by the acknowledged law of nations, nor necessary for any useful purpose, nor consistent with a proper and just sense of the relative position in which the aggressive measure of the United States had placed the two countries. But that the refusal of Mexico to submit to that additional contumely should have been considered as an insult to the United States betrays the pride of power, rather than a just sense of what is due to the true dignity and honor of this nation.

It has been demonstrated that the republic of Texas had not a shadow of right to the territory adjacent to the left bank of the lower portion of the Rio Norte; that, though she claimed, she never had actually exercised jurisdiction over any portion of it; that the Mexicans were the sole inhabitants and in actual possession of that district; that, therefore, its forcible occupation by the army of the United States was, according to the acknowledged law of nations, as well as in fact, an act of open hostility and war; that the resistance of the Mexicans to that invasion was legitimate; and that therefore the war was unprovoked by them, and commenced by the United States.

If any doubt should remain of the correctness of these statements, let them be tested by the divine and undeniable precept, "Do unto others as you would be done by."

If at this moment France was to contract a treaty of defensive and offensive alliance with Mexico, a treaty taking effect immediately and pending the war between the United States and Mexico, and binding herself to defend it with all her forces against any and every other power, would not the United States at once consider such a treaty as a declaration of war against them?

If, in lieu of declaring war against Great Britain in the year 1812, the United States had only suspended the ordinary diplomatic relations between the two countries, and Great Britain had declared that she would not enter into any negotiation for the settlement of all the subjects of difference between the two countries unless the United States should, as a preliminary condition, restore those relations, would not this have been considered as a most insolent demand, and to which the United States never would submit?

If the United States were, and had been for more than a century, in possession of a tract of country exclusively inhabited and governed by them, disturbed only by the occasional forays of an enemy, would they not consider the forcible military invasion and occupation of such a district by a third power as open and unprovoked war commenced against them? And could their resistance to the invasion render them liable to the imputation of having themselves commenced the war?

Yet it would seem as if the splendid and almost romantic successes of the American arms had for a while made the people of the United States deaf to any other consideration than an enthusiastic and exclusive love of military glory; as if, forgetting the origin of the war, and with an entire disregard for the dictates of justice, they thought that those successes gave the nation a right to dismember Mexico, and to appropriate to themselves that which did not belong to them.

But I do not despair, for I have faith in our institutions and in the people; and I will now ask them whether this was their mission; and whether they were placed by Providence on this continent for the purpose of cultivating false glory, and of sinking to the level of those vulgar conquerors who have at all times desolated the earth.

VII.—THE MISSION OF THE UNITED STATES.

The people of the United States have been placed by Providence in a position never before enjoyed by any other nation.

They are possessed of a most extensive territory, with a very fertile soil, a variety of climates and productions, and a capacity of sustaining a population greater in proportion to its extent than any other territory of the same size on the face of the globe.

By a concourse of various circumstances, they found themselves, at the epoch of their independence, in the full enjoyment of religious, civil, and political liberty, entirely free from any hereditary monopoly of wealth or power. The people at large were in full and quiet possession of all those natural rights for which the people of other countries have for a long time contended and still do contend. They were, and you still are, the supreme sovereigns, acknowledged as such by all. For the proper exercise of these uncontrolled powers and privileges you are responsible to posterity, to the world at large, and to the Almighty Being who has poured on you such unparalleled blessings.

Your mission is to improve the state of the world, to be the "model republic," to show that men are capable of governing themselves, and that this simple and natural form of government is that also which confers most happiness on all, is productive of the greatest development of the intellectual faculties, above all, that which is attended with the highest standard of private and political virtue and morality.

Your forefathers, the founders of the republic, imbued with a deep feeling of their rights and duties, did not deviate from those principles. The sound sense, the wisdom, the probity, the respect for public faith, with which the internal concerns of the nation were managed made our institutions an object of general admiration. Here, for the first time, was the experiment attempted with any prospect of success, and on a large scale, of a representative democratic republic. If it failed, the last hope of the friends of mankind was lost or indefinitely postponed; and the eyes of the world were turned towards you. Whenever real or pretended apprehensions of the imminent danger of trusting the people at large with power were expressed, the answer ever was, "Look at America!"

In their external relations the United States, before this unfortunate war, had, whilst sustaining their just rights, ever acted in strict conformity with the dictates of justice, and displayed the utmost moderation. They never had voluntarily injured any other nation. Every acquisition of territory from foreign powers was honestly made, the result of treaties not imposed, but freely assented to by the other party. The preservation of peace was ever a primary object. The recourse to arms was always in self-defence. On its expediency there may have been a difference of opinion; that in the only two instances of conflict with civilized nations which occurred during a period of sixty-three years (1783 to 1846) the just rights of the United States had been invaded by a long-continued series of aggressions is undeniable. In the first instance war was not declared, and there were only partial hostilities between France and England. The Congress of the United States, the only legitimate organ of the nation for that purpose, did, in 1812, declare war against Great Britain. Independent of depredations on our commerce, she had for twenty years carried on an actual war against the United States. I say actual war, since there is now but one opinion on that subject; a renewal of the impressment of men sailing under the protection of our flag would be tantamount to a declaration of war. The partial opposition to the war of 1812 did not rest on a denial of the aggressions of England and of the justice of our cause, but on the fact that, with the exception of impressments, similar infractions of our just rights had been committed by France, and on the most erroneous belief that the Administration was partial to that country and insincere in their apparent efforts to restore peace.

At present all these principles would seem to have been abandoned. The most just, a purely defensive war, and no other is justifiable, is necessarily attended with a train of

great and unavoidable evils. What shall we say of one, iniquitous in its origin, and provoked by ourselves, of a war of
aggression, which is now publicly avowed to be one of intended conquest?

If persisted in, its necessary consequences will be a permanent increase of our military establishment and of executive
patronage; its general tendency to make man hate man, to
awaken his worst passions, to accustom him to the taste of
blood. It has already demoralized no inconsiderable portion
of the nation.

The general peace which has been preserved between the
great European powers during the last thirty years may not
be ascribed to the purest motives. Be these what they may,
this long and unusual repose has been most beneficial to the
cause of humanity. Nothing can be more injurious to it, more
lamentable, more scandalous, than the war between two
adjacent republics of North America.

Your mission was to be a model for all other governments
and for all other less-favored nations, to adhere to the most
elevated principles of political morality, to apply all your
faculties to the gradual improvement of your own institutions
and social state, and by your example to exert a moral influence most beneficial to mankind at large. Instead of this, an
appeal has been made to your worst passions; to cupidity; to
the thirst of unjust aggrandizement by brutal force; to the
love of military fame and of false glory; and it has even been
tried to pervert the noblest feelings of your nature. The attempt is made to make you abandon the lofty position which
your fathers occupied, to substitute for it the political morality and heathen patriotism of the heroes and statesmen of
antiquity.

I have said that it was attempted to pervert even your virtues. Devotedness to country, or patriotism, is a most essential
virtue, since the national existence of any society depends

upon it. Unfortunately, our most virtuous dispositions are perverted not only by our vices and selfishness, but also by their own excess. Even the most holy of our attributes, the religious feeling, may be perverted from that cause, as was but too lamentably exhibited in the persecutions, even unto death, of those who were deemed heretics. It is not, therefore, astonishing that patriotism carried to excess should also be perverted. In the entire devotedness to their country, the people everywhere and at all times have been too apt to forget the duties imposed upon them by justice towards other nations. It is against this natural propensity that you should be specially on your guard. The blame does not attach to those who, led by their patriotic feelings, though erroneous, flock around the national standard. On the contrary, no men are more worthy of admiration, better entitled to the thanks of their country, than those who, after war has once taken place, actuated only by the purest motives, daily and with the utmost self-devotedness brave death and stake their own lives in the conflict against the actual enemy. I must confess that I do not extend the same charity to those civilians who coolly and deliberately plunge the country into any unjust or unnecessary war.

We should have but one conscience; and most happy would it be for mankind were statesmen and politicians only as honest in their management of the internal or external national concerns as they are in private life. The irreproachable private character of the President and of all the members of his Administration is known and respected. There is not one of them who would not spurn with indignation the most remote hint that, on similar pretences to those alleged for dismembering Mexico, he might be capable of an attempt to appropriate to himself his neighbor's farm.

In the total absence of any argument that can justify the war in which we are now involved, resort has been had to a most extraordinary assertion. It is said that the people of the

United States have an hereditary superiority of race over the Mexicans, which gives them the right to subjugate and keep in bondage the inferior nation. This, it is also alleged, will be the means of enlightening the degraded Mexicans, of improving their social state, and of ultimately increasing the happiness of the masses.

Is it compatible with the principle of democracy, which rejects every hereditary claim of individuals, to admit an hereditary superiority of races? You very properly deny that the son can, independent of his own merit, derive any right or privilege whatever from the merit or any other social superiority of his father. Can you for a moment suppose that a very doubtful descent from men who lived one thousand years ago has transmitted to you a superiority over your fellow-men? But the Anglo-Saxons were inferior to the Goths, from whom the Spaniards claim to be descended; and they were in no respect superior to the Franks and to the Burgundians. It is not to their Anglo-Saxon descent, but to a variety of causes, among which the subsequent mixture of Frenchified Normans, Angevins, and Gascons must not be forgotten, that the English are indebted for their superior institutions. In the progressive improvement of mankind much more has been due to religious and political institutions than to races. Whenever the European nations which from their language are presumed to belong to the Latin or to the Sclavonian race shall have conquered institutions similar to those of England, there will be no trace left of the pretended superiority of one of those races above the other. At this time the claim is but a pretext for covering and justifying unjust usurpation and unbounded ambition.

But admitting, with respect to Mexico, the superiority of race, this confers no superiority of rights. Among ourselves the most ignorant, the most inferior, either in physical or mental faculties, is recognized as having equal rights, and he has an equal vote with any one, however superior to him in all those respects. This is founded on the immutable principle that no one man is born with the right of governing another man. He may, indeed, acquire a moral influence over others, and no other is legitimate. The same principle will apply to nations. However superior the Anglo-American race may be to that of Mexico, this gives the Americans no right to infringe upon the rights of the inferior race. The people of the United States may rightfully, and will, if they use the proper means, exercise a most beneficial moral influence over the Mexicans and other less enlightened nations of America. Beyond this they have no right to go.

The allegation that the subjugation of Mexico would be the means of enlightening the Mexicans, of improving their social state, and of increasing their happiness, is but the shallow attempt to disguise unbounded cupidity and ambition. Truth never was or can be propagated by fire and sword, or by any other than purely moral means. By these, and by these alone, the Christian religion was propagated, and enabled, in less than three hundred years, to conquer idolatry. During the whole of that period Christianity was tainted by no other blood than that of its martyrs.

The duties of the people of the United States towards other nations are obvious. Never losing sight of the divine precept, "Do to others as you would be done by," they have only to consult their own conscience. For our benevolent Creator has implanted in the hearts of men the moral sense of right and wrong, and that sympathy for other men the evidences of which are of daily occurrence.

It seems unnecessary to add anything respecting that false glory which, from habit and the general tenor of our early education, we are taught to admire. The task has already been repeatedly performed, in a far more able and impressive manner than anything I could say on the subject. It is sufficient to say that at this time neither the dignity or honor of the nation demand a further sacrifice of invaluable lives, or

even of money. The very reverse is the case. The true honor
and dignity of the nation are inseparable from justice. Pride
and vanity alone demand the sacrifice. Though so dearly purchased, the astonishing successes of the American arms have
at least put it in the power of the United States to grant any
terms of peace without incurring the imputation of being
actuated by any but the most elevated motives. It would
seem that the most proud and vain must be satiated with
glory, and that the most reckless and bellicose should be sufficiently glutted with human gore.

A more truly glorious termination of the war, a more splendid spectacle, an example more highly useful to mankind at
large, cannot well be conceived than that of the victorious
forces of the United States voluntarily abandoning all their
conquests, without requiring anything else than that which
was strictly due to our citizens.

VIII.—TERMS OF PEACE.

I have said that the unfounded claim of Texas to the territory between the Nueces and the Rio Norte was the greatest
impediment to peace. Of this there can be no doubt. For if,
relinquishing the spirit of military conquest, nothing shall be
required but the indemnities due to our citizens, the United
States have only to accept the terms which have been offered
by the Mexican government. It consents to yield a territory
five degrees of latitude, or near 350 miles, in breadth, and extending from New Mexico to the Pacific. Although the greater
part of this is quite worthless, yet the portion of California
lying between the Sierra Nevada and the Pacific, and including the port of San Francisco, is certainly worth much more
than the amount of indemnities justly due to our citizens. It
is only in order to satisfy those claims that an accession of
territory may become necessary.

It is not believed that the Executive will favor the wild

suggestions of a subjugation or annexation of the whole of Mexico, or of any of its interior provinces. And, if I understand the terms offered by Mr. Trist, there was no intention to include within the cessions required the province of New Mexico. But the demand of both Old and New California, or of a sea-coast of more than thirteen hundred miles in length (lat. 23° to 42°), is extravagant and unnecessary. The peninsula is altogether worthless, and there is nothing worth contending for south of San Diego, or about latitude 32°.

In saying that if conquest is not the object of the war, and if the pretended claim of Texas to the Rio del Norte shall be abandoned there cannot be any insuperable obstacle to the restoration of peace, it is by no means intended to assert that the terms heretofore proposed by either party are at this time proper. And I apprehend that the different views of the subject entertained by those who sincerely desire a speedy and just peace, may create some difficulty. There are some important considerations which may become the subject of subsequent arrangements. For the present, nothing more is strictly required than to adopt the principle of *status ante bellum,* or, in other words, to evacuate the Mexican territory and to provide for the payment of the indemnities due to our citizens. The scruples of those who object to any cession whatever of territory, except on terms unacceptable to the Southern States, might be removed by a provision that would only pledge a territory sufficient for the purpose, and leave it in the possession of the United States until the indemnities had been fully paid.

Was I to listen exclusively to my own feelings and opinions, I would say that, if the propositions which I have attempted to establish are correct, if I am not mistaken in my sincere conviction that the war has been unprovoked by the Mexicans and has been one of iniquitous aggression on our part, it necessarily follows that, according to the dictates of justice, the United States are bound to indemnify them for having invaded their territory, bombarded their towns, and inflicted all the miseries of war on a people who were fighting in defence of their own homes. If all this be true, the United States would give but an inadequate compensation for the injuries they have inflicted by assuming the payment of the indemnities justly due to their own citizens.

Even if a fair purchase of territory should be convenient to both parties, it would be far preferable to postpone it for the present, among other reasons, in order that it should not have the appearance of being imposed on Mexico. There are also some important considerations, to which it may not be improper to call at this time the public attention.

Our population may at this time be assumed as amounting to twenty millions. Although the ratio of natural increase has already been lessened from thirty-three to about thirty per cent. in ten years, the deficiency has been, and will probably continue for a while to be, compensated by the prodigious increase of immigration from foreign countries. An increase of thirty per cent. would add to our population six millions within ten, and near fourteen millions in twenty, years. At the rate of only twenty-five per cent. it will add five millions in ten, and more than eleven millions in twenty, years. That the fertile uncultivated land within the limits of the States admitted or immediately admissible in the Union could sustain three times that number, is indubitable. But the indomitable energy, the locomotive propensities, and all the habits of the settlers of new countries are such that not even the united efforts of both governments can or will prevent their occupying within twenty, if not within ten, years, every district as far as the Pacific, and whether within the limits of the United States or of Mexico, which shall not have previously been actually and *bona fide* occupied and settled by others. It may be said that this is justifiable by natural law; that, for the same reason which sets aside the right of discovery if not followed by actual occupation within a reasonable time, the rights of Spain and Mexico have been forfeited by their neglect or inability, during a period of three hundred years, to colonize a country which, during the whole of that period, they held undisputed by any other foreign nation. And it may perhaps be observed that, had the government of the United States waited for the operation of natural and irresistible causes, these alone would have given them, without a war, more than they want at this moment.

However plausible all this may appear, it is nevertheless certain that it will be an acquisition of territory for the benefit of the people of the United States and in violation of solemn treaties. Not only collisions must be avoided and the renewal of another illicit annexation be prevented, but the two countries must coolly consider their relative position, and whatever portion of territory not actually settled by the Mexicans and of no real utility to them they may be disposed to cede, must be acquired by a treaty freely assented to and for a reasonable compensation. But this is not the time for the discussion of a proper final arrangement. We must wait till peace shall have been restored and angry feelings shall have subsided. At present the only object is peace, immediate peace, a just peace, and no acquisition of territory but that which may be absolutely necessary for effecting the great object in view. The most simple terms, those which will only provide for the adjustment of the Texas boundary and for the payment of the indemnities due to our citizens, and, in every other respect, restore things as they stood before the beginning of hostilities, appear to me the most eligible. For that purpose I may be permitted to wish that the discussion of the terms should not be embarrassed by the introduction of any other matter. There are other considerations, highly important, and not foreign to the great question of an extension of territory, but which may, without any inconvenience or commitment, be postponed, and should not be permitted to impede the immediate termination of this lamentable war.

I have gone farther than I intended. It is said that a rallying-point is wanted by the friends of peace. Let them unite, boldly express their opinions, and use their utmost endeavors in promoting an immediate termination of the war. For the people no other banner is necessary. But their representatives in Congress assembled are alone competent to ascertain, alone vested with the legitimate power of deciding, what course should be pursued at this momentous crisis, what are the best means for carrying into effect their own views, whatever these may be. We may wait with hope and confidence the result of their deliberations.

I have tried in this essay to confine myself to the questions at issue between the United States and Mexico. Whether the Executive has in any respect exceeded his legitimate powers, whether he is for any of his acts liable to animadversion, are questions which do not concern Mexico.

There are certainly some doubtful assumptions of power and some points on which explanations are necessary. The most important is the reason which may have induced the President, when he considered the war as necessary and almost unavoidable, not to communicate to Congress, which was all that time in session, the important steps he had taken till after hostilities, and indeed actual war, had taken place. The substitution for war contributions of an arbitrary and varying tariff, appears to me to be of a doubtful nature, and it is hoped that the subject will attract the early attention of Congress. I am also clearly of opinion that the provisions of the law respecting volunteers, which authorizes them to elect their officers, is a direct violation of the Constitution of the United States, which recognizes no other land force than the army and the militia, and which vests in the President and Senate the exclusive power of appointing all the officers of the United States whose appointments are not otherwise provided for in the Constitution itself. (With respect to precedents, refer to the Act of July 6, 1812, chap. 461 (cxxxviii.), enacted with due deliberation, and which repeals in that respect the Act on same subject of February 6, 1812.)

Selective Index to Gallatin's Thought

INDEX

THE AMERICAN HERITAGE SERIES

THE COLONIAL PERIOD

Adams, John *The Political Writings of John Adams: Representative Selections* AHS 8 George A. Peek, Jr.
The English Libertarian Heritage: From the Writings of John Trenchard and Thomas Gordon in The Independent Whig *and* Cato's Letters AHS 32 David L. Jacobson
The Great Awakening AHS 34 Alan Heimert, Perry Miller
Puritan Political Thought AHS 33 Edmund S. Morgan

THE REVOLUTIONARY ERA

The American Revolution as a Democratic Movement AHS 36 Alfred Young
The Antifederalists AHS 38 Cecelia Kenyon
Early American Libertarian Thought: Freedom of the Press from Zenger to Jefferson AHS 41 Leonard W. Levy
Franklin, Benjamin *The Political Thought of Benjamin Franklin* AHS 64 Ralph Ketcham
Paine, Thomas *Common Sense and Other Political Writings* AHS 5 Nelson F. Adkins

THE YOUNG NATION

Calhoun, John C. *Disquisition on Government and Selections from the* Discourse AHS 10 C. Gordon Post
Channing, William Ellery *Unitarian Christianity and Other Essays* AHS 21 Irving H. Bartlett
Democracy, Liberty, and Property: The State Constitutional Conventions of the 1820's AHS 43 Merrill D. Peterson

TOPICAL VOLUMES